Women's Work in Industrial England

Regional and Local Perspectives

Women's Work in Industrial England

Regional and Local Perspectives

Edited by

NIGEL GOOSE

A LOCAL POPULATION STUDIES SUPPLEMENT

Published in 2007 by
LOCAL POPULATION STUDIES
Hatfield, Hertfordshire

© Local Population Studies
Department of Humanities, University of Hertfordshire,
Hertfordshire AL10 9AB

ISBN 0 9541621 1 0

The publication of this volume has been
assisted by an award from the
Marc Fitch Fund,
which is gratefully acknowledged.

Typeset by Cambrian Typesetters, Frimley, Surrey
Printed by Halstan & Co. Ltd, Amersham

Contents

List of contributors

MICHAEL ANDERSON, Professor of Economic History, University of Edinburgh

OWEN DAVIES, Reader in Social History, University of Hertfordshire

MARGUERITE DUPREE, Reader in Social History and the History of Medicine, University of Glasgow and Fellow of Wolfson College, Cambridge

EILIDH GARRETT, Senior Research Fellow, Cambridge Group for the History of Population and Social Structure, University of Cambridge

NIGEL GOOSE, Professor of Social and Economic History and Director of the Centre for Regional and Local History, University of Hertfordshire

EDWARD HIGGS, Reader in History, University of Essex

CHRISTINE JONES, Research Assistant, UK Data Archive, University of Essex

JOHN McKAY, retired customs and excise officer, formerly part-time tutor for the Open University and University of Dundee, currently writing a history of the Scottish shale oil industry.

STANA NENADIC, Senior Lecturer in Social History, University of Edinburgh

OSAMU SAITO, Professor in the Institute of Economic Research, Hitotsubashi University

PAM SHARPE, Professor of History, University of Tasmania

LEIGH SHAW-TAYLOR, Lecturer in Eighteenth and Nineteenth-Century British Economic and Social History, University of Cambridge

NICOLA VERDON, Senior Lecturer in History, Sheffield Hallam University

List of figures

List of tables

Preface

This book originates in a Local Population Studies Society conference held at Charlotte Mason College, Ambleside, in September 1996, a stimulating and enjoyable meeting that produced enthusiasm to publish the proceedings. Subsequent discussion of the project by the *Local Population Studies* Editorial Board led to a decision to add to the papers delivered at the conference by commissioning new material, in order to produce a fuller, more wide-ranging volume, and to reprint some key articles that first appeared in *Local Population Studies*. It was hoped to be able to represent the full range of work, both formal and informal, in which women engaged during the years when England was at its industrial height, taken roughly to correspond to the nineteenth century, as well as to engage with some key methodological issues. It would probably be fair to say that the volume is only partly successful in its first aspiration for—although it includes chapters on agriculture, centralised industry, cottage industry, service, business and alternative medicine—obvious gaps remain, most notably women's crucial role in the domestic economy and self-provisioning. Moreover, women in business are represented by a case study of Edinburgh, while the title of the book is confined to England to avoid any possible misrepresentation of its main preoccupation. Greater success might be claimed for the second aspiration, for the volume includes some key methodological debates, each chapter incorporates discussion of methodological issues, and the whole volume is underpinned by insistence upon the crucial importance of the adoption of regional and local perspectives in any attempt properly to understand women's work in industrial England.

Given the long gap between the conference that generated some of these papers and the production of this volume, it is not surprising that two of them have been published in the interim. Chapter 3 by Pam Sharpe, 'The female labour market in English agriculture in the industrial revolution: expansion or contraction?', appeared in the *Agricultural History Review*, 47 (1999), and I am most grateful to the editor for permission to reprint it here. Chapter 8 by Michael Anderson, 'What can the mid-Victorian censuses tell us about married women's employment?', also first presented at the Ambleside conference, was published in *Local Population Studies*, 62 (1999). The other articles reprinted from *Local Population Studies* are chapter 7, John McKay, 'Married women and work in nineteenth-century Lancashire: the evidence of the 1851 and 1861 census reports' (*LPS* 61, 1998); chapter 9, Osamu Saito, 'Who worked when? Life-time profiles of labour force participation in Cardington and Corfe Castle in the late eighteenth and mid-nineteenth centuries' (*LPS* 22, 1979); chapter 11, Edward Higgs, 'The tabulation of occupations in the nineteenth-century census with special reference to domestic servants' (*LPS* 28, 1982); and chapter 12, Michael Anderson, 'Mis-specification of servant occupations in the 1851 census: a problem revisited' (*LPS* 60, 1998). Chapter 15 by Eilidh Garrett, 'The dawning of a new era? Women's work in England at the turn of the twentieth century', is reprinted from *Histoire Sociale/Social History*, 28 (1995), and I am most grateful to the co-directors of the journal for their permission to do so. The remaining eight chapters are new, although chapter 6 by Marguerite Dupree, 'Women as wives and workers in the Staffordshire potteries in the nineteenth century', is substantially based upon material first published as *Family structure in the Staffordshire Potteries 1840-1880* (Oxford University Press, 1995). The resulting volume, therefore, combines a range of important, published contributions to the history of women's work in industrial England that deserve fuller exposure and accessibility, with some of the more important new research recently undertaken.

I am grateful to Eildih Garrett and Christine Jones for organising the conference from which this volume has arisen, and to all of the contributors for offering their papers, for responding so willingly to suggested alterations, and for showing such patience in awaiting its production. I would also like to thank the *Local Population Studies* Editorial Board for their enduring support for this project, the realisation of which has taken far too long. I would like to record a personal debt of gratitude to the numerous Hertfordshire local historians and genealogists, without whom my interest in the history of women's work in Hertfordshire, and in industrial England more generally, might never have arisen.

1

Working women in industrial England[1]

NIGEL GOOSE

> . . .when I got married I had work plenty and thou knows I was
> not lazy . . . And we had a good furnished house, and Mary need
> not go to work. I could work for the two of us; but now the world
> is upside down. Mary has to work and I have to stop at home and
> mind the childer, sweep and wash, bake and mend; and when the
> poor woman comes home at night, she is knocked up. Thou
> knows, Joe, its hard for one that was used different.
>
> > F. Engels, *The condition of the working class in England*,
> > p. 174 (1844–5).

Frederick Engels' well known relation of a conversation between Joe
and Jack, where Jack passionately bemoans his sad plight as a house
husband of three years standing, reduced to 'women's work'—
domestic chores—while his wife has become the breadwinner, reveals
very clearly a gender stereotyping of the male breadwinner family as
the right and natural state of affairs, an ideal that Engels perceived as
having been subverted by the march of capitalist relations of
production in the factory towns of the Midlands and the North that
he regarded as the heartland of a new, exploitative industrial society.
His judgement could not be more categorical: 'Can anyone imagine
a more insane state of things . . .? And yet this condition, which
unsexes the man and takes from the woman all womanliness . . . this
condition which degrades, in the most shameful way, both sexes, and,
through them, Humanity, is the last result of our much praised

[1] I would like to thank Eilidh Garrett and Leigh Shaw-Taylor for their helpful
comments on this chapter, and the participants at the First Modern Labour
Market Seminar, All Soul's, Oxford 22nd September 2006, organised by Jane
Humphries and Leonard Schwarz, for providing stimulating discussions which
informed the final version.

civilisation . . . .'.[2] Engels comments are, of course, context-specific, and he was not alone in suggesting that the employment of women in factories tended to supplant the labour of men. From a very different position on the political spectrum Andrew Ure, in his *Philosophy of Manufactures*, argued that 'It is, in fact, the constant aim and tendency of every improvement in machinery to supersede human labour altogether, or to diminish its cost, by substituting the industry of women and children for that of men, or that of ordinary labourers for trained artisans'.[3] By the 1840s such remarks, as a generalisation at least, may have been out of date. While it is true that in the early stages of industrialisation extensive use was made of female and child labour in factories, as it was both cheaper and more flexible, it has been argued that the conditions which had encouraged this state of affairs had largely ceased to exist by the mid-nineteenth century, even if, outside of cloth production, some further migration of women's work from home to factory still occurred.[4] Engels figures, 'furnished by a manufacturer', for 412 Lancashire factories, identify only 821 unemployed husbands of female operatives out of a total of 10,721, or just two per factory.[5]

It is also often suggested that by the 1840s, if not earlier, there had been a profound shift in attitudes towards the working woman as compared with the late eighteenth century. Middle class disapproval of working women was now commonplace, and was rooted in the notion of 'separate spheres', reinforced by humanitarian concern, sharpened by the development of stereotypes of immoral working girls and mothers and assisted by the failure of the middle classes to understand the economics of working-class life. The Victorian middle-class ideal of the woman as the 'angel in the house', her role relating primarily to home and family, was well established by the early Victorian period, having been facilitated by the emphasis that evangelical Christianity placed

---

[2] Engels, *Condition*, p. 174. For Engels, of course, domestic employment did not equate with 'work', a view strongly rejected in much recent writing, and not necessarily shared by his working class contemporaries: see Schwarzkopf, *Unpicking gender*, pp. 139–41.

[3] Ure, *Philosophy of manufactures*, p. 23. He also thought, however, that the consequent lowering of the price of the finished product would expand demand, provide additional employment for all operatives and hence sustain male wages even in the face of such displacement (pp. 321–6), a view supported by R.M. Hartwell: *Industrial revolution*, pp. 318–19.

[4] Honeyman, *Women, gender and industrialisation*, pp. 42 and fn. 39, 71; Berg, 'Women's work', p. 71; for late nineteenth century expansion of women's employment in Leicester hosiery factories see Osterud, 'Gender divisions', p. 63.

[5] Engels, *Condition*, p. 175 fn. 1.

upon the relationship between religious and domestic virtues, giving women a key role in the moral regeneration of the nation through their centrality to the private sphere but absence from the public.[6] Quite how new the notion of separate spheres was is open to question. While Deborah Valenze asks 'why were female workers praised for their industriousness in the eighteenth century, but a century later, damned or pitied?', Bythell suggests that, 'The Victorians may have pushed the doctrine of "separate spheres" to its limits, but they did not invent it'.[7]

Humanitarian concern was also rooted in patriarchal notions, which lumped women together with children as the proper objects of paternalistic concern, in need of protection from exploitation while men could look after themselves. The 1842 Mines and Collieries Act—the first gender-specific piece of legislation—clearly highlights, however, the juxtaposition of humanitarian concern with moral disapprobation, for it was feared that the effect of mine work upon the woman was likely to 'destroy that purity and delicacy of character which ought ever to invest her with a hallowed atmosphere; and to lay the foundation for a life of sensual indulgence, domestic thriftlessness, dirt, dissipation and quarrels'.[8] Women working in cramped and over-heated conditions in close proximity to unrelated men were in danger of moral harm, but the effect upon their character could also compromise their role as wife and mother, the latter being a conclusion the Commissioners drew even though it was not convincingly supported by the evidence to hand.[9]

If mine work was seen by some as a recipe for female moral depravity, the factory girl also came in for extensive criticism, and was frequently stereotyped as unduly independent, coarse in manner and habits, sexually promiscuous and untrained in those domestic skills that properly befit a woman.[10] In the words of Deborah Valenze, 'The factory female acquired a reputation as a fallen creature disposed to indecency'.[11] Legislation to restrict the hours of female labour in factories followed hard on the heels of that for the mines, the Act of 1844 limiting their daily hours of labour, along with children, to 12,

[6] Hall, 'Early formation'; Davidoff and Hall, *Family fortunes*, pp. 149–92.
[7] Valenze, *First industrial woman*, p. 3; Bythell, 'Women in the work force', p. 51.
[8] Quoted in John, *By the sweat*, p. 46. The first explicitly 'protective' legislation with regard to women's employment was the 1878 Factory Act: Harrison, *Not only the 'dangerous trades'*, p. 27.
[9] Humphries, 'Protective legislation', pp. 17–18, 25–7.
[10] Valenze, *First industrial woman*, p. 86. Their independent spirit was commented upon also by sympathetic observers: see, for example, Gaskell, *Mary Barton*, pp. 40–3.
[11] Valenze, *First industrial woman*, p. 99.

while a further Act in 1847 restricted weekly work to 63 hours for women and children over 13. Hours of work were more flexible and less visible in domestic industry, and hence much harder to regulate, but adverse moral judgements were not reserved for women employed in factories and mines. If William Cobbett viewed straw plaiting as the ideal female occupation within the context of the rural family economy, a host of contemporary observers condemned the plait girl as precociously independent, ignorant, prone to both illegitimacy and prostitution, and unsuited to domestic service, while 'the fact of the girls being engrossed from early childhood by plaiting, they grow up as a class very ignorant of domestic economy'.[12] Glovers fared little better, for as one commentator wrote in 1867 'their morality is very low, their ignorance often excessive, and their language and behaviour often rough and coarse', and it was concluded that they were generally 'reckoned of rather easy virtue'.[13] Women field workers came in for criticism on the grounds that such work was inappropriate to the female constitution and had a brutalising effect, while those who worked in the notorious labour gangs were regarded as in similar moral jeopardy to their sisters in the mines, and condemnation of female agricultural employment gathered momentum after 1850.[14]

In the last half, and particularly the last quarter, of the nineteenth century the focus of attention, and disapproval, shifted more firmly towards the employment of married women. To a Unitarian minister such as John James Tayler, the home was 'the nursery of all kind and pure and humane affections', the very 'seedpot of the state', the domestic role of the wife an essential civilising—indeed, moral—influence, not only in the middle-class family but potentially too for the working classes of Victorian Manchester to whom he preached. Unsurprisingly, he complained of the 'too early and exclusive employment of females in manufacturing labour', which, he felt, contributed to the moral depravity of the working classes.[15] But in the later part of the century concern extended beyond considerations of domestic skills, the provision of domestic comfort or 'civilising' influences, and an extensive debate

---

[12] Cobbett, *Cottage economy*, p. 153; Goose. 'How saucy did it make the poor?', pp. 534–6.

[13] BPP 1867–8, XVII, *First Report of the Commissioners on the Employment of Children, Young Persons and Women in Agriculture*, quoted in Samuel, *Village life and labour*, p. 118.

[14] Verdon, 'Physically a splendid race', pp. 225–36. For similar thoughts on agriculture and a fuller discussion of mining see Humphries, 'Most free from objection', pp. 937–42.

[15] Wach, 'A "still small voice"', pp. 433–8, quotes at pp. 435, 436.

ensued about the effect of married women's work upon infant mortality. This was to lead to additional legislation designed to protect and prioritise motherhood, while also implying the culpability for high rates of infant mortality of both the working mother *and* the working husband who failed adequately to fulfil the breadwinner role.[16] In the view of Chiozza Money writing in 1905, in the interests of the well-being of children, 'The nation must set its face against the employment of married women in factories and workshops. . . . There is only one proper sphere of work for the married woman and that is her own home'.[17] By this time such views had already resulted in the imposition of a marriage bar in some industries, and hence in the centralised branches of the boot and shoe industry in Northampton, in hosiery in Nottingham, and in the Huddersfield woollen industry the employment of married women was prohibited.[18] At Dickinson's paper mills in Hertfordshire the manager thought their employment both 'quite unnecessary' and 'bad for the home', and here too their employment was eventually banned, although they had been regularly employed in the mills at mid-century as rag and paper sorters, paper colourers and even overlookers.[19] In the expanding area of clerical work in the later nineteenth and early twentieth centuries the situation was the same, with most employers hiring only single women or, occasionally, widows.[20]

Across the nineteenth century, therefore, there was protracted debate about the issue of women's work, and that debate increasingly extended beyond the question of factory employment that was of central concern to Engels. The factory as a locus for female employment dominated contemporary discussion out of all proportion to its significance, and, in consequence, until relatively recently historians of industrial England also tended to concentrate their attention upon the employment of women in factories. Ivy Pinchbeck's early contribution, however, provided a much needed corrective to the views of commentators such as Engels, by pointing up the advantages of factory labour over domestic industry in terms of the required work effort, conditions and wages. She

[16] Rose, *Limited livelihoods*, pp. 71–3.
[17] Quoted in Land, 'Family wage', p. 61.
[18] Rose, *Limited livelihoods*, pp. 45–7; Lewis, *Women in England*, pp. 146–9; Garrett, 'Trials of labour'.
[19] Rose, *Limited livelihoods*, p. 46; digitised Hertfordshire census enumerators' books, 1851, Watford Registration District: TNA, HO 107/1714. Available on CDRom from the Centre for Regional and Local History, University of Hertfordshire: Goose, *Hertfordshire census 1851*.
[20] Zimmeck, 'Jobs for the girls', p. 162. Separation of spheres was retained by the concentration of women in 'mechanical' as opposed to 'intellectual' work and by the strict physical segregation of men and women (p. 160).

also demonstrated that most female factory operatives were single, and argued that if they were indeed guilty, as often accused, of 'moral degradation', they merely shared in the mores of the working classes at large. Factory employment, Pinchbeck argued, gave single women a distinct social and economic independence, and this was a blessing, not a curse.[21] These themes were elaborated by Hewitt in her classic study of the Lancashire textile industry published in 1958, *Wives and mothers in Victorian industry*, which concluded that the worst evils associated with the employment of women in factories had been exaggerated, perhaps with the exception of effects upon infant mortality, that female factory employment was often a financial necessity as well as financially advantageous, but also that there was little evidence of women supplanting men as the family breadwinner.[22]

More recent research has confirmed that it is probably true that some female factory employment was better paid, and more regular, than many of the alternatives available to women. Cotton powerloom weaving in Lancashire was, however, wholly exceptional in paying the same piece rates to women and men. Here women were overwhelmingly dominant in the early nineteenth century, men only entering the trade in significant numbers from the 1840s and being paid the same low rate earned by the established female operatives.[23] Men may still have earned more than women overall, however, because they more commonly worked four to six looms while women worked two to four. Furthermore, it was only men who became overlookers and hence earned the very best rates of pay, while women may also have been more vulnerable to periodic cutbacks than men.[24] Nevertheless, it has been suggested that 'Women weavers . . . made better wages than any other women workers in the country', although this is a subject that has yet to be systematically explored.[25]

Women's wages in Cortauld's silk mill at Halstead in Essex were lower than wages in many other parts of the country, though they were higher than those available in alternative local employments. Here boys and girls aged 12–17 worked as winders earning 2s. – 4s. 6d. in 1861, after which most boys left the mill while those that remained were trained for higher grade positions. For females there was a very different career path which led almost exclusively to another low paid job,

---

[21] Pinchbeck, *Women workers*, esp. pp. 183–201, 306–16.
[22] Hewitt, *Wives and mothers*, pp. 35–152.
[23] The classic study of the rise and decline of male handloom weaving in the cotton industry is Bythell, *The handloom weavers*.
[24] Rose, *Limited livelihoods*, pp. 154–60.
[25] Rose, *Limited livelihoods*, p. 156.

usually in the weaving sheds where wages ranged from 5s. 8d. – 8s. Although women dominated the workforce numerically, virtually all of the higher grade posts were held by men, and those few women who did achieve overseeing positions were assistants to male overseers in the winding department.[26] Furthermore, women commonly entered the mill in their early teens and remained millworkers throughout their lives, with just temporary breaks for childbearing, a very different scenario to industrial Preston where only 23 per cent of wives with children were at work in 1851 (nearly half of whom were in non-factory occupations) and where women tended to stop working altogether once their families grew in size.[27] Hence, Judith Lown concludes, 'The circumstances of poverty, hardship and the "double burden" of employment and family responsibilities characterizing the lives of Halstead's female millworkers do little to support a stereotype of newly found freedom and independence . . . '.[28]

Notwithstanding the qualifications that more recent research has produced, the main focus of this earlier work was upon the factory, and its thrust was to indicate the advantages it brought to women to counterbalance a prior emphasis on the disadvantages, advantages in terms of female earnings and independence in particular. This emphasis was picked up by economic historians such as R.M. Hartwell, who argued that the industrial revolution marked 'the beginning of that most important and most beneficial of all the social revolutions of the last two centuries, the emancipation of women', again emphasising the employment of women outside of the domestic context.[29] These views were fundamentally challenged by Eric Richards in 1974.[30] Richards argued that, far from emancipating women, industrialisation resulted in a contraction in many of their traditional economic functions. Thus whilst in some sectors of the economy, most notably cotton textiles, there was a disproportionate expansion of female employment opportunities, this was more than offset by contraction elsewhere—in other branches of the textile industry, in the metal trades and in agriculture—while the new heavy industries offered little in the way of female employment. Furthermore, the typical factory girl was aged 16–21, and thus even here employment was little more than a life-cycle phase. The number of jobs for women may have risen until 1820, he

[26] Lown, *Women and industrialization*, pp. 45–59.
[27] Lown, *Women and industrialization.*, p. 60; Anderson, *Family structure*, pp. 71–2 and Table 22.
[28] Lown, *Women and industrialization*, p. 61.
[29] Hartwell, *Industrial Revolution*, pp. 57, 343.
[30] Richards, 'Women in the British economy'.

suggests, but undoubtedly contracted thereafter to produce the figures revealed in the national censuses of 1851–81 of just 20 per cent of all women in officially-recorded employment. Domestic service, the most widespread employment and the largest single occupational category, Richards characterised as a form of 'disguised underemployment'. Thus while pre-industrial female employment had stood close to a notional maximum, he argued, it fell drastically during the industrial revolution, and did not recover until the mid–twentieth century.

Richards was entirely correct about the predominance of domestic service in female employment by the mid–nineteenth century. The census of 1851 recorded 1,069,865 female servants in England and Wales (9.8 per cent of the female population), and a further 154,554 in Scotland (10.2 per cent of the female population).[31] In contrast to the sixteenth, seventeenth and eighteenth centuries, domestic service had now become overwhelmingly a female occupation, with just 13 male servants to every 100 female by this date.[32] The eighteenth century, particularly the latter half, witnessed the development of new standards of domestic housekeeping, the increasing feminisation of housework, greater wealth among middle-class employers, and a growing gentility that increasingly represented household tasks as demeaning.[33] Other factors at work were the reduction of female opportunities as servants in husbandry, the decline of hand spinning (particularly in the east and south of England) and sustained and rapid population growth through the late eighteenth and early nineteenth centuries—all of which served to increase the supply of female domestic servants alongside the increasing demand for their services. Nor should we forget the role that the lower middle classes played as employers of servants, for far from all domestics were to be found in the households of the wealthy. In Rochdale, the censuses of 1851, 1861 and 1871 reveal that retailers were the largest servant-employing group, while in 1871 16 per cent of servant-employing heads of household were artisans or manual workers, possibly reflecting the availability of workhouse girls who worked for board and without wages.[34]

---

[31] Roberts, *Women's work*, Table 2.1, p. 19.

[32] Valenze, *First industrial woman*, p. 158; Hill. *Women, work and sexual politics*, pp. 125–7; Kussmaul, *Servants in husbandry*, p. 4.

[33] Hill, *Women, work and sexual politics*, pp. 120–4, 128; Rouyer-Daney, 'Representations of housework', p. 34. The precise timing of the feminisation of housework remains open to debate: Lehmann, 'Birth of a new profession', p. 10 and sources cited therein.

[34] Higgs, 'Domestic service', pp. 133–5; Prochaska, 'Female philanthropy', pp. 82–3. For servant-keeping by tradesmen and shopkeepers in the eighteenth century see Kent, 'Ubiquitous but invisible'.

In absolute terms the number of female domestic servants continued to expand through to 1891, by when there were 1,759,555 in England and Wales and a further 190,051 in Scotland, but as a proportion of the female population the peak had been reached in 1871. It should be noted, however, that these figures include washerwomen and laundry workers, classified together in the census from 1871 forwards, and thus probably understate the decline in the number of strictly domestic servants, a decline that was clearly underway by the turn of the century, though remaining more marked in proportional than in absolute terms.[35] By this time complaints could be heard about the shortage of domestic help, a product of the declining rural population as well as the rise of alternative employment in shop and clerical work, for which—as noted in the 1901 Census Report—there is evidence of a preference where the choice could be made. That choice was often unavailable in the countryside, however, and notwithstanding the growth of female employment opportunities in both the tertiary sector of the economy and in a wider range of light manufacturing industries, domestic service remained the largest employer of female labour deep into the twentieth century.[36]

In a number of other respects, Richards' argument is now widely regarded as seriously flawed. It has commonly been argued that because the pre-industrial economy was subject to low levels of productivity it was simply essential for most women to work and, moreover, that they participated in a wide range of employments. But, as Jane Humphries noted in 1987, the evidence is largely qualitative, and dissenting voices to this orthodoxy could already be heard.[37] It is quite difficult to square Richards' view of female employment in pre-industrial England with a seventeenth-century labour market characterised by some economic historians as subject to endemic underemployment, while the most recent interpretation of early modern women's employment prospects concludes that between the later fifteenth and early seventeenth centuries 'a cluster of conjoined demographic, economic and cultural changes made it much more difficult for women to engage in profitable economic activities'.[38] In the eighteenth century spinning was the archetypal female

---

[35] Roberts, *Women's work*, Table 2.1 and pp. 19–20. The difficulties in interpreting the census data with respect to women's work in the late nineteenth and early twentieth centuries are discussed in detail by Garrett, 'Dawning of a new era?', chapter 15 below.

[36] Horn, *Rise and fall*, pp. 171–7; Banks, *Prosperity and parenthood*, pp. 134–5; Higgs, 'Domestic service', pp. 143–5.

[37] Humphries, 'Most free from objection', p. 931.

[38] Coleman, 'Labour in the English economy'; McIntosh, *Working women*, p. 252.

pursuit, but while it provided widespread employment it rarely guaranteed full-time work, and wage rates were so low that the unmarried or widowed spinster often had to resort to the parish to support an independent subsistence.[39] Writing in 1993 Bythell went so far to conclude that, 'At *no* time in the "pre-industrial" past was there a "golden age" when women were not confined—either by prevailing notions of "separate spheres", "complementarity", or "partnership", or by the institutional structures and mentalities created by patriarchy—to marginal, unskilled and poorly paid work', while he also insisted that distinctions needed to be made *within* the pre-industrial era.[40] The availability of work for women prior to industrialisation, and how this changed over a time, is another topic requiring further exploration.

It is in relation to what Richards had to say about the later eighteenth and nineteenth centuries that his views have been particularly strongly criticised. Like Hewitt and Pinchbeck before him, he focused unduly on female employment in factory towns, as if this was the only new employment available to women. This in turn reflects an outmoded view of the process of industrialisation as synonymous with large-scale, centralised production that should have died a death as a result of the work of John Clapham in the 1930s.[41] Four years after Richards' essay was published, Patricia Branca identified the contribution of the textile factory sector to female employment prior to the mid-nineteenth century as 'minute', and suggested that it required only a small absolute number of workers thereafter, but it has taken a long time for this to become more generally appreciated.[42] The substantial and sustained increase in demand associated with the industrial revolution affected industries both new and old, creating new forms of production in some sectors, but having a far wider impact upon traditional forms which also benefited from increased opportunities for employment. Richards does not even do justice to centralised production, neglecting the role that women played in the potteries, and in silk and linen manufacture. But, more importantly, he fails to appreciate the continued importance of women in a wide range of handicraft and retail trades, the growing importance of which in the early nineteenth century has recently been re-emphasised.[43] In particular Richards ignored those industries that can be characterised under the broad heading of outwork, sometimes described as the 'sweated trades', trades such as nail and chain-making,

[39] Berg, *Age of manufactures*, pp. 139–40.
[40] Bythell, 'Women in the workforce', p. 34.
[41] Clapham, *Economic history*, passim.
[42] Branca, *Women in Europe*, pp. 10–11, 39–40.
[43] Wrigley, 'Men on the land'; Goose, *St Albans*, pp. 79–80.

lace-making, shoebinding, garment-making, bonnet-sewing, straw-plaiting, hosiery and glove-making.[44]

Continuity between the pre-industrial and industrial eras is one theme in this discussion: as Gareth Stedman Jones wrote of London 'The effect of the Industrial Revolution on London was to accentuate its pre-industrial characteristics'.[45] But we are not merely dealing with continuity, for some traditional outwork trades expanded considerably during the later eighteenth and first half of the nineteenth centuries, creating industries that were of an entirely different order of scale and, to quote Bythell, 'those industries which continued to rely on outwork in the course of the nineteenth century, or which expanded for a time by using it, almost invariably increased their proportion of women workers'.[46] Indeed, growing mechanisation and an expansion of handicraft outwork often went hand in hand. Mechanisation of textile production necessitated the employment of more hands to make up the cloth into clothing, and even after the invention of the sewing machine much of this work took place within the home.[47] The boot and shoe industry combined factory production with decentralisation of the unskilled processes of the trade, while in hosiery the cheaper lines were produced in the factory and the more intricate 'fancy' work continued to be produced by hand.[48] A cheap and plentiful supply of female labour discouraged mechanisation, and helps to explain the slow rate of technical progress and capitalisation of nineteenth-century English industry. To neglect outwork as Richards did is to do a serious injustice to the extent of female employment during the nineteenth century, for 'Not only were most outworkers women: until the last quarter of the nineteenth century, most of the women who worked in industry probably did so as outworkers'.[49]

It is still not clear, however, how the balance sheet worked out, despite the additional contributions to the debate that that have been made in the last twenty years or so. Berg and Hudson, implicitly rejecting Richards' thesis, suggest that 'the role of women and children in both capital and labour intensive market-orientated manufacturing (in both the 'traditional' and the 'modern' sectors) probably reached a peak in the industrial revolution, making it a unique period in this

[44] Bythell, *Sweated trades*, passim. It is a moot point whether all of these trades should indeed be classified as 'sweated'.
[45] Stedman Jones, *Outcast London*, p. 26.
[46] Bythell, *Sweated trades*, p. 145.
[47] Pennington and Westover, *Hidden workforce*, pp. 32–3.
[48] Pennington and Westover, *Hidden workforce*, pp. 34–6.
[49] Bythell, *Sweated trades*, p. 145.

respect', even if by the mid-nineteenth century 'female and child labour was declining in importance'.[50] The overall picture suggested by Horrell and Humphries' analysis of 1,781 household budgets is more complex, but suggests greater participation during the Napoleonic Wars, a sharp drop in the post-war slump, some improvement during the 1830s, and long-term decline setting in during the 1840s. However, they also point out that experiences varied, and it is possible to discern different trends in women's work related to differences in the occupation and earning capacity of the male household head.[51]

Agricultural employment for women is a topic that has generated considerable interest and debate in its own right, and again has been the subject of both economic and cultural interpretations. Keith Snell has added considerable weight to the pessimistic view of female employment prospects, using settlement certificates allied to government reports to argue for a long-term decline of female participation in agriculture across much of the south and east, partly related to technological changes in grain growing areas but also the product of increasing uncertainty of employment amongst male agricultural labourers.[52] In dairying, it has been suggested, the prevailing matriarchal authority evident in the late eighteenth century was soon to be challenged by the development of new scientific approaches to production, approaches that were inherently masculine rather than feminine and which, allied to mechanisation, were in the short term to change the balance of authority within the industry and eventually to diminish the traditional female contribution.[53] However, the south and east, as Snell appreciated, is not the whole of England, and his arguments do not apply to the pastoral south-west, nor to much of the North where women continued to participate until well into the later part of the century.[54] Many historians have demonstrated the informal or part-time nature of much of female agricultural employment, which may obscure their contribution in the documentary record.[55] Furthermore, in the case of dairy production it is too easy to overstate the speed at which the changes that have been identified took place, and to pay

---

[50] Berg and Hudson, 'Rehabilitating the industrial revolution', pp. 35, 37. For an excellent discussion of the complexity of the issue of female employment in the early industrial period see Berg, 'Women's work'.

[51] Horrell and Humphries, 'Women's labour force participation', pp. 99–100.

[52] Snell, *Annals*, pp. 49–66.

[53] Valenze, *First industrial woman*, pp. 48–67.

[54] Valenze, *First industrial woman*, p. 64; Roberts, *Women's work*, pp. 33–4.

[55] Horn, *Labouring life*, pp. 60–89; Horn, *Victorian countrywoman*; Miller, 'Hidden workforce'.

insufficient regard to the strength of regional and local cultural traditions, while comparative work on England and America has indeed identified a decline in female participation in cheesemaking in the latter country but in 'English farmhouse cheesemaking between 1800 and 1930, the basic division of labour according to gender persisted'.[56] These issues are further explored by Pam Sharpe in chapter three, below.

One feature of the changing nature of women's work that is generally agreed upon is the importance of the growth of tertiary employment towards the end of the nineteenth century. Inroads into the professions were made only slowly, and women constituted only 6 per cent of the higher professions by 1911, and only 8 per cent as late as 1951.[57] Much greater gains were made in lower status 'white blouse' employment: as shop assistants, clerks, elementary schoolteachers and nurses. There were almost half a million female shop assistants in England and Wales by 1914, while by the same date nearly three-quarters of all elementary teachers were women. Both the typewriter and the telephone exchange quickly became the province of women towards the end of the nineteenth century, and the Post Office provided unprecedented opportunities for single, middle-class women to gain respectable employment, albeit with inferior status, prospects and pay than those achieved by men.[58] Nevertheless, women were not completely powerless, and were prepared to use the weapon of mobility in search of better pay and conditions, a strategy that Clara Collet's survey of rates of pay, conducted in 1907, suggests was beginning to bear fruit. As Zimmeck puts it, 'Women clerks thus exercised a good deal of autonomy in their choice of work. They decided what they wanted and then went after it, even if this meant changing jobs several times over'.[59]

Despite some areas of clarity and agreement, after well over half a century of historical interest and an upsurge of activity during the past thirty or so years, many fundamental questions about women's work remain open to debate, such as the role women played in the process of transition from a pre-industrial to an industrial economy, the impact that industrialisation had upon their employment patterns and prospects, and the changing value systems and gender relationships that accompanied these developments. For, despite all of these efforts, two recalcitrant problems remain. First, we remain uncertain about the extent and nature

[56] McMurry, 'Women's work in agriculture', p. 269. See also Bouquet, *Family, servants and visitors*, pp. 34–6, 42.
[57] Lewis, *Women in England*, p. 194.
[58] Lewis, *Women in England*, pp. 195–200; John, 'Introduction', pp. 17–20; Zimmeck, 'Jobs for the girls', pp. 158–64.
[59] Zimmeck, 'Jobs for the girls', pp. 166–8.

of women's work in the pre-industrial period. As Pam Sharpe has recently written, 'Attempts to consider the amount of work, type of work, and sexual division of labour in the industrial revolution founder on this problem of lack of information regarding the early modern period'.[60] It is also true, however, that much remains unclear about the extent and importance of female participation in the labour force of industrial England, for although we have more information than we did two decades ago, that information remains fragmented and disjointed: 'the ingredients have been collected but the cake has yet to be mixed'.[61] But Sharpe goes further, suggesting that there may well be more ingredients to collect before we are in a position to achieve culinary success: 'We still need more specific studies of women's employment in different areas. We have not yet progressed from a situation where in the early 1970s Richards had to deal 'mainly in aggregates in a subject where local studies are sparse'.[62]

It is, of course, correct to suggest that national aggregates often obscure as much as they illuminate, and the importance of regional and local perspectives is the very essence of the present volume. Interestingly, while offering an analysis drawn from a national sample of household budgets, Horrell and Humphries first important conclusion was that

> accounts of women's and children's contributions to family incomes must be conditional on their occupational and regional identity, which limits 'grand theories' of the causes of women's marginalization. Theories that depict women, whatever their circumstances, as undifferentiated victims of allied economic and ideological forces must give way to detailed analyses of institutional changes at occupational and regional levels.[63]

Appreciation of the need for regional and local perspective does, in fact, echo through the extant literature on women's work. Here is Bythell: 'What women did depended largely on the peculiar economic structure of the place where they were born, and generalizations based on crude national totals ignore the essential element of regional variety'.[64] In similar fashion Hudson and Lee, in their historical overview of women's work and the family economy, emphasise the importance of the local

---

[60] Sharpe, 'Continuity and change', p. 356. In a valuable recent discussion Sara Horrell finds little to support De Vries' notion of increased female participation in the later seventeenth century due to an 'industrious revolution': 'Women and the industrious revolution'.

[61] Sharpe, 'Continuity and change', p. 353.

[62] Sharpe, 'Continuity and change', p. 357.

[63] Horrell and Humphries, 'Women's labour force participation', p. 105.

[64] Bythell, 'Women in the work force', p. 38.

and regional dimension, to agriculture, rural manufacturing, factory employment and informal economic activity, concluding that

> the process of industrialization needs to be examined as a highly diverse regional phenomenon, involving a variegated pattern of sectoral balance and attendant levels of technological development. This, in turn, generated regionally divergent gender-specific labour markets and local configurations of female employment opportunities in both formal and non-formal activities.[65]

It was not simply a case of sectoral diversity, however, for there were also enormous local variations *within* sectors. With regard to outwork Bythell notes its 'extreme diversity', while Pennington and Westover write that, 'During our research for this book we uncovered many more home industries which are too numerous to mention, many being specific to a particular locality'.[66] The importance of laundry work is undeniable given its representation in Victorian censuses, but it was particularly heavily concentrated in London, and evolved in its structure as large steam laundries emerged from the 1890s.[67] Verdon stresses how hard it is to generalise about women in agriculture: significant regional variations existed even within the southern arable zone between 1790 and 1850, while in the period 1850–70 there were 'regional variations not only between different counties, but also between different areas within counties'.[68] The best recent surveys echo this view, and hence Katrina Honeyman notes regional variations—not only in agriculture and industry—but also more generally in 'the extent to which the working-class family shifted from a family economy to a family wage economy'.[69] Kathryn Gleadle similarly highlights the 'highly diverse labour market for women', and advises that the 'enormous regional and sectoral variations in both employment practices and customs of gendered labour division forewarn against simple analyses of female exploitation in the workplace'.[70] For the late nineteenth and early twentieth centuries, Harrison too stresses how 'overall patterns obscure many changes which occurred in the kinds of work women did and regional as well as more local patterns of employment'.[71]

---

[65] Hudson and Lee, 'Women's work', pp. 10, 15, 16, 28–9, quote from p. 33.
[66] Bythell, *Sweated trades*, p. 48; Pennington and Westover, *Hidden workforce*, p. 65.
[67] Malcolmson, *English laundresses*, pp. 7–9.
[68] Verdon, 'A diminishing force?', p. 210; Verdon, 'Physically a splendid race', p. 236.
[69] Honeyman, *Women, gender and industrialisation*, pp. 79, 113, 140.
[70] Gleadle, *British women*, p. 9.
[71] Harrison, *Not only the 'dangerous trades'*, p. 6.

The importance of regional and local perspectives extends beyond the simple question of numbers of women employed and types of employment available, however, for it is also relevant to the issue of attitudes to women's work, a topic so frequently subject to overarching generalisation. While it may indeed be possible, as discussed above, to detect broad shifts of opinion about the proper role of women in general or married women in particular, these views were often refracted through the glass of local labour market requirements and cultural traditions. Hence in the case of Courtauld's silk mill at Halstead, both George and Samuel Courtauld espoused the 'domestic ideal' for women, an ideal that was played out within their own families as the women withdrew from active involvement in the industry. At the same time, however, their mill was dependent upon cheap, female labour, and hence they had to reconcile their ideological and practical positions by presenting the mill as a locus of paternalism, recreating the family within the workplace.[72] Paternalistic employment regimes in family-owned businesses proliferated in the second half of the nineteenth century, at the apogee of which stood the Cadbury family of Birmingham, who rigidly enforced gender distinctions from an early age, provided opportunities appropriate for the different destinies of their male and female employees, and hence recreated gendered familial structures within the workplace. While this may have been astute managerial practice, it is clear too that it was a means to resolve the conflict of separate spheres ideology with reliance upon cheap, female labour.[73] The Cortaulds and Cadburys were by no means alone in adopting such practices, though one must wonder how many firms could afford them, and how deeply troubled by the conflict between this hegemonic ideology and practical necessity most employers really were. As Hudson and Lee have argued, a 'general societal attitude which deplored heavy work for women was conveniently forgotten in areas where female labour remained vital'. Hence in the north-east of England female 'bondagers' continued to be employed in field gangs into the late nineteenth century, despite the restrictions of the Gangs Act of 1867 and the furore over the issue that had led to its passage.[74] Indeed, in the same year the Hexham Board of Guardians argued that, 'to prohibit female labour in this district would simply be to prohibit

---

[72] Lown, *Women and industrialisation*, pp. 8, 29, 96–135, 163.

[73] Rose, *Limited livelihoods*, pp. 33–45; Joyce, 'The new paternalism', in *Work, society and politics*, pp. 134–57.

[74] Hudson and Lee, 'Women's work', p. 10; Verdon, *Rural women workers*, pp. 110–13, 198–9.

farming'.[75] Both 'bondagers' and 'cottars'—independent female labourers who worked in return for a rent free cottage—remained vital to the agrarian economy of Northumberland into the 1890s, constituting fully one-quarter of its farm labour force, at a time when women in many other parts of the country were withdrawing from agricultural work and rural populations were declining.[76]

It was not only among employers that perspectives on women's work varied regionally and locally, however. Writing in 1896, Clara Collet suggested that the basic north/south divide in women's employment patterns that she found in the 1891 census reflected fundamentally different attitudes to work: in northern England women commonly considered work as a lifelong occupation, whereas in the south it was generally regarded as a necessary—if unfortunate—prelude to marriage, wedlock providing a 'release from wage-earning employment'.[77] Collet's view was itself, of course, a very sweeping generalisation, and differences in attitudes have also been identified on an occupational basis. Despite the growing acceptance, even within the working class itself, of notions of patriarchy in the later nineteenth century, in the pottery industry the male breadwinner ethos appears to have failed to take hold, and here women's contribution to the labour force remained crucial, while they also participated in trade union activity.[78] Indeed, there was a substantial increase in the number of wives of potters working outside of the home between 1861 and 1881, and the tradition continued into the twentieth century.[79] Lancashire textiles also witnessed growing numbers of married and widowed women working in factories across the second half of the nineteenth century, while fewer married women were employed in textile factories in the West Riding of Yorkshire.[80] Employment in cotton weaving in Lancashire was a source of great pride to its female workforce in the late nineteenth and early twentieth centuries, while—notwithstanding the negative opinion of Engels—for men to undertake domestic work was quite normal, not a reason for shame.[81] Even within an industry that has been universally

---

[75] Quoted in Long, *Conversations in cold rooms*, p. 83.

[76] Long, *Conversations in cold rooms*, pp. 81–8; Hostettler, 'Women farm workers', p. 40. Seccombe also notes how employers who relied on female labour could be hypocritical in this respect: 'Patriarchy stabilized', pp. 73–4.

[77] Cited in Harrison, *Not only the 'dangerous trades'*, p. 6.

[78] Whipp, 'Kinship, labour and enterprise'; Hudson and Lee, 'Women's work', p. 32.

[79] Dupree, *Family structure*, p. 171; Whipp, *Patterns of labour*.

[80] Joyce, *Work, society and politics*, p. 112.

[81] Schwarzkopf, *Unpicking gender*, pp. 139–41.

characterised as a 'sweated trade' by the late nineteenth century, that of tailoring, there were distinct differences between the organisation of the industry in Leeds and in London. In Leeds factory production was more common than in London, women's wages—although still low—were higher too, and one must wonder how this might have affected both the employment patterns of married women and attitudes towards their employment outside of the home.[82] In the Leicester hosiery industry, the development of mechanised seaming after 1870 drew women out of the home and into the factory, at the very time that concern about married women's employment outside the home was gathering pace.[83] Local labour market conditions could also engender different attitudes to women's work within particular trades: brickmaking was women's work in the Black Country because male employment in ironworks and coalpits was plentiful, whereas in the textile areas of Lancashire, where male employment was more precarious, it was a male preserve.[84] The very existence of employment opportunities for women could itself engender different attitudes. This finds reflection in the regularity with which women's work was recorded by local enumerators in the decennial census returns. In areas where women commonly worked, such as in industrial Preston and Lancashire more generally, or in the straw plait and hat regions of the south Midlands, the work of women— whether single or married—was generally quite faithfully recorded.[85] Where women's employment was more sporadic, or only on a part-time footing, there was a much greater chance of under-recording.[86] Local practice, therefore, could engender very different perceptions and expectations of women's economic role and contribution, rather than that involvement being largely determined by an ideology of paternalism and belief in separate spheres.

It is not only regional and local variation that makes it difficult fully to map out the changing incidence of women's work in industrial England: source material is either sparse, or problematic. This is particularly true of the eighteenth and early nineteenth centuries, when very little systematic information on women's employment is available. Often excluded from the formal procedures of apprenticeship and

---

[82] Morris, 'Characteristics of sweating', pp. 113–14; Honeyman, 'Gender divisions', 48–9.

[83] Osterud, 'Gender divisions', p. 63.

[84] Lewis, *Women in England*, p. 162.

[85] Anderson, 'Married women's employment', chapter 8 below; McKay, 'Married women and work', chapter 7 below; Goose, *St Albans*, pp. 86–8; Goose, 'Straw plait and hat trades, chapter 5 below.

[86] For similar views see Shaw-Taylor, 'Diverse experiences', chapter 2 below.

denied entry to borough freedoms and guilds, largely absent from probate documentation unless they were widowed, and most commonly found working in a subsidiary role within the domestic context, women as workers were 'ignored, unrecorded and invisible'.[87] Most women's work in London was 'casual, intermittent, or seasonal', and thus difficult to trace in the documentary record.[88] Much of what we know about women's employment in this period comes from contemporary comment by authors such as Daniel Defoe, Thomas Firmin or Frederic Eden, the periodical publications that grow in number from the mid-eighteenth century, the unofficial contemporary estimates of writers such as Gregory King, Joseph Massie or Patrick Colquhoun, or extrapolation back from the early occupational censuses of 1841 and 1851.[89] Depositions made in ecclesiastical court proceedings can prove valuable where a considerable volume of documentation survives, but even for London between 1695 and 1725 a search of three courts produced a female employment sample of only 851, of which 613 declared an occupation.[90] We can, of course, deduce trends in female employment from the rise and decline of particular industries and sectors, from which it does seems likely that in both East Anglia and the West Country, as their textile industries came under pressure and then contracted during the eighteenth century, women's work as spinners for the cloth trade contracted too.[91] But although the ubiquity of female spinsters is attested in much contemporary comment, as Pinchbeck remarked, 'when we try to discover what proportion of women was so engaged, and how many might be assumed to be in receipt of wages and contributing to the support of their families, the material becomes tantalisingly vague'.[92] Even the pictorial record provides but scant representation of female employment, and where women do feature they are commonly either idealised or ridiculed.[93] So while Valenze has argued that 'The work of women was everywhere in evidence in eighteenth-

[87] Quote taken from the heading to chapter 9 of Hill, *Women, work and sexual politics*, p. 148. For a discussion of female apprenticeship, which again emphasises their relative invisibility, see Hill, *Women, work and sexual politics*, pp. 85–102; Earle, 'Female labour market', p. 344 fn. 45. For formal exclusion and strategies for involvement in towns, see Simonton, 'Claiming their place in the corporate community'.

[88] Earle, 'Female labour market', p. 342.

[89] Hill, *Women, work and sexual politics*, pp. 148–9; Pinchbeck, *Women workers*, p. 2 and Appendix and bibliography, pp. 317–31.

[90] Earle, 'Female labour market', Tables 2 and 8, pp. 332, 337.

[91] For a discussion of the reasons for this: Berg, *Age of manufactures*, pp. 108–22.

[92] Pinchbeck, *Women workers*, p. 132.

[93] Baudino, 'Eighteenth-century images'.

century England', that evidence is far from comprehensive, and rarely reveals precisely how many women worked or in what capacities.[94]

From the early nineteenth century, parliamentary reports and commissions of enquiry provide a growing body of evidence for the work of both women and children, but the evidence they contain is often disappointing in its geographical coverage, chronologically selective and subject to distortion through special pleading. These sources were extensively used by Pinchbeck and other early historians of women's work, but the purposes for which they were written need to be carefully considered, as does the social background of the authors and witnesses whose views were drawn upon, and hence they should be viewed as social constructs rather than as objective evidence.[95] Furthermore, the Royal Commissions of Enquiry established in the 1830s, 1840s and 1860s investigated employment, wages and conditions in domestic industries during periods of trade depression, and their findings cannot, therefore, be taken to represent the situation in more normal years.[96] Furthermore, even the most comprehensive reports, notably the 1834 Royal Commission on the Poor Laws, provide at best patchy geographic coverage. The 'Answers to Rural Queries' that the Poor Law Report contains have been systematically employed to investigate the particular contribution to family budgets of gleaning, and rural women's and children's employment more generally.[97] It is, however, by no means an easy document to use, for the questions it contains are often poorly phrased, and the qualifications of the respondents to answer them might also be called into question.[98] Notwithstanding the advantage presented by its national coverage, only about 10 per cent of the parishes of England and Wales are represented, the number which returned useful information on female employment was smaller still, and those that provided data on the contribution of women and children to family budgets was tiny, most commonly either none or just a single parish per county.[99] Conclusions about the broad regional pattern of female employment might be drawn from this

---

94 Valenze, *First industrial woman*, p. 13. Such remarks, if taken to imply ubiquitous employment, sit uncomfortably alongside Sara Horrell's conclusion that the 'existence of an industrious revolution in the late seventeenth century finds little support' form extant evidence on female employment: 'Women and the industrious revolution'.

95 Sayer, *Women of the fields*, p. 3; Verdon, *Rural women workers*, p. 35.

96 See also Goose, 'Straw plait and hat trades', chapter 5 below, pp. 111–12.

97 King, 'Customary rights'; Verdon, 'Rural labour market'.

98 Verdon, 'Rural labour market', pp. 302–3.

99 Verdon, 'Rural labour market', pp. 303, Figure 6, p. 317.

evidence, but precise quantification is impossible and much local detail is inevitably obscured.

Another form of evidence that has recently been the subject of extensive analysis and discussion is that drawn from family budgets. Horrell and Humphries' sample of 1,781 family budgets drawn from 59 sources between 1787 and 1865 has formed the basis for a string of illuminating articles on various aspects of female and child employment— in particular female participation rates and the contribution of their earnings to total family budgets.[100] This is not, of course, in any sense a 'representative' sample, and as some of these budgets are taken from Parliamentary Papers and the work of contemporary social commentators it is possible that they were influenced by the purpose of the investigation in hand. They do, however, provide evidence for a period where other sources are sparse, and for a key period in England's industrialisation. The occupationally weighted aggregate participation series that Horrell and Humphries construct from these data reveal a sharp decline in participation in the post Napoleonic War slump, an increase during the 1830s, and renewed decline in the 1840s which continued after mid century.[101] But while the broad, long-term picture is one of decline, the trend varied between occupational groups, which again reflect different regional experiences. As the data employed by Horrell and Humphries is divided into broad categories according to the occupation of the male head of household, however, it is not possible to determine the experience of precise regions, let alone particular localities or trades, for even a sample as impressive in size as this one is quickly reduced to very small numbers indeed when broken down both chronologically and geographically.[102] This may explain why, although the county of Hertfordshire was undoubtedly what Horrell and Humphries would call a 'low-wage agriculture' area, there is little congruence between their results—either for participation or earnings—and those from the detailed regional analysis of the straw plait and hat trades here presented in chapter 5 below.[103]

From 1841 onwards the decennial census provides the opportunity to conduct local and regional research into female employment on a firmer foundation. Most historians have relied upon the published census

---

[100] Most notably Horrell and Humphries, 'Women's labour force participation'.

[101] Horrell and Humphries, 'Women's labour force participation', p. 100.

[102] See the sample sizes presented in Horrell and Humphries, 'Women's labour force participation', Table 3, p. 107.

[103] Horrell and Humphries are, of course, aware of these shortcomings, and emphasise the need for more regional, and occupationally specific, research: 'Women's labour force participation, pp. 105–6.

reports, while more intensive, usually local, studies employ the individual Census Enumerators Books (hereafter CEBs) from which the reports were derived. These too, of course, have been severely criticised for understating women's employment, and some judgements have been quite extreme.[104] Higgs has suggested that, because the census returns were compiled by male enumerators and the schedules were filled in by heads of households who were usually male, 'women tended to be defined as dependants, whatever their productive functions'.[105] Although the instructions to householders in 1851 required the recording of women's occupations when they were *regularly* employed either away from home, or at home in any but domestic duties, it is possible that much part-time, casual or seasonal female employment went unrecorded, an issue explored in relation to the 1851 census by Shaw-Taylor in chapter two, below.[106] Seasonal work may also have gone unnoticed if enumerators and householders recorded only those occupations actually being conducted on census night itself, March 30th in 1851, which would obviously exclude much seasonal agricultural work.[107] The census will also fail to represent women's work that emerged only temporarily, such as the beadwork that briefly thrived in Warwickshire in the later 1860s. While at its peak this industry may have employed several hundred women and children, only a solitary female 'trimming and beadworker' is recorded in the 1871 census.[108] There is indeed some evidence of erratic recording of female occupations and a few instances where entries for married women are suspiciously standardised which might reflect these difficulties, though the more informed critics of the census data have concluded that the jury remains out on the question of general under-enumeration.[109]

---

[104] Hudson has described them as 'hopelessly inaccurate in recording female work': *History by numbers*, p. 14; Davidoff and Hall described them as 'almost useless' for the determination of women's occupations unless they were household heads: *Family fortunes*, p. 273. See also Gleadle, *British women*, pp. 10, 21, 96; Roberts, *Women's work*, table 1.2, p. 11.

[105] Higgs, 'Women, occupations and work', pp. 60–2.

[106] Higgs, 'Women, occupations and work', pp. 61–3; and see Shaw-Taylor, 'Diverse experiences', chapter 2 below, pp. 32–42.

[107] Seasonal agricultural work was not *invariably* excluded, however. The 1851 return for Corfe Castle in Dorset , for example, lists a small number of individuals as employed in weeding, stone picking or 'occasionally works on the farm'. This may, of course, represent merely the tip of an iceberg, as Saito suggests, but it is at least possible too that it represents the reality of the situation. See Saito, 'Who worked when?', chapter 9 below, pp. 215–16.

[108] Kingman, ' "Doing the beads" ', p. 85.

[109] Higgs, 'Women, occupations and work', pp. 64–8; and see Anderson, 'What can the mid-Victorian censuses tell us?', chapter 8 below.

There may well have been particular problems in relation to the recording of women working in the agricultural sector, apart from the exclusion of seasonal harvest workers and the failure to record activities such as gleaning, clearly not an official occupation but potentially a valuable contribution to the family budget.[110] Numerous other part-time or seasonal agricultural activities performed by women, such as weeding, stone-picking, dairying, hoeing turnips, digging and pulling potatoes and other roots, planting beans and so on may also have gone unrecorded.[111] Local specialities, the chronology of which failed to match that of the census, may also have been ignored, amongst which we can include lavender growing in the region of Hitchin in Hertfordshire. Although approximately 100 acres in the vicinity of the town were devoted to lavender in the later nineteenth century, it left no trace in the census record, no doubt because it was harvested (by women) in July.[112] Some female farm servants may have been mistakenly entered as domestic servants rather than as agricultural workers, and there may be some confusion too with regard to those entered as 'farmer's wife' or 'farmer's daughter'.[113] Comparison between farm wage books and the 1871 census for five Gloucestershire parishes has revealed considerable under-enumeration of women who worked on the land for perhaps as much as one-third of the year, as well as discrepant treatment of female agricultural work between parishes.[114] Investigation of women's employment in agriculture, therefore, as Verdon demonstrates in chapter 4 below, requires the deployment of a range of other sources—farm accounts, parliamentary papers, contemporary reports and descriptions—in addition to the census.

This does not exhaust the problems that have been identified regarding female occupational designations in the census. There may also be a tendency for the published census reports to exaggerate the number of true domestic servants, possibly including those simply providing support to relatives and perhaps also the employees of retailers who might more properly be described as shop assistants, though such distinctions can usually be made through an examination of the census enumerators books themselves.[115] More problematic is the unstated contribution of wives (and possibly also daughters) in particular trades,

---

[110] Sharpe, 'Continuity and change', p. 357; King, 'Customary rights'.
[111] Horn, *Life and labour*, pp. 75–7.
[112] Festing, *Story of lavender*; Goose, *Hertfordshire census 1851*.
[113] Higgs, 'Occupational censuses', pp. 704–5, 709–11.
[114] Miller, 'Hidden workforce'.
[115] Higgs, 'Tabulation of occupations', chapter 11 below, and Anderson, 'Mis-specification of servant occupations', chapter 12 below.

notably in the service sector. It is most unlikely that the wives of innkeepers and victuallers, for example, failed to contribute towards the running of these establishments, but that contribution is not always clear in the CEBs.[116] Indeed, the compilers of the 1851 Census Report themselves acknowledged this difficulty which, they felt, extended beyond the service trades, and hence in that report, 'The "Wives" of "Innkeepers", "Beershop-keepers", "Shoemakers", "Shopkeepers", "Butchers", "Farmers" are specifically returned in the Table, as they are generally engaged in the same business as their husbands'.[117] If studies based upon CEBs frequently exclude those described as 'wife' and possibly understate the contribution of women, therefore, for these occupations at least the published report can only exaggerate female involvement by assuming that each and every wife of these tradesmen and craftsmen was occupationally active.

Certainly, the published reports must be handled with care, for—as this example shows—they introduce an additional layer of interpretation between the historian and the original returns. Furthermore, they were not consistent over time, and changes in systems of classification, as well as in the instructions given to enumerators, pose further challenges to the historian of women's work.[118] But with regard to the CEBs themselves it is possible to become unduly sceptical, to focus only upon instances of apparent omission and to ignore the clear evidence that many enumerators did a very good job indeed. If the CEBs *invariably* under-represent female employment, as some critics have suggested, it is very difficult to understand how they have so frequently been employed to highlight very high levels of female employment in cottage industries in particular localities and regions, such as Cardington in Bedfordshire, Colyton in Devon, Great Horwood in Buckinghamshire or south and west Hertfordshire.[119] These studies have shown that in areas where a culture of women's work clearly existed, usually itself the product of regular female employment over a considerable period of time, the work of both single and married women was *generally* faithfully

---

[116] Even descriptions such as 'innkeepers' wife' are ambiguous, and it is clear that some enumerators completely misunderstood the instructions they were given. One amongst many examples is the town of Great Berkhamsted, Hertfordshire, in 1851, where virtually *all* wives are recorded in this way, whatever the occupation of the male household head.

[117] BPP 1852–3, LXXXVIII, *Population tables II: ages, civil condition, occupations and birthplace of the people*, p. 13 fn.

[118] See, for instance, Garrett, 'Dawning of a new era?', chapter 15 below.

[119] Tranter, 'Social structure'; Saito, 'Who worked when?', chapter 9 below, Table 9.2; Wall, 'Work, welfare and family', pp. 279–80; Horn, 'Victorian villages', Table 2, p. 27; Goose, 'Straw plait and hat trades', chapter 5 below.

recorded. Recent work on industrial Lancashire and Cheshire, using both the published census reports and local CEBs, supports this conclusion, finding little evidence of under-recording of female domestic or factory-based textile work, and consistent recording of the work of married women through into the early twentieth century.[120] Regional analysis of the patterns of female employment found in the 1851 census across England also encourages confidence in the general reliability of this data.[121] This is not to say that the local enumerations can always be relied upon, as those examined below for Hertfordshire reveal.[122] Careful inspection and analysis of the evidence for individual enumeration districts may be necessary to detect any lapses, but it is encouraging that their detection *is* possible—at least within the context of a broader regional study.

This brief review of some key sources for the history of women's work is not, of course, by any means comprehensive, and passes over some of the evidence deployed below by contributors to this volume, such as the ethnographic evidence used by Davies to identify female healers in chapter 10, and the detailed business and personal records used by Nenadic in chapter 13 to throw light upon the operations of female entrepreneurs in late nineteenth-century Edinburgh.[123] In each of these chapters, however, census records are used in conjunction with these other sources, and might also be fruitfully deployed to investigate female investors (commonly identified as annuitants, property-holders or 'of independent means') in support of the work currently being undertaken on this subject by David Green and Lucy Newton using probate, taxation and banking records.[124] It is fitting, therefore, that the census

---

[120] McKay, 'Married women and work', chapter 7 below; Anderson, 'What can the mid-Victorian censuses tell us?', chapter 8 below.

[121] Shaw-Taylor, 'Diverse experiences', chapter 2 below.

[122] See chapter 5, p. 103.

[123] We must also look forward to publication of the full results of Jane Humphries' analysis of working-class autobiographical evidence, reported at the Economic History Society Annual Conference, 8–10 April 2005, University of Leicester: 'Sons and mothers: family relations and sources of family income in early industrial Britain'. The literature on women in business is expanding rapidly: for valuable recent additions see Barker, *Business of women*; Beachy, Craig and Owens (eds), *Women, business and finance*; Phillips, *Women in business*. For the early twentieth century oral evidence has proved valuable, while for a limited number of female trades trade union records can also be used: see, for instance, Roberts, *A woman's place*; Schwarzkopf, *Social construction of gender*.

[124] David Green, 'Feathering the nest: men's and women's wealth in nineteenth-century London', and Lucy Newton, 'Women investors in early nineteenth-century English joint-stock banks', reported at the Economic History Society Annual Conference, University of Reading, 31 March–2 April 2006. See also Green and Owens, 'Gentlewomanly capitalism?'.

should take pride of place in this discussion, given its prominence in so many of the chapters in this book, and the enormous scope that exists for its further exploitation in the analysis of female employment and livelihood at the local and regional level from the mid–nineteenth century forwards. Historians of women's work have barely begun to exploit its full potential—for the detailed analysis of individual trades and crafts, the local and regional geography of female occupations, the investigation of age and life-cycle employment, the relationship between women's work and family structure, or the occupational experiences of never-married and widowed women, to name just a few avenues of enquiry.[125] Notwithstanding its shortcomings and the interpretative difficulties it sometimes poses, and while best practice is ever likely to involve its use in conjunction with additional documentation, the census will inevitably remain central to the further examination of female employment in industrial England.

Only once more work along these lines had been completed will it be possible to resolve certain tensions—even contradictions—that currently exist within the historiography of women's work, for there are many issues that remain to be resolved quite apart from the basic question relating to changing participation over time. How crucial was female employment, formal and informal, to family economies? On the one hand some historians emphasise the inadequacy of 'many' or even 'most' male working-class incomes to maintain a family, while on the other family budget studies seem to indicate that working women made only a modest contribution to total family incomes, even if this did vary between occupational groups.[126] Did women work for 'pin money', as Clementina Black appears to have thought in the early twentieth century, or were their earnings essential to family maintenance?[127] Similarly, there is a tension between the view that female earnings were crucial—even in the later nineteenth century when the real wages of men were improving—and the emphasis upon the increasing marginalisation of women apparent in some (often feminist) interpretations: how can they have been effectively marginalised, yet found to be making a crucial and

---

[125] For never-married women see Christine Jones, 'From Hartland to Hartley', chapter 14 below.

[126] Rose, *Limited livelihoods*, pp. 84, 100, 185; Horrell and Humphries, 'Women's labour force participation', Table 3, p. 107. Booth emphasised the necessity for women to contribute towards family incomes in late nineteenth-century London: Schmiechen, *Sweated industries*, p. 64.

[127] Pennington and Westover, *Hidden workforce*, pp. 75–6, citing Black's *Married women's work*, published in 1915.

multi-faceted contribution, at one and the same time.[128] This also introduces the question of their role in self-provisioning and the 'informal' economy, which—notwithstanding the views of Engels reported at the start of this chapter—often involved hard physical toil, as well as ingenuity in management and diplomatic skills, even if the end product was not a cash wage. In this respect, of course, sources are more intractable and the evidence often less easy to quantify, but there are already some excellent extant discussions of such topics, while the census again provides systematic evidence on the keeping of lodgers and the way in which households could be structured to enhance economic security in response to regional or local economic circumstances.[129]

The development of the ideology of the male breadwinner family and trade union demands for a family wage may have gathered momentum towards the later nineteenth century, but how large was the gap between ideology and reality, and to what extent was this occupationally or regionally specific?[130] We have already noted that employers could themselves be hypocritical, defending women's work when they needed female labour.[131] It may well be that working-class attitudes concerning fit work for women—*and* for men—could also be compromised by economic necessity, as the relatively high number of adult men working in the straw industry in Bedfordshire in 1871, or the appearance of male milkmen in Buckinghamshire, would seem to indicate.[132] There are important interpretative issues to be resolved too.

---

[128] Compare, for example, Rose, *Limited livelihoods*, pp. 84, 100, 185; Honeyman, *Women, gender and industrialisation*, pp. 92, 112; Zimmeck, 'Jobs for the girls', p. 153; August, 'How separate a sphere?' Hilary Land goes so far as to suggest that married women were no longer *expected* to make a financial contribution by the end of the century: Land, 'Family wage', p. 60.

[129] Lane, 'Work on the margins'; Humphries, 'Enclosure, common rights and women'; Humphries, 'Female-headed households'; Ross, *Love and toil*, esp. pp. 21–84; Chinn, *They worked all their lives*, esp. pp. 12–79; Rose, 'Widowhood and poverty'; Robin, 'Family care of the elderly'; Gittins, 'Marital status, work and kinship'; Wall, 'Work, welfare and the family'; Cooper and Donald. 'Households and "hidden" kin'; Goose, *Berkhamsted region*, pp. 74–5; Goose, *St Albans and its region*, pp. 158–9, 166–7; Goose, 'Poverty, old age and gender', pp. 368–71; Armstrong, *Stability and change*, pp. 180–2; Dupree, *Family structure*, p. 108, and Dupree, 'Women as wives and workers', chapter 6 below.

[130] Rogers, 'The good are not always powerful', p. 612; Seccombe, 'Patriarchy stabilized', p. 68; Pennington and Westover. *Hidden workforce*, pp. 4–5. For the notion of a family wage in London as early as the middle of the century, in all but the most casual of occupations, see Alexander, *Becoming a woman*, p. 26.

[131] Above, p. 16; Seccombe, 'Patriarchy stabilized', pp. 73–4.

[132] BPP 1873, LXXI, part I, p. 148; Sharpe, 'Female labour market', chapter 3 below, p. 60.

Do we characterise the migration of women to towns as a sign of the 'crushing effects of industrialisation', or a reflection of 'women's economic initiative'?[133] Should women's work be defined as a feature of the 'survival strategies' of an oppressed underclass, or as occupations and employment?[134] Was the existence of the 'sweated trades'—the definition of which seems in some accounts to be infinitely elastic—altogether a 'bad thing', or did they provide crucial means of support to both single and widowed women, as well as to women within the family context?[135] Did established gender roles actually work to the advantage of some women, particularly though not exclusively among the elderly, by providing them with training in domestic tasks that could provide employment that was simply unavailable to men, even to the extent of keeping them from the workhouse?[136] Were women increasingly *denied* opportunities in the labour market, or did they increasingly *choose* the role of wife and mother as a means of optimising family comfort?[137]

Many authors have highlighted the gap that so often existed between ideology and practical necessity in relation to such issues, as well as the veritable chasm that yawned between the moralising of the middle classes and the economic exigencies of working-class life.[138] But it is equally true that generalisations about the gender division of labour are constantly rendered hazardous by the complexity of the economic and social changes that were the very essence of English industrialisation, involving relatively rapid but diverse changes, in town and countryside alike, that inevitably had regional and local dimensions. If this volume helps to raise greater awareness of these dimensions, and to stimulate further local and regional research, it will have performed its task.

---

133 Gleadle, *British women*, p. 22.
134 Gleadle, *British women*, p. 22.
135 For a more positive gloss than is often found, see Alexander, *Becoming a woman*, pp. 46–52. For an extended definition of sweated trades see Blackburn, '"No necessary connection with homework"'.
136 Goose, 'Poverty, old age and gender', pp. 367–8.
137 Bourke, 'Housewifery', *passim*.
138 Pennington and Westover, *Hidden workforce*, pp. 4–5; Rogers, 'The good are not always powerful', p. 612; Seccombe, 'Patriarchy stabilized', pp. 54–5, 68; August, 'How separate a sphere?'; Wach, 'A "still small voice"', pp. 433–8; Goose, 'How saucy did it make the poor?', p. 551.

2

Diverse experiences: the geography of adult female employment in England and the 1851 census[1]

LEIGH SHAW-TAYLOR

Introduction

Historians concerned with women's experience of work before the twentieth century are faced with very serious problems in finding satisfactory source material with which to document that work systematically. But the problems they face for the period before the 1841 census are very different from those they face thereafter. Before the 1841 census there is a profound paucity of systematic data. The data presently available are in fact so thin that historians have found it

[1] The work from which this chapter derives was part of a research project funded by the Economic and Social Research Council: *Male occupational change and economic growth in England 1750–1851* (RES 000-23-0131). All the maps were produced by Dr Max Satchell who also created the electronic boundary data for the 1851 registration districts. Without his work this chapter would not have been possible. The creation of the boundary data was funded partly by the ESRC as part of the aforementioned project and partly by two grants awarded by the British Academy to Professor E.A. Wrigley (The creation of the boundary data was dependent upon two pre-existing datasets. Kain, R.J.P. and Oliver, R.R., *Historic parishes of England and Wales: An electronic map of boundaries before 1850 with a gazetteer and metadata*. Colchester, Essex: UK Data Archive, May 2001. SN: 4348; Burton, N., Westwood, J. and Carter, P., *GIS of the Ancient Parishes of England and Wales, 1500–1850*. Colchester, Essex: UK Data Archive, March 2004. SN: 4828). The new boundary data will shortly be available from the Arts and Humanities Data Service. The data entry for the occupational data was undertaken by Ms Rebecca Tyler and the database was constructed by Dr Peter Kitson. I am grateful to them all. I am also indebted to Joyce Burnette, Amy Erickson, Nigel Goose, Eddy Higgs, Peter Kirby, Richard Wall and Tony Wrigley for comments on earlier versions of this chapter. I alone am responsible for any errors.

possible to sustain a number of entirely divergent views on trends in
female participation in the formal economy. They have variously held
that over the course of the industrial revolution paid employment for
women was increasing; decreasing; stable; increasing and then
decreasing.[2] No doubt other more complex permutations can be
identified in the literature.[3] To some degree these differences may arise
from individual historians generalising from particular sectors or regions
with which they are familiar but in the absence of datasets with
complete coverage of the national economy. Such contradictory
viewpoints can only be sustained in a field where the data remain
radically inadequate.

From 1841 onwards two rather different problems with source
material come to centre stage. The first is that, instead of a paucity of
data, the sheer superabundance of data both in the published census
reports and the manuscript census enumerators' books (hereafter CEBs)
has been, and remains, an obstacle to making full use of the available
material. The second problem, and the more serious of the two, is that
many historians have voiced serious doubts as to the reliability and
accuracy of the census data.

Most of this chapter is taken up with a discussion of the English data
published in the 1851 census report and a selection of maps based on
those data accompanied by a brief discussion of the geographical
differences in patterns of adult female employment in 1851. It thus deals
with a very small fraction of the available nineteenth century census
material. But it is worth stressing that the published 1851 census alone
contains a vast body of data covering all parts of the country and
virtually every sector of paid employment: the only obvious omission is
prostitution. It should be noted at the outset that the census tells us
relatively little about unpaid housework or other forms of non-market

---

[2] Neil McKendrick is perhaps the best known proponent of the view that the
industrial revolution increased work opportunities for women and children:
McKendrick, 'Home demand'. Historians who have advocated decline
include Pinchbeck, Richards, Horrell and Humphries: Pinchbeck, *Women
workers*; Richards, 'Women in the British economy'; Horrell and Humphries,
'Women's labour force participation'. For London Peter Earle has suggested
there was little change between *c*.1700 and 1851, an argument Judith Bennett
has advanced more generally: Earle, 'Female labour market'; Bennett, 'History
that stands still'. Maxine Berg and Pat Hudson have argued that female
employment rose and then fell over the industrial revolution: Berg and
Hudson, 'Rehabilitating the industrial revolution'; Berg, 'What difference did
women's work make?'

[3] A number of historians have, more cautiously, suggested that experience was
very varied: Sharpe, *Women's work*; Verdon, *Women workers*.

economic activity. This chapter is concerned with economic activity which was market oriented—either paid work or unpaid work within a family business.

We can begin with a brief discussion of the occupational data published for 1851. Firstly, there are three summary tables recording female occupational data for Britain, for Scotland and for England and Wales. Females were allocated to one of 196 categories by five-year age intervals. These tables have been relatively widely used by historians.[4] Then there is a second series of very similar tables for every county in England and Scotland. Wales is somewhat less well served, with tables for North Wales, South Wales and Monmouthshire. These too give occupational breakdowns in five-year age intervals. Only a handful of these county-level tables have ever been subject to detailed analysis.[5] C.H. Lee published summary tabulations derived from the published county-level census material from 1841 through to 1971 and made use of these data to make important arguments about regional development and the service sector, though the focus was on male employment.[6] Ellen Jordan's study of female unemployment in England and Wales in 1851 is a rare example of a study of women's work making use of data from a large set of county tables, though only a very limited amount of data is drawn from each table.[7]

Thirdly there are tables giving the occupations of women aged 20 and over for every registration district in England and Wales again in 196 different categories. The data provided for the 576 English registration districts are the primary focus of this chapter. The only published study I am aware of, drawing heavily on the registration district data, is John McKay's important paper on married women's participation rates in nineteenth century Lancashire, though again this uses only a small proportion of the data available in the Lancashire tables.[8]

Fourthly there are tables enumerating the occupations of adult women in 'principal' towns (there were 72 towns so described for England). I am not aware of any published work making extensive use

---

[4] See, for instance, Deane and Cole, *British economic growth*; Valenze, *First industrial woman*, Kirby, *Child labour*.

[5] That for London has attracted most attention: see Schwarz, *London;* Ball and Sunderland, *London;* Kirby, 'How many children were "unemployed"?'; Kirby, 'London child labour market'.

[6] Lee, *British regional employment statistics*; Lee, 'Regional growth'; Lee, 'The service sector'. See also Lee, *British economy,* chapter 7, 'Regional growth'.

[7] Jordan, 'Female unemployment.'

[8] McKay, 'Married women and work', chapter 7 below.

of this material though there must be local studies making some use of it. It is important to note that none of the published data records female employment by marital status, though this is recorded in the manuscript CEBs.

Clearly, then, by the mid-nineteenth century there is no shortage of systematic data on female occupations, but only a small fraction of this very rich body of data has ever been used by historians.[9] The reasons for this can only be guessed at but presumably relate to the two problems outlined above. Firstly, that the body of data is very large and has not been available in machine-readable form. That is now history. As part of a project, funded by the Economic and Social Research Council, on the changing occupational structure of England during the course of the industrial revolution, all of the English county, registration district and principal towns data for 1851 have been made fully machine-readable.[10] The second and more serious problem—that the data are widely believed to under-record female employment—may have reinforced the first problem by serving as a disincentive to making the data machine-readable. There can be little doubt that increasing awareness of the problems over the last 20 years has served to discourage the use of the published census material. However, further investigation shows that, despite the problems of under-recording, the data can tell us a great deal about female employment in the mid-nineteenth century. This chapter provides some basic mapping of these data and a very limited provisional analysis of the geography of adult female employment. Before doing so it is necessary to review the problems regarding the under-enumeration of female occupations.

The problems with the 1851 census data

No-one has done more than Eddy Higgs to draw attention to the deficiencies of the nineteenth century censuses with regard to the

---

[9] In contrast Eddy Higgs, writing in 1982 was inclined to stress how extensively the occupational tables had been used. However, he was presumably referring to the national level tables: Higgs, 'Tabulation of occupations', chapter 11 below.

[10] *Male occupational change and economic growth in England 1750–1851* (RES 000-23-0131). Despite the title of the grant the project was, in part, concerned with female occupations. In due course these datasets will be made publicly available through the Arts and Humanities Data Service. Further census datasets being created as part of a second E.S.R.C. funded project, *The occupational structure of nineteenth century Britain*, covering England, Scotland and Wales over the period 1851–1911 will also be made publicly available through AHDS.

recording of female occupations, and no-one should work on either the CEBs or the printed material without being fully apprised of his work.[11] In his early work Higgs was cautious about the implications, writing in 1987 that it might be premature to 'claim there was considerable under-enumeration . . .'[12] By 1995 he had concluded that 'the quality of the data in the Victorian census tables is indeed problematic', and he chose to illustrate this 'by way of a study of one economic sector, agriculture.'[13] However, as we will see later, agriculture is unlikely to be representative of other sectors.

In a similar vein Pam Sharpe has concluded that 'investigation of the census material has now revealed it to be a poor tool for use in analysing Victorian women's participation.'[14] Similarly Davidoff and Hall have written that the occupational recording for women who were not household heads is 'so unreliable as to be almost useless.'[15] Jane Humphries and Sara Horrell have claimed that 'the census enumeration of women's employment is demonstrably inaccurate.'[16] Michael Anderson rightly describes these views as part of a new orthodoxy and notes that it 'would be easy to read Horrell and Humphries as arguing that the reporting of married women's employment in the CEBs is so bad that the data are almost useless for serious analytical purposes.'[17] Anderson's view, and the one advanced here, is that the census remains the best and most comprehensive source we have on female employment. It follows that historians should make extensive use of the census data and that we need to move beyond the mere identification of problems and towards an evaluation, preferably quantitative, of the impact of the problems on the recorded data.

Before discussing the problems raised in the historiography, it is important to clarify what the General Register Office (hereafter G.R.O.) wanted householders and enumerators to record in terms of women's occupations. The instructions put to householders were as follows:

[11] Higgs, 'Domestic servants'; Higgs, 'Tabulation of occupations', chapter 11 below; Higgs, 'Women, occupations and work'; Higgs, 'Occupational censuses'; Higgs, *Clearer sense.*
[12] Higgs, 'Women, occupations and work', p. 68
[13] Higgs, 'Occupational censuses', p. 700.
[14] Sharpe, 'Continuity and change', p. 24.
[15] Davidoff and Hall, *Family fortunes*, p. 273.
[16] Horrell and Humphries, 'Women's labour force participation', p. 95.
[17] Anderson, 'Mid-Victorian census', p. 10. But see footnote 10, p. 28 of Anderson for a further elucidation of Horrell and Humphries' views on this issue. In fact Horrell and Humphries' remarks were not restricted to married women but applied to all women.

WOMEN AND CHILDREN – The Titles or occupations of ladies who are householders to be entered according to the above Instructions [for men]. The occupations of women who are regularly employed from home, or at home, in any but domestic duties, to be distinctly recorded. So also of children and young persons. Against the names of children above five years of age, if daily attending school, or receiving regular tuition under a master or governess at home, write "*scholar*" and in the latter case add "at home."

It is immediately obvious that the census will provide only very limited direct evidence on unpaid housework. Furthermore, these instructions make it quite clear that children and women who were not household heads and who were not employed 'regularly' or who were employed at home in domestic duties, were not to be attributed an occupation. The word 'regularly' is unfortunately highly ambiguous.

However, this is the question that was asked and it is important to distinguish clearly between whether or not the 1851 CEBs fully enumerate female employment (which, as we shall see, they do not) and whether they satisfactorily record 'regular' employment (which they probably do) and to consider what exactly 'regular' employment might mean. Some of those writing about the deficiencies of the census have not made this distinction at all and do not appear to be aware that only 'regular' employment was supposed to be recorded, while others have noted the use of the phrase but do not seem to have taken on board its full significance. This has led to a widespread misrepresentation of the nature of under-recording of female occupations in the census: a problem which primarily pertains to irregular work done by married women has been presented as if it pertained to all work done by all adult women.

There is a conflation in the literature between the fact that the census does not always record what historians of women's work would ideally like to know and the census being unreliable. The evidence that it does not fully enumerate female employment is overwhelming. But this is entirely unsurprising given that, female householders apart, only 'regular' work was supposed to have been recorded. The 'reliability' of the census should be judged not against whether all women who worked were ascribed occupations but against (a) whether all non-householder women who worked 'regularly' were ascribed occupations, and (b) whether all female householders were ascribed an occupation.

In general householders and enumerators are thought to have tried to provide accurate information. No historian that I am aware of has suggested that the CEBs are seriously defective in recording the names and sexes of household members. Some doubts have been expressed as to the precision with which ages and places of birth are recorded.[18] With minor caveats, the recorded relationships between household members are thought to be reliable. It could be suggested that male occupational descriptors mask a more complex reality of multiple employment, but no-one is suggesting that men were not generally returned with their 'principal' occupation as requested. Unless there is evidence to the contrary, it would be sensible to assume that householders and enumerators tried to answer the question about 'regular' employment to the best of their ability. The widely cited evidence that irregular employment was not *always* recorded is not evidence to the contrary. It is entirely possible that the CEBs, while failing to give a full enumeration of female employment, record 'regular' employment quite satisfactorily. It is, of course, crucial to confront the difficulties posed by how the word 'regularly' was understood by householders and enumerators and how this might have varied.

Whilst the phrase 'regularly employed' is ambiguous, it is worth noting that it is not ambiguous with respect to all forms of employment. Any work that was both full-time and took place throughout the year would have been very difficult to construe as irregular. Factory work must have conformed to this model and, as we shall see shortly, the evidence is that this was very fully enumerated. Similarly there can have been no real doubt that women who were occupied as live-in domestic or agricultural servants were employed regularly. Although it has been suggested that domestic servants may be over-enumerated in the census, no-one has yet suggested that they are under-enumerated.[19]

A number of distinct claims about the inadequacies of recording of female occupations in 1851 can be identified in the secondary literature:

[18] On age reporting see Tillott, 'Sources of inaccuracy', pp. 107–8; Anderson, 'Family structure', p. 75; Razzell, 'Evaluation', pp. 123–7; Thomson, 'Age reporting', pp. 13–25; Perkyns, 'Age checkability', pp. 19–38; Higgs, *Clearer sense*, pp. 78–82. On birthplace reporting see Tillott, 'Sources of inaccuracy', pp. 108–9; Anderson, 'Family structure', p. 75; Razzell, 'Evaluation', p. 123; Wrigley, 'Baptism coverage', p. 299–306; Perkyns, 'Birthplace accuracy', pp. 39–55; Higgs, *Clearer sense*, pp. 83–7.

[19] It has been suggested that the way in which agricultural servants were sometimes recorded may have led to significant numbers of them being tabulated in the printed returns as agricultural labourers rather than agricultural servants: Goose, 'Farm service in southern England', pp. 77–82. For a revised view, however, see Goose, 'Farm service, seasonal unemployment and casual labour'.

(1) child labour (both male and female) is under-recorded.[20]
(2) women's work as domestic servants is exaggerated.[21]
(3) women's work in agriculture is under-recorded.[22]
(4) married women's work is particularly poorly recorded.[23]
(5) women's work is generally under-recorded.[24]

The first of these claims is not relevant to the subject of this chapter—adult female employment—and will not be discussed further here. The remaining claims will be discussed in turn.

The over-enumeration of servants

Higgs has argued that the printed census reports overstate the number of domestic servants by a factor of about two largely on the basis of evidence from Rochdale in Lancashire.[25] In the Rochdale CEBs Higgs found that 40 per cent of the women ascribed what he classified as servant occupations were not described as servants in the relationship column and the vast majority of these were ascribed kin relationships with the household head.[26] But Lancashire textile towns turned out to be unrepresentative of the country as a whole in this respect, and in a national sample Anderson found that 19 per cent was a more generally representative figure.[27]

Based on a further examination of CEBs Higgs argues that 25 per cent of servants in Rutland in 1871 were resident with persons not described as their employers.[28] This is closer to the figure found nationally by Anderson. But these figures may be interpreted as less problematic for the census than Higgs suggests. He himself has noted that women might well work in service occupations but nevertheless be listed in the relationship column as kin rather than servant. This could arise, either, if they were employed as day-servants but lived with their kin, or, if they did indeed work for individuals to whom they were

---

[20] Kirby, *Child labour*, pp. 11–13.
[21] Higgs, 'Domestic servants'.
[22] Higgs, 'Occupational censuses'; Miller, 'Hidden workforce'; Verdon, *Rural women workers*, p. 119.
[23] Higgs, 'Women, occupations and work', pp. 63–4.
[24] Horrell and Humphries, 'Women's labour force participation', p. 95; Sharpe, 'Continuity and change', p. 24.
[25] Higgs, 'Women, occupations and work', p. 75.
[26] Higgs, 'Tabulation of occupations', chapter 11 below, p. 256.
[27] Anderson, 'Mis-specification of servant occupations', chapter 12, below, p. 263.
[28] Higgs, 'Domestic servants', p. 20.

related.[29] In addition Anderson points out that in 1851 census day was Mothering Sunday and suggests, though he does not cite evidence, that 'in certain parts of the country, it was conventional to give servants leave to pay a visit to their parents.'[30] In such cases the confusion would arise in the relationship to household head column (visitor or relative) rather than in the occupation column. But if parents were being visited by their non-resident children on census night, it would be unsurprising if the household head opted for kinship relations rather than 'visitor' to describe his or her relationship with his or her children.

Higgs also makes the point that many domestic servants worked in farm households and were probably involved, to some degree, in farm labour, leading to some understatement of agricultural employment. Equally some female farm servants must have undertaken domestic work. Why we should suppose one of these effects was larger than the other is not clear. Thus it seems clear that Higgs has overestimated the importance of this problem and a halving of domestic servants in the printed census tables cannot be justified.

The under-enumeration of women's employment in agriculture

There are a number of studies which demonstrate conclusively that many women who worked in agriculture were not recorded as so doing in the census. The best known and most cited of these is Celia Miller's pioneering linkage of payments to female workers recorded in Gloucestershire farm accounts with the 1871 CEB material. This showed that most of the women she found recorded in the accounts were not attributed an occupation in the census, even though some of them worked more than half the days in the year.[31] Nicola Verdon found that only one of the fourteen women recorded in the wage books of Laxton Manor Farm in the East Riding was recorded as an agricultural labourer in the 1881 census, though in this case none of these women worked more than 78 days in the year. Other work by Verdon for Norfolk and by Helen Speechley for Somerset shows women working on farms but not recorded in the CEBs.[32] None of this is particularly surprising given the instruction only to record

---

[29] Higgs, 'Tabulation of occupations', chapter 11 below, pp. 251–4.
[30] Anderson, 'Mis-specification of servant occupations', chapter 12, below, p. 264.
[31] Miller, 'Hidden workforce'.
[32] Verdon, 'Changing patterns of female employment', pp. 214–17; Speechley, 'Female and child day labourers', pp. 29–31.

employment that was 'regular.' And the undoubted under-recording of agricultural employment should not lead us, of itself, to suspect all occupational sectors of under-recording.

The under-enumeration of married women's employment

Higgs cites a number of studies suggesting that married women's work was particularly prone to under-recording.[33] He has even gone so far as to suggest the possibility that the belief that factory work was dominated by the young and single might be a statistical artefact of such under-recording, a claim repeated by Horrell and Humphries.[34] This argument has been emphatically rejected by Michael Anderson on convincing evidential grounds.[35]

Anderson's work on the CEBs provides compelling evidence that married women's work in factory and domestic textile employment in Cheshire and Lancashire was very well recorded indeed.[36] For instance, Anderson shows that in Preston, 34 per cent of all married women were recorded as working but that this rose to 74 per cent for women married to low paid factory operatives.[37] But when he looked at women under 30 married to low paid factory operatives, the figure rose to over 90 per cent.[38] Looking at childless married women under 40 across Lancashire and Cheshire, Anderson found 85 per cent of power loom weavers' wives, 92 per cent of handloom weavers' wives and 97 per cent of the wives of unspecified weavers had recorded occupations.[39] Clearly the scope for under-enumeration here is very low indeed. McKay's work on the employment of married women in the registration districts of Lancashire in 1851 and 1861 lends further support to the view that textile employment was well enumerated.[40] This does not appear to be a peculiarity of recording in Lancashire and Cheshire. Lown's work on the Essex silk factories suggests that married women's employment in factories was pretty fully enumerated.[41]

Given the regularity of factory work, one would expect to find it

---

[33] Higgs, 'Women, occupations and work', pp. 63–4.
[34] Higgs, 'Women, occupations and work', p. 64; Horrell and Humphries, 'Women's labour force participation', p. 95.
[35] Anderson, 'Mid-Victorian censuses', chapter 8, below.
[36] Anderson, 'Mid-Victorian censuses', chapter 8, below, pp. 188–95.
[37] Anderson, 'Mid-Victorian censuses', chapter 8, below, pp. 189–90.
[38] Anderson, 'Mid-Victorian censuses', chapter 8 below, p. 193.
[39] Anderson, 'Mid-Victorian censuses', chapter 8 below, p. 196.
[40] McKay, 'Married women and work', chapter 7 below.
[41] Lown, *Women and industrialization*, p. 91.

fully enumerated, if householders and enumerators had attempted to answer the questions posed in the householders schedules as best as they could. The evidence appears to be that, in general, this is exactly what happened. If the work of married women in factories was very fully enumerated, then it is not very likely that regular work by married women in other sectors was any less well recorded than that of unmarried women.

Domestic industry

How well enumerated was domestic or cottage industry? Anderson's work on married women suggests that domestic textile employment was well enumerated in Lancashire and Cheshire.[42] Osamu Saito's work on the lace-making village of Cardington in Bedfordshire is also suggestive of high levels of enumeration of cottage industry there.[43] Nigel Goose's work on the straw-plait industry in south and west Hertfordshire is similarly indicative of very high participation rates.[44]

In 1851 straw plait and lace remained important cottage industries in the counties of Buckinghamshire, Bedfordshire and Hertfordshire. The existence of a machine-readable database of the Buckinghamshire CEBs for 1851 (created by the Buckinghamshire Family History Society) allows us to investigate the recording of female occupations across the whole county.[45] Critically, the CEBs allow the examination of women's employment by marital status which the printed material for 1851 does not. How 'regular' domestic employment in these industries was is not entirely clear. But, as Figures 2.2, 2.3 and 2.6 make clear, recorded employment for women in these counties was high.

A priori, the women most likely to be in regular employment would be unmarried adults. In Buckinghamshire in 1851 82 per cent of unmarried women aged 20 and over were in fact recorded as in employment. There may be some under-enumeration of regular employment, but the scope for under-enumeration is limited. Clearly this is an area where the opportunities for female employment were high, and amongst the group of female workers most likely to be in employment we do indeed find very high levels of employment enumerated. By comparison only 42 percent of married women were

[42] Anderson, 'Mid-Victorian censuses', chapter 8 below.
[43] Saito, 'Who worked when?', chapter 9 below.
[44] Goose, *Berkhamsted region*; Goose, *St Albans*; Goose 'Straw plait and hat trades', chapter 5 below.
[45] I am very grateful to the Buckinghamshire Family History Society for allowing me to use this database and to David Thorpe for his help with this.

recorded as in employment. It is entirely probable that married women's regular employment was considerably less than that of unmarried women. No doubt there were both unmarried and married women whose part-time, casual or seasonal employment was not regarded as regular and was not therefore recorded.

If the enumerations were carried out in line with the instructions of the G.R.O., one would expect very full enumeration of widows because the majority of them would have been household heads who were supposed to record occupations whether they were employed 'regularly' or not. In fact 67 per cent of widows were recorded as in employment and a further 22 per cent indicated they were in receipt of poor relief or alms. Thus 89 per cent of all widows recorded, if not an occupational descriptor, what one might call a livelihood descriptor. Only 11 per cent did not return a livelihood descriptor. This falls to 6 per cent for widows who were household heads. Once again the evidence suggests that the instructions of the G.R.O. were complied with pretty fully.

The under-recording of female employment

The evidence, such as it is, is consistent with very high levels of recording of regular employment. However, it is very clear that irregular work by women was under-recorded in 1851, but largely because the G.R.O. did not want to know about such work. Any work that was seasonal was necessarily irregular and it is unsurprising that the problems appear greatest in agriculture and least in factory employment.[46]

As long ago as 1982 Higgs, in noting that his work did not 'attempt to measure the overall discrepancies', expressed the hope that his work would encourage others to do so.[47] He also noted that 'more work needs to be done on the relationship between the enumerators' books and the tabulations in the published census reports for which they formed the raw material.'[48] Such work has been a long time coming. In

---

[46] It is sometimes asserted that the recording of female occupations was related to their activity at that time of year. It is possible that seasonal work that happened to be in season in late March and early April was more likely to be reported that other seasonal work but we have no evidence that this was so and this would not be consistent with a strict interpretation of the question that was asked. It seems likely that there was some tendency of this sort but how one might assess the quantitative importance of any such effect remains unexplored.

[47] Higgs, 'Tabulation of occupations', chapter 11 below, p. 250.

[48] Higgs, 'Tabulation of occupations', chapter 11 below, p. 253.

1987 Higgs published some speculative revisions of the nineteenth century census figures. For 1851 he increased the numbers of women in agriculture by a factor of 4.2, increased the numbers in dealing by a factor 2.5 and halved the numbers of domestic servants.[49] He went on to note that these 'figures are really an invitation to others to make more refined calculations and probably represent hypothetical upper bounds to any suggested changes.'[50] More recently Higgs himself has produced more refined estimates for agriculture suggesting a multiplication factor for 1851 of 3.4 and repeated his call for further work especially on agricultural under-enumeration.[51] The only historian who has taken up this invitation to date is Joyce Burnette. Her work, based on detailed empirical research, suggests that a doubling of the figures in agriculture would be more appropriate than a multiplication factor of 3.4 or 4.2, which is in line with Higgs' early work.

As discussed above, Anderson's recent work on servants has suggested that Higgs has considerably overestimated the scale of the problem and it is not clear that there is a serious quantitative problem with respect to domestic servants. The evidence also suggests that factory and domestic employment were well recorded. Agriculture is clearly under-recorded and no doubt much other irregular work will have escaped recording. Nevertheless, the view promoted by some historians (though not, it should be emphasised, by Higgs) that the census enumeration of female work is so poor that it is not worth using cannot be sustained. Higgs himself has argued, and there can be no doubt that he is correct in this, that 'the census enumerators' books are still our best source for understanding the economic activities of women in the Victorian period.'[52] Moreover, the census remains far and away the most comprehensive source of data we have on female employment in the nineteenth century.

None of this is to suggest that the census forms a perfect record of female occupations. Clearly it does not. In addition to the problems already noted there are reasons to think that some enumerators systematically failed to enumerate the occupations of married women.[53] How widespread this problem was remains unclear, but if it were widespread, it would create some downward bias in apparent

---

[49] Higgs, 'Women, occupations and work', p. 74.
[50] Higgs, 'Women, occupations and work', p. 76.
[51] Higgs, 'Occupational censuses', pp. 710, 714.
[52] Higgs, *Making sense of the census revisited*, p. 103. See also chapter 1 above, pp. 21–5.
[53] See for instance, Wall, 'Work, welfare and the family'; August 'How separate a sphere?', p. 289.

participation rates in the published census.[54] However, there is no obvious *a priori* reason to think that the proportion of enumerators who thus flouted the instructions of the Census Office would vary much from one part of the country to another. If that supposition is broadly correct then the relative geographical patterns apparent in the maps with which the rest of this chapter is concerned should be broadly reliable.

The geography of adult female employment in 1851

Many of the problems discussed above need to be explored at considerably greater length than is possible here, and much further research is still necessary if we are to move beyond an awareness of the problems to a capacity to assess their quantitative effects satisfactorily. Nevertheless, the rest of this chapter comprises a preliminary discussion of the patterns recorded in the printed census tabulation for 1851 and their geography. The aim of this section of the chapter is simply to put novel spatial data into the public domain. This is done in the belief that the accompanying maps will be of value to those working on, or with an interest in, local or regional studies of female employment in the mid-nineteenth century by providing a wider context for local and regional studies, and in the hope that the geographical patterns revealed by the maps will stimulate further research. The discussion is largely a descriptive exercise restricted to picking out some basic features of interest and occasionally highlighting patterns that shed further light on the reliability of the data. The underlying data deserve a much fuller discussion incorporating a full-scale statistical analysis. Such a treatment is planned in conjunction with the analysis of comparable data from later nineteenth century censuses. [55]

In most of the figures that follow no adjustment has been made to the raw data. However, since there are strong grounds for thinking that female employment in agriculture is under-enumerated and the unoccupied are consequently over-enumerated, Figures 2.3, 2.5 and 2.11 are modified versions of Figures 2.2, 2.4 and 2.10 respectively in which, following Joyce Burnette, female employment in agriculture has been doubled. Figure 2.1, which shows all the English registration

---

[54] Those working from enumerators' books can rectify the problem by excluding suspect enumeration districts as Richard Wall does in 'Work welfare and the family', though there might sometimes be problems in distinguishing defective enumeration districts from those with genuinely low participation rates.

[55] This work forms part of a larger project being funded by the ESRC: *The occupational structure of nineteenth century Britain* (RES-000-23-1579), which will lead, amongst other things, to the publication of a historical atlas.

English registration counties

1. Bedfordshire	22. London
2. Berkshire	23. Middlesex
3. Buckinghamshire	24. Norfolk
4. Cambridgeshire	25. Northamptonshire
5. Cheshire	26. Northumberland
6. Cornwall	27. Nottinghamshire
7. Cumberland	28. Oxfordshire
8. Derbyshire	29. Rutland
9. Devonshire	30. Shropshire
10. Dorset	31. Somerset
11. Durham	32. Staffordshire
12. Essex	33. Suffolk
13. Gloucestershire	34. Surrey
14. Hampshire	35. Sussex
15. Herefordshire	36. Warwickshire
16. Hertfordshire	37. Westmorland
17. Huntingdonshire	38. Wiltshire
18. Kent	39. Worcestershire
19. Lancashire	40. Yorkshire. East Riding with York
20. Leicestershire	41. Yorkshire. North Riding
21. Lincolnshire	42. Yorkshire. West Riding

Figure 2.1 Registration counties of England

counties, may be useful to readers not familiar with the locations of these administrative units. The registration counties differed somewhat from the ancient counties and were constructs created by the Census Office as an administratively convenient way of tabulating the data for publication. All of the occupational data have been coded into the Primary, Secondary, Tertiary (PST) scheme devised by Tony Wrigley.[56] The primary sector subsumes agriculture and mining. The secondary sector refers to the production of other physical commodities and includes handicrafts, manufacturing and construction. The tertiary sector refers to services and includes retailing, dealing and transport.

Figure 2.2 shows the percentage of adult females reported as economically active in each of England's 576 registration districts. As noted earlier, these figures refer to participation in market-oriented work and exclude domestic labour at home. Moreover, it should be noted that because of the vagaries regarding the recording of irregular work the figures should be regarded as indicative rather than exact. To the extent that irregular employment was not recorded the data on which these maps are based will understate female participation rates. However, it is also the case that the data capture many women who may not have been working full-time and it is therefore unclear whether these data will over or under-enumerate adult female employment *vis a vis* male employment in the formal sector.

Figure 2.3 also shows adult female participation rates but, in line with the discussion above, with the proportion of women in agriculture doubled. The two maps thus give two somewhat different geographies for female participation rates. The most striking feature of both these maps is the huge range over which participation rates varied. In Figure 2.2 the unadjusted adult female participation rate ranges from a low of 17 percent in the Easington registration district (north-east Durham) on the north-eastern coal-field to a high of 78 per cent in the hat-making registration district of Luton (south-western Bedfordshire).

Low adult female participation rates are to be expected in coal-field areas, in part because of the extra-domestic labour associated with coal-mining.[57] High participation rates are also to be expected in the straw hat and pillow-lace districts of the south-east Midlands in parts of

---

[56] See Wrigley, *Poverty*, pp. 166–9, for a description of the PST scheme. I am very grateful to Tony Wrigley and Ros Davies for the coding of the occupational data to PST.

[57] One could argue that such household labour was essentially ancillary to coal-production and thus market-oriented. Female participation rates remained low on the coalfields well into the second half of the twentieth century: Hudson and Williams, *The United Kingdom*, pp. 64, 68, 71.

Northamptonshire, Bedfordshire, Buckinghamshire and Hertfordshire. That the published census data show such extreme variations in adult female participation rates and indicate high rates where we know we should expect high rates and low rates where we might expect them is, in itself, strong evidence that the printed census data are a very good source of evidence on the geographical variations in female employment.

Reported participation rates were over 50 per cent in parts of Lancashire and the West Riding of Yorkshire. This was clearly related to the importance of employment in cotton and wool/worsted textiles respectively. Interestingly, though, the areas of high participation rates and high textile employment (compare Figures 2.2 and 2.3 with Figures 2.16 and 2.17) were not entirely coincident. This intriguing feature deserves more detailed exploration than is possible here. Elsewhere there were only isolated localities where reported participation rates were above 50 percent. In most of the country reported unadjusted participation rates ranged between 30 and 50 per cent. The lowest rates of female participation were to be found in the south and east in an arc sweeping south from the East Riding of Yorkshire down through Lincolnshire and East Anglia and west as far as the eastern end of Dorset. In some parts of this zone, there were substantial areas where reported unadjusted participation rates fell below 30 per cent.

Inevitably the participation rates shown in Figure 2.3 are rather higher since the figures have been adjusted upwards. Many of the same patterns remain visible especially the very low participation rates in south-eastern England. The North Riding and Lincolnshire no longer fit the same pattern of ubiquitously low participation rates. The uplands of northern England now stand out more clearly as areas of unusually high female participation with rates generally over 70 per cent and frequently over 80 per cent, probably because of the prevalence of small family farms in these areas. The female participation rates revealed by Figures 2.2 and 2.3 may go a long way to explain the geography of per capita poor relief expenditure in the nineteenth century, though this hypothesis will need to be subjected to statistical scrutiny. If the hypothesis can be validated statistically, then a comparative statistical analysis of the geographical relationship between rates of poor relief and the two female participation rates mapped in Figures 2.2 and 2.3 might shed light on the appropriateness or otherwise of the blanket doubling of agricultural employment in Figure 2.3.

Figures 2.4 and 2.5 show adult female participation rates in agriculture. Figure 2.5 brings out the relationship between the uplands and very high levels of adjusted female participation in agriculture (over

30 per cent) very clearly, most notably in the Cheviots, the Pennines and the North Yorkshire Moors. These were areas with very heavy concentrations of small family farms.[58] There were also large areas with high levels of female participation in agriculture in the south west of England, at the intersection of the Gloucestershire, Wiltshire and Berkshire borders, and in northern parts of Cornwall, Devon and Somerset. Elsewhere, apart from isolated patches, female participation rates in agriculture were below 20 per cent (Figure 2.4) or below 30 per cent on the adjusted figures (Figure 2.5). The lowest rates were in the south and east with female participation rates in agriculture commonly below 10 per cent on the unadjusted figures (Figure 2.4) or below 20 per cent on the adjusted figures (Figure 2.5). The low rates in the south and east correspond closely to the area in which large-scale labour-employing or capitalist farms predominated.[59]

Figure 2.6 shows the percentage of adult women employed in the secondary sector. In most parts of the country less than 10 per cent of adult women were employed in the secondary sector. A number of distinct clusters with much higher levels of female secondary sector activity stand out. The largest of these were: the cotton districts of south-east Lancashire and north-eastern Cheshire; the woollen and worsted districts of the West Riding; and the straw plait and pillow lace districts in the south-east Midlands (parts of Northamptonshire, Bedfordshire, Buckinghamshire and Hertfordshire). A number of other smaller regions can be identified: the silk districts at the western end of the Essex Suffolk border and around Coventry (on the Warwickshire Leicestershire border); the textile and lace districts in the south west; the worsted area around Norwich (Norfolk) and a number of other districts in the Midlands including lace making in Staffordshire, Nottinghamshire and Leicestershire and clothes-making in Leicestershire.

A conventional cartographic representation of this kind is very good at picking out which economic activities were of relative importance within particular areas. However, areas with similar *rates* of a particular economic activity but very different population densities cannot be distinguished from one another. Areas with high population densities will form a larger share of national employment in a given sector than equal areas with a similar sectoral rate of employment but a much lower population density. Thus nationally important concentrations of an industry may not be distinguishable from ones which were nationally

---

[58] Shaw-Taylor, 'Family farms', p. 183.
[59] Shaw-Taylor, 'Family farms', pp. 184–5.

unimportant. The conventional cartographic representation is not, therefore, a reliable way of identifying which areas were important for an activity at national level. Figure 2.7 is intended to show the importance of individual registration districts for national employment in the secondary sector. Each registration district has been allocated one of ten colours. Collectively all the areas in any one colour accounted for 10 per cent of secondary sector employment nationally. The key indicates the number of registration districts in each colour. Thus the four registration districts shown in dark purple (Bradford in the West Riding, Stockport in north-east Cheshire, and Manchester and Ashton-under-Lyme in Lancashire) between them accounted for a full 10 per cent of all adult female secondary sector employment in England. At the other extreme, around half the area of the country (272 out of 576 registration districts) is shaded in light yellow. This indicates that these 272 registration districts between them accounted for only 10 per cent of all secondary sector employment. The colours from pink through to dark purple between them accounted for a full 50 per cent of secondary sector employment, although these districts formed a relatively small area (57 registration districts out of 576). I have termed this kind of map a spatial concentration map. Figures 2.9, 2.15 and 2.17 are also maps of spatial concentration.

Figure 2.6 indicates that in most of the country the secondary sector was not a major employer of adult female labour in 1851. In most registrations districts (shown in shades of green) between 5 and 15 per cent of occupied women worked in the secondary sector. In a few areas the rate fell below 5 per cent. A number of clearly defined areas with radically higher levels of adult female secondary sector employment stand out. The textile districts of the West Riding and Lancashire together with north-eastern Cheshire, the hat and straw-plait districts of the south-east Midlands and the clothing districts of Nottinghamshire and Leicestershire all stand out with the secondary sector accounting for between 30 and 50 per cent of female employment in these areas, and occasionally more. Parts of Somerset and Devon also had high rates of secondary sector adult female employment. A number of smaller districts with high levels of adult female secondary sector employment were dotted around the country, including the centres of the silk industry on the Essex-Suffolk border, at Coventry and in the East End of London.

When we turn to Figure 2.7, which shows the spatial concentration of secondary sector employment, the much greater numerical weight of the north-western textile districts compared to the Midlands clothing districts and the straw-plait and lace districts of the south-east Midlands becomes apparent. The importance of London as an employer of secondary sector female labour also becomes clearer while the dearth of secondary sector female employment elsewhere in south-eastern England and in north-eastern England appears more starkly than in Figure 2.6.

Figure 2.8 shows the percentage of adult women reported as being in tertiary employment in 1851 and Figure 2.9 shows the spatial concentration of tertiary employment at the same date. As Figure 2.8 indicates, the local importance of tertiary employment generally varied between 10 and 30 per cent of adult female employment across most of England. In a few places, most notably in and around London, higher figures of between 30 and 40 per cent prevailed. Hampstead and St George, Hanover Square, registration districts had the highest proportions of occupied women in tertiary employment with rates of 48 per cent and 44 per cent respectively.

When we turn to Figure 2.9 we can see, very clearly, just how misleading the conventional cartographic representation can be of the importance of local areas to the national picture. The major importance of the north-west to national service sector employment, entirely hidden in Figure 2.8, is now abundantly clear, while London's leading role shows through both more clearly and over a significantly larger area.

Figure 2.10 simply shows which of the three sectors was the largest employer, on the unadjusted figures for agriculture, and Figure 2.11 shows which was the largest sector using the adjusted figures. The areas where the secondary sector was most important are clear enough. Whether agriculture or the service sector was the largest employer in most of the rest of the country is clearly dependent on how one adjusts the data to allow for any under-recording in agriculture. The leading role of the service sector in adult female employment in and around London is plain from Figure 2.11.

Figure 2.12 shows the spatial concentration of population growth from 1801–1851. In other words what is shown is how much of the national population growth over the period from 1801 to 1851 was accounted for by each registration district. In general mortality tended to be higher in the areas that were growing most rapidly in population.[60] Since fertility showed no great regional differences it follows that these disparate patterns of population growth were driven by migration from the slower growing to the faster growing areas. Figure 2.13 shows the spatial concentration of male non-agricultural employment in 1851.

---

[60] Compare Woods and Shelton, *Atlas*, p. 29, with Figure 2.12.

Comparing Figures 2.12 and 2.13 it clear that the geography of population growth over the first five decades of the nineteenth century was very closely related to the work opportunities for men outside agriculture. The relationship between local population growth and female work opportunities outside agriculture, however, was much less straightforward. In most cases high levels of employment for women outside agriculture tended to be in areas which also had high levels of non-agricultural employment for men (see Figure 2.13).

There were, however, two major exceptions, which can be seen by comparing Figure 2.13 with Figure 2.2. One was the north-eastern coal-field which was (in employment terms) concentrated in the north-east of the County of Durham. Here, as can be seen in Figure 2.2, female participation rates were very low but work opportunities outside agriculture for men, principally in coal-mining, were plentiful (see Figure 2.13). Despite the poor employment opportunities for adult women, as Figure 2.12 shows, the area experienced very rapid population expansion between 1801 and 1851.[61] The other major exception was the south-east Midlands where the straw hat and lace industry offered substantial employment opportunities for women outside agriculture (see Figures 2.6 and 2.7) but not for men (see Figure 2.13) and where population growth (see Figure 2.12) was low. Thus good employment opportunities outside agriculture for women but not for men, as in the south-east Midlands, did not lead to major population growth, while good non-agricultural employment opportunities for men but for not women, as in north-east Durham, were compatible with high population growth levels. High levels of sustained relative population growth required in-migration by both men and women.[62] The evidence is only indirect but is seems reasonable to interpret these patterns as suggesting that large numbers of men would not migrate into areas with good employment opportunities for women only, whereas large numbers of women would migrate into areas without good employment opportunities for women. This led to skewed sex ratios and higher than average proportions of women who never married.[63] Thus male employment opportunities appear to have been significantly more important in determining the relative population growth rates of different areas. This is readily explicable. We know from Horrell and

[61] An alternative interpretation, equally consistent with the occupational and population data, would be that female participation rates were low, not because female employment opportunities were low but because male wages in mining were high and women were thus able to stay at home.

[62] However, see Goose 'Cottage industry' for a gloss on this argument.

[63] Goose, *Berkhamsted*, pp. 31–2; Goose, *St Albans*, pp. 45–50.

Humphries' work that married men had much higher earning capacities than married women and this would obviously loom large in the migration decisions made by families.[64]

Figure 2.14 shows the percentage of adult women in domestic service in 1851 while Figure 2.15 shows the spatial concentration. In most of the country between 5 and 15 per cent of adult women worked in domestic service. In much of London and the surrounding area the figure was generally higher. In the West End over 25 per cent and in Hampstead over 30 per cent of adult women worked in domestic service. Bath, Cheltenham and Clifton also stand out with very high rates of domestic service employment at over 20 per cent. The importance of domestic service in and around London is unsurprising but the textile districts of the north-west show up as important nationally in Figure 2.15.

Figure 2.16 shows the percentage of adult women employed in textile manufacture in 1851 while Figure 2.17 shows the spatial concentration. The concentration of the textile employment in the north-west is extremely pronounced. The extent of the relative decline of the traditional centres of cloth-making in East Anglia and in the West Country, when viewed in terms of national importance in Figure 2.17, is remarkable. If spinning really was the ubiquitous by-employment for women in pre-industrial England that it is usually assumed to have been, it had suffered a catastrophic decline in most parts of England by the mid-nineteenth century.

This leads to a more general point. Patterns of female employment in 1851 were extremely geographically diverse. That suggests that any simple aggregate national narrative about women's experience of the labour market during the industrial revolution is likely to be seriously misleading. If we return to Figures 2.2 and 2.3, it would seem improbable that the female participation rate had been rising on the north-eastern coal-field or in the agricultural districts of the east and south-east. It is equally improbable that female participation rates had suffered any serious decline in the north-western textiles districts or in the hat and straw making areas of the south-east Midlands. These somewhat speculative generalisations direct our attention to the pressing need for more quantitative local and regional studies of changes in female employment over time and in particular to the vexed problem of how to obtain reliable evidence on female employment for the pre-census period.

---

[64] Horrell and Humphries, 'Women's labour force participation', pp. 100–8.

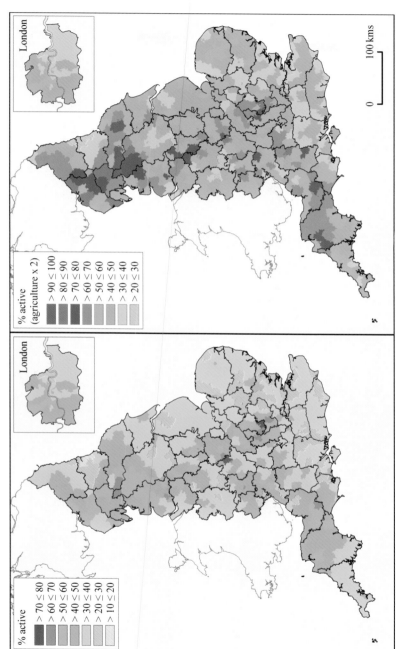

> 70 ⩽ 80
> 60 ⩽ 70
> 50 ⩽ 60
> 40 ⩽ 50
> 30 ⩽ 40
> 20 ⩽ 30
> 10 ⩽ 20

London

% active
(agriculture x 2)

> 90 ⩽ 100
> 80 ⩽ 90
> 70 ⩽ 80
> 60 ⩽ 70
> 50 ⩽ 60
> 40 ⩽ 50
> 30 ⩽ 40
> 20 ⩽ 30

London

0   100 kms

Figure 2.2 Percentage of adult women reported economically active

Figure 2.3 Percentage of adult women reported economically active (with reported agricultural employment doubled)

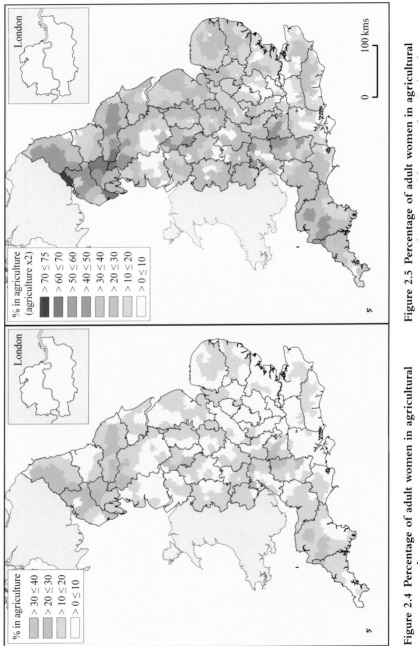

% in agriculture

> 30 ≦ 40
> 20 ≦ 30
> 10 ≦ 20
> 0 ≦ 10

London

Figure 2.4 Percentage of adult women in agricultural employment

% in agriculture (agriculture x2)

> 70 ≦ 75
> 60 ≦ 70
> 50 ≦ 60
> 40 ≦ 50
> 30 ≦ 40
> 20 ≦ 30
> 10 ≦ 20
> 0 ≦ 10

London

0   100 kms

Figure 2.5 Percentage of adult women in agricultural employment (with reported agricultural employment doubled)

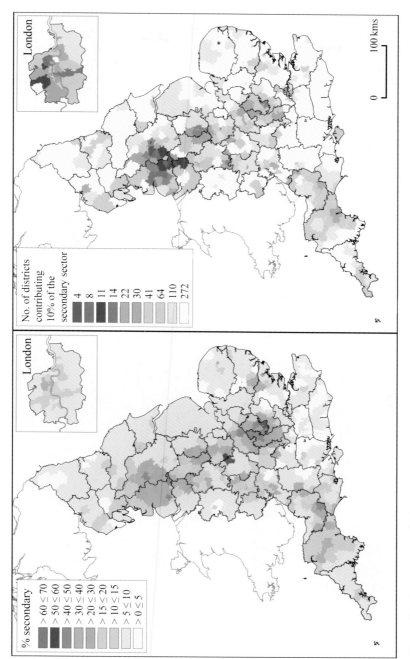

Figure 2.7 Spatial concentration of adult women in secondary employment

Figure 2.6 Percentage of adult women in secondary employment

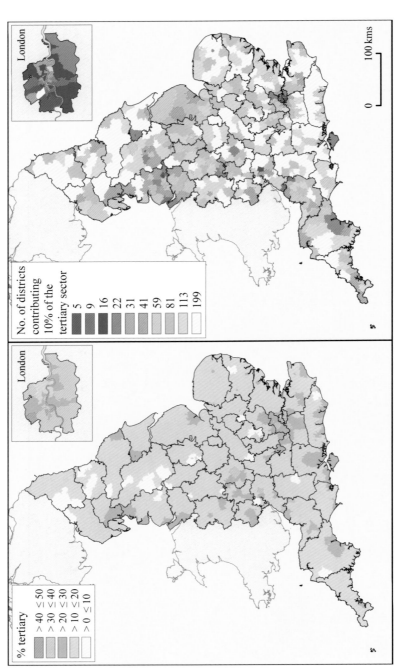

Figure 2.8 Percentage of adult women in tertiary employment

Figure 2.9 Spatial concentration of adult women in tertiary employment

% tertiary
> 40 ≤ 50
> 30 ≤ 40
> 20 ≤ 30
> 10 ≤ 20
> 0 ≤ 10

London

No. of districts contributing 10% of the tertiary sector
5
9
16
22
31
41
59
81
113
199

London

0   100 kms

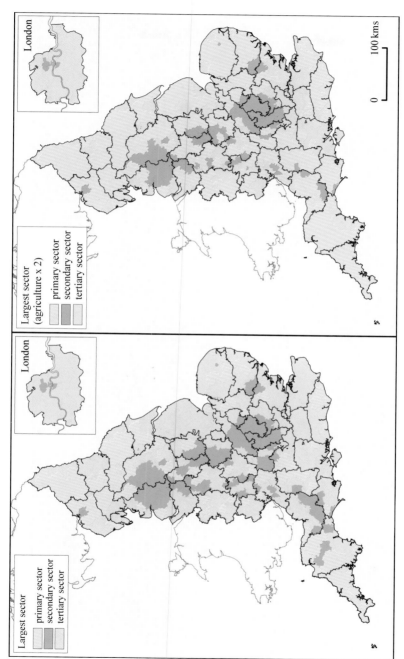

Largest sector

primary sector

secondary sector

tertiary sector

London

Largest sector
(agriculture x 2)

primary sector

secondary sector

tertiary sector

London

0   100 kms

Figure 2.10 Female employment by largest sector

Figure 2.11 Female employment by largest sector (with
reported agricultural employment doubled)

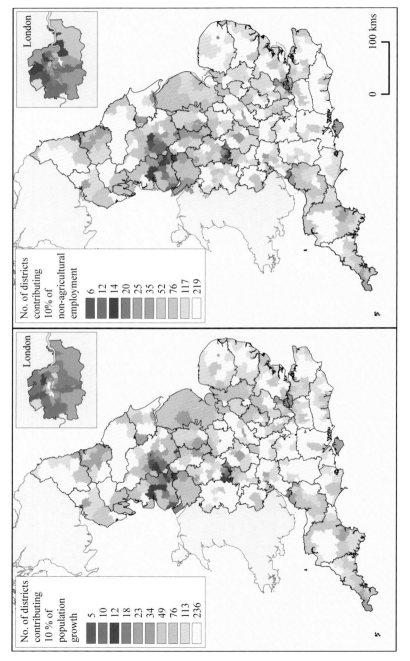

No. of districts contributing 10% of population growth	
	5
	10
	12
	18
	23
	34
	49
	76
	113
	236

London

No. of districts contributing 10% of non-agricultural employment	
	6
	12
	14
	20
	25
	35
	52
	76
	117
	219

London

0   100 kms

Figure 2.12 Spatial concentration of population growth 1801–51

Figure 2.13 Spatial concentration of adult men in non-agricultural employment

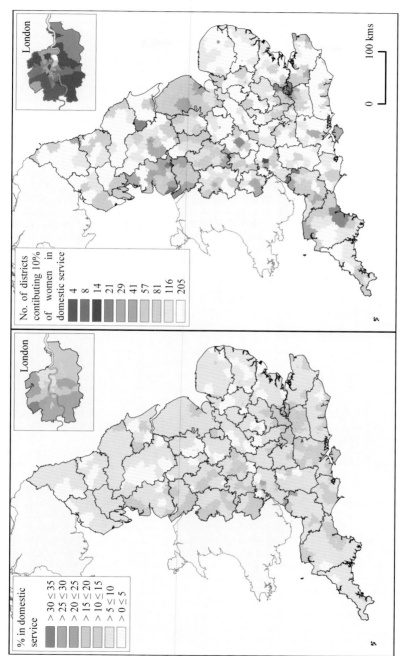

Figure 2.14 Percentage of adult women in domestic service

Figure 2.15 Spatial concentration of adult women in domestic service

% in domestic service
- > 30 ≤ 35
- > 25 ≤ 30
- > 20 ≤ 25
- > 15 ≤ 20
- > 10 ≤ 15
- > 5 ≤ 10
- > 0 ≤ 5

London

No. of districts contibuting 10% of women in domestic service
- 4
- 8
- 14
- 21
- 29
- 41
- 57
- 81
- 116
- 205

London

0   100 kms

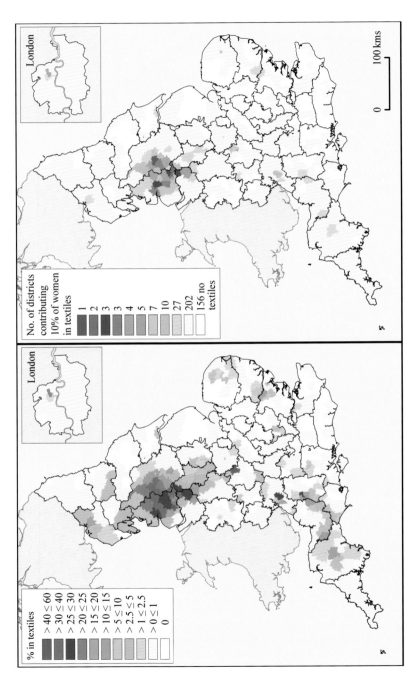

No. of districts contributing 10% of women in textiles	
1	
2	
3	
3	
4	
5	
7	
10	
27	
202	
156 no textiles	

Figure 2.17 Spatial concentration of adult women in textiles

% in textiles	
> 40 ≤ 60	
> 30 ≤ 40	
> 25 ≤ 30	
> 20 ≤ 25	
> 15 ≤ 20	
> 10 ≤ 15	
> 5 ≤ 10	
> 2.5 ≤ 5	
> 1 ≤ 2.5	
> 0 ≤ 1	
0	

Figure 2.16 Percentage of adult women in textiles

3

The female labour market in English agriculture during the Industrial Revolution: expansion or contraction?

PAMELA SHARPE

Introduction

Thomas Hardy describes Tess of the d'Urberville's slavery to the threshing machine thus:

> For some probably economical reason it was usually a woman who was chosen for this particular duty, and Groby gave as his motive in selecting Tess that she was one of those who best combined strength with quickness in untying and both with staying power . . .[1]

While by some accounts Tess's labours were anachronistic by the 1880s, this article considers the extent to which English women carried out farm work from the seventeenth to the nineteenth centuries. Were female farm workers 'economical' to employ? Did their aptitudes suit agricultural labour? Research and writing in social and economic history has been concerned with patterns of women's work, particularly since the 'new wave' of women's history from the 1970s, but we still have little idea of where and when women worked on farms. Widening our knowledge of the female labour market enables us to develop our understanding of the 'release' of labour from the land to mills and factories (for the main Industrial Revolution labour force was female) as well as to local cottage industries. Nevertheless, we cannot assume that expanding opportunities for women in agriculture would have been welcome if more attractive work were available in other sectors of the economy. More generally, historians still disagree on whether or not capitalist agriculture meant more or less work for women. This chapter

---

[1] Hardy, *Tess of the D'Urbervilles*, p. 406.

will first consider when and where women worked on farms, and will proceed to the related question of the extent to which women's work in farming became more specific in terms of the type of work women undertook. The degree to which work was gender segregated and whether this was more rigidly applied over time will be explored next, followed by a review of the wage rate evidence and examination of the 'female marginalisation' thesis.

The current differences of opinion between historians mainly concern areas of developed capitalist farming, so this discussion will tend to concentrate on the east and the Midlands rather than smaller farms of the west and uplands which, until recent times, employed more family labour. The focus will not be on live-in farm servants (unmarried young women) but on day or piece-workers (wives or widows). Feminist historians have taken exception to the term 'family labour', with its implicit devaluing of the contribution of members other than the (male) household head, but a close examination of the identity of female workers in farm accounts show that they are usually related to the farm labourers who worked on the same farm. Their wives and children found periodic employment, as did adult daughters (some of whom seem to have been women who had illegitimate children and perhaps found themselves excluded on grounds of respectability from domestic service), and widows of former farm workers.[2] Moreover, at this stage it is easier to review some of the debates and difficulties rather than aiming to produce a definitive view. Ultimately, exploration of the regional context of women's work will provide a fuller and more nuanced picture.

When and where women worked on farms

An impressionistic overview suggests that, in the eighteenth century at least, female farm work was less common in England than in other European countries. As Peter Mathias has recently held, 'Judged against other societies, perhaps the unusual thing is that women's role in agriculture was so limited in England'.[3] Only a cursory glimpse at the writings of late eighteenth-century agricultural observers is sufficient to suggest that they saw a lack of work for women and children in rural

[2] Sharpe, 'Time and wages', pp. 66–8.
[3] Mathias, 'Labour and the process of industrialisation', pp. 41–2. More research appears to have been carried out on women's farm work in Scotland and Continental Europe than in England: see Devine, 'Women workers, 1850–1914'. Deborah Simonton provides an excellent summary of the literature for European regions. Much of what we know for early modern England is provided by Kussmaul, *Servants in husbandry*, but the evidence for women is scanty.

areas, especially in the cereal growing areas of south-east England, and connected this with soaring levels of poor relief.

Some recent research on the history of farm labour in England suggests that agrarian capitalism led to a decrease in the work possibilities for women. Robert Allen has pointed out that larger, capitalised, arable farms were likely to employ fewer women and children.[4] This echoes Arthur Young's observations on his *Northern Tour* (1770) that 'great farmers do not keep near the proportion of servants, maids and boys that smaller ones do. Their superiority . . . lies totally in labourers'.[5] Burnette's recent research collates wage data for the country as a whole and shows a growing wage gap between males and females over the period of industrialisation. She suggests that this was due to a declining demand for women's skills.[6] Her detailed study of a farm near Sheffield shows that work opportunities for female labourers fell between the 1770s and 1830s and it appears that generally increasing agricultural productivity led to a decreasing demand for women workers.[7] The theoretical basis for 'female marginalisation' with the development of capitalism is also well established in sociological texts. Ever since Engels published *The origin of the family, private property and the state*, it has been argued that women have been progressively excluded from productive activities as economies develop.[8] Esther Boserup, in her important empirical work on comparative economic development, also argued that women's status was high where they had a full role in production and tended to decline with progressive economic development and specialisation.[9]

The argument for women's declining involvement is at odds with Ivy Pinchbeck's classic work on the Industrial Revolution written in 1930. By drawing on parliamentary reports and a wide variety of other evidence, Pinchbeck produced a detailed picture of what women actually did on farms. She argued, for the country as a whole, that 'whenever new crops were grown and improved methods adopted, the employment of women as day labourers rapidly increased' and that as 'capitalistic farming developed, and with it the desire to lower the cost

---

[4] Allen, *Enclosure and the yeoman*; Allen, 'Growth of labour productivity'.
[5] Quoted by Alan Armstrong in Mingay, (ed.), *Agrarian history*, *VI*, p. 673.
[6] Burnette, 'Investigation into the female-male wage gap'.
[7] Burnette, 'Labourers at the Oakes'.
[8] Engels, *Origins of the family*. For sociological approaches see MacEwan-Scott, 'Women and industrialisation'. A comprehensive introduction to historical and sociological approaches is Bradley, *Men's work, women's work*.
[9] Boserup, *Women's role in economic development*.

of production, women's labour was increasingly in demand'.[10] From a situation where women had only intensively worked in agriculture at haytime and harvest, Pinchbeck argued that the conditions of the late eighteenth century forced women to undertake more agricultural labour.[11] Inadequate male wages and falling alternative opportunities, particularly in spinning, coincided with more work suited to the perceived skills of women. Large farms and improved methods meant a more intensive seasonal demand for planters, hoers, weeders and harvesters of intensively grown crops. Pinchbeck was mistaken in her emphasis on the novelty of turnip cultivation in the century after 1750, but evidence from large farms in Essex, an area of advanced, commercial agriculture in the eighteenth century, confirms the role of both women and children in setting crops, stone-picking and weed gathering, and as the main workers employed to deal with specialist crops, such as medicinal herbs for the London market, in seed growing, in commercial vegetable production and on fruit farms.[12] On the point that women were a cheap source of labour and capitalist farming methods needed low costs of production, Pinchbeck argued that, had women and children not been available, 'it is probable that much of the work demanded by the new cultures would have remained undone, or that the expense of employing extra men would have deterred many from adopting new methods'.[13] Recent detailed research on Somerset supports the Pinchbeck view.[14] Helen Speechley finds a rise in the proportion of women employed on farms over the period from the seventeenth century to the era of 'high' farming, with a rapid decline before the agricultural depression of the last quarter of the nineteenth century. Until the mid-nineteenth century, female agricultural labourers constituted an average of 20 per cent of the annual day labour force in Somerset. Women's employment declined only in line with the overall trend in agricultural employment in the course of the nineteenth century.

Keith Snell argued for women's reduced role in agriculture in the eighteenth-century south-east of England in his *Annals of the Labouring Poor*.[15] His data, drawn from seasonal patterns of work and wages recorded in settlement examinations, suggested that women's work in

---

[10] Pinchbeck, *Women workers*, pp. 66, 100.
[11] Pinchbeck, *Women workers*, pp. 53–66.
[12] Sharpe, *Adapting to capitalism*, pp. 92–9.
[13] Pinchbeck, *Women workers*, p. 66. Pinchbeck's view is adopted by Armstrong, in Mingay (ed.), *Agrarian history, VI*, p. 684.
[14] Speechley, 'Female and child agricultural day labourers', p. 49.
[15] Snell, *Annals*.

predominantly arable counties such as Essex, Suffolk, Cambridgeshire, Hertfordshire, Bedfordshire and Northamptonshire became more confined and less well paid as the eighteenth century advanced. Whereas in the early modern period through to the early eighteenth century, the patterns revealed a reasonably equitable sharing of tasks and the involvement of women in multifarious farm jobs, Snell showed that a sexual division of labour developed in the second half of the century. Women no longer worked in harvest operations, and indeed by the mid-nineteenth century had very little involvement in farm work at all. The pastoral west of England presented a different pattern because of female work opportunities in dairying that may, in fact, have increased in the nineteenth century. Snell's views have become widely influential, being recounted in textbooks on women's history, and more widely in general works of economic and social history.[16] Yet Snell himself readily acknowledged that the explanations for his results were tentative.

The broad patterns of women's work are unclear until the onset of the French Wars. We must balance Snell's trend of declining female participation in the cornlands against the evident areas of growth identified by Pinchbeck. The French Wars (1793–1815) are thought to have created more work for women, leading to reports of 'petticoat harvests' in some parts of the country.[17] Can this be substantiated? If we turn to Essex, farm account books show an increase in women employed on farms in the first few years of wartime conditions. As the cost of living soared, some cottage industries collapsed and, with many men away on service, there is little doubt that women would have been actively seeking farm work. Demographic conditions of early and near universal marriage, and a high birth rate from the end of the eighteenth century, make it obvious that the supply of family labourers increased. But so did the glut of male farm workers, with farmers using the poor law to subsidise the practice of maintaining agricultural labourers through low points of the year to meet peak seasonal labour demands.[18] Moreover, the incomparably high prices and profits may have meant that farmers placed a premium on expert harvesters. Farm accounts for Essex show that as the wars progressed, harvests were brought in by contracted labour, or sometimes by the militia on large farms, while

---

[16] Most recently Mark Overton cites the story of declining participation in his *Agricultural Revolution*. Hill, *Women, work and sexual politics*, follows Snell's line of argument. For examples of more general textbooks see Brown, *Society and economy in modern Britain*, pp. 321–2; Rule, *Albion's people*, pp. 190–1.

[17] Emsley, *British society and the French wars*, p. 111; Mingay (ed.), *Agrarian history, VI*, p. 684.

[18] See Boyer, *Economic history of the English Poor Law*.

women continued in the areas seen as traditional 'women's work' such as weeding, stone-picking, haymaking, and turnip singling.[19] Rather than employing more women in threshing, the wartime saw the first use of threshing machines. Other positive evidence of women working in Essex during the wars comes from the prizes provided by agricultural societies to women workers. Such measures, and the indications of women and children 'dibbling' wheat rather than sowing broadcast, seem more like efforts to reduce the poor rate by artificially creating work for labourers' families than proof that women's agricultural work was plentiful.[20] Poor relief evidence also casts doubt on a picture of buoyant work opportunities for women. For example, in the typical grain-growing parish of Terling in Essex, women's earnings from agriculture were very small. The poor women on listings were only able to earn a third of their livelihood from farm work and many of them were listed as doing 'nothing'. The Terling vestry investigated the situation in 1811 and resolved that they must introduce measures to employ labourers' families.[21] Even in the low-lying area of south Essex, which experienced labour shortages in normal conditions, the exigencies of wartime do not seem to have been met with increased casual female labour. This district seems to have maintained live-in farm servants for longer than the claylands. The surviving accounts of Skinnerswick Farm in Tolleshunt d'Arcy do show wives predominating in sowing and haymaking, but the harvest workforce was supplied by professional reapers who hailed from villages in north Essex and Suffolk.[22]

Whatever the level of female employment in wartime, the demand for women workers seems certain to have shrunk in the agricultural depression from 1815 to 1835. There are grounds for arguing for a revival in women's work between 1835 and 1850, particularly in the cornlands. On the demand side, this was because some farmers diversified away from wheat into other cereals or livestock.[23] On the supply side, the stipulations of the New Poor Law seem to have propelled more women—particularly single women and widows— towards farm work. Although women agricultural workers formed only 1.2 per cent of agricultural labourers in Essex in the 1851 census, there

---

[19] Sharpe, *Adapting to capitalism*, pp. 38–70.

[20] Armstrong, *Farmworkers*, p. 51. See also Anon., *An account of the Essex society for the encouragement of agriculture and industry* (Bocking, 1793), copy held at Essex Record Office (hereafter ERO).

[21] ERO, D/P 299/12/4-5; D/P 299/8/3, 30 December 1811.

[22] ERO, D/DU 623/183.

[23] Wilkes, 'Adjustments in arable farming'.

was an increasing barrage of middle-class condemnation of women participating in field work in the mid-nineteenth century. The invective against women's agricultural employment ran alongside the factory and mine legislation of the 1830s and 1840s and expressed the conflict between women's work and their domestic role. The Commissioners on Women and Children's Employment in Agriculture reported in 1843 on the notorious gang system in operation in East Anglia, although such gangs continued into the 1850s and 1860s.[24] But factors such as higher male wages and male unionisation, agricultural depression in the last quarter of the nineteenth century, mechanisation of agricultural processes and compulsory education for children only went so far towards changing the position of women and children as a reserve pool of casual labour which fed the capitalist farming system. Oral reports from twentieth century Essex still mention forms of women and children's rural work which had gone virtually unchanged for centuries, work such as weeding, bird scaring, stone-picking, collecting acorns to feed pigs, clover turning, potato picking and singling of root crops.[25] Women found little work in cereal production, but vegetable cultivation could keep them in sporadic work through the summer. As a result, Steve Hussey's recent oral history might be describing the seventeenth century: work was sex specific, men worked alongside women but in different, more skilled occupations.[26]

This discussion suggests that, given the problems of comparability of evidence and the ebb and flow of work for women over time, perhaps the existing views of historians are differences of degree rather than being directly contradictory. Pinchbeck describes expanding demand for female labour in the improved sectors of the economy. Snell's evidence reflects female unemployment in localised areas where former servants in husbandry were now cast off in an increasingly casualised and seasonal farming regime. A modern chronology might also suggest that some of the labour intensive production described by Pinchbeck emerged as early as the seventeenth century. Estimates of overall labour productivity rise during the mid-seventeenth century because convertible husbandry led to better land preparation by ploughing and harrowing and more time spent on pruning and hoeing. De Vries' recent formulation of an 'industrious revolution' preceding the Industrial Revolution suggests that much of this new work reflects a

[24] Armstrong, *Farmworkers*, pp. 80, 96.
[25] ERO, T/Z 25/241 (Old people's essays, 1961).
[26] Hussey, 'Out in the fields in all weathers'. Hussey suggests the sexual division of labour in field work may have been the result of the mechanisation of cereal operations, but I would argue it had a much longer history.

greater input of women and children's labour galvanised by the stirrings of an emergent consumerism.[27]

Comparability over time is vexed by the fact that the reference points for the rise or decline of work availability all lie in the nineteenth century. Except for the few farms which kept comprehensive records, there is no way of measuring the extent of female participation in an earlier period. Many interpretations of decline in women's employment in the nineteenth century have been influenced by census figures. Eric Richards, for example, drew up a U-shaped curve of female labour participation in the industrialising period, drawing on the declining census trend.[28] But Edward Higgs has recently argued that the censuses massively underestimate women's agricultural work in the mid-nineteenth century.[29] Celia Miller's earlier comparison of farm accounts for Gloucestershire with the census enumerator's books for 1871 and 1881 revealed that women were employed in a wide range of farm work as cheap labourers, even as harvesters, but they were not noticed in the census as participating in work.[30] This lack of firm information on the numbers of female workers leads us to explore other avenues to secure a picture of female labour participation.

Work and gender segregation

Although the supply of female labour to farmers increased after 1750, women's work depended on the sexual division of labour. The thrust of Burnette's recent argument for 'occupational crowding' is that work was not rigidly gender-segregated in agriculture, but that differences in strength between males and females affected the allocation of tasks.[31] Regarding the sexual division of labour, Snell argued that 'There is abundant supportive evidence for a very wide range of female participation in agricultural tasks before 1750 in the south-east, when their work extended to reaping, loading and spreading dung, ploughing, threshing, thatching, following the harrow, sheep shearing, and even working as shepherdesses'. Indeed, he claimed that there was then 'a traditionally fuller and more sexually equal participation in agriculture' than what was to follow.[32] He did not provide much 'abundant' supporting evidence, however, referring readers to writers on women's

[27] De Vries, 'Between purchasing power and the world of goods'.
[28] Richards, 'Women in the British economy'.
[29] Higgs, 'Occupational censuses'; Higgs, 'Women, occupations and work'.
[30] Miller, 'Hidden workforce'.
[31] Burnette, 'Testing for occupational crowding'.
[32] Snell, *Annals*, pp. 52, 56.

work in the early modern period, such as Alice Clark. Clark's book sees the seventeenth century as an era in which women participated in a wide range of work hitherto closed to them, and, she believed, this conferred upon them a degree of equality in family relationships which subsequently declined.[33] More recent research questions the extent to which work was in fact carried out as a partnership, and suggests that, in urban areas at least, both male and female contributions to the household might be wages from completely different sorts of employment.[34]

Farm accounts can give us a comparable, detailed picture for the countryside, even if there tends to be a bias towards the survival of larger and more capitalised farms where accounts were more likely to be kept and which provide more detail.[35] A. Hassell Smith's research on the late sixteenth-century account books of Nathaniel Bacon of Stiffkey in Norfolk is suggestive.[36] He found women's farm work to be complementary to men's, but not the same. Certain tasks seem to have always been women's work, especially spring weeding and stone-picking. On Bacon's estates, women did not take part in ploughing, hedging and ditching, reaping or threshing, which were distinctively male tasks. Henry Best's farming and memorandum books for Elmswell, Yorkshire, in 1642 give some of the richest descriptions of farm organisation available for the early modern period. In Best's world there was a strict gender division of labour, farm tasks were not interchangeable, and their allocation depended on age, strength and its application to the soil, or prevailing weather conditions.[37]

On the Antony estate in Torpoint in Cornwall in the seventeenth century, the range of women's employment was much wider. Although they did the planting and cleaning operations, they also winnowed barley and threshed oats.[38] Carol Shammas' study of Swarthmoor Hall in Lancashire in the seventeenth century also revealed gender-specific employment patterns in day labour.[39] Women were involved in harrowing and haying in the arable fields but not in weeding. They

---

[33] Clark, *Working life of women.*

[34] Earle, 'Female labour market'. Sharpe, 'Literally spinsters.

[35] The main difficulty is locating such accounts. They now mainly reside within collections of private papers in county record offices. However, more research could be carried out on the large collection held at the Rural History Centre, Reading University.

[36] Hassell Smith, 'Labourers in late sixteenth-century England' (parts I and II).

[37] Woodward, (ed.), *Farming and memorandum books of Henry Best.*

[38] Sharpe, 'Time and wages'.

[39] Shammas, 'The world women knew'.

were weeders in the garden and flax fields. On the Thornborough estate in Yorkshire studied by Mrs Gilboy, in the third quarter of the eighteenth century women were employed in 'shearing' or reaping, but they took no part in mowing, threshing hedging, ploughing or stubbing.[40] Considered together, these various case studies suggest that there were important regional and local differences in the gender-specificity of employment.

Another source, William Marshall's *Review and abstract of the county reports to the Board of Agriculture* made between 1787 (Norfolk) and 1815 (Cornwall), is well trodden.[41] Here the historian relies on whether or not the reporters considered women to fall into the category of 'work people'. As their *raison d'etre* demanded, the authors of the county reports were concerned with the efficiency of the workforce and the degree to which new farming methods had been adopted, and as a result often comment only on particularly good or bad practice. Moreover, the reports were compiled over a 30-year period, during much of which there was a wartime economy. The shortcomings are obvious, but, nevertheless, the information which Marshall's *Review* can provide on women's employment has not been given adequate attention. Regional specificity is apparent throughout these reports, but the broad patterns show men's involvement with mowing corn, ploughing, and hedging and ditching, while women were concerned with poultry, sheep, weeding, planting and any husbandry which was garden-like such as flax-pulling, hemp cultivation, orchards, vegetables or herb growing.[42] The most distinctive difference was the primary association of women with the dairy and men with arable, but even this was not universal. Men were reported as milking in Buckinghamshire.[43] In other areas, women were reported to be ploughing, as in Berkshire where the Mole Plow was 'drawn by one horse, and sometimes by women, as occasion requires'.[44] In Westmoreland female servants were 'toiling in the severe labours of the field, they drive the harrows or plough . . .' and also

---

[40] Gilboy, 'Labour at Thornborough'.

[41] Marshall, *Review and abstract*.

[42] Marshall, *Review and abstract*, IV, pp. 66–7; V, p. 130. For Welsh women working in market gardens around London see Williams-Davies, 'Merched y Gerddi'.

[43] Marshall, *Review and abstract*, IV, p. 505.

[44] Marshall, *Review and abstract*, V, p. 84. This was used by Mr Loveden of Buscot Park and the footnote comments on 'the *magic* of *invention*, drawn by one horse, – and even by the women!' It is notable that development economists have drawn attention to the fact that ploughing is almost always a male job in agrarian systems worldwide.

carried dung on their backs to the fields.[45] In general, women did a wider variety of farm tasks in the north and west of the country, particularly where male labour was needed in industry. For instance, in Northumberland, 'Most of the corn is cut with sickles, by women; seven of whom, with a man to bind after them'; the picture was similar in the North Riding of Yorkshire.[46] In Cornwall, 'The women, everywhere in the county, perform a large share of the rural labours, particularly in the harvest work, weeding the corn, hoeing turnips, potatoes, etc., attending the thrashing machines; by the latter business they have more employment in the winter than they formerly had'.[47] An overview of the regional patterns of women's work evident from comment in Marshall's *Review* can be gained from Table 3.1. Broadly, a highland/lowland contrast is evident, with far less farm work reported for women in the lowlands to the south and east of a line drawn from the Wash to the Severn.

For Snell, the crucial change in the south-eastern arable lands towards male labour took place in harvesting. Drawing heavily on the research of Michael Roberts but making more of the late eighteenth-century evidence, Snell argued that women's progressive withdrawal from farm labour in arable areas was connected with the replacement of the sickle by the scythe in corn-growing regions, the scythe being less physically manageable for women[48]. But there is little wholesale evidence for the replacement of the female reaper by the male mower, or for any other determinative technological change when we examine farm accounts such as those available for some Essex farms. The two technologies could, and did, co-exist and were used when most appropriate for the crop mix and the weather. As E.J.T. Collins has written, 'the exact tool mix in any one season [was] determined by labour supply and crop condition'.[49] Farmers could strike a balance between speed and care in cutting. In Marshall's *Review* we read in Northamptonshire of 'wheat reaped with sickles, barley, oats and beans moved with a scythe'. In Berkshire in 1794 'the usual practice of the county is to let the harvest work by the great; and many of the women are employed in reaping, as well as the other labour necessary for getting in crops'.[50] Scythes may have been used mainly by men, but the argument is inadequate to substantiate a wholesale change in labour practices happening in the late eighteenth century. The corn scythe may have become established in

[45] Marshall, *Review and abstract*, I, p. 234.
[46] Marshall, *Review and abstract*, I, pp. 73, 474.
[47] Marshall, *Review and abstract*, III, p. 538.
[48] Roberts, 'Sickles and scythes'.
[49] Collins, 'Harvest technology', p. 462.
[50] Marshall, *Review and abstract*, IV, p. 356; V, p. 56.

Table 3.1 Descriptions of English women's work in Marshall's *Review and abstract*

South-east	Norfolk	wheat dibbling. Reaping is unusual and day labourers wages do not mention women
	Middlesex	fruit, market gardening
	Surrey	hoeing turnip
	Kent	weeding, dairy, domestic work
	North-east Essex	women as servants mentioned
	South Essex	house servants
	Cambridgeshire	service for women is stressed
	Suffolk	no tasks given for women
South-west	Herefordshire	sheep shearing, fruit work
	Worcestershire	harvest, dairying
	Gloucestershire	haymaking, harvest
	Somerset	weeding, common work
	Devon	shortage of women's employment
	South Wiltshire	getting in harvest and gleaning
	Hampshire	dairymaids and cooks
	Cornwall	harvest work, weeding corn, hoeing turnips, potatoes, tending threshing machines
Midlands	Oxfordshire	haying, reaping in harvest
	Buckinghamshire	dairymaids difficult to get
	Bedfordshire	little
	Hertfordshire	straw plait only
	Berkshire	reaping, dairy, plough, planting
	Leicestershire	common work and hay time
	Northamptonshire	hay harvest
	Rutland	little employment except in summer
North-east	Northumberland	harvesting, hoeing turnips, haymaking, scaling and weeding corn, reaping
	Durham	weeding, haying, reaping
	Yorkshire N.Riding	dairy, harvest, weeding corn, haymaking, manuring, same work as men
	Yorkshire E.Riding	men and women day labourers hired
	Lincolnshire	dairying but women lazy
North-west	Cumberland	haymaking, harvest
	Westmoreland	carting dung, driving harrows or ploughs
	Cheshire	dairying

Source: Marshall, *Review and abstract.*

southern England during the medieval period: the 'revolution' in adoption of heavier tools in the rest of the country was delayed until 1835–70. Overton suggests that whereas in 1790 some 90 per cent of the wheat harvest was cut with a sickle, by 1870 it was 20 per cent.[51] Not only does this suggest a slow transition in the nineteenth century rather than a late eighteenth-century transformation, but it seems that in areas where women already formed the bulk of harvest workers, as in the Borders, the scythe was unlikely to be adopted at all.

Marshall commented on a broad contrast between the north-west and the south-east of England at the end of the eighteenth century. In the north harvesting was mainly in the hands of women, but this was certainly not evident in the counties of the south-east.[52] For Essex, it is the case that descriptions of harvest work in the late eighteenth and early nineteenth centuries are male-orientated. Harvest operations were invested with a great deal of symbolic importance. Boys became men when they first took their place in the line of harvesters. On some farms, the first cut was taken by the oldest male villager present. However, the evidence not only suggests that the role of women was limited at the end of the eighteenth century, but that this had long been the case. In the extant sixteenth and seventeenth century Essex farm accounts, such as those of the Petre family—the largest landowners in Essex—women were mainly involved in spring weeding and haymaking. Women's work in the harvest was confined to raking oats.[53] It might be argued that these documents are providing an early view of the 'Allen effect'. However, the accounts of Thomas Cawton, who was farming on a much smaller scale in Wivenhoe and Great Bentley in eastern Essex in the early 1630s, give a very similar picture. As in the Petre accounts, most of the workers are in family groups. The women were spring weeders, sometimes working with their husbands. Again many women were involved in haymaking. For the grain harvest, however, women's role was relatively marginal, with a limited involvement in the oat harvest alongside their husbands. Women had the additional jobs of gathering up the wool from sheep shearing in Great Bentley and picking seed rye in Wivenhoe. Just as Hassell Smith found, all the winter work of ploughing, hedging, ditching, and threshing was done by men.[54] Evidence from this local economy suggests another significant change

---

[51] Collins, 'Harvest technology', pp. 456–7, 463. See also the discussion in Middleton, 'The familiar fate of the *famulae*'; Overton, *Agricultural Revolution*, p. 124.

[52] Quoted in Gilboy, 'Labour at Thornborough', p. 391.

[53] ERO, D/DP A18–22, A57.

[54] ERO, TA287.

due to alterations in the crop mix. In the sixteenth century, hops were grown in almost every parish in Essex and provided an intermittent amount of work for women, from tending the plants through to meticulous harvesting from March to late September.[55] When economic circumstances favoured grain production, hops were judged to be too liable to crop failure and too demanding of manure, and their acreage shrank on the Essex heavy clays in the late eighteenth century. The result was a substitution of male for female labour.

In summary, close analysis of the sexual division of labour does not give as straightforward a view as Snell and those who have repeated and extended his arguments have maintained, and would lead us to eschew a view of technological change explaining female expulsion in favour of a more nuanced approach which gives greater weight to local variations due to geography, regional culture and time-honoured patterns of customary work. Despite the availability of more labour by the end of the eighteenth century, we can argue that there is evidence of a long standing sexual division of labour on capitalist farms in the south-east. While an explanation based on technology transfer may be too limited, it is possible that a drive for efficiency may have excluded less productive parts of the labour force, except in specific, limited ways. It was also the case that, as the nineteenth century advanced, a growing sense of domestic ideology encouraged married women to move away from the more strenuous types of outdoor work. We should not underestimate the fact that, like labouring men, poor women, especially those who were single, could and did exercise considerable mobility, both geographically and in terms of shifting occupation.[56] Back-breaking labour, low pay, and long-standing customary practices which relegated women to the most degrading and monotonous tasks would not be endured if alternatives were available.

Female wage rates

Turning to wage rates, Snell accumulated a large amount of evidence of declining female wages, comparing the south-east of England with the south-west, to support his view of a declining participation rate and increasing gender division of labour in the south-east. Burnette, by contrast, has recently argued that agricultural work was not well defined by gender, but that women's lack of strength and relative productivity

---

[55] Shrimpton, 'Landed society and the farming community', p. 306
[56] For speculations on this in a European context see Ankarloo, 'Agriculture and women's work'.

had an impact on the low wages offered for farm work.[57] It should be noted that she assumes women farm labourers were unskilled and therefore substitutable, but this is not borne out by Pinchbeck's assumption that women's dexterity made them the best workers to carry out new agricultural tasks, or by evidence such as Valenze's regarding the expertise necessary for dairying operations. There are also, of course, very many problems in assessing female farm worker's wages, not least the prevalence of wives doing task work for a family wage.[58] However, the evidence from both farm accounts and Marshall's *Review* is that female day labourer's wages show little movement or variability, being normally 6d. a day. This rate was 'sticky' through the year and between regions from the seventeenth century onwards. This is demonstrated if we revisit the Cawton farms in eastern Essex and examine the case of a single labourer and his wife in the 1630s. Thomas Toball of Wivenhoe joined his wife and some other women for a week's weeding in June. They were both paid 6d. a day. By July they were both still employed in weeding but Mr Toball was paid 8d. while his wife received 6d. a day. At the end of July he had a shilling a day 'for makeing the stake of hay'. Goodye Toball, along with the rest of the women, still received 6d. a day. At the beginning of September, when rye, oats and barley were harvested, Toball bound the oats at a shilling a day, while his wife stayed at 6d. for 'makeing of bandes for the oates' for three days and then for 'layeing of oats for the binding'. He went on to stack the 'brank' (buckwheat) at a shilling a day whereas his wife raked up at the usual 6d. she had been paid all summer.[59] Following Burnette's argument, this payment may be a true reflection of Mrs Toball's productivity. It is possible that wives started work much later in the day than their husbands, perhaps well after daybreak, and that this explains the lower wage rate. Perhaps it is, in effect, a sort of piece rate.[60] Another factor is that women's unpaid labour within the rural community was of vital importance to the well-being of labouring

---

[57] Burnette, 'Testing for occupational crowding'.

[58] As reported in the 1843 Report of Women and Children in Agriculture for Kent, Surrey and Sussex, cited by Pinchbeck, *Women workers*, p. 91.

[59] ERO, D/DA A3.

[60] The suggestion of a later start is made by Judy Gielgud, 'Nineteenth-century farm women', p. 459. In a personal communication Mark Overton has suggested that 6d. may have represented a certain agreed amount of work. Speechley argues that the discrepancy with male wage rates 'was not only due to higher daily wage rates for men but also because they [men] worked more days per year, they were more likely to receive harvest wages, and they were more frequently employed in piece rate work, which could bring in higher wages: 'Female and child agricultural day labourers', p. 113.

Table 3.2 **Female wage rates given in Marshall's** *Review and abstract*
(1780s–1810s)

	Day Work	Harvest
Northumberland	6d.	1s.–1s. 3d.
Durham	6d.	2s.– 2s. 6d.
Cumberland	8d.	10d.
Herefordshire	6d.	
Worcestershire	6d.–8d.	
Warwickshire	1s.–1s. 6d.	
Somerset	6d.–8d.	
Cornwall	6d.–8d.	
Suffolk	6d.	
Leicestershire	6d.–8d.	9d.–10d. haying
Oxfordshire	1s. 2d.	
Berkshire	6d.–8d.	
Kent	8d.–10d.	

Source: Marshall, *Review and abstract.*

families. Women were the main procurers of fuel and water, they prepared the meals for the men after their long hard days of work, and they managed the informal exchanges of farm products to which historians are now paying more attention, for example, trading eggs or vegetables to the large farms in the district. Time spent on these tasks would have been weighed against that allocated to the labour market for those with some land or produce of their own.[61]

Alternatively, perhaps women's wages contain a large customary element and the rate paid may bear little relationship to the task carried out. This explanation is rejected by Burnette, but the endurance of 6d. a day across geographical areas and time is striking, particularly when compared to changing male rates. From Best's Yorkshire in 1642, to the Spindleston, Northumberland farm account for 1676 analysed by Gielgud, to the eighteenth-century Cornish barton farms studied by Pounds, the rate was 6d.[62] Table 2 shows, for the counties for which

[61] See Reed, 'Peasantry', pp. 59–60; Mills, *Lord and peasant*. For the endurance of family labour on small farms see Winstanley, 'Industrialisation and the small farm'.

[62] Woodward (ed.), *Henry Best*, pp. 45, 60; Gielgud, 'Nineteenth-century farm women', p. 129; Pounds, 'Barton farming'. I am grateful to Mark Overton for the latter reference.

evidence is available in Marshall's *Review*, the prevalence of 6d., sometimes rising to 8d. in summer, for female day labour. So despite their multifarious activities noted in the *Review*, in Cornwall 'The women have from 6d. to 8d. per day'.[63] The exceptions were only two in number, both of which show that the market certainly had some effect. Firstly, women were paid more when they did more specialised work, as with reapers in northern England who might be paid 1s. a day. Secondly, in areas where there was competition for their labour their wages could be double, as in Warwickshire agriculture due to the effect of the Birmingham and Coventry trades. But even within living memory in Essex, the rate had risen to only 8d. for female day labourers. It is startling to note that this rate, including food, was also paid to women in 1377![64]

Looking at this in more detail, however, some differences are apparent. Going back to the sixteenth–century Petre farms in Essex, we find a difference among women, which seems to have arisen because wives were paid less than widows.[65] A widow was paid 5d., but a woman working alongside her husband was only paid 3d., less than a girl who had 4d. The women involved in these operations were usually the relatives of agricultural labourers, sometimes accompanied by children, and this suggests the payment of a family wage to widows must be seen within a context of local paternalism. It is, of course, possible that farmers felt they were maintaining the stability of the male workforce by employing married women. Unless, in fact, widows were able to work longer hours, this suggests that there was a 'social' element to women's wage payments which cannot be entirely explained by economic theory, or indeed, fully comprehended given only the limited detail of bare figures recorded in the pages of farming accounts.

It is also clear that lower wage rates for women were justified by the Bible. Leviticus 27:3–4 suggests that women should receive three-fifths of the male rate, which is precisely the rate they did receive in many recorded cases.[66] Burnette's argument that women's wage rates reflect the actual work they carried out also fails to explain comments like that made by Frederick Eden in his survey of the poor of the parish of Bromfield (Cumberland):

[63] Marshall, *Review and abstract*, V, p. 538.
[64] ERO, T/Z 25/63; Penn, 'Female wage earners', p. 10.
[65] ERO, D/DP A18–22, A57.
[66] For further justification of a customary wage see Woodward, *Men at work*, pp. 112–14.

The wages of man-servants employed in husbandry, who are hired from half-year to half-year, are from 9 to 12 guineas a year, whilst women, who here do a large portion of the work of the farm, with difficulty get half as much. It is not easy to account for so striking an inequality and still less easy to justify it.[67]

In summary, we need to know much more about the social history of wage entitlement, especially for women, before we can draw any significant conclusions about labour demand and supply from patterns of wage movements. However, there is every justification for Pinchbeck's view that female labour would be used where possible on capitalist farms because it lowered the costs of production. Yet there is no firm basis for the belief that this was a post-1750 development.

Marginalisation of female labour?

If low wages and a sexual division of labour were not new in the south-east, are there alternative explanations for the current view that women were marginalised in the eighteenth century? Snell's debate with Norma Landau concerning the function of the settlement examination has, if anything, diverted attention from the interpretation and explanation of the patterns which Snell has drawn from them.[68] To prove that female farm employments were changing in the south-east, it must be clear that we are considering farm servants, rather than domestic servants or industrial workers. Data on domestic servants can tell us very little about changes in the type and timing of women's agricultural work as the moments at which they were likely to find themselves unemployed might have only a limited relationship to agricultural imperatives. In Essex, and probably in other areas of capitalist agriculture where farm sizes were large, indoor and outdoor service would seem to have been well-defined. Maids who did domestic work were not farm workers, except for perhaps tending the garden and poultry. Moreover, some of Snell's settlements for Essex are drawn from urban areas and these are likely to have formed a higher proportion of female settlement examinations, especially as unemployed women gravitated towards towns to find work. Further, if hiring fairs and the institution of farm service were waning in the south-east at the end of the eighteenth-century, it is not clear that the Snell sample could contain many farm servants anyway. As a result, it is not evident that Snell's evidence encapsulates only the rural labour market.

---

[67] Eden, *State of the poor*, II, p. 47.
[68] Landau, 'Law of settlement'; Snell, 'Pauper settlement'; Landau., 'Eighteenth-century context'.

While Snell provides unemployment patterns for yearly servants, we know from the writings of contemporaries that the supply of female farm workers was affected by the prevalence and prosperity of alternative forms of employment. In some regions there was an inverse relationship between the female labour supply for farming and the availability of other types of work. Of Marton (Westmorland), to take a negative example, David Davies commented in 1795; 'There is no kind of manufactory carried on in this neighbourhood, for which reason women and children earn little, except in hay and corn harvest'.[69] 'Spring' unemployment would have been alleviated in many of the south-eastern counties by the development of the London-based fashion trades and services with their production closely related to the London season. Not only were employments a draw in London itself, but fashion industries created work for women in the countryside, such as lace-making and straw-plaiting, which pulled women away from service or farm work.[70] This was the type of work in which women were perceived as having a comparative advantage. Snell has presented us with a distribution of cases, so that a factor creating employment can be just as significant as one reducing employment. In fact, the greatest economic change in the eastern counties like Essex (but also Suffolk, Norfolk and even parts of Cambridgeshire) was the decline in spinning opportunities in the late eighteenth century. Indeed the fall-off in women's 'work', which contemporaries such as David Davies wrote about, is undoubtedly the collapse of spinning rather than agricultural work. This is likely to have had the most marked effect on Snell's wage rates. Part of his argument for the increasing sexual division of labour concerned the failure of women's wages to move in tandem with male wages, which he used to prove that women were an increasingly devalued part of the agricultural labour force. But given a year-round alternative employment, farms would have to compete with clothiers for female labour. When spinning ceased to be viable, it is not surprising that the effect was the stagnation of female wage rates.

There is another explanation for why women were not participating in the labour market at harvest time. Women's customary role was in gleaning, picking up the waste or leftover crop after the harvest. Gleaning was probably seen as the married women's and widow's main role in the harvest and is, in fact, sufficient of itself to explain why women did not engage in cutting the crop. As a reporter describing

[69] Davies, *The case of the labourers in husbandry*.
[70] Sharpe, 'Women's harvest'; Sharpe, *Adapting to capitalism*, pp. 38–70; Eden, *State of the poor*, II, pp. 1–28.

women's employment in August in the Stowmarket area of Suffolk in the 1840s said, 'when gleaning comes in they are all engaged in that and will not leave it'.[71] From medieval times gleaning was seen as beneficial to the farmer as a cleaning operation.[72] Added to the evidence that weeding and stone-picking were women's jobs, this further aspect of clearing the ground may have had almost symbolic importance. Jane Humphries has written of the importance of common rights as an area of women's 'self-employment' and their erosion in the late eighteenth century as private property was vigorously defended and gentry farms consolidated.[73]

Gleaning is an exception to this because the activity was one way in which capitalist farming enhanced the potential of common rights, for gleaning was far more profitable in areas where there was specialisation in cereal production and higher grain yields. Where farms employed a crop rotation, peas, beans, barley and wheat might all be gleaned in one village in a single season. Peter King, using evidence from Essex court cases, has pointed to the importance of gleaning to the eighteenth-century labouring family.[74] Once threshed, the gleanings could provide a household with flour for the year and could account for from an eighth to a tenth of total labouring family income. For women on their own, such as widows, this could be especially beneficial, providing about a quarter of their annual income. Gleaning was particularly important after the decline of spinning, when all labouring families, but widows in particular, were increasingly dependent on the poor law. From the overseers' point of view, gleaning was an effective form of self-help for the poor.[75] King found that most gleaners were married women, while a quarter were widows, children or single women. Gleaning was being increasingly regulated by the late eighteenth century as farmers resisted trespassing on private property, but the

---

[71] BPP 1843, XII, *Reports from the Commissioners: Employment of Women and Children in Agriculture*, p. 229.

[72] Ault, 'By-laws of gleaning'.

[73] Humphries, 'Enclosures, common rights and women'. See also Neeson, *Commoners*.

[74] King, 'Customary rights and women's earnings'. Pinchbeck recognised the importance of gleaning but confused the issue by believing it was only worthwhile on open fields: *Women workers*, pp. 56–7.

[75] Wells, 'Development of the English rural proletariat'. In 1795 Terling overseers restricted gleaning to widows who had to give notice of their intentions and inform on trespassers (ERO, D/P 299/8/2, 1/7/1795). Those who contravened this faced a reduction in their bread allowance. In the 1820s, however, they supplied bread and cheese to women gleaners (ERO, D/P 299/12/7).

common right was sustained, if regulated.[76] The importance of gleaning to the family budget and women's primary role as providers of family subsistence largely explains why women did not work as harvesters. Gleaning started in a field as soon as the harvester had carted the grain out of it and moved on to another one.[77] Gleaning and working in the harvest are, then, not strictly compatible activities and, in themselves, reinforce a sexual division of labour at harvest time. The persistently low wage for women, with no change over the year, unlike that paid to men, may also suggest why women did not do reaping in the south-east. It was more profitable to glean than to harvest.

It is, then, possible to provide several explanations for declining female labour market participation in rural areas and the associated fluctuations in wage rates in the early industrial period without arguing that this was entirely the result of the expansion of capitalist farming. Alternative employment opportunities for women remind us that while some of the characteristics of rural women's work may not have changed over the centuries, taking rural and urban labour markets as a whole, the overall picture of the female labour market was dynamic rather than static as it has often been portrayed.

Conclusion

Alun Howkins has recently argued that our picture of farmworkers—and he is considering both female and male workers—is dominated by the traditional concerns of economic history.[78] As a result, they are seen as factors of production, and it is their contribution to a distinctive English model of development which is seen as important. There is no denying that the approach taken here does not escape these criticisms. At the same time, the intention has been to bring into play some of the more 'immeasurable' aspects of women's work. Howkins draws our attention to the importance of regional and local cultures.[79] Agrarian historians obviously have to weigh the differences between arable and pastoral areas or the Highland and Lowland zones. We need to unravel the role of custom at the level of the micro-economy. Despite the emphasis on efficiency on capitalist farms, there is evidence for the importance of cultural factors outweighing rational, economic decision-making. Celia Fiennes, for example, noted on her visit to Cornwall at

---

[76] King, 'Gleaners'; King, 'Legal change'.
[77] Smith., 'In harvest time', p. 246.
[78] Howkins, 'Peasants, servants and labourers'.
[79] Howkins, 'English farm labourer'.

the end of the seventeenth century that the harvest was put onto yokes on horses that were led by women and supported by two men. She wondered why they did not use carts but commented 'the common observation of a custom being as a second nature people are very hardly convinc'd or brought off from, tho' never soe inconvenient'.[80] Some 150 years later the 1843 Commission drew its reader's attention to the 'habits of narrow localities. . . . The women of one village have always been accustomed to reap whilst to those of another in the immediate neighbourhood, the practice is unknown. Turnip hoeing is by no means an uncommon occupation for women, yet in many villages they never undertake it'.[81] The point here is not only should we be mindful of local distinctiveness, but also that our explanations may be flawed if we assume that only economic rules held sway.

By taking both *la longue durée* and a regional view of what we know about women's involvement in farm work in the period of industrialisation it is apparent that, at this moment, we are actually better informed about the type and amount of work women did in the medieval period, and in the late nineteenth and early twentieth century, than we are for the long eighteenth century. The manorial and micro-community basis of much research in medieval economic and social history has provided us with a detailed picture. Judith Bennett, for example, found that in Brigstock in Northamptonshire, women looked after small animals, tended fruit trees, cultivated herbs and vegetables, and grew hemp and flax. Their work complemented that of their husbands in the more specialised production of grain.[82] For the second half of the nineteenth century, Karen Sayer charts the change in attitudes in artistic representations of female farm workers, from their taking centre stage as part of a rural idyll to becoming a despised part of the labour force.[83] Criticism of women's agricultural employment started from the mid-nineteenth century with parliamentary commissions which expressed the conflict between women working and their domestic role. Nevertheless, Eve Hostetler and Judy Gielgud have considered the work of a distinctive group for whom demand increased over the nineteenth century, the female bondagers of the

---

[80] Morris, (ed.), *Journeys of Celia Fiennes*, p. 265.
[81] BPP 1843, XII, *Reports from the Commissioners: Employment of Women and Children in Agriculture*, p. 3, cited in Bradley, *Men's work, women's work*, p. 82.
[82] Bennett, *Women in the medieval English countryside*, p. 117. See also Middleton, 'Familiar fate'. An impressive, detailed analysis of medieval women's rural work is Penn, 'Female wage earners'.
[83] Sayer, *Women of the fields* and Kitteringham, 'Country work girls'.

farms of the north-east of England.[84] In fact, comparing arable areas in the north-east and the south-east of England during the same time period produces two contrasting views of female participation in the agricultural labour market. While Snell found women's employment narrowing and becoming more acutely seasonal into the nineteenth century in the south-east, Judy Gielgud, in her recent dissertation, shows the opposite pattern for the north-east with women moving from a traditional work pattern of haymaking and harvesting to a wider involvement throughout the year.[85] Furthermore, whereas Snell saw the position of the dairymaid of the western counties becoming enhanced in the nineteenth century, Deborah Valenze argues that the expertise of dairying was increasingly being seen as the province of men.[86] Although it may go against the grain of feminist projects which seek to rescue women from invisibility in the historical sources, it may be apposite, as the quote from Mathias suggested, to accept that women are simply invisible because they are not part of the workforce and that locating areas in which women did not participate in the labour market is a valuable exercise in itself.[87] There are also temporal considerations inherent in making comparisons. Conflicting pictures from different regions suggest that we should be analysing cyclical, not linear, patterns of women's work and questioning how they fit together between sectors and geographical areas.[88] A useful study would also give attention to the life-cycle of female farm workers, perhaps by linking farm records to parish reconstitutions or listings to establish work patterns through the life course.[89]

This article has argued that in trying to take early steps to fill a gap in our knowledge of women's farm work on capitalist farms in the early industrial period, little evidence has been found of a change in the sexual division of agricultural labour over time. The types of farm work women did, in the south-east at least, was not much different in the nineteenth century from the sixteenth century. Keeping regional differences and parish peculiarities in mind, in this area women's day work was probably always relatively limited in arable agriculture on

---

[84] Hostetler, 'Women farm workers', pp. 40–1; Gielgud, 'Nineteenth-century farm women'.

[85] Snell, *Annals*, pp. 15–66; Gielgud, 'Nineteenth-century farm women', p. 168.

[86] Snell, *Annals*, p. 40; Valenze, 'Art of women'.

[87] A point made by Michael Anderson, 'Mid-Victorian censuses', reprinted here as chapter 8, below.

[88] See the analysis of Hudson, *Industrial Revolution*, p. 231.

[89] See, for example, the life-cycle analysis of Speechley, 'Female and child agricultural labourers'.

large farms. If anything, the amount of work in weeding and planting increased in the second quarter of the nineteenth century, as Pinchbeck suggested. Before that, however, coupled with population rise, the lack of work suggests an avenue for the early release of labour from the land to go into the industrial or service sectors of the economy. It can be linked with the female migration of women from rural areas to towns and cities which was such a marked feature of late seventeenth and eighteenth-century England. As a result, this is a direct route by which the 'agricultural revolution' fed the 'consumer revolution'. Women who moved to towns formed a labour supply for the proliferating fashion industries and services of the urban milieu. As research on other European countries finds fieldwork to have a depressing effect on both fertility and the survival of infants, it may be possible to link low participation in fieldwork with population rise in the English regions where female farm work was relatively minimal and seasonally short-lived.[90] The 'labour release' is less clear for other parts of England, particularly highland areas, where there is little evidence that women's participation had fallen by the end of the eighteenth century, and in some areas it may have increased.

Turning to wages, it is the case that, as Snell found, female wages did not keep pace with male wages over the course of the eighteenth century. For Essex, the wages for female agricultural workers lie at the bottom of the scale of wage payments for women's work by 1800. Whereas they had been between a half and three-quarters of the male rate in the seventeenth century, they were now between a third and a quarter, or even less, because they did not change. As Charles Feinstein has demonstrated for England as a whole in his recent pessimistic, quantitative summary of the standard of living in the Industrial Revolution, taking benchmarks of 1778–82 and 1846–52, all female agricultural workers ended at a lower level than they began. The ratio of the female to male wage showed an initial decline from 50 per cent in 1770 to 40 per cent in the 1820s and was then stable.[91] An element of the female wage was certainly 'sticky' and governed by custom rather than the market. As a result, a clear connection between work opportunities and wage rate movements is questionable. Falling female wages do not necessarily reflect declining labour participation in that there may be no proportionate difference in the amount of work they represent. Industrial work increased for women in the late eighteenth

---

[90] Lee, 'Women's work and the family', pp. 50–75.
[91] Feinstein, 'Pessimism perpetuated', Tawney lecture at Economic History Society conference, University of Oxford, March 1999.

and early nineteenth-centuries whilst their wages fell because employers wanted cheap, docile, nimble-fingered labour and had a labour surplus economy to draw on.

This takes us to the heart of current research in women's economic history which considers how women's position changed with capitalism. Sara Horrell and Jane Humphries drew on wage rates in their collection of budgets for married women to argue that women's opportunities declined.[92] They found that women generated 5 per cent of family incomes in high wage and 12 per cent in low wage agricultural counties and that women's share fell over time. They argue that 'women were losing what employment opportunities they had through the commercialisation of agriculture and the decline in outwork activities. . . The high proportion of households still engaged in agriculture largely ameliorates the increased participation of women found in other occupations'. The problem here is deciding whether we should see falling wages as indicating reduced opportunities, or rather accept that women carried a large burden in supporting an economy in transition. This is not to suggest that custom rules entirely as the market had some effect. For example, in Essex during the French Wars, there was a noticeable rise in payments to women of up to 10d. or a shilling a day. After 1800, Helen Speechley's Somerset farms also show the first noticeable rises in female wage rates for two centuries.[93] If female marginalisation with capitalism does apply, we need to see its effect operating from far back in time and encompassing a much longer time span than that traditionally associated with the Industrial Revolution. The suggestion made by Beneria and Sen, when reviewing Boserup's *Women's role in economic development* (1970) was that 'capitalist accumulation can have a variety of effects on women's work depending on the specific form accumulation takes in a particular region'. Perhaps this is more apposite to the case of English rural labour than a unilinear pattern of female marginalisation.[94] Overall, in comparison with other countries, work for women in agriculture does seem limited and this surely is the other side of the coin for an explanation of women's extensive involvement in other economic sectors. Only further local research, which considers both economic explanations and less quantifiable aspects of human experience in tandem, can take us beyond this necessarily sketchy picture.

[92] Horrell and Humphries, 'Women's labour force participation', quotation at p. 112.

[93] ERO, D/DJN E5; Speechley, 'Female and child agricultural labourers', p. 107.

[94] Beneria and Sen, 'Accumulation, reproduction and women's role', p. 288.

4

Hay, hops and harvest: women's work in agriculture in nineteenth-century Sussex

NICOLA VERDON

Introduction: women's work in nineteenth-century English agriculture

The importance of regional distinctions in nineteenth-century English agriculture has long been recognised by historians. Differences in farm size, agricultural systems, modes of hiring, technological innovation and investment meant the constitution of the farm workforce varied considerably across the British Isles. Until relatively recently, however, research has centred on the male worker. Gender-blindness in agrarian history has meant the distinctive characteristics of the female agricultural labour force have been overlooked or disregarded. This oversight is now being corrected and a number of studies have shown that local factors had a significant impact on the type and amount of work performed by women in nineteenth-century English agriculture. Indeed it is now acknowledged that researching women's employment at the local level offers a more refined assessment of the conditions faced by rural female workers in the past. Pamela Sharpe has argued that many accounts of women's work in agriculture 'suffer from a lack of detailed case studies to back them up'. She writes,

> We still need more specific studies of women's employment in different areas . . . For agricultural workers themselves a wealth of detail can be gathered in local archives using household and farm accounts. It is necessary to build up a corrective picture at the local level by developing new sources, in which, as far as is possible, we can discover the feminine aspect. What women actually did needs to be established from the bottom up, paying attention to localised differences and to such factors as seasonal change, age-specificity, and marital status.[1]

---

[1] Sharpe, 'Continuity and change', pp. 357–8. See also Sharpe, 'Female labour market', chapter 3 above.

Local studies of women's work enable generalisations to be questioned and dismantled, and allow a comparative framework to be established. This chapter aims to show how a county study of female agricultural workers using archival as well as traditional printed sources, can aid our understanding of this complex and under-researched topic.

The earliest and still one of the most comprehensive accounts of women's work in agriculture is Ivy Pinchbeck's study, published in 1930.[2] Based on an exhaustive survey of printed primary material, Pinchbeck's analysis of the impact of industrialisation on women workers highlights the broad regional trends in the employment of women on farms between 1750 and 1850. A key division emerges between northern and southern counties. Writing specifically about day labourers, Pinchbeck claims,

> The greatest amount of work was provided in turnip and potato districts, and consequently in the North, where the population was thinner and the demand for labour greater, women had more regular employment than in the South . . . The more regular employment of women, and the addition of their earnings which were really appreciable, not only permitted a better standard of living in the North, but it also prevented many families being pauperised . . . The greater demoralisation of labourers in the South was due to various causes, but the more regular employment of women was not the least important factor in preserving the independence of the North.[3]

According to Pinchbeck, women's employment as day labourers peaked between 1780 and 1815 due to the widespread introduction of root crops, innovations in cultivation and shortages of male workers, and again in the 1830s and 1840s when both economising farmers and needy families benefited from women's labour.[4] After the 1850s, however, the demand for female day labourers receded dramatically so that 'By the end of the nineteenth century women had almost ceased to be employed as wage earners in agriculture'.[5] Keith Snell's more recent study of women's agricultural work, based on settlement examinations, places the origins for reduced demand for women earlier than Pinchbeck, in the late eighteenth century. Several factors including changes in agricultural technology, the enlargement of farms, and male unemployment were influential in altering the seasonal demand for

---

[2] Pinchbeck, *Women workers*.
[3] Pinchbeck, *Women workers*, p. 79.
[4] Pinchbeck, *Women workers*, pp. 59–63, 84–6.
[5] Pinchbeck, *Women workers*, p. 110.

women. This trend towards sexual specialisation (with women more likely to be employed in spring and early summer tasks such as weeding and haymaking rather than harvesting and winter work) was temporarily halted during the Napoleonic Wars but continued unabated after 1815. These changes were most profound in the corn lands of south-east England: where small-scale pastoral farming predominated, particularly in areas of western and northern England, women's work remained important.[6]

Set against regional studies of farm labour books, how do these conclusions hold up? Farms in several northern counties, including Northumberland and East Yorkshire, corroborate Pinchbeck's claim that the large-scale introduction of root crops led to an increased demand for female labourers.[7] But this pattern was not unique to the north: in Somerset, increased arable output and the extensive cultivation of new crops also contributed to a noticeable enlargement of the female day labour force in the late eighteenth and early nineteenth century.[8] Labour records from the large corn-growing farms of Norfolk, Cambridgeshire, Suffolk and parts of Essex, confirm the marginalisation of female labourers from the late eighteenth century. In this region, women's participation in agricultural day labour was casual and sporadic, limited to certain tasks and poorly paid, as Snell found. The French Wars did not disrupt this pattern significantly and by the 1830s it was the usual practice on many farms to substitute the labour of women with that of boys.[9] But the decline of women in the agricultural labour force should not be overstated. Where local demand or crop patterns dictated it, the employment of women in agriculture remained significant throughout the nineteenth century, even in some areas of the south. Women often formed the core of the workforce in planting and harvesting specialist crops such as hops, flax, saffron, fruit and flowers.[10] Women also continued to be employed on many arable or mixed farms.

---

6 Snell, *Annals*, chapter 1.
7 Gielgud, 'Nineteenth-century farm women', pp. 155–8; Verdon, *Rural women workers*, pp. 102–4.
8 Speechley, 'Female and child agricultural day labourers', p. 64. On farms where livestock production dominated however, opportunities for women to find remunerative work on farms at this time was restricted. Joyce Burnette's study of the Oakes farm, near Sheffield, reveals a substantial decrease in the employment of women day labourers between the 1770s and 1830s, linked the fall-off in demand to changes in husbandry which followed enclosure: Burnette, 'Labourers at the Oakes', pp. 55–6.
9 Verdon, 'A diminishing force?'
10 See Sharpe, *Adapting to capitalism*, pp. 92–3; Speechley, 'Female and child agricultural day labourers', pp. 101–3.

In late nineteenth-century Gloucestershire, for example, female day labourers continued to perform a substantial proportion of work on farms, and were engaged on a wide variety of tasks including reaping, spreading manure, threshing, haymaking, weeding and hoeing.[11]

Women's work in nineteenth-century agriculture was complex and contradictory. Patterns of female labourer differed both within and between counties. Local systems of farming and hiring affected when and where women worked. The size of population settlements, the availability of non-agricultural work, the extent of male employment, as well as other ideological and lifecycle factors, also influenced the position of women in the agricultural labour force. Although much insightful analysis has been carried out on the nature of female agricultural work over recent years, further research at the local level is needed to extend our understanding of this topic. The remainder of this chapter will use a case study of the county of Sussex to show how local research can augment the debate.

Sussex in the nineteenth century

The county of Sussex contains considerable regional variation. Brian Short has identified ten agrarian regions in Sussex.[12] These included the prosperous region of the Coastal Plain and South Downs, which was dominated by arable and mixed farming in the nineteenth century, famous for its sheep and entrepreneurial farmers such as John Ellman. In this region landownership was concentrated, the large estates at Goodwood, Petworth and Arundel exerting huge influence over south-west Sussex, whose parishes were largely closed and strictly controlled.[13] In contrast, the High and Low Wealds were characterised by a wood-pasture economy, with cattle and dairy farming being carried out on small-scale subsistence units, although larger farms were also found in the region. Several features mark the Weald out as distinctive. Many farms continued to hire living-in servants in the nineteenth century and two distinguishing industries were adopted in the High Weald: hops and chicken cramming. In addition, Wealden landownership was scattered, with mobile, open communities prevailing.[14] Mr Little, reporting to the Royal Commission on Agricultural Interests, captured the key division within Sussex farming

---

[11] Miller, 'Hidden workforce', pp. 139–55.
[12] See Leslie and Short, *Historical atlas of Sussex*, chapter 48.
[13] Short, 'Changing rural society and economy of Sussex', p. 153.
[14] Short, 'Changing rural society and economy of Sussex', p. 154.

in 1880, juxtaposing the capitalist farming system of the Downlands against the more antiquated structure of the Weald:

> The WEALD . . . is for the most part the country of small farmers, of little inclosures . . . few sheep, and generally speaking, an old fashioned style of farming . . . the CHALK range of the South Downs . . . has given a name and a character to Sussex as an agricultural county . . . Here are large farms, extensive sheep breeding . . . On the south side of the Downs the soil is remarkably well adapted for the growth of wheat.[15]

Inevitably, the different farming systems and economic bases of Sussex influenced the nature of the rural workforce, and the type and amount of work available for women. Henry Vaughan, who investigated the counties of Kent, Surrey and Sussex for the 1843 commission on the employment of women and children in agriculture, recognised that regional distinctions in female labour were produced by differences in soil type and crop patterns. As the nature of soil varied, he writes, 'the opportunities of employing different kinds of labour are changed also. So the hop-grounds furnish employment to women and children more generally than corn-land, and some kinds of corn-land more than others'.[16] He goes on,

> The peculiar nature of all agricultural produce, too, has a strong influence in the same direction . . . all occupations in agriculture have their seasons more or less general in their condition . . . as these opportunities occur and disappear, the work of course increases and diminishes, so as at one time to suspend some portion of the adult men from their occupation, and at another to crowd the field with women and children.[17]

In Sussex then, women's access to remunerative work in agriculture differed across the county. The survival of farm service, the cultivation of hops and the demands of arable farming will be investigated here to assess how local farming systems could influence the provision of work for rural women.

[15] BPP 1880, XIV, *Royal Commission on Agricultural Interests. Reports from the Assistant Commissioners.* Mr Little's Report, pp. 405–6.
[16] BPP 1843, XII, *Reports of Special Assistant Poor Law Commissioners on the Employment of Women and Children in Agriculture.* Mr. Vaughan on the counties of Kent, Surrey and Sussex, p. 130.
[17] BPP 1843, XII, Report by Vaughan, p. 131.

Farm service

While many areas of southern England witnessed the irrevocable decline of living-in service in the aftermath of the Napoleonic Wars, turning to a reliance on a day labour force, areas of Sussex, particularly the Weald, retained their dependence on farm servants well into the nineteenth century.[18] The system represented the most reliable way of retaining a regular workforce to tend the livestock on the mixed and grassland farms.[19] Both large and small Wealden farmers continued to hire servants in the nineteenth century, although they were more crucial to the smooth running of smaller units (of less than 100 acres).[20] Farm service represented a particular stage in the lifecycle: young, unmarried men and women were hired as servants on long-term contracts (normally six or twelve months), receiving an agreed wage plus board and lodgings. Mid nineteenth-century census figures point to the survival of farm service in Sussex.[21] Although male agricultural labourers (all ages) outnumbered farm servants in the county as a whole by about 11 to 1 in 1851, in the age group 15–24 there were less than 5 labourers for every servant. In certain Wealden parishes the average ratio of servants to other unmarried males in the same age group was 1:2.10.[22] The female occupational figures are also interesting. Table 4.1 shows the number of female farm servants and agricultural labourers in Sussex as recorded in the census returns for 1851, 1861 and 1871.[23] In 1851 for every female agricultural labourer, there were fifteen female farm servants. Most of these servants were young, unmarried women: 47 per cent of servants in 1851 were aged 15 to 19 years, whilst 21 per cent fell into the age group 20 to 24 years. In 1851 female farm service was not unique to the High Weald though as parishes situated in the south-west of the county, such as Westbourne and Westhampnett, also returned relatively high numbers of women in farm service. After 1851 the

---

[18] The decline of living-in farm service is documented in Kussmaul, *Servants in husbandry*. Since the publication of her book, several historians have pointed to the survival of this institution in many areas of the British Isles. See for example, Howkins, 'Peasants, servants and labourers'; Caunce, *Amongst farm horses*; Gritt, 'The census and the servant'; Goose, 'Farm service in southern England'.

[19] Short, 'Decline of living-in servants'.

[20] Reed, 'Indoor farm service', p. 229.

[21] Farm service also survived in areas of neighbouring Kent in the nineteenth century: Reay, *Microhistories*.

[22] Reed, 'In-door farm service', pp. 228–9.

[23] After 1871 farm servants and agricultural labourers were classified under one heading.

Table 4.1   Female farm servants and agricultural labourers in Sussex, 1851–1871 (all ages)

Year	Female farm servants (in-door)	Female agricultural labourers (out-door)
1851	1,760	117
1861	313	149
1871	117	192

Sources: BPP 1851, LXXXVIII, *Ages and Occupations*, 1 (1852-3), BPP 1861, LIII, *Abstracts of Ages, Occupations and Birthplaces of People*, vol. 2 (1863), BPP 1871, LXXI, *Ages, Civil Condition, Occupations, and Birthplaces*, vol. 3 (1873).

census records a drastic reduction in the number of women being engaged as farm servants. Between 1851 and 1871 the number of women (of all ages) classified in this category declined by some 93 per cent. Over the same period the number of females recorded as general domestic servants grew by 28 per cent. In fact domestic service accounted for by far the largest proportion of employed females in the county at this period: in 1851 there were 13,213 women (of all ages) classified as domestic servants (general), rising to 18,467 by 1871.

But these figures are problematic. It is likely that many women who worked as servants on farms were officially recorded as domestic servants. The 1851 census specified 'The return for farm servant (in door) includes Dairy-women and all Female Servants living in farmhouses, except those employed in domestic duties, as cooks, housemaids, nurses, etc'. Yet for most women who worked as servants on farms, the nature of their daily work was multifaceted, with a blurring between 'domestic' indoor duties and dairy work or other outdoor labour. It would have been very difficult for enumerators to determine whether a servant was hired purely for 'domestic duties'. In fact evidence suggests that very few women employed as servants on farms in nineteenth-century Sussex were engaged for specific tasks. The typical experience of a female servant on a small farm revolved around a combination of jobs in the farmhouse (cooking, cleaning and washing), in the dairy (milking and processing the milk), in the farmyard (tending small animals) and at peak seasons assisting in the fields if needed. Most worked alone, under the supervision of the farmer's wife, or with one other general servant. Autobiographical evidence from Sussex emphasises the wide range of tasks undertaken by servants on farms. The following account comes from a servant at Wadhurst and describes the weekly work routine of the 1820s and 1830s:

I'd churning twice a week, and cheesing twice a week, and brewing twice a week, besides washing and baking; and six cows to milk every night and morning, and sometimes a dozen pigs to feed. There were four men lived in the house, and I'd all the bilin' to do – the cabbage and the peas and pork for their dinners – besides all the beds to make . . .[24]

A woman who worked as a servant in the mid 1850s has left another description of the unremitting and varied nature of work:

Three men boarded in the farmhouse. There were ten cows for the men to milk. Milking did not come into my work, but they taught me how to do it. Except for a couple of hours during the afternoon, I worked from five in the morning till nearly ten at night. You see there were six people in the house: Master, Missus, three men and myself. We baked, brewed, churned, made up fifty to seventy pounds of butter a week, besides doing all the washing, clothing and cleaning that was needed. Then I had the little chicks and ducklings to mind, till they were big enough to sell to the higgler, and it was my place to catch them before he came, and take the money every week for those he bought. We had a very big oven; kneading all the bread was part of my work, and I can tell you the quantity of dough needed strength to work it.[25]

This woman was not hired in the usual way as a farm servant on a fixed long-term contract. She was nineteen when she entered service, approaching the 'missus' of the farm for work, describing herself as a 'general' servant and paid a weekly wage of 3s. 9d. Women like her were, in all probability, classified as domestic servants in the census returns, although their work clearly went beyond the 'domestic' sphere.[26] Thus the decline of farm service for women in farms in Sussex in the nineteenth century should not be exaggerated. Many young unmarried women were likely to spend at least part of their early working life as general servants on farms, carrying out a variety of

---

[24] Coker Egerton, *Sussex folk and Sussex ways* (1924), quoted in Reed, 'Indoor farm service', p. 231. A similar range of tasks has been found for women employed as farm servants in other English counties. See Gielgud, 'Nineteenth-century farm women', chapters 4 and 5; Bouquet, *Family, servants and visitors*; Green, 'A survey of domestic service', pp. 65–9; Verdon, *Rural women workers*, chapter 3.

[25] Day, *Glimpses of rural life in Sussex*, p. 16.

[26] Edward Higgs has argued that general female servants on farms were under-enumerated by nineteenth-century censuses, being placed in the category of domestic service: Higgs, 'Occupational censuses', p. 707.

laborious and exhausting tasks, facilitating the productivity of the farm. This group of workers are not easily classified, but their presence on farms in Sussex was important and indicates the persistence of a form of labour too often presumed to have disappeared from south-eastern England by the mid nineteenth century.

Special industries: hops

The hop gardens of east Sussex formed part of the large band of hop cultivation of south-east England which also stretched into Surrey and the Weald of Kent. The planting, tending and harvesting of this crop was notoriously tricky to successfully oversee, 'for no plant is more fickle and so difficult to manage' as one nineteenth-century observer remarked.[27] Arthur Young, visiting Sussex in the late eighteenth century, believed that hops were 'the gambling of farmers'.[28] He was not alone in questioning the zeal for this crop. James Caird, writing on Sussex during his tour of English agriculture in the mid nineteenth century, believed that 'uncertainty of prices and crops, and the peculiar bearing of the duty, are such that very few hop farmers are enriched by it; while many are ruined, and still more are kept on the verge of bankruptcy'.[29] But such insecurity did not prevent farmers in east Sussex from enthusiastically adopting the crop. Between 1821 and 1874, hop cultivation in the High Weald doubled, with over 16,062 acres being given over to hops by the 1870s.[30] This growth continued, Mr Little noting in 1880 'Sussex ranks next to Kent as a hop-growing county, there being nearly 10,000 acres of that crop'.[31]

The amount of labour expended on hop cultivation was appreciable. The usual mode of employment in Sussex was to hire workers by the task. Men, women and children were all involved in tending the hop gardens, often working in family groups, as Vaughan describes in 1843:

> There is, perhaps, no produce in the country that requires so much or such varied human labour as the hop at the different periods of its

[27] Whitehead, 'On recent improvements', p. 336.
[28] Young, 'A tour in Sussex', p. 256. Young calculated that the average loss on an acre of hops was £7 15s. 3d. 'The number of men here that are fond of hops is great; and we are hardly to suppose they are all fools', he wrote, 'But, on the other hand, I desire, and may very rationally request, *shew me by what means hops are profitable?*' (pp. 254–5).
[29] Caird, *English agriculture in 1850–51*, p. 127. For a similar view see also Farncombe, 'On the farming of Sussex', p. 85.
[30] Leslie and Short, *Historical atlas of Sussex*, p. 97.
[31] BPP 1880, XIV, Report by Mr Little, p. 405.

progress . . . it must be trained and tended from its first shoot to its ripening . . . It thus levies its tax of labour upon all ages and either sex. The soil is handled and subdued by the man; the plant is tended and trained by the woman; in the gathering are united all, – man, woman, and child.[32]

Thus certain tasks associated with hop growing were specifically gendered. Men dug the hop ground, whilst tying the vines to the poles was a female occupation. The latter occupied women for around six to eight weeks in the year.[33] Male labourers undertook other jobs with the assistance of their wives and children. Examples of this team work included poling the hops in the springtime (poles being fixed into the earth to support the growing shoots) and stacking the poles after they had been stripped or shaved. As Vaughan put it, 'By the task work of the man, however, both woman and boy, and sometimes the girl, are engaged in the more laborious treatment of the land'.[34] Both men and women were employed in shaving the hop poles in winter, whilst during that season women also found work chopping rags for manure. Whole families took part in hop picking in September, although it was often the application of women and children that made the largest contribution to family earnings. Women were therefore seen as being suited to particular categories of labour in the hop grounds; those which required concentration, flexibility and dexterity.

The complementary nature of male and female labour on the hop grounds can be seen in the accounts of the Courthope estate at Whiligh, in the parish of Ticehurst. The accounts most likely belong to the home farm, a large mixed enterprise, which concentrated on sheep husbandry and the cultivation of wheat, oats, barley and hops. In 1824 the farm grew 19 acres of hops, consisting of over 23,000 hop hills. In that year several men were paid on account for digging and dressing the hop ground in the winter months. In April and May they were engaged in hop poling. Women were also paid by the piece for hop pole shaving (being paid according to the size of the pole) and by the acre for hop tying. The record of female labour in these two tasks on the farm in 1825 is shown in Table 4.2. Some men and children were also employed in hop-pole shaving. In March of that year for example the

---

[32] BPP 1843, XII, Report by Vaughan, p. 134.

[33] BPP 1867–8, XVII, *First Report from the Commissioners on the Employment of Children, Young Persons and Women in Agriculture.* Report by Rev James Fraser on Norfolk, Sussex, Gloucestershire and two detached districts of Suffolk, p. 9.

[34] BPP 1843, XII, Report by Vaughan, p. 134.

Table 4.2   Women's work at hop pole shaving and hop tying at Whiligh in 1825

Month	Name and task	Earnings
March	Dame Wallis tying 2800 hop hills	16s 4d
April	Dame Irzard for shaving 950/13@6d.; 700/12@4d; 766/10@3d.*	8s 11½d
June	Dames Wisdom, Clifton and Avards tying 10,483 hop hills	£3 1s 0d
June	Dame Manser tying 4966 hop hills	£1 8s 11d
June	Dame Wilson tying 2725 hop hills	15s 10¾d

Source: East Sussex Record Office, Acc SAS 1276 H, Courthope Estate, wages book, 1824–5.

Note : * These entries record the number of poles shaved, their size in feet, and the price paid per 100 poles. This was usually a winter occupation and this payment may refer to work carried out prior to April.

ledger records 'William Waghorn children for shaving new hop poles £2 8s. 10½d.', but tying appears to have been an exclusively female task. This pattern of work is replicated in the accounts into the mid nineteenth century. Unfortunately the Courthope records do not fully detail the labour force employed at hop picking, which usually lasted from four to six weeks. Instead the cost of the operation appears as a total at the end of September. In 1821 for example the cost is noted as 'Total of the hop picken account excluding beer and supper £35 0s.1d.'.[35] Only a daily journal of 1861 records the names of 18 women and girls who were engaged in hop picking. In the week ending September 26 they collectively picked 731 bushels of hops at 2d. per bushel.[36] Unlike neighbouring Kent, hop picking in Sussex was undertaken by the resident population, whole families often migrating into different villages to take part in the hop harvest.[37]

The value of task work in the hop fields of Sussex fluctuated year by year. In an exceptional hop picking season for example, pickers could be paid up to 7d. a bushel, but this price could fall to just 1¼d. per

[35] East Sussex Record Office (hereafter ESRO), Acc SAS 1276L, Courthope estate, wages book, 1820–1821.
[36] ESRO, Acc SAS 1276C, Courthope estate, Farmer's daily journal, 1861–2.
[37] BPP 1867–8, XVII, Report by Fraser, p. 9.

bushel in meagre years.[38] It is difficult then to accurately assess how far the earnings gained in hop work by various family members contributed to the subsistence of the labouring population in nineteenth-century Sussex. But official reports and written testimony time and again affirm the value of women's work in this mode of cultivation. Several replies to the Rural Queries of the 1834 Poor Law Report stated that women in Sussex could make considerably more by hop work than any other type of agricultural employment. As the respondent from Ticehurst explained: 'The women have employment in the hop-pole shaving, hop-tying, weeding and haymaking; but the principal profit to the Women and Children arises from hop-picking, which, in favourable seasons, gives a considerable sum to large families'.[39] Vaughan contended that 'the wife's skill in tying, a task which the husband never performs, and her rapidity and adroitness in picking, in which she commonly excels him' enabled her to add a considerable sum to the family income in the 1840s.[40] Wages from hop work provided purchasing power for expensive items that could not usually be met from weekly earnings such as clothes, footwear, linen and other household bills. The recollections of a shepherd's wife from east Sussex who went hop picking in the 1870s indicates the significance of the hop harvest to her family:

> For hop-picking . . . we used to be in the gardens at 7am. As a rule we worked till half-past five or six pm . . . The number of bushels varied with the size of hops and abundance of yield . . . I have, with my children's help, earned five pounds during a single hop-picking. That paid our firing for the year, and found a new pair of boots for everyone of the family.[41]

Even at the end of the nineteenth century the status of the hop-picking season had not declined in importance. As the 1890s Royal Commission on Labour reported:

> The month of hop-picking is the harvest for the workpeople; schools closed, so all children over say, six or seven years can earn a little, and some families rely on this to pay their year's shoe bill. It will be readily seen much depends on the hop season.[42]

[38] BPP 1843, XII, Report by Vaughan, p. 179.
[39] BPP 1834, XXX, *Report from His Majesty's Commissioners for Inquiring into the Administration and Practical Operation of the Poor Laws.* Appendix (B.1). Answers to Rural Queries in Five Parts. Part 1, Ticehurst, pp. 28–9a.
[40] BPP 1843, XII, Report by Vaughan, p. 139.
[41] Day, *Glimpses of rural life in Sussex*, pp. 19–20.
[42] BPP 1893–4, XXXV, *Royal Commission on Labour. The Agricultural Labourer.* Report by Mr William E. Bear upon the Poor Law Union of Thakeham, p. 58.

Arable agriculture

Previous research has shown that women day labourers were a marginal component of the workforce on the large arable and mixed farms of south-eastern England in the nineteenth century, their roles restricted to a limited number of tasks in the spring and summer months. Is this pattern replicated in Sussex, or can we find evidence to suggest wider participation of female labourers in the county? On the surface official sources seem to document a familiar model: women in Sussex formed a casual pool of labour whose utility declined drastically over the course of the nineteenth century. James Fraser, reporting on the county for the 1867–9 Royal Commission on the Employment of Children, Young Persons and Women in Agriculture, found plenty of evidence to suggest that the hiring of women had contracted noticeably since Vaughan's account of the 1840s. In the Weald Fraser observed 'Females, whether old or young, married or single, are rarely employed by the farmer: not to a tithe of the extent that they were 20 years ago', whilst in south-west Sussex, women's labour 'once largely used in the district, is now scarcely employed at all, except at haymaking and harvest, or for an occasional job of trimming roots'.[43] According to the census returns, the number of women employed as agricultural labourers (out door) in the second half of the century was small (see Table 4.1). Contemporary commentators cited several reasons for the withdrawal of women labourers from the fields. As one witness in Fraser's report explained, 'the women are indisposed to work in the field; their husbands can keep them without. Their place has been taken to some extent by machinery. It would be quite an exception to find a young unmarried girl at work in the fields; the farmers present don't wish to see it encouraged'.[44] But again we need to exercise caution with this material. It has been convincingly demonstrated that census enumerators persistently under-recorded female day labourers in agriculture as their work patterns did not conform to official definitions of an 'occupation'.[45] Moreover, a systematic re-reading of parliamentary reports reveals a wider participation of female labourers in Sussex than first impressions suggest. This is corroborated by farm labour and wage books, and can be best illustrated by analysing two themes: the role of women workers at harvest time, and the employment of female day labourers on farms in the second half of the nineteenth century.

[43] BPP 1867–8, XVII, Report by Fraser, pp. 8, 9.
[44] BPP 1867–8, XVII, Evidence to Fraser's report, p. 77.
[45] See for example Higgs, 'Occupational censuses', pp. 706–8; Miller, 'Hidden workforce', pp. 145–7; Verdon, *Rural women workers*, pp. 117–19.

Printed and archival evidence indicates that in many areas of southern and eastern England women found very little separately paid employment in the harvest fields in the nineteenth century.[46] Sussex deviates from this pattern. The 1834 Poor Law Report (Rural Queries) reveals—unsurprisingly—that women in northern English counties were more likely to be engaged in harvest work. But the number of responses from Sussex which mention women's work in harvest time is sizeable, suggesting that female involvement in the harvest fields in some parts of the south-east was still important.[47] In many cases replies to the Rural Queries are vague: it is not clear what those filling in the returns meant by 'harvest work'. In some Sussex parishes the responses mention only gleaning (Bolney, Hamsey, Hartfield, Herstmonceaux, Kirdford, Ringmer, Willington and Wisborough Green). But other parishes specifically state that women were employed to reap or cut corn in the harvest (Framfield, Glynde, Hartfield, Herstmonceaux, Sedlescomb and Westfield, Singleton, Waldron, Willington and Wisborough Green).

Women were often employed alongside their husbands to assist with reaping and binding the corn, the final payment going to the male head of the team. In 1843 Vaughan notes 'as the boy and woman are generally helpmates of the father of the family their exertions may depend upon their strength and inclination'.[48] But women were also engaged in their own right to cut corn by the acre in the nineteenth century. Both men and women used sickles to cut the 100 acres of wheat on Stanton's Farm, located at East Chiltington in the early Victorian period. Moreover, the female harvesters were paid a wage commensurate with male one for this task:

> Now and then a strong woman would yield a sickle, bind the corn into sheaves, and build the shocks, and the work might go on long after sundown, sometimes by moonlight; the pay would be, as for the men, twelve shillings an acre.[49]

The farm accounts from the Courthope estate at Whiligh also record women being engaged to cut wheat at harvest time, even after the mid nineteenth century. The daily work journal from 1861 has left us with a particularly full record of women's employment in the harvest fields. This has been replicated in Table 4.3. At Whiligh, although men

---

[46] See Verdon, 'A diminishing force?'; Snell, *Annals*; Sharpe, *Adapting to capitalism*, pp. 80–5.
[47] Verdon, 'Rural labour market', pp. 314–5. Kent also returned a large proportion of responses which mention harvest work for women.
[48] BPP 1843, XII, Report by Vaughan, p. 135.
[49] Woodward, *The mistress of Stanton's Farm*, p. 38.

Table 4.3 Women harvesters at Whiligh in September 1861

Cutting wheat in Chapple Field:	Amount (acres, roods and perches)*
Dame Blackburn	1a. 2r. 9p.
Dame Friend	1a. 1r. 0p.
Dame Jarrett	1a. 3r. 8p.
Dame Avard	1a. 1r. 8p.
Total	5a. 3r. 25p. @11s. per acre £3 4s. 11½d.
Cutting wheat in Wadhurst Field:	
Dame Blackburn	0a 2r 7p
Dame Friend	0a 3r 14p
Dame Jarrett	0a 3r 2p
Dame Avard	0a 1r 31p
Total	2a 2r 14p @ 11s. per acre £1 8s. 5½d.
Cutting wheat in Gato Field:	
Dame Friend	0a 1r 36p
Dame Jarrett	0a 1r 32p
Total	0a 3r 28p @ 8s. per acre £0 7s. 4¾d.

Source: ESRO, ACC Sas 1276C, Courthope Estate, farmer's daily journal, 1861–2.

Note: * There were 40 perches in a rood and 4 roods in an acre.

performed the bulk of the labour in the harvest fields, women workers were in demand for key tasks, as well as the subsidiary roles of gathering and tying the crops after cutting. In certain localities women's work in the harvest was still desirable and necessary in the nineteenth century and the Sussex evidence reminds us that generalisations about female agricultural employment can mask distinct regional trends.

Nor did women disappear from the Sussex fields in the second half of the nineteenth century. Although many observers announced the departure of female agricultural labourers, other witnesses in the late 1860s point to the need for farmers to continue hiring women. 'Under the present system of cultivation it cannot entirely be dispensed with' was the conclusion of a meeting at West Grinstead, whilst at Yapton it was stated 'The farmers do not consider women's labour absolutely indispensable . . . but it is very useful'.[50] Female agricultural day labour remained integral to certain tasks on many Sussex farms throughout the century: cleaning the land by weeding and stone-picking in springtime;

[50] BPP 1867–8, XVII, Evidence to Fraser's report, pp. 81, 87.

planting, tending and picking root crops in spring and autumn months; haymaking and harvesting in the summer. These were jobs usually labelled as 'women's work' in nineteenth-century agriculture as they demanded dexterity and speed. Female labour therefore did not substitute male labour but women's work should not be dismissed as inconsequential because of this. Although census enumerators did not recognise women's contribution to farm productivity as constituting an occupation, farm records show that individual women could amass an impressive work record over the year and their earnings could be significant even in the 1870s and 1880s.

Day books from the Courthope estate cease recording work performed by individual female labourers in the later decades of the nineteenth century. This may point to the declining use of female labourers on the estate farm, but it is clear that women were still central to some tasks. In August 1866 the ledger notes 'Women haymaking and weeding £10 10s. 9d.'.[51] Similar entries appear every summer. In August 1878 for example 'Cash to women haymakers' totalled £23 7s. 2½d.[52] By the 1880s and 1890s the amount expended on women for haymaking had declined, but still represented a significant proportion of day labour costs every August. The labour ledgers from the Petworth estate (which survive from 1869) were kept in a similar way, with the work details of male labourers thoroughly itemised for each employee, whilst women's labour appears at the end of the weekly accounts as a supplementary cost. However, the entries provide interesting details about the seasonal nature of the demand for female labour in the late nineteenth century. The work record for women in one year, 1875, is shown in Table 4.4, a pattern that was replicated year after year. The number of women employed on the estate, and the days they worked each year, was small in comparison to male labour. On Stag Park Farm over 30 men (and boys) were engaged for year-round work. The workforce on the Petworth estate was clearly a male-dominated one, but women's labour retained its utility for cleaning the land, hay and harvest work in the late nineteenth century.

Two farms, Selhurst Park Farm in Boxgrove (part of the Goodwood estate) and the home farm of the Wiston estate, have left more comprehensive accounts of their workforces. The accounts from Selhurst Park Farm only survive intact from April to November 1861, but they provide full details of all workers, recorded under the headings

---

[51] ESRO, Acc SAS 1276U, Courthope estate, day book, 1865–8.
[52] ESRO, Acc SAS 1276T, Courthope estate, day book, 1877–80.

Table 4.4   Women's labour on Stag Park Farm, Petworth, in 1875

Month	No. of women	Tasks performed	No. of days worked	Daily rate	Total payment
January	-	-	-	-	-
February	-	-	-	-	-
March	3	Trimming mangold	16	1s.	16s.
April	5	Trimming mangold and picking stones	83	1s.	£4 3s. 0d.
May	5	Trimming mangold and picking stones	52	1s.	£5 7s. 0d.
	5	Weeding corn	55	1s.	
June	5	Weeding corn	91	1s.	£4 11s. 0d.
July	5-7	Hay work and cutting thistles	161	1s.	£8 1s. 0d.
August	6	Hay work and cutting thistles	42	1s.	
	3	Harvest work	32	1s. 3d.	
September	4	Harvest and hay work	38	1s. 3d.	£4 6s. 6d.
	4	Cutting thistles	39	1s.	
October	5	Cutting thistles	32	1s.	£2 19s. 0d.
	4	Couch carting and picking apples	27	1s.	
November	2	Couching	12	1s.	12s.
December	-	-	-	-	-

Source: West Sussex Record Office, 1949 Stag Park Farm, Petworth, labour accounts, 1873–1875

'men', 'women' and 'boys'.[53] This was an arable farm, with wheat and oats its main cash crops, although barley, clover, turnips and swedes were also grown. The farm engaged around 15 regular male labourers, with a number of men employed on a more casual basis. Several women and children also worked on the farm, most of them related to the regular male labourers. As in Kent, farmers in Sussex often engaged men on the condition they had healthy family members willing to undertake farm work when needed.[54] Six boys worked on the farm, three being

[53] West Sussex Record Office (WSRO), Goodwood MS E5435, Selhurst Park farm labourers.
[54] Reay, *Microhistories*, p. 111.

regularly employed, and seven women appear in the accounts. Men and boys were paid different daily rates according to age, skill and task performed. Male rates varied from 1s. to 3s. 4d. a day for usual tasks, with 2s. 6d. to 5s. a day for harvest day labour. Boys received 4d. to 10d. a day, with up to 1s. 8d. at harvest. The usual day rate for female labourers was 10d. a day, rising to 1s. 6d. in harvest work. Women's labour accounts for 16 per cent of total 'man' days worked between April and November, boys 18 per cent and men 66 per cent. However, men were also paid by the piece for mowing, hoeing, dung spreading and during the harvest month, whereas women were not engaged in their own right in any task work. Thus, although women on this farm were not full-time workers, they were employed for an appreciable number of days across the spring and summer months, accruing not inconsiderable wages.

The same trends are evident on Wiston Home Farm in the late 1880s.[55] Again women were more casually employed than men, with seven women working between April and November. Like the female labourers at Selhurst, women at Wiston did not work constantly during this time, some weeks being employed for six days, other for just one or two days when needed by the farmer. They found no employment during the winter months between December and March. Nor were women separately employed on task work. At Wiston, female labour was remunerated at 1s. per day throughout these months but, as at Selhurst Park Farm, individual women could accumulate a significant wage for their farm work over the months they worked. The labour record of women who worked on these two farms is shown Table 4.5. Women's earnings on this scale would have represented a small, but significant contribution to the family budget in the second half of the nineteenth century. Female wages on Selhurst Park Farm, for example, ranged from £2 8s. 9d. to £6 1s. 11d., whilst the annual money wage (not including extras) of a regularly employed, married agricultural labour in Sussex in the 1860s was around £33.[56] Thus although female earnings were secondary to male wages (and to the wages contributed by older male children of the family if there were any), they were important. Put another way, the earnings of all but one woman on Selhurst Park Farm would have covered the average rent on a cottage

---

[55] WSRO, Wiston Estate MS 7060, Wiston Home farm, 1886–90.

[56] BPP 1867–8, XVII, Report by Fraser, p. 9. The basic weekly wage of male agricultural workers in Sussex is recorded at between 12s. and 13s. 6d (not including task work or extras).

Table 4.5   Women employed on Selhurst Park Farm and Wiston Home Farm

Name	Days worked @ daily rate	Total wage
Selhurst Park Farm, April–November 1861		
Martha Bennett	90 @ 10d.	£5 8s. 0d
	22 @ 1s. 6d.	
L. Wight	112½ @ 10d.	£5 4s. 11d.
	7½ @ 1s. 6d.	
C. Neal	105½ @ 10d.	£6 1s. 11d.
	23 @ 1s. 6d.	
Ann Bennett	93 @ 10d.	£4 4s. 3d.
	4½ @ 1s. 6d.	
E. Oakley	84 @ 10d.	£4 17s. 0d.
	18 @ 1s. 6d.	
E. Whittington	58½ @ 10d.	£2 8s. 9d.
S. Whittington	57 @ 10d.	£2 17s. 2d.
	6½ @ 1s. 6d.	
Wiston Home Farm, January to December 1888		
Mrs Garman	135 @ 1s.	£6 15s. 0d.
E. Garman	120½ @ 1s.	£6 0s. 6d.
Mrs Golds	91½ @ 1s.	£4 11s. 6d.
Mrs Bolden	106½ @ 1s.	£5 6s. 6d.
Mrs Terry	30 @ 1s.	£1 10s. 0d.
Mary Terry	92½ @ 1s.	£4 12s. 6d.
Mrs Clements	57½ @ 1s.	£3 17s. 6d.

Sources: WSRO, Goodwood MS E5435; Wiston Estate MS 7060.

in the Boxgrove region in the 1860s, with money left over for other expensive goods.[57]

Of course, married women's contribution to total family income in the nineteenth century varied considerably according to regional and life-cycle factors. Not all women were in a position to work in the fields for a considerable number of days a year. Familial and domestic responsibilities often kept women out of the labour market for large periods of time. Some farms did not employ women in the same volume as they did at Selhurst or Wiston. Moreover, these accounts cannot tell us about the changing nature of women's work on these

---

[57] BPP 1867–8, XVII, Evidence to Fraser's report, p. 95. The average rent in Boxgrove was 1s. a week, or £2 12s. a year.

farms in the second half of the nineteenth century as they only survive for odd years. Nevertheless, the presence of female labourers at Selhurst in the 1860s and Wiston in the 1880s indicates that women still had a role to play in agriculture in Sussex after the mid nineteenth century in some instances. Although agricultural depression and the increasing use of machinery undermined women's work on farms in the late nineteenth century, the withdrawal of women from the agricultural labour force was not uniform across south-eastern England.

Conclusion: Sussex in context

In many ways women's agricultural employment in Sussex does not conform to general assumptions about female farm work in south-eastern England in the nineteenth century. Particularly on the Weald of Sussex, the persistence of farm service and the availability of well-remunerated task work in the harvest and hop fields meant single and married women played a notable role on some farms. Even for usual day labour tasks such as weeding, stone picking and haymaking, women in this region of Sussex normally received wages in excess of female labourers in East Anglia and the south-west.[58] Away from the Weald, the pattern of women's agricultural work has more in common with that found in other corn-growing counties of the south and east. The workforces on the large cereal-growing estate farms at Goodwood, Petworth and Wiston were composed of a large number of regularly employed male labourers, assisted by boys and women when needed. Female day labourers were usually married women, employed by the day to weed, pick stones, trim root crops, make hay and help out in the harvest fields, and receiving between a half and a third of the usual male daily rate. This sexual division of labour and wage-gap are found repeatedly in nineteenth-century farm accounts from across southern England. However, in Sussex women's labour remained attractive to large arable farmers so that even in the last quarter of the nineteenth century, women day labourers did not simply 'disappear' from the fields. In Sussex, then, local farming systems and crop patterns presented some women with wider employment opportunities in agriculture than has previously been supposed in southern England by this time. Moreover, the nature of women's agricultural labour in Sussex had much in common with neighbouring Kent. Barry Reay's detailed analysis of the Blean area of Kent led him to conclude 'There is not much evidence here for a decline in the rural female labour force' over the nineteenth

[58] See Verdon, *Rural women workers*, p. 65.

and early twentieth centuries.[59] It is time, therefore, to lay aside well-worn generalisations about women's work in agriculture and look to future local analyses of other areas of the British Isles in order to assemble a more refined and perceptive understanding of female labour at the local level.

[59] Reay, *Microhistories*, p. 112.

5

The straw plait and hat trades in nineteenth-century Hertfordshire

NIGEL GOOSE

Introduction

The straw plait and hat trades never feature prominently in histories of industrialisation in England, and if they feature at all it is almost invariably as a distinctly local phenomenon, a low-wage and labour-intensive symptom of agricultural distress or as a wholly inadequate replacement for the declining textile trades of southern England.[1] Even when their local importance is acknowledged, it is often suggested that their efflorescence was strictly temporary, and that they only paid well in the exceptional circumstances of the late eighteenth and early nineteenth centuries. In the words of one modern authority, 'Straw plaiting had started in the late eighteenth century . . . [produced] . . . good wages until the end of the Napoleonic Wars . . . [and] . . . the industry finally died in 1870', the short paragraph devoted to the industry featuring in a chapter devoted to 'industrial decline'.[2] Similarly, in a study that does focus upon straw plaiting as an example of a female-dominated cottage industry, its strictly temporary prosperity in the late eighteenth and early nineteenth century is again noted, as are the difficulties created by the return of Italian competition by the 1830s, but we learn little more about its progress across the Victorian period apart from its slide into 'proletarianization'.[3]

There are a number of possible explanations for this marginalisation, one of which is the continued tendency to associate industrialisation with a number of traditional and clearly defined regions: the West

[1] Hudson, *Industrial revolution*, passim; Hudson, 'Industrial organization and structure', p. 35; Berg, *Age of manufactures*, pp. 118, 122–3, 146; Snell, *Annals*, pp. 59, 125; Sharpe, 'Women's harvest'.

[2] Berg, *Age of manufactures*, pp. 123–4.

[3] Valenze, *First industrial woman*, pp. 119–21.

Riding of Yorkshire, Lancashire, the west Midlands, and Northumberland and Durham in particular.[4] Related to this, it is also because the classic contribution of female labour to industrialisation lay in selected industries in some of those very same areas, most notably the cotton textile factories of industrial Lancashire, the woollen and worsted mills of the West Riding, the Staffordshire potteries or in the nailmakers' cottages of the Black Country. Although it has long been appreciated that the most characteristic female employment across the later nineteenth and early twentieth centuries was domestic service, and that the importance of the factory in industrialisation has been exaggerated, the literature does not always show full appreciation of the implications of this, and the consequent need to—at least partially—redraw the map of female employment.[5] A cursory glance at the leading trades followed by either sex listed in the 1851 census report provides an immediate corrective. Here straw plait manufacture stood in 46th position, with 32,062 employed, and straw hat and bonnet makers in 63rd position with 21,902. But although the industry clearly could not compete with cotton and calico manufacture, in 3rd place with 501,465 employees, the combined total of 53,964 in the straw plait and hat trades did not represent a wholly different order of magnitude to woollen cloth manufacture (137,814), or the silk industry (114,570), or worsted production (104,061), all of which are accorded a far more prominent place in English industrial history, both in general and in terms of the employment opportunities they afforded to women.[6] Furthermore, as employment in the straw industries—as we will see—was so heavily skewed toward women and girls, the disparity between these trades in terms of female employment was considerably smaller than the bare figures for both sexes suggest.

There are other reasons for the marginalisation of the straw plait and hat trades, prominent among which is the fact that a modern economic and social history of the industry remains to be written, and hence the true longevity of the industry and its economic significance is often understated. That said, John Dony's study published in 1942—still valuable and by far the best available—appreciated that straw hat-making outlived straw plaiting by several decades, extending the life of

---

[4] Hudson, *Industrial revolution*, pp. 115–32; Honeyman, *Women, gender and industrialisation*, p. 86;

[5] Roberts, *Women's work*, pp. 19–22; Nardinelli, *Child labor*, pp. 103–22; and see Shaw-Taylor, 'Diverse experiences', chapter 2 above.

[6] BPP 1852–3, LXXXVIII, *Census of Great Britain, Population Tables*, II, Vol. I, Table 41, p. c. These figures exclude the 16,975 described simply as 'Hatter, Hat manufacture'.

the industry and the employment opportunities within it long after the collapse of indigenous plaiting in the face of foreign competition. Furthermore, far from being a trade of merely local or regional importance for home consumption, both plait and hats were exported, some 250,000 dozen hats by the mid-1870s rising to a peak of approximately 700,000 dozen by the 1890s, gradually declining thereafter.[7] Straw hats, therefore, may have suffered the same fate as the English almshouse, their quaint and apparently peripheral place in the modern world serving to colour historians' views and detract from the more important position that they once held, both economically and socially. The main purpose of this chapter will be to restore the straw plait and hat trades to their rightful place in the history of women's work, to underline their importance to the local and regional economy of the south Midlands in general and Hertfordshire in particular, and to examine the significance of the trade for the family economy.

The rise and decline of the straw plait and hat trades

Despite the marginal place they usually occupy in general histories of industrialisation, the straw plait and hat trades were of considerable importance to the economies of Hertfordshire and Bedfordshire, and—to a lesser degree—Buckinghamshire, Essex and Suffolk in the nineteenth century. Straw plaiting and hat-making did not suddenly appear towards the end of the eighteenth century, but was already in evidence in the later seventeenth and eighteenth centuries, benefited considerably from the embargo on imported straw during the Napoleonic Wars, and continued to thrive—despite periodic setbacks—into the third quarter of the nineteenth century. The figures presented in Table 5.1, for males and females employed in all branches of the straw plait and hat trades from 1841 to 1891 in the six English counties where the trade was most significant, indicate its importance and progress over time.

The number recorded in the census report for 1841 is almost certainly a considerable understatement, for there were no particular circumstances that might explain an almost fourfold increase during the course of the next decade. By mid-century, its workforce numbered over 39,000, 89 per cent of them female. Far from disappearing towards the mid-nineteenth century as mechanisation took hold in many industries and England became the 'workshop of the world', straw plait and hat-making continued to expand, not reaching its peak until 1871 when it employed approaching 45,000 workers, 93 per cent of them

---

[7] Dony, *Straw hat industry*, statistical appendix pp. 194–7.

Table 5.1   **Employment in the straw plait and hat trades in five English counties, 1841–1901**

		Beds	Bucks	Herts	Essex	Suffolk	Total
1841	Males	349	184	437	28	10	1,008
	Females	2,387	1,276	4,590	605	303	9,161
	Total	2,736	1,460	5,027	633	313	10,169
1851	Males	2,290	505	1,143	342	131	4,411
	Females	15,156	3,180	10,518	3,440	2,572	34,866
	Total	17,446	3,685	11,661	3,782	2,703	39,277
1861	Males	2,097	163	750	51	36	3,097
	Females	19,262	3,364	10,694	2,647	2,001	37,968
	Total	21,359	3,527	11,444	2,698	2,037	41,065
1871	Males	2,357	112	715	50	26	3,260
	Females	20,701	3,412	12,089	2,839	2,335	41,376
	Total	23,058	3,524	12,804	2,889	2,361	44,636
1881	Males	2,258	87	339	8	5	2,697
	Females	15,058	1,654	7,543	922	776	25,953
	Total	17,316	1,741	7,882	930	781	28,650
1891	Males	2,885	27	283	13	1	3,209
	Females	10,191	515	3,133	37	38	13,914
	Total	13,076	542	3,416	50	39	17,123
1901	Males	3,531	14	363	182	11	4,101
	Females	8,230	185	1,979	68	14	10,476
	Total	11,761	199	2,342	250	25	14,577

Notes: Terminology changes between censuses. All those described as workers, manufacturers or dealers in straw plait or straw hat or bonnets are included. The 1851 data includes 'Other workers in cane, rush and straw', the only category where males feature in this report. Unspecified hatters, trimming makers and embroiderers are excluded. From 1891 only those age 10 or over are included, but the 1891 CEBs for Hertfordshire identify few workers below this age.

Source: Census Reports 1841–1901.

female, by which time some other traditional, local handicraft industries—such a lace-making—had long since started to decline.[8] Decline set in during the 1870s, although straw hat-making held on better than straw plaiting, for it was the import of cheap straw plait from Japan and China that killed the plaiting trade, not mechanisation from

[8] Spencely, 'English pillow lace industry', p. 70; Horn, 'Child workers', p. 782; Bythell, *Sweated trades*, p. 104.

within, and the impact was dramatic. In these five counties collectively the number of straw workers fell by just over one-third within a decade. In Hertfordshire the number of female straw plait and hat-makers also fell by over one-third in the 1870s, and more than halved again in the 1880s, although even in 1891 it retained a significant—if rapidly declining—presence in a number of Hertfordshire parishes. It was plaiting by children that fell away most dramatically, no doubt helped by the introduction of compulsory education in the legislation of 1870 and 1881, and hence the rate of decline indicated in Table 5.1 was lower among adult plaiters. Bonnet sewing may have provided compensation in some localities, and the appearance of a new occupational descriptor in the Hertfordshire census enumerators' books, 'straw hat machinist', indicates adaptability to new technology. Nevertheless, while employment held up better in Bedfordshire than it did in any of the other straw counties, by the final decade of the century the industry was in an advanced state of contraction, and wages fell simultaneously. In Buckinghamshire, it has been claimed, the social status of the plaiter diminished rapidly as the century drew to a close, and plaiting increasingly became the mark of poverty.[9] In Essex, where the trade had always possessed a more marginal presence and declined even more rapidly, the straw trade was 'starving work' according to the few plaiters remaining around Chelmsford in Essex in 1881.[10] In Hertfordshire, by 1910, Mr Maberly Phillips could write of Hertfordshire in *The Connoisseur* that 'only a few veterans of the art are left', and by this time the rewards were derisory.[11]

Straw plait and hat-making in Hertfordshire

Even less well known than the chronology of the industry is its precise regional location, to establish which recourse must be had to the Census Enumerators' Books (hereafter CEBs), which have been digitized for the ancient county of Hertfordshire.[12] The reliability of the recording of female employment in the CEBs (and hence, at one remove, in the census reports) has been questioned by Edward Higgs, who has argued that 'women tended to be defined as dependants, whatever their

[9] Grof, *Children of straw*, p. 103; Horn, 'Buckinghamshire straw plait trade', p. 52.
[10] Sharpe, *Adapting to capitalism*, p. 62.
[11] Page (ed.), *VCH Hertfordshire*, vol. 4, p. 255; Goose, *St Albans*, pp. 70–2.
[12] The data is available on CDRom from the Centre for Regional and Local History at the University of Hertfordshire: Goose (ed.), *Hertfordshire Census 1851*.

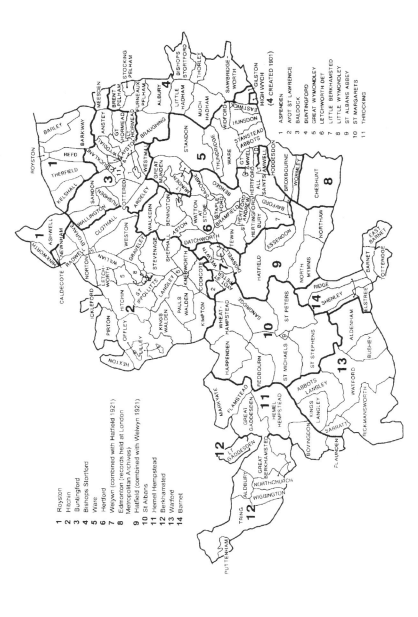

Figure 5.1 Hertfordshire Poor Law Unions and Registration Districts

1 Royston
2 Hitchin
3 Buntingford
4 Bishops Stortford
5 Ware
6 Hertford
7 Edmonton (records held at London Metropolitan Archives)
8 Welwyn (combined with Hatfield 1921)
9 Hatfield (combined with Welwyn 1921)
10 St Albans
11 Hemel Hempstead
12 Berkhamsted
13 Watford
14 Barnet

(4 CREATED 1901)

1 ASPENDEN
2 AYOT ST LAWRENCE
3 BALDOCK
4 BUNTINGFORD
5 GREAT WYMONDLEY
6 LETCHWORTH DET
7 LITTLE BERKHAMSTED
8 LITTLE WYMONDLEY
9 ST ALBANS ABBEY
10 ST MARGARETS
11 THROCKING

productive functions', but the sheer number recorded as working in the straw plait and hat trades indicates that—in this region at least—this simply was not the case.[13] In areas where a trade of particular importance was specifically associated with women one might expect this to be recognised by the census enumerators; indeed, it would have been wholly perverse to deny so many women their occupational identity. That said, close scrutiny of the CEBs does suggest that, even here, in a small number of parishes or parts of parishes female employment may have been under-recorded. This was certainly true in two of the three enumeration districts that constituted the parish of Wheathampstead in the St Albans district, and is indicated by the inexplicably low proportion of married women recorded as employed.[14] Within the Hitchin district, female employment in straw was almost entirely absent in three adjacent parishes to the north—Bygrave, Caldecote and Newnham—in three towards the south—Knebworth, Shephall and St Paul's Walden—as well as in Great Wymondley. The discovery of numerous straw plaiters in St Paul's Walden in the 1891 census returns has led one author to question the consistency of the recording of female occupations in the 1851 CEBs, and examination of the 1881 census reveals as many as 155 female plaiters at this date compared to just one in 1851, while in five of the other six parishes there were at least a few plaiters at this later date.[15] While this may possibly reflect the continued growth in the industry up to 1871, the St Paul's Walden figures do appear to suggest under-recording at mid-century. In both Pirton and Little Wymondley there is a considerable discrepancy between the number of single and married women recorded as in work, and it is again possible that some under-recording occurred here. Elsewhere, however, the data offers a high degree of internal consistency, and although these examples show how important it is carefully to examine the data when working on individual parishes, on a regional level the results will not be markedly affected.

The data presented in Table 5.2 indicates that within Hertfordshire the straw plait and hat trades were very heavily concentrated in the west

---

[13] Higgs, 'Women, occupations and work', pp. 60–2. They can certainly not generally be regarded as 'hopelessly inaccurate in recording female work': Hudson, *History by numbers*, p. 14.

[14] Goose, *St Albans*, pp. 87, 89.

[15] Crompton, 'Rural service occupations', p. 202; K. Schürer and M. Woollard (2002), 1881 Census for England and Wales, the Channel Islands and the Isle of Man (Enriched Version) [computer file]. Genealogical Society of Utah, Federation of Family History Societies [original data producers]. Colchester, Essex: History Data Service, UK Data Archive [distributor]. SN:4519.

Table 5.2 Employment in the straw industry in Hertfordshire, 1851

SRD	Total	Population M	F	Sex ratio	% total population in straw All	M	F	% occupied in straw All	M	F
Berkhamsted	11,471	5,427	6,044	90	18	5	29	32	8	63
Hemel Hempstead	12,985	6,251	6,734	93	16	5	27	30	8	62
Hitchin	24,345	11,929	12,416	96	11	2	19	22	4	56
St Albans	17,748	8,453	9,295	91	13	3	23	24	4	50
Hatfield & Welwyn	8,358	4,257	4,101	104	4	0	8	8	0	25
Royston	14,326	7,283	7,043	103	2	0	4	4	0	17
Watford	18,491	9,075	9,416	96	2	0	4	4	0	13
Hertford	14,840	7,565	7,275	104	1	0	2	2	0	8
Barnet	5,530	2,819	2,711	104	1	0	1	1	0	4
Ware	16,319	8,260	8,059	103	0	0	0	0	0	1
Bishop's Stortford	13,086	6,508	6,578	99	0	0	0	0	0	1
Edmonton	4,815	2,379	2,436	98	0	0	0	0	0	1
Hertfordshire	162,314	80,206	82,108	98	6	1	11	13	2	35

Source: Digitized census enumerators' books.

and particularly the south-west of the county and had relatively little impact elsewhere, despite the fact that they were also found in parts of Essex to the east. They were in fact only a general presence in four of the twelve Superintendent Registrar's Districts (hereafter SRDs) that lay within, or across, the county boundary: Berkhamsted, St Albans, Hemel Hempstead and Hitchin, and even in Hitchin appear to have failed to take root on any scale in a number of parishes, although the possibility of a degree of under-recording must be borne in mind.[16] This

---

[16] These remarks, and the figures in Table 5.2, apply to the ancient (or geographical) county, which either wholly or partly embraced 12 Superintendent Registrar's Districts (SRDs), although only 10 were largely situated within Hertfordshire and formed the registration county as defined in the published census reports: Ware, Bishop's Stortford, Royston, Hitchin, Hertford, Hatfield, St Albans, Watford, Hemel Hempstead and Berkhamsted. Parts of the Barnet and Edmonton SRDs lay in the ancient county, while part of the Royston SRD was situated in Cambridgeshire. The SRDs correspond to the Registration Districts of the Registrar General's *Annual Reports*; the 28 Registrar's Districts into which the county was divided correspond to the sub-districts in the *Annual Reports*.

concentration is reflected in the extent of both female and child employment, for among adults the trade of straw plaiting was very predominantly a female pursuit, while it provided extensive employment for young children of both sexes—producing proportions of children employed in some localities that are as high as previously reported for any English parish studied to date.[17] Specific analysis of the employment of younger children (ages 5–9) of both sexes also reveals a concentration in Berkhamsted, St Albans, Hemel Hempstead and Hitchin, and the picture is similar for older girls (aged 10–14), while older boys tended to graduate to agricultural labour.[18] Hence while Edwin Grey in his reminiscences of Harpenden (in the St Albans SRD) in the 1860s recorded that 'The children, both boys and girls, learned to plait when very young', and that even 'some of the men and the lads were also good at the work, doing it at odd times, or in the evening after farm work . . .', he adds that 'this home industry was always looked upon really as women's work', noting too that at the age of 9 or 10 boys began to take up employment with local farmers.[19] Similarly, in 1867 it was reported from Toddington in Bedfordshire that 'At the age of 10 or 12 most of the boys exchange plaiting for farm work, but resume plaiting when severe weather or a scarcity of work prevents them from labouring in the fields'.[20] The data in Table 5.1 indicates that males formed a larger proportion of the workforce in Bedfordshire throughout the period, their proportional significance growing in the final third of the century as the industry waned. Furthermore, the published census reports also show much greater involvement of adult men in Bedfordshire than in Hertfordshire, perhaps testifying to the depth and the continuity of agrarian poverty there, as well as the well-documented determination of the Bedfordshire Poor Law Guardians to withhold outdoor relief from able-bodied males.[21]

Local variations are obscured in the data in Table 5.2, but can be seen clearly in the more detailed breakdown provided in Appendices 5.1 and 5.2 to this chapter.[22] While Appendix 5.1 confirms the broad regional

[17] Goose, *Berkhamsted*, pp. 40–3; Goose, *St Albans*, pp. 97–100; Cunningham, 'Employment and unemployment', Tables 3 and 4, pp. 144–5.

[18] For details for the Berkhamsted and St Albans regions see Goose, *Berkhamsted*, pp. 40–3; Goose, *St Albans*, pp. 97–100.

[19] Grey, *Cottage life*, pp. 57, 68, 70.

[20] BPP 1867–68, XVII, *Royal Commission on the Employment of Children, Young Persons and Women in* Agriculture (1867), Appendix Part II, pp. 498–9.

[21] BPP 1873, LXXI, Part I, *Census of England and Wales, 1871*, p. 148; Apfel and Dunkley, 'English rural society'; Williams, 'Earnings, poor relief and the economy of makeshifts'.

[22] Below, pp. 125–37.

distribution of the straw industry and its particular concentration in the Berkhamsted, Hemel Hempstead, Hitchin and St Albans SRDs, it also shows that as a major employer it extended south into Abbots Langley and Sarratt, east into Hatfield, North Mimms, Aston and Walkern, and north into Ashwell and Hinxworth. In each of the main towns in these four districts a distinctly lower proportion of both the total and the occupied female population were employed in straw, reflecting their more variegated economies and the wider range of female employment options available, largely in the service trades and in domestic service. In the rural parts of Berkhamsted, Hemel and St Albans, however, it formed a major presence in virtually every parish. The rank order listings in Appendix 5.2 reveals that in 50 Hertfordshire parishes out of 135 over 25 per cent of the occupied female population worked in the straw industry, while in 62 it was insignificant, accounting for under 2 per cent. In 45 parishes it employed over 10 per cent of the total female population (of all ages), while in 69 under 1 per cent worked in straw. Towards the top of these rankings the industry was of overwhelming importance, providing employment for fully 30 per cent of the total female population in 15 parishes, and accounting for 75 per cent of female employment in the same number. In such parishes, the occupational participation rate of women stood far in excess of that for both Hertfordshire and England and Wales as a whole, underlining the local and regional importance of the trade which can be obscured by county-wide figures.

Female employment by age and marital status

Table 5.3 provides further breakdowns by SRD for adult females by age and marital status, distinguishing the straw industry from other sources of employment, and reveals that the straw plait and hat trades were by no means the prerogative of single women and girls. For females aged 15 and over, between 57 and 60 per cent were in employment in the three leading straw SRDs, with 32–34 per cent employed in the straw industry and related trades.[23] Overall employment opportunities for women were clearly boosted considerably by the presence of the industry, although towards the fringes of London those parts of the Edmonton and Barnet districts that fell within the county offered

---

[23] Included in this age group in the St Albans data are 251 brazilian hat-makers or grass splitters, and 132 hat trimming makers or trimming weavers. In the Watford SRD 39 brazilian hat workers were identified, 34 in Hatfield, 2 in Hemel and a solitary hat trimmer in Hertford. Brazilian hats were woven from split palm leaves.

Table 5.3   Working women by age and marital status, Hertfordshire, 1851

SRD	Age 15+								Married								
	No.	All		Occupied Straw		Other			No.	All		Occupied Straw		Other		
		No.	%	No.	%	No.	%			No.	%	No.	%	No.	%	
Berkhamsted	3,942	2,258	57.3	1,286	32.6	972	24.7		1,913	667	34.9	503	26.3	164	8.6	
Hemel Hempstead	4,188	2,365	56.5	1,339	32.0	1,026	24.5		2,170	758	34.9	579	26.7	179	8.2	
Hitchin	7,834	3,584	45.7	1,781	22.7	1,803	23.0		4,096	972	23.7	695	17.0	277	6.8	
St Albans	6,069	3,660	60.3	2,080	34.3	1,580	26.0		2,980	1,146	38.5	845	28.4	301	10.1	
Hatfield & Welwyn	2,635	1,188	45.1	312	11.8	876	33.2		1,379	304	22.0	157	11.4	147	10.7	
Royston	4,332	1,420	32.8	208	4.8	1,212	28.0		2,412	311	12.9	87	3.6	224	9.3	
Watford	6,009	2,543	42.3	351	5.8	2,192	36.5		3,060	553	18.1	142	4.6	411	13.4	
Hertford	4,643	1,715	36.9	119	2.6	1,596	34.4		2,394	288	12.0	55	2.3	233	9.7	
Barnet	1,811	760	42.0	32	1.8	728	40.2		853	109	12.8	9	1.1	100	11.7	
Ware	5,133	1,507	29.4	19	0.4	1,488	29.0		2,700	181	6.7	9	0.3	172	6.4	
Bishop's Stortford	4,145	1,206	29.1	11	0.3	1,195	28.8		2,214	179	8.1	4	0.2	175	7.9	
Edmonton	1,661	651	39.2	5	0.3	646	38.9		798	84	10.5	2	0.3	82	10.3	
Total	52,402	22,857	43.6	7,543	14.4	15,314	29.2		26,969	5,552	20.6	3,087	11.4	2,465	9.1	

Table 5.3 continued

| SRD | Never Married Age 20+ | | | | | | | Widows | | | | | | |
| | No. | All | | Occupied Straw | | Other | | No. | All | | Occupied Straw | | Other | |
		No.	%	No.	%	No.	%		No.	%	No.	%	No.	%
Berkhamsted	981	797	81.2	358	36.5	439	44.8	410	275	67.1	101	24.6	174	42.4
Hemel Hempstead	968	776	80.2	321	33.2	455	47.0	422	307	72.7	106	25.1	201	47.6
Hitchin	1,742	1,290	74.1	478	27.4	812	46.6	780	458	58.7	127	16.3	331	42.4
St Albans	1,521	1,282	84.3	578	38.0	704	46.3	638	466	73.0	157	24.6	309	48.4
Hatfield & Welwyn	611	466	76.3	67	11.0	399	65.3	285	198	69.5	26	9.1	172	60.4
Royston	830	532	64.1	54	6.5	478	57.6	487	230	47.2	10	2.1	220	45.2
Watford	1,398	1,023	73.2	86	6.2	937	67.0	731	442	60.5	34	4.7	408	55.8
Hertford	1,056	747	70.7	32	3.0	715	67.7	536	293	54.7	7	1.3	286	53.4
Barnet	480	361	75.2	12	2.5	349	72.7	228	140	61.4	6	2.6	134	58.8
Ware	1,082	678	62.7	6	0.6	672	62.1	639	312	48.8	2	0.3	310	48.5
Bishop's Stortford	892	507	56.8	3	0.3	504	56.5	444	242	54.5	3	0.7	239	53.8
Edmonton	483	336	69.6	2	0.4	334	69.2	172	117	68.0	1	0.6	116	67.4
Total	12,044	8,795	73.0	1,997	16.6	6,798	56.4	5,772	3,480	60.3	580	10.0	2,900	50.2

Source: Digitized census enumerators' books.

compensating opportunities in the service trades, while in Watford the presence of a smaller plait and hat industry was reinforced by female employment in silk and paper manufacture. The discrepancies for married women, however, are greater still. In the same three leading straw districts overall employment levels for married women stood at 35–39 per cent, figures which stand above those reported for many localities and regions traditionally associated with the industrial employment of married women, such as Preston (26 per cent), Lancashire (30 per cent) and the Staffordshire potteries (14 per cent).[24] Of these the great majority were employed in the straw trades, which alone accounted for 26–28 per cent of married women's employment. The overall county figure for the employment of married women, at 20.6 per cent, is almost identical to that found by Andrew August in three poor London districts in 1881 (20.2 per cent), but where work in plaiting and hat-making was available the figures were much higher and, conversely, where it was absent they were generally substantially lower.[25] The Watford district again provided some alternative employment opportunities, but to a lesser degree for married than for single women. Given the overall proportion of the occupied female population identified as working in the straw trades in the Hitchin district shown in Table 5.2, the figures for adult and married women for this district given in Table 5.3 are surprisingly low. While this may reflect a greater relative reliance here on child as opposed to adult female labour, it may also reflect a degree of under-recording, suspicions concerning which have been discussed above.

Across Hertfordshire 73 per cent of those women who remained unmarried at the age or 20 or over were in employment—again a very similar figure to that found in three poor areas of London in 1881—but the difference between the straw and non-straw districts was now one of degree rather than of kind.[26] While the straw trades remained an important source of employment for this category, employing a higher proportion though a lower absolute number compared to married women, a much higher proportion found employment in other capacities in those areas where the industry was unimportant. The same was true of the widowed female population. For these two categories, therefore, employment outside of the straw industry was far more

---

[24] Anderson, *Family structure*, 71, 208 fn.32; Dupree, *Family structure*, 147–8, 169–70.

[25] August, 'How separate a sphere?', p. 294.

[26] The age-categories used by August are more detailed than those adopted here, but he found that over 72 per cent of single women were employed in every adult age group up to 60–64: August, 'How separate a sphere?', p. 295.

important across the county as a whole, and was also more important—though much less clearly so—in the prime straw plait and hat areas. This is not to suggest that the straw trades had no impact upon the lives of never-married or widowed women, and it may have helped some women avoid having recourse to poor relief. For each of the ten districts which lay within the registration county of Hertfordshire, the average numbers in receipt of out-relief across the five-year period 1859–63 has been compared with the total population given in the census of 1861, and for both 1 January and 1 July Hemel Hempstead, St Albans and Berkhamsted occupy the bottom three places in the rankings, with a collective proportion of outdoor paupers for the two dates of 4.2 and 3.9 per cent compared with county averages of 5.8 and 5.4 per cent.[27] Nevertheless, the outstanding feature of Table 5.3 is the substantial involvement of married women in the straw plait and hat trades, and this must have had a considerable impact upon family economies.

Earnings and the regularity of employment

Just how significant that impact was depends, of course, upon both the level and regularity of earnings. Some historians, while appreciative of the employment domestic industries such as straw plaiting created, have tended to generalise unduly about both levels of remuneration and conditions of work, with little attempt to distinguish either between trades or across time. Hence Pinchbeck wrote:

> Among lacemakers, straw plaiters, glovemakers, frame-work knitters, nailmakers and other domestic workers, women and children were still working in overcrowded insanitary cottages for long hours each day; few of them, despite unremitting toil, could earn a living wage, and they were powerless to resist payments in truck, petty exactions and such tyrannies as might be imposed by the greed and dishonesty of the middlemen.[28]

Unfortunately there are no extant wage series for female employment in straw plait or hat-making, only scattered indications of earnings, while the regularity of employment, both within and between years, is also problematic. Particularly high wages were reported during the Napoleonic Wars, when there was an embargo on imported plait. In

---

[27] Calculations from BPP 1857–8, 49 pt. II; 1859, 24; 1860, 58; 1861, 53; 1862, 48; 1863, 51. As outdoor relief was skewed towards women in a ratio of approximately 2:1, these figures will more faithfully reflect the experience of women than would those for indoor relief.

[28] Pinchbeck, *Women workers*, p. 308.

1797 Eden reported adult female earnings in Dunstable of 6–12s. per week, and 2–4s. for children.[29] In 1804 Arthur Young reported earnings for female plaiters of 21s. per week at Redbourn and Dunstable, 14–18s. at Berkhamsted and up to 5s. per day in St Albans, while for 'a short time' some women earned 42s. per week, and even 10 year old children could earn 12s. per week or more.[30] Another early nineteenth-century source reported that at Hatfield 'one woman had earned 22s. in a week by plait'.[31] These were extraordinary sums at a time when male agricultural labourers in Hertfordshire could command no more than 10–12s. per week, possibly only 7–9s. in cash.[32]

Such sums were also extraordinary in the sense of being untypical, and rates fell considerably once the import of plait was restored; and just as there were particularly good times for the industry, there were distressed periods too. Respondents to the Poor Law Commission noted the slump in trade in 1832–4, St Peters parish in St Albans reporting that the trade was 'very low', Shenley that it was 'very poor', and Welwyn that it 'affords at present but a scanty subsistence'.[33] Consequently, estimated earnings were meagre at this time, just 1s. 6d. to 3s. 6d. per week in Hemel Hempstead, Redbourn, Welwyn, and in both St Michaels and St Peters in St Albans, though reaching as much as 6s. or even 8s. per week in Watford where the silk industry also offered employment for women.[34] In 1842 the Board of Guardians of the Hitchin Union blamed overcrowding in their workhouse on 'a concurrence of want of employment among Mechanics and Agricultural Labourers through the wetness of the season, with a particular depression of the Straw Plait manufacture'.[35] These difficulties were not helped by the removal of protective tariffs in the same year and they continued into the following year, the Children's Employment Commission Report of 1843 noting that 'the earnings now of the plaiters were at least a third less than they were in former years', children being kept at home to plait to avoid the cost of sending them to plaiting

---

[29] Eden, *State of the poor*, 2, p. 2. Throughout this chapter, 's.' indicates a pre-decimal shilling, 'd.' a pre-decimal penny.

[30] Young, *General view*, pp. 221–3.

[31] BPP 1831, VIII, *Report from the Select Committee of the House of Lords on the Poor Laws*, p. 277.

[32] Young, *General view*, pp. 217–20; Mingay (ed.), *Agrarian history*, Table IV.6, p. 1095; Purdy, 'On the earnings of agricultural labourers', p. 342; Eden, *State of the poor*, 2, p. 275.

[33] BPP 1834, XXX, *Report of the Royal Commission of the Poor Laws*, pp. 217, 224, 226.

[34] BPP 1834, XXX, pp. 217, 219, 222, 227.

[35] Gutchen (ed.), *Hitchin union workhouse 1842*, unpaginated.

schools. Women, the report claimed, needed to work a 12–14 hour day to earn 3–4s. per week.[36] Reports from Bedfordshire and Buckinghamshire in 1867 of earnings as low as 2s. 6d. per week for plaiters over 16 years of age again reflect a period when the trade was 'unusually depressed'.[37]

These depressed years should not, however, be taken as typical, and there is evidence of far better wages in more normal trading conditions.[38] In 1831, for example, it was reported that although earnings at Hatfield, Hertfordshire, had fallen from their peak, they still stood at 8–10s. per week for women and 3–5s. for children, figures far higher than those given in 1834.[39] In 1864 William Horley, postmaster and registrar for Toddington in Bedfordshire, reported earnings for most adult plaiters of 1s. per day when trade was good, 'though many will make more, up to 8s. or 10s., and some earn 12s. a week'.[40] Similarly in 1867 George Culley reported for Bedfordshire and Buckinghamshire, 'on very good evidence', that when the trade was good, plaiters from 16 years of age could earn 6–10s. per week.[41] A particularly comprehensive account of the trade and potential earnings was provided in 1860 by A.J. Tansley, a Luton hat manufacturer, in an address to the Society of Arts.[42] He reported earnings in straw plait for very young children of 1s.–1s. 6d, 2–3s. at ages eight or nine, 4–5s. on leaving the plait schools, and as much as 7s. 'after they become skilful'. The earnings of a good, adult plaiter, after allowing for deduction of the cost of straws, would be from 5s.–7s. 6d. per week when trade was good, and hence 'a well ordered family will obtain as much or more than the husband who is at work on the neighbouring farm'—a view that is echoed in successive

---

[36] BPP 1843, XIII, *Children's Employment Commission: Second Report (Trades and Manufactures)*, p. 132.

[37] BPP 1867–1868, XVII, *Royal Commission on the Employment of Children, Young Persons and Women in* Agriculture (1867), Appendix Part I, p. 135. Verdon similarly notes the coincidence of Royal Commissions of inquiry with periods of depression in lace-making and straw-plaiting: *Rural women workers*, p. 152.

[38] Some modern authorities, following Dony and relying upon evidence from depressed years reported in parliamentary papers, have over-emphasised the instability of the industry: for instance, Valenze, *First industrial woman*, pp. 118–21.

[39] BPP 1831, VIII, *Report of the Select Committee of the House of Lords on the Poor Laws*, pp. 277, 279.

[40] BPP 1864, XXII, *Children's Employment Commission: Second Report of the Commissioners on Children's Employment*, p. 203.

[41] BPP 1867–1868, XVII, *Royal Commission on the Employment of Children, Young Persons and Women in* Agriculture (1867), Appendix Part I, p. 136.

[42] Tansley,' On the straw plait trade', 69–77.

parliamentary reports as well as in reminiscences of the parish of Harpenden in the 1860s written by Edwin Grey.[43]

Plaiting, however, was only one stage in the production of straw hats, and bonnet sewing—largely an urban occupation, though only an important source of employment in Hertfordshire at St Albans—was regarded as a superior occupation, as well as being better remunerated. Tansley reported that sewers engaged in 'sale work', the cheaper ranges, earned from 5–8s. per week, while the earnings of the more skilful 'room hands' were 'superior to any similar class in the kingdom', ranging from 8–12s. per week for 'medium' hands, to 16–20s. for 'the best fancy hands', although these earnings too would fluctuate according to the state of trade as well as with the season. J.E. White's report to the Children's Employment Commission of 1864, drawing upon evidence from Luton, similarly records 'remarkably good' wages for plait sewers, indifferent workers earning 10–12s., the best over 20s. per week, with an average of 18s.[44]

It has also been suggested that straw plait and hat trade was distinctly seasonal, raising the further crucial issue of the regularity of earnings, one discussion of the industry in north Essex suggesting that 'The demand for hats was confined to the summer and plait manufacture was a springtime activity, lasting for a maximum of three months'.[45] Lucy Luck in her autobiography refers to the 'dull season', and reports 'the straw-work is very bad, as a rule, from July up to about Christmas', but there is considerable contrary testimony.[46] Tansley reported that 'plait is made all year round, except during the interruption of harvest time'.[47] Similarly Edwin Grey gives no suggestion of seasonality in Harpenden in the 1860s, describing women strolling in the lanes or plaiting in the fields in groups during the summer months. Only on market day, 'or at least the better part of it', was there a general cessation of plaiting, while gleaning appears to have taken priority over plaiting for a short time, 'though undoubtedly the stay-at-homes still kept on with their plait

[43] Tansley,' On the straw plait trade', pp. 71–2; BPP 1818, V, *Report from the House of Lords Select Committee on the Poor Laws* (1817), V, p 94; BPP 1864, XXII, *Children's Employment Commission: Second Report of the Commissioners on Children's Employment*, p. 203; Grey, *Cottage life*, p. 67.

[44] BPP 1864, XXII, *Children's Employment Commission: Second Report of the Commissioners on Children's Employment*, pp. 200, 206–8.

[45] Sharpe, 'Women's harvest', p. 136. For a similar emphasis upon seasonality see Valenze, *First industrial woman*, pp. 119–20; John, 'Introduction', p. 14; Verdon, *Rural women workers*, pp. 144–5.

[46] Burnett (ed.) *Useful toil*, p. 77.

[47] Tansley, 'On the straw plait trade', p. 71.

work'.[48] Even during the depression of 1832–4 the Poor Law Commissioners noted that straw plaiting provided employment in Redbourn 'throughout the year', and that it was particularly important in providing winter work in Shenley, Stevenage and Welwyn.[49] In 1864 William Hardy of Toddington in Bedfordshire reported that while 'sewing work will not sell in summer . . . Plait, however, sells all year round', and George Philpotts reported that his sewing room was busy 'From about Christmas until the end of May, and from August till November'.[50] Messrs. Munt and Brown, straw bonnet and hat manufacturers of Luton, noted an exodus of female sewers from the town during July, only for them to return once again in August.[51] Some specialised branches of the trade may, however, have been more distinctly seasonal: in 1843 it was reported that fancy straw weaving at St Albans was 'only carried on for about two months of the year' but—equally instructive—'the rest of the year they work at straw plait'.[52] Contemporaries recognized the difference between summer plait and winter plait, the former being superior to the latter and commanding a higher price, but this in itself testifies to year-round plaiting.[53] Any seasonality, in employment or earnings, can only have represented a difference of degree rather than kind, and does not undermine the importance of the industry to the women of south and south-west Hertfordshire. Before the slump in earnings that accompanied the late-nineteenth century decline of the industry, therefore, reported earnings appear to have been considerable enough to have made a substantial contribution to family budgets.

Straw plait and hat-making and the family economy

We can estimate that contribution more precisely through a detailed examination of individual parishes, a sample of which are analysed in Table 5.4. Harpenden, in the St Albans SRD, stood towards the top of the parish rankings in terms of the proportion of both the total and the

---

[48] Grey, *Cottage life*, pp. 70, 90, 118–19.
[49] BPP 1834, XXX, *Report of the Royal Commission of the Poor Laws*, pp. 222, 224, 225, 227.
[50] BPP 1864, XXII, *Children's Employment Commission: Second Report of the Commissioners on Children's Employment*, p. 204.
[51] BPP 1864, XXII, p. 207.
[52] BPP 1843, XIV, *Children's Employment Commission: Second Report (Trades and Manufactures)*, Appendix, p. A13. Cf. Sharpe, 'Women's harvest', p. 137.
[53] Tansley, 'On the straw plait trade', p. 72; Freeman, *Luton and the hat industry*, p. 12; Horn, 'Child workers', p. 789.

Table 5.4 The straw plait and hat trades and the family economy, selected Hertfordshire parishes, 1851

Parish	Pop.	No. h'holds	No. craft/ labouring h'holds	Children (<15) Plait	Bonnets	Adults Plait	Bonnets	Elderly (>59) Plait	Bonnets	Total weekly earnings (shillings)	Weekly earnings per h'hold (shillings)	Weekly earn. per craft/lab. h'hold (shillings)
Harpenden	1,979	428	361	91	4	337	28	37	6	2,670	6.24	7.40
Wigginton	638	121	110	56	0	104	0	1	0	795	6.57	7.23
St Peters (Urban)	2,523	578	502	9	25	46	100	6	2	1,229	2.13	2.45
Lilley	528	104	96	48	5	80	24	13	0	875	8.41	9.11
Kings Walden	1,162	226	195	20	0	95	4	7	0	683	3.02	3.50
Hitchin (Urban)	5,087	1,058	948	150	1	340	33	4	1	2,774	2.62	2.93
Flamstead	1,852	376	342	191	16	238	85	28	1	2,833	7.53	8.28
Bovingdon	1,131	226	189	48	0	98	2	3	0	757	3.35	4.01
Redbourn	2,084	451	409	127	14	271	68	20	3	2,679	5.94	6.55
Stevenage	2,117	462	393	79	0	146	7	4	0	1,181	2.56	3.01
Rural parishes	11,491	2,394	2,095	660	39	1,369	218	113	10	12,473	5.21	5.95
Urban parishes	7,610	1,636	1,450	159	26	386	133	10	3	4,003	2.45	2.76
Total	19,101	4,030	3,545	819	65	1,755	351	123	13	16,476	4.09	4.65

Notes: Children under 15 include boys and girls; adults include females only, aged 15–59.
Plait includes all straw workers and trimming weavers.
For estimated earnings see text.

Source: Digitized census enumerators' books.

occupied female population employed in the straw industry. Here it was plaiting rather than hat-making that dominated, and the trade occupied children, single women, widows and married women too. Indeed, the parish was exceptional for the number of married women employed, for fully 224 out of a total of 336 married women worked in the straw industry here in 1851 (67 per cent), with a further 24 in other occupations to produce an overall level of employment among married women of 74 per cent. Perhaps more typical of the straw parishes of rural Hertfordshire is Wigginton in the Berkhamsted region, where there were 41 straw workers out of 112 married women (37 per cent), plus five working in other occupations to produce an overall employment level of 41 per cent. St Albans was a special case, for here there were considerable numbers of bonnet sewers as well as straw plaiters, probably able to command generally higher wages, while in the town suburbs brazilian hat-making assumed importance too. St Albans is represented by the central parts of the parish of St Peters. For the Hitchin region these three parishes are loosely paralleled by, respectively, Lilley, Kings Walden and the more clearly urban portion of the large parish of Hitchin, and from the Hemel region Flamstead and Bovingdon are included to achieve a more representative urban/rural balance, as are Redbourn and Stevenage. The population, number of households, and numbers of children (under 15) and adults working in the straw industry in these ten parishes in 1851 is shown in Table 5.4.[54] The final two columns estimate the total weekly earnings of children and adult females, and earnings per household, assuming average earnings for children and elderly plaiters (age 60 or over) of 3s., 6s. for adult plaiters, and for bonnet sewers 4s. and 8s. respectively. Two calculations are offered: the first includes all households in the respective parishes, the second includes only craft, trade and labouring households, on the assumption that few professional or propertied families would engage in the straw trade.

The sample encompasses a total population of 19,101 individuals divided between 4,030 households, within which were found 2,242 adult straw workers (136 of them elderly) and 884 children. The ratio between children and adults varied considerably between parishes, children constituting only 16 per cent of the total in Kings Walden but 37 per cent in Flamstead, the average for the whole sample standing at

---

[54] The number of households shown for some of these parishes differ slightly from previously published analyses because there all inns, lodging houses, pubs, victualling houses, beershops and hotels were excluded: Goose, *Berkhamsted*, pp. 60–79; Goose, *St Albans*, pp. 145–81.

28 per cent.[55] The calculations presented in Table 5.4 suggest that the average weekly earnings of these 4,030 households were enhanced by 4.09s.; if the households of professional and propertied persons are excluded that sum rises to 4.65s. In the two urban parishes represented the contribution was considerably lower, reflecting the smaller proportion of the female population engaged in the straw industry here and the more diverse occupational opportunities that towns offered. In rural Hertfordshire, however, across 2,095 craft, trade and labouring households, weekly earnings were increased by an average of 5.95s. per week. Between them there was considerable variation, Stevenage and Kings Walden standing at the bottom of the rural rankings at 3.01s. and 3.50s. respectively, while at the top stood Lilley and Flamstead, at 9.11s. and 8.28s. respectively. Given that these figures are averages across all households whether or not they were engaged in the straw trades, the significance of these earnings for the families that did participate in the industry is quite clear. Estimates of agricultural labourers' wages in Hertfordshire at mid-century vary from as low as 8 or 9s. in cash to an average of 10s. 6d. for the Michaelmas and Christmas quarters.[56] In areas where the straw industry was most important, the earnings generated could almost match these figures, while in parishes where it was of lesser importance it could still provide a useful supplement. Furthermore, even if there was indeed a degree of seasonality to the straw industry, with slightly less work or poorer returns available in the winter months, it may have been at that very same time that these earnings were most crucial, for it was then that male agricultural employment was at its most precarious, and task work in agriculture for women and children most scarce.[57]

The distribution of these earnings between households can be further investigated through a closer examination of the parish of Harpenden, largely a plaiting rather than a hat-making parish, part of which formed the subject matter of Edwin Grey's reminiscences of Hertfordshire life in the 1860s.[58] Here, out of a total of 428 households, 279 included at

---

[55] Particularly large numbers of boys and men were employed in the industry in Flamstead, many of them described as 'straw cutter' or 'straw drawer'. Of the 207 children included in Table 5.4 for this parish, 82 were boys, while there were also 76 adult male straw workers.

[56] Purdy, 'On the earnings of agricultural labourers', p. 332; Wilson Fox, 'Agricultural wages in England and Wales', p. 325; Orwin and Felton, 'A century of wages and earnings in agriculture', p. 238.

[57] For women and children see Purdy, 'On the earnings of agricultural labourers', pp. 332–3.

[58] Grey, *Cottage life*.

Table 5.5 Female and child straw plait earnings in Harpenden, 1851, by household head

No. earning weekly (shillings)	Head of household							Total
	Married male	Widower	Married female	Widow (straw)	Widow (non-straw)	Unmarried female (straw)	Unmarried female (non-straw)	
3–4	17	0	1	1	1	1	1	22
6	115	5	0	2	3	2	0	127
8–9	32	1	0	8	0	1	0	42
11–12	28	2	0	5	1	2	0	38
14–16	10	0	1	4	1	1	0	17
17–18	13	0	1	3	1	1	0	18
20–21	10	0	0	2	0	0	0	13
25–26	2	0	0	0	0	0	0	2
Total	227	8	3	25	7	8	1	279

Source: Digitized census enumerators' books.

least one woman and/or child who participated in the straw industry (65 per cent). If the 67 professional or propertied households are excluded, 7 of which themselves participated in the straw trade, the number is 272 out of 361 households (75 per cent), and hence exactly three-quarters of all craft, trade or labouring households participated to at least some degree in the straw industry in Harpenden in 1851. In the great majority of cases this represented a contribution to a family income, not a means to establish independence. As the data in Table 5.5 shows, 227 of the 279 households participating in the straw industry (81 per cent) were headed by a married male, only four of whom were also occupied in the straw industry. There was, in fact, only one clearly solitary female straw worker recorded in the parish: Mary Attwood who lived alone on Turnpike Lane, an unmarried bonnet sewer, aged 67. Three widows are recorded as residing alone apart from a visitor on census night—Ellen Proctor aged 67, Sarah Lovett aged 58 and Mary Munt aged 43—as was another unmarried woman, Elizabeth Crane of Staker's Lane, aged 56. If their 'visitors' (three of whom were themselves straw plaiters) were strictly temporary, and were indeed visitors rather than lodgers, just five women straw workers in total usually lived alone.[59] Mary Attwood and Elizabeth Crane apart, there were six unmarried female straw workers heading their own households, among which Eliza Marrin, aged 30, supported her—presumably illegitimate—son William, a scholar aged 8. One, Sarah Dimmock, lived with her elderly, widowed mother, who also plaited straw, whilst the remaining four lived in small households with one or two sisters, brothers or brothers-in-law, all working either in the straw industry or (in the case of the males) as agricultural labourers.

A more common scenario was to find a widowed mother maintaining herself with the assistance of one or more children. Of the total of 428 households in the parish, 47 were headed by a widow. As Table 5.5 indicates, 25 straw-working widows headed their own households, while another seven households which contained one or more straw workers were also headed by widows. As nine of the widows who headed their households were farming, propertied or professional people, 32 out of 38 of the trade, craft or labouring widow-headed households drew at least part of their income from the straw industry. Of these 32, 22 included at least one daughter working in the trade (two with an additional granddaughter), two lived with nieces, one with a granddaughter, one with a sister-in-law and one with her

---

[59] Davidoff has suggested that the terms could be used interchangeably: 'Separation of home and work?', pp. 66–7.

son, an agricultural labourer, and a straw-plaiting visitor. Four of the remainder have been accounted for (three with visitors and one alone), and the final plaiting widow shared her house with her son, an agricultural labourer, as well as a labouring lodger and his wife and child. While most widows connected with the straw trade, therefore, maintained their independence with the help of their immediate offspring, there are a few instances of co-residence with siblings and more distant kin to add to those provided by unmarried female household heads. There is only one indication in the census return of reliance upon the poor law: Charlotte Johnson of Turnpike Road, a widow aged 80 years, is recorded as receiving 'relief from the parish', while living with her daughter and granddaughter, both of whom plaited straw.

Table 5.5 also contains estimates of the earnings generated by straw working in these 279 households, calculated on the same basis as in Table 5.4, divided according to household head. Those earning 3–4s. weekly represent households where just one child (under 15) or one elderly woman (60 or over) were working in the industry, and these were relatively few, constituting no more than 8 per cent of the total. The large number generating between 6s. and 8s. per week reflect the prominence of adult women earning 6s. as a plaiter or (in just 8 cases) 8s. as a bonnet sewer, as well as the fact that most households included only one straw worker, which accounted for 156 out of the total of 279 (56 per cent). In only a handful of cases, as we have seen, did such earnings constitute a living wage for widowed or unmarried women: most of the small number of households included in Table 5.5 under this category also contained working sons or lodgers. However, given a male agricultural labouring wage of 8–10s. per week, 6–8s. was clearly a significant addition to family incomes, and was enjoyed by fully 40 per cent of the 308 households in the parish that were headed by a married male.

Despite the prominence of households containing just a single straw worker, Table 5.5 also reveals a substantial number that represented the 'well ordered family', described in 1860 by A.J. Tansley as being able to generate a sum equivalent to, or in excess of, male agricultural earnings.[60] Those households headed by a married male able to generate such a sum number 87 (38 per cent of the total), 63 of which (28 per cent) generated incomes in excess of even the highest reported earnings of male agricultural labourers in Hertfordshire at mid-century, while 25 (11 per cent) earned approximately double, or more than double, the

[60] See above, p. ooo

average male agricultural wage, from the straw plait and hat trades alone. Although their total number is small, a particularly high proportion of the 25 households headed by a straw-working widow (14, or 56 per cent) generated earnings above the level of the male agricultural wage, and in many cases this was in addition to the agricultural earnings of sons, and/or the income from taking in lodgers.

Among these 279 households are some particularly interesting instances of families piecing together a sufficient income from various sources. Generating the highest income of all from the straw trade was the family of Daniel Biggs of Lewin's Green, whose wife Sarah plaited straw, while two adult daughters and one child sewed bonnets, producing a potential income of 26s. weekly, in addition to which Daniel, aged 57, worked as an agricultural labourer, while the household also included a lodger, Emily Attwood, aged 26, herself a bonnet sewer. Probably generating an even higher income was the eleven-person household headed by William Wheeler in Pimlico. Still reasonably young at the age of 40, William worked as an agricultural labourer, as did three of his sons, aged 16, 14 and 11, while two more sons, aged 9 and 7, plaited straw. His wife Martha was also a straw plaiter, as was his nineteen-year old daughter Mary, while three young children were yet to be drafted into the family workforce. A similarly productive household was that of George Hardy of Turnpike Road, which included two adult agricultural labourers, two adult straw plaiters, two young daughters also plaiting straw, and a twelve-year old son employed as a butcher's boy. James Ivory's household in Hatchen Green also included two adult agricultural labourers, one of them a lodger, in addition to a total of five female straw plaiters (two adults, three children). While some contemporaries were inclined to associate large families with poverty, such examples amply bear out Cobbett's view that, 'little children are as arrows in the hands of giants, and blessed is the man that hath his quiver full of them . . . [for they] become, very soon, so many assistants and props to the parents . . .'.[61]

Lodgers also provided additional income for households headed by unmarried or widowed women, as in the case of Elizabeth Andrew, a widowed 63 year-old plaiter of Broad Croft, who lived with two adult daughters and two adult lodgers, all of whom were straw plaiters or bonnet sewers. Similarly, Jane Sharman of Staker's Lane was a widowed 40 year-old plaiter, who lived with her sons James and William, aged 16 and 14, both agricultural labourers, her 13 year-old daughter Maria who plaited straw, besides three lodgers—Samuel Bent, aged 23, an

---

[61] Cobbett, *Cottage economy*, p. 5. Cobbett is, of course, paraphrasing Psalm 127.

unmarried agricultural labourer, Fanny Simmonds, aged 20, an unmarried straw plaiter, and her (presumably illegitimate) six-month old son Frederick. Indeed, across the St Albans SRD as a whole it has been found that the highest mean number of lodgers per household by occupation of household head was in those headed by straw workers, followed by clothing and textile workers, both of which categories included considerable numbers of households headed by women. These households also contained fewer children compared to other craft and labouring households, either because the female head had never married, or the loss of a spouse had ended child-bearing earlier or because the higher average age of the household head meant that more children had already left home. Hence the absence of a spouse and fewer than average numbers of children created more space for lodgers, at the same time as the absence of a wage-earning partner and the relatively low economic status of these occupations placed a premium upon the additional income a lodger could bring.[62]

Precisely the same circumstances made it both more possible and more desirable to take in kin, particularly where the straw industry provided such ready employment. An example from Harpenden is Elizabeth Rolt, aged 32, an unmarried plaiter who lived with two sisters, a brother-in-law and a nephew, to create a five-person household all of whom were employed either in agriculture or in straw plaiting. Others were extended downwards rather than laterally to include married children and grandchildren, including those headed by Elizabeth Dunkley and Mary Wright, both widows aged 74 and 71 respectively. Again it has been discovered for the St Albans region as a whole that households headed by straw and textile workers included relatively large numbers of kin in their households, subverting the more general positive association between numbers of co-resident kin and social class.[63] More broadly, comparison of the relative tendencies of households to include different categories of kin in the straw working areas of Hertfordshire with other parts of the county where the straw industry was absent produced interesting results. For while there was little difference between the two regions with respect to the tendency to take in elderly relatives (although women were favoured over men in both regions), in the straw areas a considerably higher proportion of households included siblings (and siblings-in-law). Furthermore, the sex ratio of these siblings stood as low as 36 (males per 100 females) compared to 82 in the non-straw region, a clear reflection of the

[62] Goose, *St Albans*, pp. 170–3.
[63] Goose, *St Albans*, pp. 169, 173–4.

preference for female lateral kin where opportunities for them to contribute to family incomes existed.[64]

Conclusion

Lack of reliable occupational data prior to 1851 makes it difficult to accurately assess the period for which the straw plait and hat trades assumed prominence, but as plaiting was important enough regularly to attract contemporary comment from the late eighteenth century forwards, did not start to decline until the end of the nineteenth century, and as hat-making continued into the twentieth century, as a significant presence the industry spanned approximately 100 years. At its peak in the third quarter of the nineteenth century, it employed labour on a scale that put it in the same league as silk or worsted production, and was particularly important as an employer of female labour. In those parts of the south Midlands were it assumed greatest importance it provided employment opportunities both for women and for children that were superior to any other industrial region, and could boast figures for individual parishes that are among the very highest that have been reported to date. It was not, however, a significant presence across the county as a whole, but was concentrated in the south and the south-west, while even here it assumed far greater importance in some parishes than in others, underlining the importance of a local perspective on women's work. In these areas married women particularly benefited, for it was an occupation that could be conducted in conjunction with other family responsibilities. While in those parts of the county where there was little or no plaiting never-married and widowed women gravitated of necessity to alternative occupations, no such opportunities were available to those who were married, and hence the overall female occupational participation rate in these areas was significantly lower than it was in the straw plait and hat region.

Notwithstanding periodic fluctuations in the straw plait and hat trades, potential earnings were significant too, and on balance the evidence suggests that in most branches of the trade these were available all year round. The highest earnings, of course, accrued in those parishes where the industry was particularly heavily concentrated, but they provided a substantial supplement to family budgets in perhaps 50 of the 135 parishes that have been examined for Hertfordshire. The parish of Harpenden, one of the leading straw-plaiting parishes and a particularly

---

[64] Goose, 'Poverty, old age and gender', pp. 368–71. A similar though less marked tendency existed to prefer nieces over nephews.

heavy employer of married women, indicates the full extent of the financial benefits that could accrue from the trade, and fully bears out the contemporary testimonies regarding its significance made by observers such as A.J. Tansley and Edwin Grey. But it also reveals that the industry was one that was most commonly enmeshed with the family economy, only rarely providing the opportunity for single women to attain complete independence, though helping a number of single women and widows to maintain themselves within the context of additional family support, while it also encouraged the extension of a welcome to more distant kin, particularly if they were female. The examples offered here of families that pieced together what must have been comparatively substantial incomes through the participation of various family members and by the taking in of lodgers, suggests that an approach to family budgets based upon prior analysis of household structure is particularly fruitful, while the additional evidence provided by Edwin Grey of the importance of pig-keeping, allotments, cottage gardens and gleaning in Harpenden underlines the potential complexity of the incomes of the labouring classes, indicating a variegated family economy to parallel the 'economy of makeshifts' of the labouring poor.[65] Above all this discussion endorses the view of Horrell and Humphries that 'accounts of women's and children's contributions to family incomes must be conditional on their occupational and regional identity', for the earnings available to families in the straw plait and hat districts of Hertfordshire—unavailable to their counterparts just 20 miles away to the east of the county—comfortably exceed the averages that have been revealed in recent analyses of extant family budgets.[66] As part of the wider straw plait and hat region, therefore, the south and west of Hertfordshire was both exceptional and significant, and serves to re-emphasise the contribution made by women to the complex process of nineteenth-century industrial development.

---

[65] Grey, *Cottage life*, pp. 112–26; King and Tomkins (eds), *The poor in England*. The family life-cycle approach was, of course, pioneered in Anderson's seminal study of Preston, but few have attempted to emulate his achievement: *Family structure*.

[66] Horrell and Humphries, 'Women's labour force participation', pp. 102–7.

Appendix 5.1 Employment in the straw industry in Hertfordshire in 1851, by SRD and parish

	Population			Occupied population			No. in straw			% total pop in straw	% total male pop. in straw	% total fem. pop. in straw	% occ. pop in straw	% occ. male pop. in straw	% occ. fem. pop. in straw
	Total	M	F	Total	M	F	Total	M	F						
Berkhamsted SRD															
Aldbury	816	412	404	452	271	181	193	37	156	23.7	9.0	38.6	42.7	13.7	86.2
Gt Berkhamsted	3,303	1,543	1,760	1,689	930	759	420	20	400	12.7	1.3	22.7	24.9	2.2	52.7
Little Gaddesden	435	213	222	240	138	102	68	4	64	15.6	1.9	28.8	28.3	2.9	62.7
Northchurch	1,383	670	713	750	427	323	228	12	216	16.5	1.8	30.3	30.4	2.8	66.9
Puttenham	142	77	65	95	59	36	41	13	28	28.9	16.9	43.1	43.2	22.0	77.8
Tring	4,754	2,206	2,548	2,723	1,470	1,253	933	176	757	19.6	8.0	29.7	34.3	12.0	60.4
Wigginton	638	306	332	374	213	161	164	20	144	25.7	6.5	43.4	43.9	9.4	89.4
Total	11,471	5,427	6,044	6,323	3,508	2,815	2,047	282	1,765	17.8	5.2	29.2	32.4	8.0	62.7
Hemel Hempstead SRD															
Bovingdon	1,131	563	568	622	384	238	154	6	148	13.6	1.1	26.1	24.8	1.6	62.2
Flamstead	1,852	899	953	1,181	628	553	635	158	477	34.3	17.6	50.1	53.8	25.2	86.3
Flaunden	305	162	143	119	91	28	14	0	14	4.6	0.0	9.8	11.8	0.0	50.0
Great Gaddesden	1,160	570	590	650	373	277	250	24	226	21.6	4.2	38.3	38.5	6.4	81.6
Hemel Hempstead	6,956	3,299	3,657	3,671	2,164	1,507	949	130	819	13.6	3.9	22.4	25.9	6.0	54.3
Kings Langley	1,581	758	823	759	492	267	100	1	99	6.3	0.1	12.0	13.2	0.2	37.1
Total	12,985	6,251	6,734	7,018	4,127	2,891	2,102	319	1,783	16.2	5.1	26.5	30.0	7.7	61.7
Hitchin SRD															
Baldock	1,921	930	991	958	611	347	131	10	121	6.8	1.1	12.2	13.7	1.6	34.9
Bygrave	221	115	106	76	72	4	0	0	0	0.0	0.0	0.0	0.0	0.0	0.0
Caldecote	49	29	20	17	16	1	0	0	0	0.0	0.0	0.0	0.0	0.0	0.0
Clothall	521	279	242	260	191	69	36	3	33	6.9	1.1	13.6	13.8	1.6	47.8

	Population			Occupied population			No. in straw			% total pop in straw	% total male pop in straw	% total fem pop in straw	% occ. pop in straw	% occ. male pop in straw	% occ. fem pop in straw
	Total	M	F	Total	M	F	Total	M	F						
Codicote	1,035	519	516	454	336	118	52	2	50	5.0	0.4	9.7	11.5	0.6	42.4
Graveley	412	203	209	188	131	57	21	0	21	5.1	0.0	10.0	11.2	0.0	36.8
Gt Wymondley	335	170	165	117	103	14	0	0	0	0.0	0.0	0.0	0.0	0.0	0.0
Hexton	278	145	133	124	92	32	17	0	17	6.1	0.0	12.8	13.7	0.0	53.1
Hitchin	6,402	3,000	3,402	3,191	1,851	1,340	694	74	620	10.8	2.5	18.2	21.7	4.0	46.3
Ickleford	572	273	299	229	183	46	17	4	13	3.0	1.5	4.3	7.4	2.2	28.3
Kimpton	992	504	488	413	304	109	68	6	62	6.9	1.2	12.7	16.5	2.0	56.9
Kings Walden	1,162	587	575	571	385	186	157	38	119	13.7	6.5	20.7	27.8	9.9	64.0
Knebworth	291	146	145	139	103	36	2	0	2	0.7	0.0	1.4	1.4	0.0	5.6
Langley+Preston (Hitchin)	502	246	256	272	165	107	97	18	79	19.3	7.3	30.9	35.7	10.9	73.8
Letchworth	76	36	40	47	24	23	18	0	18	23.7	0.0	45.0	38.3	0.0	78.3
Lilley	528	257	271	349	170	179	184	26	158	34.8	10.1	58.3	52.7	15.3	88.3
Lt Wymondley	300	142	158	137	97	40	24	2	22	8.0	1.4	13.9	17.5	2.1	55.0
Newnham	150	76	74	68	57	11	0	0	0	0.0	0.0	0.0	0.0	0.0	0.0
Norton	399	200	199	196	126	70	65	3	62	16.0	1.5	30.7	32.7	2.4	87.1
Offley	1,208	596	612	773	418	355	338	48	290	28.0	8.1	47.4	43.7	11.5	81.7
Pirton	895	421	474	367	248	119	95	2	93	10.6	0.5	19.6	25.9	0.8	78.2
Radwell	88	38	50	47	22	25	8	0	8	9.1	0.0	16.0	17.0	0.0	32.0
Shephall	242	121	121	110	87	23	0	0	0	0.0	0.0	0.0	0.0	0.0	0.0
St Ippollitts	965	465	500	501	311	190	150	7	143	15.5	1.5	28.6	29.9	2.3	75.3
St Pauls Walden	1,175	576	599	471	383	88	3	2	1	0.3	0.3	0.2	0.6	0.5	1.1
Stevenage	2,117	1,070	1,047	1,102	725	377	241	18	223	11.4	1.7	21.3	21.9	2.5	59.2
Weston	1,187	617	570	613	427	186	147	8	139	12.4	1.3	24.4	24.0	1.9	74.7
Willian	322	168	154	221	120	101	85	4	81	26.4	2.4	52.6	38.5	3.3	80.2
Total	24,345	11,929	12,416	12,011	7,758	4,253	2,652	275	2,377	10.9	2.3	19.1	22.1	3.5	55.9

St Albans SRD

St Albans, Abbey	3,371	1,570	1,801	1,829	994	835	265	50	215	7.9	3.2	11.9	14.5	5.0	25.7
St Albans, St Michael	2,000	944	1,056	1,114	645	469	264	46	218	13.2	4.9	20.6	23.7	7.1	46.5
St Albans, St Peter	3,744	1,753	1,991	1,974	1,115	859	328	31	297	8.8	1.8	14.9	16.6	2.8	34.6
St Albans, St Stephen	1,802	902	900	998	629	369	100	5	95	5.5	0.6	10.6	10.0	0.8	25.7
Harpenden	1,979	945	1,034	1,282	648	634	517	30	487	26.1	3.2	47.1	40.3	4.6	76.8
Sandridge	860	429	431	447	291	156	65	1	64	7.6	0.2	14.8	14.5	0.3	41.0
Redbourn	2,084	965	1,119	1,270	656	614	528	58	470	25.3	6.0	42.0	41.6	8.8	76.5
Wheathampstead	1,908	945	963	991	617	374	309	21	288	16.2	2.2	29.9	31.2	3.4	77.0
Total	17,748	8,453	9,295	9,905	5,595	4,310	2,376	242	2,134	13.4	2.9	23.0	24.0	4.3	49.5

Hatfield & Welwyn SRD

Ayot St Lawrence	147	71	76	80	49	31	1	0	1	0.7	0.0	1.3	1.3	0.0	3.2
Ayot St Peter	282	145	137	135	99	36	6	0	6	2.1	0.0	4.4	4.4	0.0	16.7
Digswell	239	112	127	121	88	33	1	0	1	0.4	0.0	0.8	0.8	0.0	3.0
Essendon	739	377	362	315	242	73	0	0	0	0.0	0.0	0.0	0.0	0.0	0.0
Hatfield	3,753	1,926	1,827	1,931	1,330	601	205	1	204	5.5	0.1	11.2	10.6	0.1	33.9
North Mimms	1,116	567	549	575	381	194	82	0	82	7.3	0.0	14.9	14.3	0.0	42.3
Norhaw	543	287	256	276	205	71	0	0	0	0.0	0.0	0.0	0.0	0.0	0.0
Welwyn	1,539	772	767	737	502	235	18	0	18	1.2	0.0	2.3	2.4	0.0	7.7
Total	8,358	4,257	4,101	4,170	2,896	1,274	313	1	312	3.7	0.0	7.6	7.5	0.0	24.5

Royston SRD

Anstey	465	257	208	190	168	22	0	0	0	0.0	0.0	0.0	0.0	0.0	0.0
Ardeley	628	322	306	249	216	33	0	0	0	0.0	0.0	0.0	0.0	0.0	0.0
Ashwell	1,415	716	699	754	482	272	181	0	181	12.8	0.0	25.9	24.0	0.0	66.5
Aspenden	539	279	260	200	170	30	0	0	0	0.0	0.0	0.0	0.0	0.0	0.0
Barkway (incl. Nuthamp.)	1,291	636	655	520	409	111	6	0	6	0.5	0.0	0.9	1.2	0.0	5.4
Barley	868	438	430	351	283	68	0	0	0	0.0	0.0	0.0	0.0	0.0	0.0
Buckland	421	212	209	164	131	33	0	0	0	0.0	0.0	0.0	0.0	0.0	0.0
Cottered	445	223	222	163	141	22	2	1	1	0.4	0.4	0.5	1.2	0.7	4.5
Great Hormead	601	313	288	243	213	30	0	0	0	0.0	0.0	0.0	0.0	0.0	0.0
Hinxworth	347	183	164	173	129	44	28	0	28	8.1	0.0	17.1	16.2	0.0	63.6
Kelshall	326	175	151	128	112	16	1	0	1	0.3	0.0	0.7	0.8	0.0	6.3

	Population			Occupied population			No. in straw			% total pop in straw	% total male pop. in straw	% total fem. pop. in straw	% occ. pop in straw	% occ. male pop. in straw	% occ. fem. pop. in straw
	Total	M	F	Total	M	F	Total	M	F						
Layston	1,057	523	534	488	343	145	1	0	1	0.1	0.0	0.2	0.2	0.0	0.7
Little Hormead	87	48	39	45	36	9	0	0	0	0.0	0.0	0.0	0.0	0.0	0.0
Meesden	185	95	90	76	66	10	0	0	0	0.0	0.0	0.0	0.0	0.0	0.0
Reed	277	148	129	113	105	8	0	0	0	0.0	0.0	0.0	0.0	0.0	0.0
Royston	2,061	976	1,085	972	613	359	5	0	5	0.2	0.0	0.5	0.5	0.0	1.4
Rushden	321	179	142	137	113	24	0	0	0	0.0	0.0	0.0	0.0	0.0	0.0
Sandon	770	408	362	346	276	70	34	0	34	4.4	0.0	9.4	9.8	0.0	48.6
Therfield	1,335	699	636	625	457	168	3	0	3	0.2	0.0	0.5	0.5	0.0	1.8
Wallington	253	132	121	118	97	21	0	0	0	0.0	0.0	0.0	0.0	0.0	0.0
Westmill	389	200	189	160	128	32	0	0	0	0.0	0.0	0.0	0.0	0.0	0.0
Wyddial	245	121	124	128	85	43	3	0	3	1.2	0.0	2.4	2.3	0.0	7.0
Total	14,326	7,283	7,043	6,343	4,773	1,570	264	1	263	1.8	0.0	3.7	4.2	0.0	16.8
Watford SRD															
Abbots Langley	2,376	1,177	1,199	1,129	761	368	117	4	113	4.9	0.3	9.4	10.4	0.5	30.7
Aldenham	1,653	821	832	773	545	228	34	1	33	2.1	0.1	4.0	4.4	0.2	14.5
Bushey	2,751	1,323	1,428	1,180	800	380	27	2	25	1.0	0.2	1.8	2.3	0.3	6.6
Rickmansworth	4,823	2,384	2,439	2,192	1,528	664	79	2	77	1.6	0.1	3.2	3.6	0.1	11.6
Sarratt	613	294	319	333	198	135	33	5	28	5.4	1.7	8.8	9.9	2.5	20.7
Watford	6,275	3,076	3,199	3,012	1,990	1,022	87	1	86	1.4	0.0	2.7	2.9	0.1	8.4
Total	18,491	9,075	9,416	8,619	5,822	2,797	377	15	362	2.0	0.2	3.8	4.4	0.3	12.9
Hertford SRD															
Aston	626	342	284	302	225	77	37	0	37	5.9	0.0	13.0	12.3	0.0	48.1
Bayford	353	187	166	149	115	34	0	0	0	0.0	0.0	0.0	0.0	0.0	0.0
Bengeo	1,520	740	780	619	455	164	1	0	1	0.1	0.0	0.1	0.2	0.0	0.6

Benington	659	344	315	264	224	40	0	0	0	0.0	0.0	0.0	0.0	0.0
Bramfield	210	98	112	98	68	30	4	0	4	1.9	0.0	3.6	4.1	13.3
Brickendon	750	367	383	353	241	112	0	0	0	0.0	0.0	0.0	0.0	0.0
Datchworth	648	318	330	252	213	39	9	0	9	1.4	0.0	2.7	3.6	23.1
Hertford, All Saints	1,273	637	636	621	396	225	3	0	3	0.2	0.0	0.5	0.5	1.3
Hertford, St Andrew	2,149	1,015	1,134	979	635	344	5	0	5	0.2	0.0	0.4	0.5	1.5
Hertford, St John	2,059	1,189	870	750	533	217	3	0	3	0.1	0.0	0.3	0.4	1.4
Hertingfordbury	750	376	374	316	243	73	1	0	1	0.1	0.0	0.3	0.3	1.4
Little Amwell	458	233	225	195	143	52	1	0	1	0.2	0.0	0.4	0.5	1.9
Little Berkhamstead	554	278	276	240	170	70	0	0	0	0.0	0.0	0.0	0.0	0.0
Sacombe	313	160	153	130	105	25	0	0	0	0.0	0.0	0.0	0.0	0.0
Stapleford	289	148	141	117	91	26	0	0	0	0.0	0.0	0.0	0.0	0.0
Tewin	522	269	253	238	186	52	9	0	9	1.7	0.0	3.6	3.8	17.3
Walkern	733	364	369	374	237	137	68	0	68	9.3	0.0	18.4	18.2	49.6
Watton	974	500	474	438	331	107	8	0	8	0.8	0.0	1.7	1.8	7.5
Total	14,840	7,565	7,275	6,435	4,611	1,824	149	0	149	1.0	0.0	2.0	2.3	8.2
Barnet SRD														
Chipping Barnet	2,235	1,131	1,104	1,006	703	303	2	0	2	0.1	0.0	0.2	0.2	0.7
East Barnet	663	312	351	319	200	119	3	0	3	0.5	0.0	0.9	0.9	2.5
Elstree	396	215	181	175	130	45	0	0	0	0.0	0.0	0.0	0.0	0.0
Ridge	356	183	173	177	130	47	4	0	4	1.1	0.0	2.3	2.3	8.5
Shenley	1,287	637	650	566	416	150	22	1	21	1.7	0.2	3.2	3.9	14.0
Totteridge	593	341	252	251	135	116	2	0	2	0.3	0.0	0.8	0.8	1.7
Total	5,530	2,819	2,711	2,502	1,702	800	33	1	32	0.6	0.0	1.2	1.3	4.0
Ware SRD														
Broxbourne	703	332	371	304	210	94	0	0	0	0.0	0.0	0.0	0.0	0.0
Eastwick	170	80	90	62	50	12	0	0	0	0.0	0.0	0.0	0.0	0.0
Gilston	263	134	129	103	88	15	0	0	0	0.0	0.0	0.0	0.0	0.0
Great Amwell	1,652	823	829	771	543	228	3	0	3	0.2	0.0	0.4	0.4	1.3
Great Munden	554	296	258	235	201	34	0	0	0	0.0	0.0	0.0	0.0	0.0
Hoddesdon	1,849	883	966	806	551	255	4	0	4	0.2	0.0	0.4	0.5	1.6

	Population			Occupied population			No. in straw			% total pop in straw	% total male pop. in straw	% total fem. pop. in straw	% occ. pop in straw	% occ. male pop. in straw	% occ. fem. pop. in straw
	Total	M	F	Total	M	F	Total	M	F						
Hunsdon	481	248	233	215	173	42	0	0	0	0.0	0.0	0.0	0.0	0.0	0.0
Little Munden	628	339	289	263	217	46	0	0	0	0.0	0.0	0.0	0.0	0.0	0.0
Standon	2,460	1,318	1,142	1,025	856	169	1	0	1	0.1	0.0	0.1	0.1	0.0	0.6
Stanstead Abbots	914	468	446	403	313	90	1	0	1	0.1	0.0	0.2	0.2	0.0	1.1
Stanstead St Margarets	97	46	51	49	34	15	0	0	0	0.0	0.0	0.0	0.0	0.0	0.0
Thundridge	572	300	272	248	199	49	1	1	0	0.2	0.3	0.0	0.4	0.5	0.0
Ware	4,950	2,448	2,502	1,956	1,478	478	10	0	10	0.2	0.0	0.4	0.5	0.0	2.1
Widford	518	292	226	218	189	29	0	0	0	0.0	0.0	0.0	0.0	0.0	0.0
Wormley	508	253	255	172	133	39	0	0	0	0.0	0.0	0.0	0.0	0.0	0.0
Total	16,319	8,260	8,059	6,830	5,235	1,595	20	1	19	0.1	0.0	0.2	0.3	0.0	1.2
Bishops Stortford SRD															
Albury	668	338	330	275	226	49	0	0	0	0.0	0.0	0.0	0.0	0.0	0.0
Bishops Stortford	4,942	2,403	2,539	2,008	1,423	585	6	0	6	0.1	0.0	0.2	0.3	0.0	1.0
Braughing	1,242	616	626	543	401	142	1	0	1	0.1	0.0	0.2	0.2	0.0	0.7
Brent Pelham	293	153	140	114	99	15	0	0	0	0.0	0.0	0.0	0.0	0.0	0.0
Furneux Pelham	688	343	345	258	219	39	0	0	0	0.0	0.0	0.0	0.0	0.0	0.0
Great Hadham	1,264	644	620	520	408	112	0	0	0	0.0	0.0	0.0	0.0	0.0	0.0
Little Hadham	878	460	418	362	300	62	2	0	2	0.2	0.0	0.5	0.6	0.0	3.2
Sawbridgeworth	2,571	1,276	1,295	1,027	810	217	2	0	2	0.1	0.0	0.2	0.2	0.0	0.9
Stocking Pelham	138	74	64	55	51	4	0	0	0	0.0	0.0	0.0	0.0	0.0	0.0
Thorley	402	201	201	139	117	22	0	0	0	0.0	0.0	0.0	0.0	0.0	0.0
Total	13,086	6,508	6,578	5,301	4,054	1,247	11	0	11	0.1	0.0	0.2	0.2	0.0	0.9

Edmonton SRD

Cheshunt	4,815	2,379	2,436	2,177	1,500	677	5	0	5	0.1	0.0	0.2	0.2	0.0	0.7
Total	4,815	2,379	2,436	2,177	1,500	677	5	0	5	0.1	0.0	0.2	0.2	0.0	0.7
Hertfordshire	162,314	80,206	82,108	77,634	51,581	26,053	10,349	1,137	9,212	6.4	1.4	11.2	13.3	2.2	35.4

Source: Digitized census enumerators' books.

Appendix 5.2 Female employment in the straw industry in Hertfordshire 1851, rank order by parish

SRD	Parish	% occupied female pop. in straw	Rank order	SRD	Parish	% total female pop. in straw	Rank order
Berkhamsted	Wigginton	89.4	1	Hitchin	Lilley	58.3	1
Hitchin	Norton	88.6	2	Hitchin	Willian	52.6	2
Hitchin	Lilley	88.3	3	Hemel Hemp.	Flamstead	50.1	3
Hemel Hemp.	Flamstead	86.3	4	Hitchin	Offley	47.4	4
Berkhamsted	Aldbury	86.2	5	St Albans	Harpenden	47.1	5
Hitchin	Offley	81.7	6	Hitchin	Letchworth	45.0	6
Hemel Hemp.	Great Gaddesden	81.6	7	Berkhamsted	Wigginton	43.4	7
Hitchin	Willian	80.2	8	Berkhamsted	Puttenham	43.1	8
Hitchin	Letchworth	78.3	9	St Albans	Redbourn	42.0	9
Hitchin	Pirton	78.2	10	Berkhamsted	Aldbury	38.6	10
Berkhamsted	Puttenham	77.8	11	Hemel Hemp.	Great Gaddesden	38.3	11
St Albans	Wheathampstead	77.0	12	Hitchin	Norton	31.2	12
St Albans	Harpenden	76.8	13	Hitchin	Langley+Preston (Hitchin)	30.9	13
St Albans	Redbourn	76.5	14	Berkhamsted	Northchurch	30.3	14
Hitchin	St Ippollitts	75.3	15	St Albans	Wheathampstead	29.9	15
Hitchin	Weston	74.7	16	Berkhamsted	Tring	29.7	16
Hitchin	Langley+Preston (Hitchin)	73.8	17	Berkhamsted	Little Gaddesden	28.8	17
Berkhamsted	Northchurch	66.9	18	Hitchin	St Ippollitts	28.6	18
Royston	Ashwell	66.5	19	Hemel Hemp.	Bovingdon	26.1	19
Hitchin	Kings Walden	64.0	20	Royston	Ashwell	25.9	20
Royston	Hinxworth	63.6	21	Hitchin	Weston	24.4	21
Berkhamsted	Little Gaddesden	62.7	22	Berkhamsted	Gt Berkhamsted	22.7	22

Region	Place	Value	Rank
Hemel Hemp.	Bovingdon	62.2	23
Berkhamsted	Tring	60.4	24
Hitchin	Stevenage	59.2	25
Hitchin	Kimpton	56.9	26
Hitchin	Lt Wymondley	55.0	27
Hemel Hemp.	Hemel Hempstead	54.3	28
Hitchin	Hexton	53.1	29
Berkhamsted	Gt Berkhamsted	52.7	30
Hemel Hemp.	Flaunden	50.0	31
Hertford	Walkern	49.6	32
Royston	Sandon	48.6	33
Hertford	Aston	48.1	34
Hitchin	Clothall	47.8	35
St Albans	St Albans, St Michael	46.5	36
Hitchin	Hitchin	46.3	37
Hitchin	Codicote	42.4	38
Hat. & Welw.	North Mimms	42.3	39
St Albans	Sandridge	41.0	40
Hemel Hemp.	Kings Langley	37.1	41
Hitchin	Graveley	36.8	42
Hitchin	Baldock	34.9	43
St Albans	St Albans, St Peter	34.6	44
Hat. & Welw.	Hatfield	33.9	45
Hitchin	Radwell	32.0	46
Watford	Abbots Langley	30.7	47
Hitchin	Ickleford	28.3	48
St Albans	St Albans, Abbey	25.7	49
St Albans	St Albans, St Stephen	25.7	50

Place	Region	Value	Rank
Hemel Hempstead	Hemel Hemp.	22.4	23
Stevenage	Hitchin	21.3	24
Kings Walden	Hitchin	20.7	25
St Albans, St Michael	St Albans	20.6	26
Pirton	Hitchin	19.6	27
Walkern	Hertford	18.4	28
Hitchin	Hitchin	18.2	29
Hinxworth	Royston	17.1	30
Radwell	Hitchin	16.0	31
North Mimms	Hat. & Welw.	14.9	32
St Albans, St Peter	St Albans	14.9	33
Sandridge	St Albans	14.8	34
Lt Wymondley	Hitchin	13.9	35
Clothall	Hitchin	13.6	36
Aston	Hertford	13.0	37
Hexton	Hitchin	12.8	38
Kimpton	Hitchin	12.7	39
Baldock	Hitchin	12.2	40
Kings Langley	Hemel Hemp.	12.0	41
St Albans, Abbey	St Albans	11.9	42
Hatfield	Hat. & Welw.	11.2	43
St Albans, St Stephen	St Albans	10.6	44
Graveley	Hitchin	10.0	45
Flaunden	Hemel Hemp.	9.8	46
Codicote	Hitchin	9.7	47
Abbots Langley	Watford	9.4	48
Sandon	Royston	9.4	49
Sarratt	Watford	8.8	50

SRD	Parish	% occupied female pop. in straw	Rank order	SRD	Parish	% total female pop. in straw	Rank order
Hertford	Datchworth	23.1	51	Hat. & Welw.	Ayot St Peter	4.4	51
Watford	Sarratt	20.7	52	Hitchin	Ickleford	4.3	52
Hertford	Tewin	17.3	53	Watford	Aldenham	4.0	53
Hat. & Welw.	Ayot St Peter	16.7	54	Hertford	Bramfield	3.6	54
Watford	Aldenham	14.5	55	Hertford	Tewin	3.6	55
Barnet	Shenley	14.0	56	Barnet	Shenley	3.2	56
Hertford	Bramfield	13.3	57	Watford	Rickmansworth	3.2	57
Watford	Rickmansworth	11.6	58	Hertford	Datchworth	2.7	58
Barnet	Ridge	8.5	59	Watford	Watford	2.7	59
Watford	Watford	8.4	60	Royston	Wyddial	2.4	60
Hat. & Welw.	Welwyn	7.7	61	Hat. & Welw.	Welwyn	2.3	61
Hertford	Watton	7.5	62	Barnet	Ridge	2.3	62
Royston	Wyddial	7.0	63	Watford	Bushey	1.8	63
Watford	Bushey	6.6	64	Hertford	Watton	1.7	64
Royston	Kelshall	6.3	65	Hitchin	Knebworth	1.4	65
Hitchin	Knebworth	5.6	66	Hat. & Welw.	Ayot St Lawrence	1.3	66
Royston	Barkway (incl. Nuthampstead)	5.4	67	Royston	Barkway (incl. Nuthampstead)	0.9	67
Royston	Cottered	4.5	68	Barnet	East Barnet	0.9	68
Hat. & Welw.	Ayot St Lawrence	3.2	69	Barnet	Totteridge	0.8	69
Bishops S.	Little Hadham	3.2	70	Hat. & Welw.	Digswell	0.8	70
Hat. & Welw.	Digswell	3.0	71	Royston	Kelshall	0.7	71
Barnet	East Barnet	2.5	72	Bishops S.	Little Hadham	0.5	72

Royston	Therfield	0.5	73
Hertford	Hertford, All Saints	0.5	74
Royston	Royston	0.5	75
Royston	Cottered	0.5	76
Hertford	Little Amwell	0.4	77
Hertford	Hertford, St Andrew	0.4	78
Ware	Hoddesdon	0.4	79
Ware	Ware	0.4	80
Ware	Great Amwell	0.4	81
Hertford	Hertford, St John	0.3	82
Hertford	Hertingfordbury	0.3	83
Bishops S.	Bishops Stortford	0.2	84
Ware	Stanstead Abbots	0.2	85
Edmonton	Cheshunt	0.2	86
Royston	Layston	0.2	87
Barnet	Chipping Barnet	0.2	88
Hitchin	St Pauls Walden	0.2	89
Bishops S.	Braughing	0.2	90
Bishops S.	Sawbridgeworth	0.2	91
Hertford	Bengeo	0.1	92
Ware	Standon	0.1	93
Hitchin	Bygrave	0.0	94
Hitchin	Caldecote	0.0	95
Hitchin	Gt Wymondley	0.0	96
Hitchin	Newnham	0.0	97
Hitchin	Shephall	0.0	98
Hat. & Welw.	Essendon	0.0	99

Ware	Ware	2.1	73
Hertford	Little Amwell	1.9	74
Royston	Therfield	1.8	75
Barnet	Totteridge	1.7	76
Ware	Hoddesdon	1.6	77
Hertford	Hertford, St Andrew	1.5	78
Royston	Royston	1.4	79
Hertford	Hertford, St John	1.4	80
Hertford	Hertingfordbury	1.4	81
Hertford	Hertford, All Saints	1.3	82
Ware	Great Amwell	1.3	83
Hitchin	St Pauls Walden	1.1	84
Ware	Stanstead Abbots	1.1	85
Bishops S.	Bishops Stortford	1.0	86
Bishops S.	Sawbridgeworth	0.9	87
Edmonton	Cheshunt	0.7	88
Bishops S.	Braughing	0.7	89
Royston	Layston	0.7	90
Barnet	Chipping Barnet	0.7	91
Hertford	Bengeo	0.6	92
Ware	Standon	0.6	93
Hitchin	Bygrave	0.0	94
Hitchin	Caldecote	0.0	95
Hitchin	Gt Wymondley	0.0	96
Hitchin	Newnham	0.0	97
Hitchin	Shephall	0.0	98
Hat. & Welw.	Essendon	0.0	99

SRD	Parish	% occupied female pop. in straw	Rank order	SRD	Parish	% total female pop. in straw	Rank order
Hat. & Welw.	Northaw	0.0	100	Hat. & Welw.	Northaw	0.0	100
Bishops S.	Albury	0.0	101	Bishops S.	Albury	0.0	101
Bishops S.	Brent Pelham	0.0	102	Bishops S.	Brent Pelham	0.0	102
Bishops S.	Furneux Pelham	0.0	103	Bishops S.	Furneux Pelham	0.0	103
Bishops S.	Great Hadham	0.0	104	Bishops S.	Great Hadham	0.0	104
Bishops S.	Stocking Pelham	0.0	105	Bishops S.	Stocking Pelham	0.0	105
Bishops S.	Thorley	0.0	106	Bishops S.	Thorley	0.0	106
Royston	Anstey	0.0	107	Royston	Anstey	0.0	107
Royston	Ardeley	0.0	108	Royston	Ardeley	0.0	108
Royston	Aspenden	0.0	109	Royston	Aspenden	0.0	109
Royston	Barley	0.0	110	Royston	Barley	0.0	110
Royston	Buckland	0.0	111	Royston	Buckland	0.0	111
Royston	Great Hormead	0.0	112	Royston	Great Hormead	0.0	112
Royston	Little Hormead	0.0	113	Royston	Little Hormead	0.0	113
Royston	Meesden	0.0	114	Royston	Meesden	0.0	114
Royston	Reed	0.0	115	Royston	Reed	0.0	115
Royston	Rushden	0.0	116	Royston	Rushden	0.0	116
Royston	Wallington	0.0	117	Royston	Wallington	0.0	117
Royston	Westmill	0.0	118	Royston	Westmill	0.0	118
Hertford	Bayford	0.0	119	Hertford	Bayford	0.0	119
Hertford	Benington	0.0	120	Hertford	Benington	0.0	120
Hertford	Brickendon	0.0	121	Hertford	Brickendon	0.0	121

Hertford	Little Berkhamstead	0.0	122
Hertford	Sacombe	0.0	123
Hertford	Stapleford	0.0	124
Barnet	Elstree	0.0	125
Ware	Broxbourne	0.0	126
Ware	Eastwick	0.0	127
Ware	Gilston	0.0	128
Ware	Great Munden	0.0	129
Ware	Hunsdon	0.0	130
Ware	Little Munden	0.0	131
Ware	Stanstead St Margarets	0.0	132
Ware	Thundridge	0.0	133
Ware	Widford	0.0	134
Ware	Wormley	0.0	135

Source: Digitized census enumerators' books.

Hertford	Little Berkhamstead	0.0	122
Hertford	Sacombe	0.0	123
Hertford	Stapleford	0.0	124
Barnet	Elstree	0.0	125
Ware	Broxbourne	0.0	126
Ware	Eastwick	0.0	127
Ware	Gilston	0.0	128
Ware	Great Munden	0.0	129
Ware	Hunsdon	0.0	130
Ware	Little Munden	0.0	131
Ware	Stanstead St Margarets	0.0	132
Ware	Thundridge	0.0	133
Ware	Widford	0.0	134
Ware	Wormley	0.0	135

6

Women as wives and workers in the Staffordshire Potteries during the nineteenth century

MARGUERITE W. DUPREE

> Future studies will have to recognise and identify a plurality of competing family options extant within any single society and region.[1]

Introduction

In Victorian Britain women's work in paid industrial employment outside the home and its effects on the structure of family life captured the attention of a long line of investigators.[2] Much of the work of these investigators in the mid-nineteenth century was preoccupied with a debate arising from anxieties over whether or not factory labour, particularly women working in factories in the north, led to the 'disruption' of family life. 'When women work in factories', wrote Engels, 'the most important result is the dissolution of family ties'.[3] In the recent outpouring of literature on women's history and on family history, major reorientations in the view of the relationship between women, especially married women, and work (and between family life and industrialisation) have shifted attention away from women in paid industrial employment outside the

---

[1] Stone, 'Family history in the 1980s', p. 82.

[2] See, for example, Engels, *Condition of the working class*, esp. pp. 145–6, 160–6, 233–5. For a summary of the contemporary debate on industrialism and the family, see Perkin, *Origins of modern English society*, pp. 149–153; Hewitt, *Wives and mothers*; Smelser, *Social change in the Industrial Revolution*; Anderson, *Family structure*.

[3] Quoted in Perkin, *Origins of modern English society*, p. 149.

household.[4] Yet, there are a number of reasons to look again at this type of employment and its effects on the social, demographic and economic structure of family life.

One reason to focus on women's participation in the factory labour force is that it provides a way to investigate the relationships between families and the economy during the nineteenth century. Surveys of the literature on family history point out major areas of disagreement over what questions to ask, what evidence to use, what interpretations to make. There is, however, agreement that the cohesion of the nuclear family during the Industrial Revolution is no longer an issue; a consensus has emerged that in England the characteristic family structure based on the principles of economic independence before marriage, nuclear family household afterwards and late ages at first marriage was in place before industrialisation (how long before is a matter of controversy). This family structure persisted despite economic development, and it made a significant contribution to the processes of capital accumulation, labour deployment and social welfare.[5] Coinciding with the theme of continuity is the idea that there was flexibility within the system. As Leonore Davidoff and Catherine Hall remark, 'the variability of family forms cannot be overstressed; there is no essential family only families'.[6] For example, there were variations in the co-residence of kin and adolescent children, differences in patterns of family employment and standards of living, and fluctuations in fertility. Conceptually there is agreement that the family and economy are not autonomous; nor is one secondary to the other. The behaviour of families both influences the economy and is in turn influenced by it. Furthermore, the mutual influence needs to be understood historically.[7]

---

[4] For surveys of recent literature see Anderson, *Approaches*; Stone, 'Family history in the 1980s'; Tilly and Cohen, 'Does the family have a history?'; Scott, 'Women in history'; Davidoff, 'The family in Britain'; Hareven, 'History of the family'.

[5] Stone, *Family, sex and marriage*; Wrigley, 'Reflections', p. 83; Laslett, 'Mean household size', pp. 125–58; Macfarlane, *Origins of English individualism*; Smith, 'Fertility, economy and household formation'; Levine, 'Industrialisation and the proletarian family'; Anderson, *Family structure*; Dupree, Family structure.

[6] Davidoff and Hall, *Family fortunes*, p. 31.

[7] Jane Humphries and Jill Rubery, for example, refer to the 'relative autonomy of social reproduction' (they use family and social reproduction interchangeably although they recognise that family practices are not exhaustively social reproduction nor is social reproduction limited to the family). They argue that the family system was not established as 'an interesting, central and dynamic variable for economic analysis' because of the

Looking at the availability of the 'option' of women's paid employment outside the household and at the family characteristics of those women who did and did not take it up makes it possible to illuminate family decisions and to explore in some detail the relationship between families and the economy.

Second, in recent studies of the experience of women in England during the nineteenth century, interest in women factory workers as a special creation of the Industrial Revolution has been replaced by an emphasis on the extent to which women's worlds came to be oriented around their home and family, or 'separate sphere'.[8] This work has usefully emphasised that 'paid employment was usually taken up at different points in the life-cycle in response to crises, as and when the family economy demanded it'.[9] For women there was no dichotomy between work and home or family; instead there was a continuum of women's occupations from paid industrial employment outside the home, to domestic service to sweated labour inside the home, to unpaid home work. Women's roles were characterised by flexibility which made it possible for families to adjust to circumstances. Recent work on

inadequacy of the two opposing methodologies employed to analyse the family system across the whole spectrum of theoretical approaches from neo-classical to Marxist and feminism. The first methodology is 'absolute autonomy' in which social reproduction is independent of the system of production which has to adapt to and operate within its constraints. Here the family system is a 'given', developing independently of the economy. In the second methodology, 'reductionist-functionalist', social reproduction is an integrated and adaptable part of the broader system of production and is analysed within the same framework. Here the family system is essentially a dependent variable within the economic system. Instead of either of these approaches, Humphries and Rubery suggest that family behaviour 'develops in response to changes in the productive system but the form of this response must be understood historically. It is neither predetermined nor smoothly accommodating to the demands of the productive system, but depends on the dynamics of social reproduction': 'Reconstitution of the supply side', pp. 331–46. Describing developments in population history, Tony Wrigley makes the same point when he refers to the 'logical status' of population history as both independent of, and dependent on, the economy: 'Population history in the 1980s', p. 218. Richard Wall recommends the use of the phrase 'adaptive family economy' to emphasise the 'flexibility of family and household patterns among different occupational groups': 'Work, welfare and the family', pp. 264–6. For a similar conclusion see Pleck, 'Two worlds in one'.

[8] For a wide-ranging collection reflecting this research, see the companion volumes John (ed.), *Unequal opportunities* and Lewis (ed.), *Labour and love*. For a useful synthesis see Rose, 'Gender at work', pp. 113–31; Rose, *Limited livelihoods*.

[9] Lewis, 'Introduction: reconstructing women's experience', p. 19.

women in paid employment emphasises the extent and the reasons why job opportunities for women contracted in some occupations and expanded in others, and the gender division of labour, with women deliberately confined to the least skilled and worst paid branches. In addition, domestic servants and women in sweated trades have captured attention because of their large numbers. However, unlike many other types of female occupation, paid industrial employment outside the household can be traced in the census enumerators' books, the most comprehensive source on family history available for the period.[10] As a result, if used with care, evidence is available for the mid–nineteenth century which allows systematic examination of this type of women's employment together with a number of aspects of their family life. It is possible, for example, to look at women's work together with that of their children, husbands and fathers. With this evidence historians can consider 'the family as a unit rather than study women or children as isolated groups'.[11]

A third reason to focus on women in the factory labour force is that women factory workers still have a prominent place in discussions of the decline in marital fertility after 1870.[12] Paid work for women outside the home is seen as a critical variable for determining fertility. Cotton textile workers were the first occupational group within the working class to experience the decline in marital fertility which other groups eventually followed. It was an industry in which women formed a substantial proportion of the labour force. At the same time occupational groups such as miners and ironworkers, which had few women workers and characteristically lived in isolated or homogeneous communities that did not offer paid industrial employment for women outside the home, had exceptionally high fertility.

Finally, despite changing views of the relations between work, women and family life, the main approach to the topics remains the investigation of individual industries, separate occupations or

---

[10] For a warning about the pitfalls of using this source for studies of women's employment which recommends their use only with a knowledge of local economic and social conditions see Higgs, 'Women, occupations and work', pp. 59–80. See also chapter 2, above, pp. 32–42.

[11] Stone, *Family, sex and marriage*, p. 19.

[12] Hewitt, *Wives and mothers*, esp. pp. 85–97; Haines, *Fertility and occupation*; Tilly, 'Demographic change'; Crafts, 'Cross-sectional study'; Woods, 'Approaches to the fertility transition'; Crafts, 'Duration of marriage, fertility and women's employment', pp. 331–5; Seccombe, 'Starting to stop', p.152; Garrett, 'Trials of labour'; Szreter, 'Decline of marital fertility '; Szreter, *Fertility, class and gender*.

communities dominated by a single industry.[13] Women cotton textile workers are especially prominent, but pit-brow lasses, hosiery workers in Leicestershire, women workers in the sweated trades of the East End of London or in Leeds or rural areas, fishergirls of the Yorkshire Coast, domestic servants, teachers and toward the end of the century clerical workers, largely make up our image of Victorian working women.[14] One reason for this concentration on cases of occupational isolation, both geographical and conceptual, is that the Industrial Revolution has been thought of as a series of classic industries or increasingly regionally specialised 'leading sectors' which transformed the economy. Naturally investigators of women's employment and of working class family life have been attracted to study places and groups that most fit that classic view. Recently a more complex view of the Industrial Revolution has emerged which replaces leading sectors with images of a variegated economy.[15] In what follows, close analysis of women's paid industrial employment outside the household and its effects on the social, demographic and economic structure of family life in an area with a dominant industry reveals surprising complexity in patterns of family employment, fertility and family standard of living. These patterns call into question the focus on occupation or single industry towns seen as synonymous with an industry as a unit of analysis and suggest emphasis instead on the local community. Such an approach, I will argue, is better suited to illuminate the complexity of Victorian society.[16]

---

[13] Pleck, 'Two worlds in one', p. 187.

[14] For the classic study of women cotton textile workers see Hewitt, *Wives and mothers*. For a study which concentrates on pottery workers alone in a later period, see Whipp, 'Women and the social organisation of work'; Whipp, *Patterns of labour*. See also John (ed.), *Unequal opportunities* and Lewis (ed.), *Labour and love*. For visual images see Hiley, *Victorian working women*.

[15] For a discussion of changes in the historiography of the Industrial Revolution see Cannadine, 'Present and the past', esp. pp. 163–6, and Hoppit, 'Counting the Industrial Revolution'. For the importance of a regional perspective see Hudson (ed.), *Regions and industries*; Hudson, *Industrial Revolution*. For, emphasis on the relative importance of different types of economic growth see Wrigley, *Continuity, chance and change*; Crafts, *British economic growth*; Dupree, *Family structure*, pp. 1–13. For emphasis on the uneveness and continuities of industrial development see Samuel, 'Workshop of the World'; Joyce, 'Work'.

[16] For the need to synthesise specialities and an attempt to overcome the 'balkanising thrust in social history', see Pleck, 'Two worlds in one', p. 178. For the need to integrate family and women's history into general history see Degler, 'Women and the family', esp. pp. 308, 326.

The Staffordshire Potteries in the mid-nineteenth century

The Staffordshire Potteries during the mid-nineteenth century is a particularly appropriate region in which to examine women's work in paid industrial employment outside the home and its effects on the social, demographic and economic structure of family life. First, it was a region in which the dominant industry—pottery manufacture—employed women and children as well as men. This increased the scope for families to mediate between the age structure and wage structure on the one hand, and the standard of living on the other. Moreover, because women's and children's work in the potworks was outside the household and is distinguishable in the census enumerators' books, it is possible to analyse systematically patterns of family employment. Second, women's and children's employment in the pottery industry was not subject to factory legislation until the mid-1860s. So, in the Potteries, unlike the textile areas where the factory acts pre-date useful census material, it is possible to examine patterns of family employment before as well as after the restriction of women's and children's employment through legislation. Finally, although the pottery industry dominated the region, three industries—coalmining and iron as well as pottery—were located in the same area. While the pottery industry employed men, women and children, the coalmines and ironworks employed only men. Thus, the mix of industries allows comparisons of patterns of family employment among different occupational groups in the same area.

Located in the North of England halfway between Birmingham and Manchester, the Potteries (see Figure 6.1)) was made up of a chain of six towns—Tunstall, Burslem, Hanley, Stoke, Fenton and Longton—which were encompassed in the Parliamentary Borough of Stoke-upon-Trent (population *circa* 100,000 in 1861). In 1861 over 80 per cent of the British pottery industry was concentrated in the Potteries. Within this relatively self-contained area, seven miles long and two miles wide, there were 180 manufactories (called 'potbanks' or 'potworks') and the residences of 30,000 employees. The potworks and residences were in close proximity.

During the early 1860s the Potteries as a whole was an area of relatively good housing conditions and comparatively high wages and employment. Moreover, there were unusually low levels of population turnover and migration for pottery workers who tended to be locally born, though not for miners and ironworkers who tended to have been born outside the Potteries in other centres of mining or ironworking. Nevertheless, despite general prosperity and relative

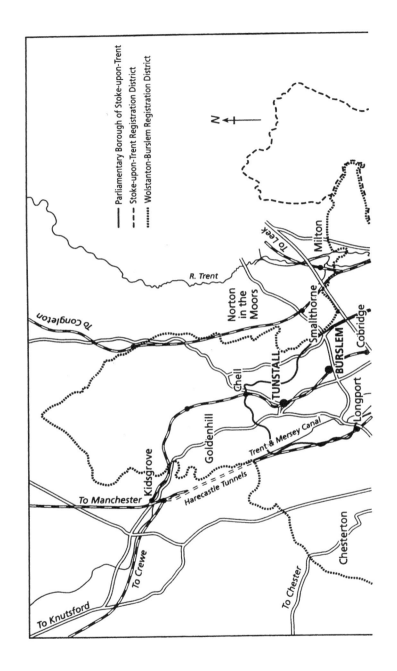

Figure 6.1 The Staffordshire Potteries, c.1861

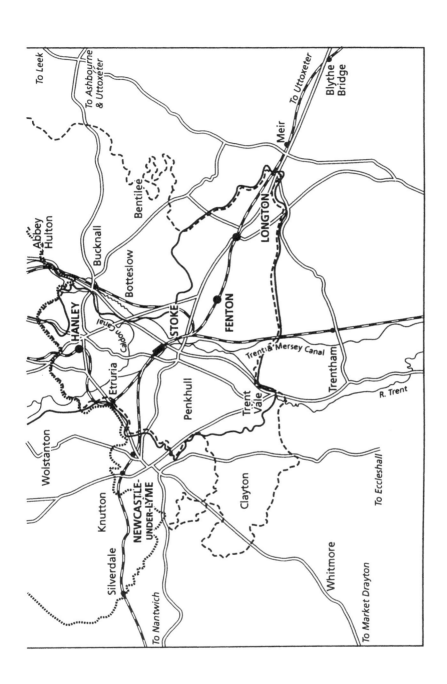

geographical stability, the Potteries was also an area of exceptionally high mortality.[17]

Female and child employment in the Potteries

Using individual level data from samples of the census enumerators' books for the Potteries in 1861 and 1881, supplemented by information from a wide variety of other sources, it is possible to reveal the extent to which women worked in the pottery labour force and to answer questions about certain aspects of their family background.[18] What was the nature of women's work in the potbanks? What were the individual and family characteristics of the women who worked there, and were there changes over the life cycle and over time? Were the wives and children of potters employed or did families diversify employment? Was the employment of women outside the home associated, as in cotton textiles, with low fertility? What was the effect of women's and children's employment in the potbanks on family standards of living?

There were two major departments within a pottery manufactory: the potting department which was made up of the various branches in which clay was prepared and ware formed; and the finishing department which included the branches in which decorating, sorting and packing the ware took place. Girls and women made up over one third (37 per cent) of the pottery labour force in 1861. They did not, however, work in all branches, and their ages and methods of hiring varied among the different branches.

In the potting department girls and women, usually 14 years or older, worked as assistants to male throwers or turners, but the majority worked in the finishing department. There, girls, apprenticed at age 11 or 12, worked as paintresses, painting earthenware in a room with 10 to 30 other girls under the supervision of an older woman. Young girls also worked as paper cutters in the printing shops where designs were printed onto tissue paper and then rubbed or 'transferred' onto the ware.

In the throwing and turning branches and in the printworks and warehouse, women and girls worked together with men or boys or were interchangeable with them. Otherwise the sexes tended to be employed in different tasks and different places in the manufactory;

---

[17] Dupree, *Family structure*, pp. 36–40, 49–99.

[18] I have taken a 1 in 15 systematic sample of the census enumerators' books for the Parliamentary Borough of Stoke-upon-Trent in 1861, and a 1 in 24 sample for 1881. The 1861 sample includes information on approximately 6,700 individuals and 1,350 households, the 1881 sample 6,000 individuals and 1,200 households.

specific tasks were age and sex graded. There were, for example, no female slipmakers, throwers, turners, flatpressers, hollow-ware pressers; instead, women were transferrers, paintresses, gilders, burnishers, scourers and warehousewomen.

There were several patterns of hiring arrangements. Women in the potting department, paintresses and warehouse girls were hired directly by the employer, while paper cutters were hired by women who in turn were hired by printers. Girls tended to begin work at a slightly later age than boys. It was exceptional for boys to start before age nine and girls before age 11. Yet, nearly 75 per cent of the female pottery workers were under 30 years of age, compared with 58 per cent of the male pottery workers. The relatively young age structure of the female labour force and the fact that only 14 of all married women worked in the pottery industry indicate that women tended to work in the industry for a limited period before marriage but then left the workforce.

Some women, however, did work in the industry after marriage. As in textile areas, married women in the pottery labour force were more likely to have no children, and particularly no children under ten years of age, compared with wives not employed in the pottery industry. Again as in the textile industries, a few women may have worked continuously after marriage, while others, particularly widows and women whose husbands were absent on census night, stopped and restarted work as necessary.

Unlike the cotton textile industry where married women tended to stop work as soon as children were able to start, mothers with children who worked in the potteries tended to continue to work.[19] For example, 12 year-old William Bardin, who worked in the biscuit warehouse at the Copeland and Garratt pottery in Stoke, told the Children's Employment Commissioner: 'I got a mother, she is a potter, 6 brothers and sisters, 3 are potters'.[20] This difference between the Potteries and cotton textile areas emphasises the flexibility of women's roles. Other evidence of the flexibility of women's participation in paid work outside the home comes from a comparison of women's employment patterns in the Potteries in 1861 and 1881. During this period the extension of factory legislation to the pottery industry together with the Education Act of 1870 restricted the employment of children in the industry. Alongside the reduction in the number of children, the most striking difference in the pottery labour force between 1861 and 1881 was the increase in the proportion of women

[19] Dupree, *Family structure*, pp. 147–71.
[20] BPP 1843, XIV, p. 249.

in the labour force from 37 per cent to 44 per cent. The women coming into the labour force included both unmarried women and some of the few previously unemployed mothers of children whose employment was restricted.

One consequence of the gender division of tasks, together with the shorter length of employment over a lifetime for women, was a difference between men and women in their susceptibility to certain diseases. Respiratory diseases such as bronchitis or potters' asthma were not as prevalent among women as among men employed in the industry, due primarily to the fact that only a small portion of women worked in the potting departments where dust was most prevalent. This is reflected in differential mortality. There was a sharp rise in male mortality rates in the middle decades of life between 25 and 64 when female rates were falling. This differential mortality of men and women meant that for families in which the male head was a pottery worker, the industry could both create the 'need' for women and children to work as well as offer an opportunity to meet the need. For example, Benjamin Taylor, age 12, who worked for Minton & Boyle earning 4s. per week making cockspurs to place ware on when it was baked told the Children's Employment Commissioner, 'got a mother, but no father; father has been dead ten years; he was a presser, working here; he died of consumption, he was forty-four when he died'.[21]

Another consequence of the sexual division of labour within a potworks was that it left little scope for a nuclear family to remain together as a work group within a potworks. It was possible, however, for members of the same family to work at different tasks within the same factory or industry.

Family employment patterns in the Potteries

Family employment patterns are the result of employers' demand for labour combined with family decisions as to which members supply labour inside and outside the home. A full explanation of the patterns would require an exploration of employers' demand for labour which this chapter cannot attempt. Suffice it to say that various economic and social factors produced a strong, continuous and increasing demand for women's labour in the pottery industry.[22] In this context it is possible to explore individual and family characteristics of those employed in the pottery labour force in comparison with the characteristics of those not

[21] BPP 1843, XIV, p. 241.
[22] Dupree, 'Family structure', pp. 45–50, 281–4, 334–40, 344–8.

employed in order to give some indication of the effect of the 'option' of women's and children's employment on family decisions about labour force participation. The comparison can also cast light on the relative autonomy of the family and economy.

'Occupation' is commonly used as a category of analysis in history and the social sciences. Its use assumes that members of different occupational groups exhibit distinctive social behaviour with regard, among other things, to certain aspects of family life, such as marriage, fertility, co-residence, family employment and mortality. In other studies miners and ironworkers have been singled out for their exceptional behaviour.[23] Due to the nature of the work and its isolated geographical location these occupational groups are associated with strong, homogeneous 'industrially based occupational cultures' characterised by families headed by a single male wage earner, little paid employment of women and children outside the home, high fertility and a high degree of role segregation between husbands and wives.[24] The fact that the pottery industry offered employment to children and women provides a test of the extent to which the Potteries population was socially segregated by occupation.[25] Given the emphasis in some of the literature relating to textile workers on the evidence that the women employed in the mills were the wives and daughters of textile workers, together with the low labour force participation of wives and daughters of miners and ironworkers and their social homogeneity, one might expect that it was the wives and children of pottery workers who worked in the potteries.[26] In addition, industrially-based occupational cultures existed in the Potteries. In the early 1860s there were separate unions within the major industries in the Potteries; different occupational groups contained different proportions of migrants; and contemporaries perceived occupational groups as separate.

Whose children worked in the Potteries? F.D. Longe, the Assistant Commissioner who investigated the area for the Royal Commission on Children's Employment in 1862, suggested that the children employed

---

[23] Haines, *Fertility and occupation*; Tilly, 'Demographic change'; Szreter, 'Decline of marital fertility'.

[24] Foster, *Class struggle*, p. 125.

[25] Other tests undertaken but not included here are the extent of occupational inter-marriage and occupational mobility both intra-generational and inter-generational based on an analysis of information from local marriage registers. See Dupree, 'Family structure', pp. 180–8.

[26] See, for example, Nardinelli 'Child labour and the factory acts'; Smelser, *Social change in the Industrial Revolution*; Joyce, *Work, society and politics*, p. 117. John, 'Introduction', p. 25. For the pottery industry in a later period see Whipp, 'Women and the social organization of work '.

in the potworks were not the children of healthy, 'respectable' working potters. Instead, they tended to be the children of widows, colliers and fathers who were 'incapable of working or of drunken habits'.[27] It is not possible to discover whether fathers were incapable of working or were of 'drunken habits' from the enumerators' books, but it is possible to estimate the extent to which the children aged 8–12 who were employed in the pottery industry were the children of potters or of widows and colliers.[28]

The relationship between the employment of children and the father's presence and occupation is set out in Table 6.1. A relatively high proportion (23 per cent) of the children who worked in the pottery industry lived with their mothers only, compared with 13 per cent of all children age 8–12 years. Moreover, it is evident that over one-third (35 per cent) of the children age 8–12 without fathers living in the household worked in the pottery industry. These relatively high proportions of children of widows confirm Longe's suggestion that widows' children tended to work in the potworks. Nevertheless, this should not obscure the fact that over three-quarters of the children who worked in the industry lived with both parents.

As might be expected given the high proportion of potters in the population, a large percentage (40 per cent) of the children employed in the potworks were the children of potters. Yet, there is a significant relationship between fathers employed in mining and children's employment in pottery as well as between fathers employed in pottery and children's employment in pottery. Moreover, surprisingly only 23 per cent of the children age 8–12 years whose fathers were potters were

---

[27] BPP 1863, XVIII, p. 99.

[28] Only six, or under 1 per cent, of the children aged 8–12 in the sample had fathers who were listed as 'not employed' or 'retired': however, it is possible that those 'incapable of working' may have recorded their most recent occupation. Contemporaries considered 'children' as an undifferentiated category with regard to employment. The Royal Commissions on the Employment of Children in 1842 and 1862 investigated the employment of both boys and girls, and factory and education legislation applied equally to boys and girls. Although, there were well-established differences between the jobs of boys and the jobs of girls within the factory and their age at starting work, the differences were not great enough to jeopardise discussion of them together as 'children'. In 1861 children made up nearly 20 per cent of the pottery labour force. The Children's Employment Commission divided children into those age 12 years and below, and those 13 to 18; the line between 12 and 13 corresponded roughly to the age when boys began apprenticeships. Furthermore, the age group specified in the factory legislation restricting the employment of children was 8–12 years. Hence, the analysis of children here uses the age category 8–12 (inclusive).

Table 6.1 Employment of children and the presence and occupation of fathers: Potteries 1861 (percentages)

Father's occupation	Children's occupation					
	Pottery	Other	Scholar	Not employed	All	(n)
No father	[23] 35	[16] 9	[9] 36	[14] 21	[13]	100 (101)
Potter	**[40] 23**	[18] 4	[36] 56	[30] 17	[34]	100 (262)
Miner	**[16] 33**	[9] 7	[7] 36	[13] 25	[10]	100 (77)
Ironworker	[4] 12	[5] 6	[7] 56	[10] 27	[7]	100 (52)
Labourer	[7] 18	[9] 9	*[5] 40*	**[12] 33**	[7]	100 (55)
Other	*[11] 8*	**[43] 11**	**[36] 68**	*[21] 14*	[29]	100 (222)
All	100 (154)	100 (56)	100 (412)	100 (147)	100 (769)	100 (769)
(n)	20	8	54	19		

Source: File of the children aged 1–12 years old in the 1861 census sample of the potteries.

Notes: [ ] = column % ; ( ) = number of cases.
Percentage numbers in **bold** type indicate the relationship between the categories is positive and significant at the 0.05 level (Haberman's adjusted residual)
Percentage numbers in *italic* type indicate the relationship between the categories is negative and significant at the 0.05 level (Haberman's adjusted residual)
'Other' is a residual category which contains shopkeepers, tradesmen, professional men, etc.

employed in the pottery industry, compared with 33 per cent of the children of miners. Thus, again coinciding with Longe's observation regarding the employment of colliers' children, a child of a miner was more likely to be employed in the pottery industry than was a child of a potter. Therefore, in general, it should not be assumed (as has been done for cotton workers) that the young children of pottery workers also worked in the pottery industry.[29]

Whose daughters and wives were working in the industry? In 1861 (Table 6.2), as expected given the high proportion of potters in the population, the largest proportion (37 per cent) of unmarried women in the pottery labour force who resided with their parents were the daughters of potters. But, although the absolute numbers are small, a slightly higher proportion of the unmarried daughters of miners (71 per cent) were employed in the pottery industry than daughters of potters (69 per cent), while 55 per cent of the daughters of labourers also worked in the potworks. There is a significant relationship between fathers employed in mining and daughters' employment in pottery as well as between fathers' and daughters' employment in pottery. Thus, an unmarried daughter of a miner who resided with her parents was as likely to work in the pottery industry as the daughter of a potter.

The relationship between the employment of married women and the occupations of their husbands in 1861 appears in Table 6.3. Although 64 per cent of married women in the pottery workforce were wives of potters, only 21 per cent of the wives of potters were employed in the industry, not much higher than the 13 per cent of the wives of miners who worked in the Potteries.

Thus, the evidence for wives in combination with the evidence for children and unmarried daughters, indicate that it is dangerous to assume that the wives and daughters of potters were necessarily employed in the industry. This coincides with Eilidh Garrett's findings in her careful study of Keighley, focusing on both the husband's and the wife's employment patterns.[30] These patterns in the Potteries also indicate that miners, who in other areas seem to be a homogeneous occupational group, displayed a considerable amount of interaction with other occupations in the Potteries. Moreover, the patterns are a further reminder of the flexibility of the roles of wives and mothers as they respond to opportunities they did not have in some single industry communities. This flexibility also becomes apparent in another, and

[29] See Nardinelli, 'Child labour and the factory acts', pp. 739–55.
[30] Garrett, 'Trials of labour', pp. 137–49.

Table 6.2 Employment of unmarried daughters (age 15+) and the presence of parents and occupation of fathers in the Potteries, 1861 (percentages)

Parent's presence/ father's occupation	Daughters' Occupation				
	Pottery	Other	Not employed	All	(n)
Mother only	62 [25]	22 [17]	17 [17]	[21]	100 (79)
Father only	50 [8]	9 [3]	41 [17]	[9]	100 (32)
Both parents, father's occupation:					
Potter	**69** [37]	*18* [19]	*14* [18]	[28]	100 (103)
Miner	71 [**8**]	19 [4]	10 [3]	[6]	100 (21)
Iron-worker	33 [2]	25 [3]	42 [6]	[3]	100 (12)
Labourer	55 [6]	30 [6]	15 [4]	[5]	100 (20)
Other	*28* [*14*]	**47** [**47**]	45 [**36**]	[27]	100 (101)
All	53	26	21	100	100 (368)
(n)	100 (194)	100 (96)	100 (78)	(368)	

Source: Potteries census sample, 1861 (see fn. 18).

Notes: [ ] = column % ; ( ) = number of cases.
Percentage numbers in **bold** type indicate the relationship between the categories is positive and significant at the 0.05 level (Haberman's adjusted residual)
Percentage numbers in *italic* type indicate the relationship between the categories is negative and significant at the 0.05 level (Haberman's adjusted residual)
'Other' is a residual category which contains shopkeepers, tradesmen, professional men, etc.

Table 6.3 Employment of wives and occupation of husbands in the Potteries, 1861 (percentages)

Husband's occupation	Wife's occupation				
	Pottery	Other	Not employed	All	
Potter	[64]	[37]	*[34]*	[38]	
	21	5	74		100 (443)
Miner	[14]	[10]	[13]	[13]	
	13	4	83		100 (151)
Ironworker	[4]	[10]	[7]	[7]	
	6	8	86		100 (79)
Labourer	[6]	[5]	[10]	[9]	
	8	3	89		100 (108)
Other	*[13]*	[40]	**[35]**	[33]	
	5	7	**89**		100 (381)
All	100	100	100	100	
	(144)	(63)	(955)	(1,162)	
	12	5	82		100 (1,162)

Source: Based upon a file of married couples in the Potteries census sample, 1861 (see fn. 18).

Notes: [ ] = column % ; ( ) = number of cases.
Percentage numbers in **bold** type indicate the relationship between the categories is positive and significant at the 0.05 level (Haberman's adjusted residual)
Percentage numbers in *italic* type indicate the relationship between the categories is negative and significant at the 0.05 level (Haberman's adjusted residual)
'Other' is a residual category which contains shopkeepers, tradesmen, professional men, etc.

surprising, way in the relationship between women's factory work and certain aspects of the demographic behaviour of occupational groups.

Female employment, marriage and fertility

Studies of occupational differences in fertility associate high female labour force participation in factory occupations with relatively low and declining fertility.[31] The relatively high fertility of coal mining areas in England, France and the United States and the relatively low fertility in

---

[31] Haines, *Fertility and occupation*; Tilly, 'Demographic change'; Szreter, 'Decline of marital fertility'.

cotton textile areas in England and France have been associated with the low levels of married women's employment outside the home in coal mining areas and the high levels of industrial employment of married women in textile areas. The Potteries provides a very different kind of area in which to examine these links. The mix of industries in the district allows comparisons of changes in patterns of family employment, in estimates of marital fertility and in marriage ages to be made among different occupational groups in the same area. Do miners' wives continue to have relatively high fertility even in an area where there was an opportunity for female employment? Do potters' wives, like the wives of textile workers, have relatively low fertility?

Given that the levels in the Potteries of women's employment outside the home are similar to those in textile areas and that the proportion of women in the pottery labour force rose between 1861 and 1881, one would expect fertility and marriage patterns in the Potteries to be similar to those in textile areas which led the fertility decline among industrial workers and where the average age of marriage for women was rising. What makes the Potteries a critically important area for study is that it does not fit these expectations. The 1911 Fertility Census shows that the potters who married 1881–1885 were among the groups with the highest fertility. They reached the levels of men in the predominantly male coal and iron industries.[32] Moreover, within the Potteries a comparison of estimates of marital fertility based on child-woman ratios in 1861 suggests that differences among the occupational groups within the area were small.[33] In an area where there were opportunities for the paid employment of women and children outside the household, there were similarities in the fertility patterns among separate occupational groups, including miners and ironworkers who are usually noted for their exceptional behaviour. Thus, it is possible that there was a 'community effect' which overrode the occupational differentials. This is plausible given the evidence of intermixing of occupations in family employment patterns.[34] What is surprising is that

---

[32] Dupree, 'Family structure', pp. 117–19; Szreter, 'Decline of marital fertility', esp. pp. 270, 326–7.

[33] Dupree, 'Family structure', pp. 196–8.

[34] Intermixing among occupational groups is also evident in marriage patterns and in inter-generational and intra-generational occupational mobility: see Dupree, *Family structure*, pp. 152–69. Eilidh Garrett also suggests the importance of the relationship to fertility of the particular pattern of the husband's and wife's employment in the textile town of Keighley in the second half of the nineteenth century: see Garrett, 'Trials of labour', pp. 137–49. Szreter, *Fertility, class and gender*, pp. 2, 5, 534 and *passim*, extends the

the 'community effect' is not that of low fertility, which one might expect given the nature of the industry that dominated the area.

Marriage ages do not appear to fit expectations either. The proportions ever-married for both men and women in the Potteries suggest that marriage ages were far younger than those in a textile town such as Preston (where only 28 per cent of women age 20–24 were married compared with 45 per cent in the Potteries). Moreover, despite the increasing proportion of women in the pottery labour force between 1861 and 1881, the average age at marriage changed little.[35] In short, the pottery workers do not follow the textile pattern. Their experience is contrary to the generalisations associating the relatively high and increasing employment of women in industry with declining fertility and increasing age of marriage.

How women were able to cope with high labour force participation and high fertility is not clear, but it is plausible to suggest that the solution lay in child care arrangements. Given that pottery employers provided little in the way of child care facilities, it is possible that child care arrangements developed as part of a 'community culture' rather than a single, separate 'industrially-based occupational culture'. Burslem's municipal day nursery closed after a short period in the 1870s due to the reluctance of working mothers to patronise it, but a detailed study of women pottery workers with children under 15 years of age in the census enumerators' books for two enumeration districts in Shelton in 1871 found a recognisable alternative adult care-giver (a relative or lodger) in about half the households, and siblings of about ten years of age who might have provided care for younger children in several others.[36] The mistress of the Hanley and Shelton Girls' National School complained in 1842 that the absence of girls 'is to be attributed to their mothers who keep them at home to do their household work and nursing'.[37] In addition, there is evidence of the provision of childcare outside the household. The minister of a chapel in Hanley commented in 1842 on the 'numerous cases in this township of little infants being left to the care of old women, who have the care of their own

---

idea that 'there were many distinct fertility and nuptiality regimes changing alongside each other' in England and Wales as a whole in the late nineteenth and twentieth centuries.

[35] For 1861 see Dupree, 'Family structure', p. 122; for 1881 see BPP 1883, LXXX, p. 236, and my sample of the 1881 enumerators' books from the Potteries cited above in n. 18.

[36] Staffordshire Sentinel, 21 Dec. 1872, p. 5; 4 April 1874, p. 5; 17 April 1875, p. 5; Hall, *Women in the labour force*, p. 43.

[37] BPP 1843, XIV, p. 273.

household, besides attending to the little charges'.[38] Also, because of the relatively high proportion of the population in the Potteries that was locally born, there was a greater likelihood that working women had relatives nearby who might provide childcare and could follow the pattern identified in Lancashire cotton towns where a coroner testified in 1871 that children are 'taken care of either by a person in the house or by some neighbour, and my impression is that it is usually done by some neighbour' who might also be a relative.[39] Finally, there is also evidence from the early twentieth century that the cost of childcare in the Potteries was lower than in Lancashire towns (70 per cent) and in England and Scotland generally (78 per cent).[40] Hence, although evidence about childcare in the Potteries is scattered, it suggests that the supply of childcare may have been greater and cost less than in Lancashire. Moreover, the provision of childcare in the neighbourhood as well as in the household means that it is necessary in considering the flexibility of women's roles to look outside as well as inside both the nuclear family unit used in neoclassical economists' analyses of labour force participation and fertility and the co-resident household unit used in some demographic and family history.[41]

The family economy

Among other things patterns of family employment and fertility such as those discussed above have implications for standards of living which in turn help to explain the patterns. It is possible to put the information about labour force participation and family composition together with estimates of incomes and compare the standards of living of families of married men in major occupational groups in the Potteries. In his study of the labour force of a paper making firm and a weaving firm in south-east Scotland in the mid-nineteenth century, John Holley, points out that two fairly clear and in some ways opposite models of the determination of family standard of living emerge from the literature.[42] The first model is that of the 'symmetrical' family in which the family standard of living was governed by the 'pre-industrial' pattern of multiple earners within the family; the second model is that of the

---

[38] BPP 1843, XIV; also quoted in Hewitt, *Wives and mothers*, p. 132.
[39] BPP 1871, VII, p. 99; Hewitt, *Wives and mothers*, pp. 128–33.
[40] BPP 1904, XXXII, paragraphs 9025–31 and Appendix V, p. 128; quoted in Hewitt, *Wives and mothers*, p. 132 and Hall, *Women in the labour force*, pp. 43–4.
[41] Anderson, *Approaches*, pp. 17–38, 65–66, 75–84.
[42] Holley, 'Re-division of labour; Holley, 'Two family economies of industrialism'.

'asymmetrical' family characterised by the 'industrial' pattern of the adult male head as the sole breadwinner. Young and Willmott among others see these models as two stages in development, and they argue that there has been a change from the 'symmetrical' to the 'asymmetrical' form over the past 150 years.[43] Holley, focusing his study on the effects of technological change, expected to find this change; instead of the asymmetrical replacing the symmetrical, however, he found that both patterns of family income determination appeared at the same time. Family standard of living was correlated with the head's income for high paid workers, but with the demographic and labour force participation characteristics of households headed by labourers. Thus to resolve these issues for the Potteries it is necessary, first, to determine the extent to which the family standard of living of married men within the various occupational groups was determined by the head's income and, second, to compare the family standard of living and its determination among the different occupational groups.

Table 6.4 shows a moderate to strong correlation (+0.78) between head's income and family standard of living for ironworkers and a moderate correlation (+0.53) for those in 'other' occupations. For potters, miners and labourers there was relatively little association between the head's income and the family standard of living. Thus, there is evidence of asymmetry for ironworkers.

The extent to which the standard of living was determined by the head's income or labour force participation of family members can be operationalised as a variable measuring the excess of earners over dependents in terms of needs. This variable (with a correlation coefficient of +0.69) explains the variation in living standard of families headed by labourers better than did the income of the head. Thus, the family composition—that is the number of people of working age and the extent of their labour force participation—was far more important for the standard of living of labourer headed families than was the income level of the head.

Comparisons of the average standard of living among various occupational groups (Table 6.5) reveals patterns which follow from these correlations. Families headed by potters and ironworkers had similar average standards of living (approximately 16s. per week above the poverty line) even though the average pay of a household head who was an ironworker was higher (over 31s. per week versus 27s. for

[43] Young and Willmott, *Symmetrical family*; and see, for example, Levine, 'Industrialization and the proletarian family', pp. 168–203; Levine, *Reproducing families*, esp. pp. 172–80; Seccombe, *Weathering the storm*, pp. 21, 111–24.

Table 6.4   Determinants of family standard of living for families headed by married men in various occupations in the Potteries, 1861

| Occupation of head | Determinants of family standard of living (coefficients of correlation) | | | |
| | Head's income | Excess of earners over dependants** | | (missing values) |
	r	r	n	
Ironworkers	0.78	0.24	65	(10)
Other	0.53	0.40	185	(200)
Potters	0.31	0.39	400	(28)
Miners	0.19	0.28	149	(2)
Labourers	0.22	0.69	100	(11)
All	0.49	0.40	912	(261)

Notes: 'Family standard of living' = the estimated income minus the minimum standard of family expenditure for each nuclear family. The aggregate income was calculated for each nuclear family headed by a married couple where the income of all family members could be estimated from the figures for the earnings of the different occupations (assuming a full week's work). Information was sufficient for incomes to be calculated for 78 per cent of the families headed by married couples in the Potteries sample. Income from lodgers was ignored and it was assumed that coresiding children gave all their income to the family. The minimum standard of family expenditure was based on Rowntree's scale of primary poverty expenditure as used by Anderson (*Family structure*, p. 201) but adjusted for lower rents in the Potteries.
'Excess of earners over dependants' = the number of earners minus the number of dependants in each nuclear family headed by a married couple where the income of all family members could be estimated.
Earners and dependants were weighted in terms of the 'adult equivalent needs' used by Foster (*Class struggle*, p. 256).
r = correlation coefficient; n = number of cases.

potters). In other words, living standards did not decline directly with the differences in the wages of heads. Families headed by potters had a higher rate of labour force participation and fewer dependants than those of ironworkers. Nor was high labour force participation directly related to low earnings by the head; potters, miners and others had higher excesses of earners over dependants and higher head's incomes than did labourers.

The contrast among the living standards of the various occupational groups can be seen more starkly when the pattern of the standard of living over the life cycle is considered (see Figure 6.2). The pattern for

Table 6.5 **Mean values of each of the three variables used in Table 6.4 for married men in various occupations who headed households in the Potteries, 1861**

Occupation of head	Head's income (s. per week)	Family standard of living (s. above or below poverty line)	Excess of earners over dependants (adult males=100)
Ironworkers	31	16	137
Potter	27	16	164
Other	26	15	164
Miners	24	12	159
Labourers	15	5	147

Notes: See Table 6.4.

each of the occupations is the same, but the level of labourers is consistently below the rest. To some extent the relatively low standard of living of labourers, however, was alleviated by taking in lodgers, which are not included in these figures.

To sum up, occupational groups embodying each of the two contrasting principles which determine family standards of living co-existed within the Potteries. For ironworkers, family standard of living was related to the income level of the head; for labourers it was related to the excess of earners over dependants within the household. Among the potters and miners, however, family standard of living was not correlated strongly with either the income of the head or the excess of earners over dependants. Moreover, the average standard of living of various occupational groups could be the same but for different reasons. Ironworkers and potters, for example, had similar mean family standards of living, yet ironworkers had relatively high income for the head, while potters had a relatively high excess of earners over dependants. Furthermore, all occupational groups displayed a similar pattern of standard of living over the life cycle, but that of labourers was considerably lower.

The availability of employment for women and children in the Potteries, therefore, provided increased scope for families to mediate between the wage structure and the age structure on the one hand, and the standard of living on the other.[44] Furthermore, at the community

---

[44] Wrigley, 'Population history in the 1980s', pp. 207–8, 225–6; Humphries and Rubery, 'Reconstitution of the supply side', pp. 331–46.

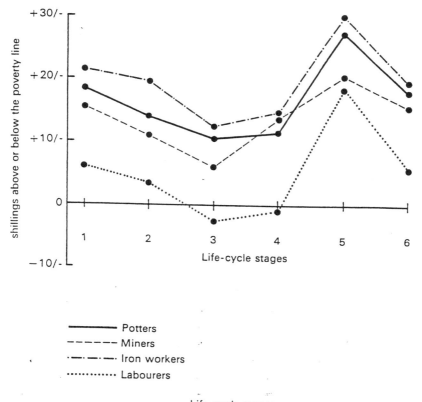

Potters
Miners
Iron workers
Labourers

Life-cycle stages
1. Wife under 45, no children at home
2. Wife under 45, one child under 1 yr at home
3. Children at home, but none in employment
4. Children at home, and some, but under half, in employment
5. Children at home, and half or over in employment
6. Wife 45 or over, no children or only children over age 20 at home

Figure 6.2 Standard of living by life-cycle stage for various occupations of husbands (married couples) Potteries sample, 1861

level the availability of employment for women and children decreased the inequality in the distribution of income, providing an economic basis for a 'community culture'. A part of any 'community culture' of particular importance to another aspect of family history are the sources of assistance such as neighbours, the Poor Law, friendly societies, churches, trade unions, voluntary hospitals, civic authorities in nineteenth century English towns, available to individuals to meet various crises in their lives.[45] The more these are investigated the more important it is that the analysis of family structure itself is community minded.

Conclusion

Two general conclusions emerge from this examination of women's work in paid industrial employment outside the home in the Potteries and its effect on aspects of the social, demographic and economic structure of family life. First, examination of family employment patterns, fertility and standard of living in the Potteries does more than show that patterns were different there than in other British communities which previously received attention. More generally, it suggests the need to consider communities rather than single occupations. The family employment and fertility patterns in the Potteries call into question the use of 'occupation' as a category with fixed prior characteristics which can be used as an explanatory variable. Instead, the social characteristics associated with occupations need to be seen as problematic. The family employment patterns in the Potteries reveal a mixing of occupations even among occupational groups such as miners and ironworkers usually characterised as relatively homogeneous. They serve as a warning against assuming that it was the wives and children of men in the industry hiring women and children who worked in that industry. Although the largest proportion of women and children employed in the potteries were the wives, daughters and children of male potters, there were substantial proportions of women and children employed who had husbands or fathers who were either dead or in other occupations. Moreover, the wives, daughters and children of potters typically did not work in the potteries. In addition, the similarity in fertility in the Potteries among different occupational groups and the relatively high fertility in an area with relatively high married women's labour force participation raise doubts about the use of 'occupation' not only as a category with fixed attributes, but also as a focus for analysis. In particular, it is plausible to argue that urban areas of mixed occupations were more typical of mid and late-Victorian Britain than homogeneous mining, iron and textile areas; hence, studies of the fertility decline in nineteenth-century Britain have over-emphasised 'occupation' at the expense of studies of particular localities where it is possible to examine fertility behaviour in

---

[45] Anderson, *Family structure*, pp. 136–9; Dupree, *Family structure*, pp. 271–345.

context. Even for 'single occupation' communities, the inevitable presence of a service sector means that a community-based rather than an occupation-based methodology may be more appropriate. It will also be more useful for any study which approaches families as one of a number of sources of assistance available to individuals. It is an approach which takes family history into the concerns of social history more generally. While there have been community studies, these have provided only tantalising glimpses of family structure. This examination of families in the Potteries suggests that studies of family history would benefit from having more community in them.

Second, the visibility of women and children's factory labour has made it possible to, 'recognise and identify a plurality of competing family options extant within' a single region.[46] The unexpected variety of responses to employment opportunities in the Potteries provides evidence of variability of employment behaviour which sets up a more complex picture of how family decisions are made about earnings and fertility and highlights the adaptability of the nuclear family. Certainly the 'structural context'—social, demographic, economic, ideological and political—imposed constraints on behaviour, but the variations in patterns of family employment, fertility and standards of living in the Potteries highlight the flexibility of the nuclear family and the key position of women as wives, mothers, daughters and workers in shaping the responses of families to their circumstances.

[46] Stone, 'Family history in the 1980s', p. 82.

7

Married women and work in nineteenth-century Lancashire: the evidence of the 1851 and 1861 census reports

JOHN McKAY

Introduction

This paper sets out to re-examine the view that there was a steep decline in the employment of married women across the second half of the nineteenth century. It relies largely on the printed census reports for 1851, 1861 and 1911, and takes into account the fact that much of the previous work in this field suggests the need for qualifications as to the accuracy of these reports. For example, Higgs argues strongly that there was a significant under-reporting of women's work in the nineteenth-century censuses. He also cites work by Davidoff, Lown and others in support of the view that this is particularly the case with married women, whose occupations were often omitted from the census enumerators' books (hereafter CEBs) by enumerators or from the original schedules by householders.[1] In a recent article, Sara Horrell and Jane Humphries utilise some innovative techniques and sources to shed light on this under-reporting in the first half of the century.[2] In so doing they comment that 'the invisibility of married women's work may well have distorted views of the nineteenth-century labour force; for example the view that factory work was confined to the young and single may well be a statistical artefact', and 'furthermore it is not easy to separate married women's work from the work of all females in the census data'.[3]

However, notwithstanding these reservations, this discussion of the decline in the employment of married women will show that the

[1] Higgs, 'Women, occupations and work'.
[2] Horrell and Humphries, 'Women's labour force participation'.
[3] Horrell and Humphries, 'Women's labour force participation', p. 95.

printed census reports of 1851 and 1861 *can* be made to tell us something about the employment of married women in the nation as a whole, and in localities as small as registration districts, in the middle of the nineteenth century.

A steep fall in the employment of married women?

Berg and Hudson have recently stated that, 'by mid century female and child labour was declining in importance through a mixture of legislation, the activities of male trade unionists, and the increasingly pervasive ideology of the male breadwinner and of fit and proper female activities'.[4] At first sight the statistical evidence seems strongly to support this view and the contention that there was a marked decline in the employment of married women in the second half of the nineteenth century. In 1911, 90 per cent of married women had no paid employment and so were 'fortunately . . . free at all ages to devote their attention to the care of their households'.[5] Hunt notes that, in 1851, nearly a quarter of married women were at work; he attributes the fall in the employment of married women over the second half of the nineteenth century to the transfer of work from homes to factories and workshops.[6]

Setting aside for the moment the causes, it is of interest to look at the figures forming the basis of this apparent fall in the employment of married women. With regard to the mid–century statistic of almost a quarter of married women being at work, Hunt makes no specific mention of the 1851 census and in fact gives no reference. Nevertheless, a search through the 1851 Census Report reveals the statement that:

> 'women . . . in certain branches of business at home render important services; such as the wives of farmers, of small shopkeepers, innkeepers, shoemakers, butchers; and others carry on businesses of various kinds or re employed in various ways. Thus Great Britain contained 3,461,524 wives of which 830,141 (about one in four) were engaged in some extraneous occupation'.[7]

It seems a fair assumption that this is the basis for Hunt's statement.

The figure of 830,141 wives engaged in some extraneous occupation

---

[4] Berg and Hudson, 'Rehabilitating the industrial revolution', p. 37.
[5] *Census of England and Wales, 1911, General report*, quoted in Hunt, *British labour history*, p. 18.
[6] Hunt, *British labour history*, p. 18.
[7] BPP 1852–3, LXXXVIII, *1851 Census of Great Britain: Population tables, pt. II, Ages, civil condition etc.*, I, pp. lxxxviii–lix.

is clearly derived from the Condition of the People and Occupation Tables published with the 1851 Census Report. Table 12, in the Appendix to the Report, gives the figure of 3,461,524 wives in Great Britain.[8] Table 54 in the body of the Report states that there were 2,631,383 women in the occupational category 'wife of no specified occupation'.[9] Deducting these from the total number of wives produces a figure of 830,141 wives 'engaged in some extraneous occupation'. This figure, however, includes not only those married women in employment, but also the 371,959 wives of farmers, small shopkeepers, innkeepers, licensed victuallers, shoemakers and butchers (see Table 7.1). It is not clear why the wives of men following these occupations were given a special occupational status. Higgs suggests that the General Register Office in the Victorian era was concerned primarily with medical and actuarial matters and that the form of the census reflected this. The wives singled out for special mention may well have been considered as exposed to the same environmental conditions as their husbands and therefore to similar risks of disease and death.[10] Whatever the reasons, some of the wives listed in Table 7.1 were given a distinct occupational status in Table 54 of the 1851 Census Report.

From 1881 the categories of innkeeper's wife, farmer's wife, etc. were discontinued, and these wives were consigned to the 'unoccupied' category: so, in setting the 1911 data against that of 1851, Hunt is not comparing like with like. Higgs points out that this difficulty in comparing pre- and post-1881 occupational tables was noted at the time, particularly by Charles Booth. Booth removed these wives and other female relatives to the 'unoccupied' category in order to present a 'more consistent time series showing the changing structure of the economy'.[11] However, Higgs argues that the removal of such women from the occupied category presents a distorted picture of the economic importance of women.[12] This is indeed the case when considering the position of working married women in 1851, 1861 or 1871—the census years for which this information is given. However, in a comparison of the 1851 census (which regards these wives as occupied) with the 1911 census (which does not) an adjustment must be made. As information on the numbers of wives of farmers, innkeepers, shopkeepers, etc. is unavailable for 1911 it is not possible to add them to the 1911 figure for

[8] BPP 1852–3, LXXXVIII, p. clxv.
[9] BPP 1852–3, LXXXVIII, p. cxli.
[10] Higgs, 'Occupational censuses', pp. 701–2; see also p. 24, above.
[11] Higgs, 'Women, occupations and work', p. 72.
[12] Higgs, 'Women, occupations and work', p. 72.

Table 7.1   **Wives of innkeepers and other selected occupations recorded in the 1851 census**

Description	Number
Innkeeper's wives	17,447
Shoemakers' wives	94,175
Shopkeepers' wives	6,002
Farmers' wives	201,736
Butchers' wives	26,015
Licensed victuallers' wives	26,584
Total	371,959

Source: BPP 1852–3, LXXXVIII, *1851 Census of Great Britain, Population tables, II*, vol. 1, pp. cxl–cxlix.

working married women.[13] This leaves, as the only option for an effective comparison, an adjustment of the 1851 figures to exclude them. The 371,959 wives listed in Table 7.1 must therefore be deducted from the figure of 830,141 wives stated earlier to have been engaged in business on their own account or in employment. This leaves 458,182 wives who may be regarded as 'working', which constitutes 13.2 per cent of all wives. Finally, the 1851 figures are for Great Britain while those quoted by Hunt for 1911 are for England and Wales only. The number of wives who may be regarded as 'working' in England and Wales in 1851 is 421,667 or 14.0 per cent of all wives (see Table 7.2).

It seems clear, therefore, that the proportion of wives stated to be working in 1851 is about 13 or 14 per cent, or slightly above half the figure used by Hunt in his comparison of the position in 1851 with that in 1911. It follows that the decline in the participation of married women in the workforce is much less steep than was supposed by Hunt. Indeed, a fall from 13 or 14 per cent in 1851 to 10 per cent in 1911 could well be regarded as of no great significance in the light of changes in methods of collecting and processing the census data.

---

[13] Higgs, 'Occupational censuses', p. 707, gives a figure of 144,000 female relatives reported by farmers in response to the 1906 census of production. However, information for the other categories of wives is unavailable.

Table 7.2 Married women recorded as being in employment, 1851 and 1861

	Total number of married women		Increase 1851–61	Number of married women employed		Increase 1851–61	% of married women employed	
	1851	1861	%	1851	1861	%	1851	1861
All married women								
England and Wales	3,015,634	3,488,952	15.69	421,667	520,213	23.37	13.98	14.91
Lancashire	342,586	428,174	24.98	68,225	94,991	39.23	19.91	22.18
Married women aged 20 years and upwards								
Lancashire	339,565	424,092	24.89	66,777	92,546	38.58	19.66	21.82
Leigh	5,099	6,417	25.84	2,321	2,985	28.60	45.51	46.51
Blackburn	14,932	20,724	38.78	5,048	7,634	51.22	33.80	36.83
Oldham	15,018	20,263	34.92	5,020	7,214	43.70	33.42	35.60
Ashton under Lyne	20,261	24,208	19.48	6,311	9,045	43.32	31.14	37.36
Burnley	10,397	12,929	24.35	3,016	3,667	21.58	29.00	28.36
Chorley	5,606	6,670	18.97	1,516	1,656	9.23	27.04	24.82
Preston	15,349	18,471	20.34	4,117	6,136	49.04	26.82	33.21
Manchester	38,870	43,061	10.78	10,036	11,746	17.03	25.81	27.27
Bury	14,906	17,406	16.77	3,436	4,783	39.20	23.05	27.47
Rochdale	12,227	16,182	32.34	2,774	4,560	64.38	22.68	29.17
Bolton	18,900	22,265	17.80	3,964	4,975	25.50	20.97	22.34
Salford	15,190	18,560	22.18	2,962	4,284	44.63	19.49	23.08
Barton-upon-Irwell	4,979	6,311	26.75	970	1,266	30.51	19.48	20.06
Warrington	5,726	7,437	29.88	978	980	0.20	17.07	13.17

Haslingden	8,413	12,113	43.97	1,316	3,045	131.38	15.64	25.13
Wigan	12,096	15,557	28.61	1,864	2,109	13.14	15.41	13.55
Clithero	3,291	3,232	1.80	498	650	30.52	15.13	20.11
Chorlton	21,349	29,483	38.10	2,999	4,388	46.31	14.04	14.88
Ormskirk	5,594	7,095	26.83	515	779	51.26	9.20	10.97
Lancaster	5,255	5,563	5.86	469	584	24.52	8.92	10.49
Liverpool	42,131	47,404	12.51	3,730	5,046	35.28	8.85	10.64
Fylde	3,334	4,044	21.95	288	498	72.91	8.63	12.24
Prescot	8,872	12,214	37.66	727	890	22.42	8.19	7.28
West Derby	25,255	38,843	53.80	1,595	3,037	90.40	6.31	7.81
Ulverston	4,596	5,584	21.49	252	347	37.69	5.48	6.21
Garstang	1,919	1,934	0.78	55	142	158.18	2.86	7.34

Sources: BPP 1852–3, LXXXVIII, *1851 Census of Great Britain, Population tables*; BPP 1863, LIII, Pt. 1, *1861 Census of England and Wales, Population tables*.

Lancashire textile industries and the employment of married women

Higgs argues that one reason for the under-enumeration of women's work was that the seasonal nature of much of their employment, particularly in rural areas, led to their exclusion from the census schedules, which were completed in March or April when they were least likely to be at work.[14] However, factory work, such as cotton manufacture, employed many women, including married women, and may well have provided more continuity of employment. An examination of the employment of married women in the county of Lancashire, a major centre of the cotton industry, provides an interesting case study with which to examine trends in women's work over the second half of the nineteenth century, and also to assess Hunt's statement that 'one cause of the long-term decline in married women's employment during the nineteenth century was the transfer of work from the home to factories and workshops'.[15]

The registration districts of Lancashire

The census reports for 1851 and 1861 provide, at the county and registration district level, data similar to those already discussed for married women at national level. It is impossible, therefore, to look at variations between different areas of the county of Lancashire in the level of employment of married women.

In the 1851 census, the population tables for the county of Lancashire show that the county contained 342,586 wives of whom 252,816 are described as having 'no specified occupation'.[16] Following the practice outlined above in obtaining the figures for Great Britain, the remaining 89,770 (or 26.2 per cent of the total) are presumed to be enumerated as following a specific occupation. Of these, 21,545 are listed as farmers' wives, innkeepers' wives, etc., leaving 68,225 (or 19.9 per cent of the total) described as following other more specific occupations.[17] Thus Lancashire had a significantly higher proportion of married women enumerated as in employment than Great Britain as a whole. Lancashire in 1851 has been described as the most urbanised county in Great

---

[14] Higgs, 'Women, occupations and work', pp. 67–8.
[15] Hunt, *British labour history*, p. 18.
[16] BPP 1852–3, LXXXVIII, *1851 Census of Great Britain: Population tables, pt. II, Ages, civil condition etc.*, II, pp. 620, 633.
[17] BPP 1852–3, LXXXVIII, pp. 633–5.

Britain.[18] That 19.9 per cent of married women were enumerated as in employment compared with 14.0 per cent in England and Wales as a whole might indicate that, on the one hand, there were more employment opportunities for married women in towns or, on the other hand, that there was more need for urban wives to seek employment because of family circumstances. It must, however, be kept in mind that Lancashire was not completely urbanised. Outside Liverpool, Manchester and the cotton manufacturing towns, large areas remained unaffected by industry or commerce. It is possible, using the data for registration districts, to identify differences in the level of married women's employment between the urban and rural areas of the county.

The population tables contain information for the registration districts. These are generally the same as the Poor Law Unions and each cover a number of parishes. In this case, however, data on wives and working women are given only for those aged 20 or over. This does not, in fact, seriously diminish their value for the present purpose, since the numbers of wives aged under 20 are very small indeed. Of the 342,586 wives enumerated in Lancashire, only 3,021 (or 0.9 per cent) were under 20 years of age.[19] In England and Wales as a whole 22,240 wives out of 3,015,634 (or 0.7 per cent) were under 20.[20]

The data from the population tables for the registration districts were treated in the same way as those for England and Wales and the county of Lancashire. The results for 1851, presented in Table 7.2, show that within the county there were substantial variations in the proportion of married women enumerated as in work. In 1851, Leigh (a small district near Manchester) had 45 per cent of its married women enumerated as in employment. Oldham, Ashton-under-Lyne and Blackburn all had over 30 per cent of wives at work. Manchester, Preston, Chorley and Burnley all had more than a quarter of their married women similarly enumerated, while Bolton, Rochdale, and Bury had more than 20 per cent. All of these are districts traditionally associated with the cotton industry. On the other hand the registration districts of Ulverston, Lancaster, Garstang, Fylde, Ormskirk, Prescot, West Derby and Liverpool all had less than 10 per cent of wives enumerated as in employment. Some of these districts were predominantly agricultural (for example Ulverston); others, like Liverpool, were urban. It seems,

---

[18] Anderson, *Family structure*, p. 32.
[19] BPP 1852–3, LXXXVIII, *1851 Census of Great Britain: Population tables, pt. II, Ages, civil condition etc.*, II, p. 620.
[20] BPP 1852–3, LXXXVIII, *1851 Census of Great Britain: Population tables, pt. II, Ages, civil condition etc.*, II, Table VIII, p. ccv.

therefore, that high levels of married women in employment were not only found in towns. The presence of the cotton industry, however, seems to have been an important factor.

The results so far lend support to Higgs's argument. The low level of employment of married women in the rural areas of the county probably partly reflects the seasonal nature of available work. It may also be the case that enumerators in such districts did not always take full cognizance of working married women. In Gloucestershire a comparison of farm wages books with the 1871 census enumerators' books showed considerable variation between districts in this respect.[21]

With regard to towns, in the mid-nineteenth century, commerce and heavy industry were predominantly male preserves and commercial centres like Liverpool and heavy industrial areas such as Warrington did not provide the same level of employment opportunity for women as did the cotton towns. This is reflected in the low levels of employment of married women.

The textile industry as a factor in the employment of married women

The importance of the presence of the cotton industry as a factor in the employment of married women can be confirmed by an examination of the relationship between the proportion of married women in employment in a registration district and the proportion of all of the district's women working in the cotton industry. It was pointed out earlier that, at registration district level, data on the employment of women are available only for those aged 20 and above. In 1851 in Lancashire 150,763 women were employed in 'cotton manufacture', of whom 64,068 were aged under 20.[22] Thus considerably more than half of Lancashire women working in the cotton industry were aged over 20, and it is considered that the proportion of women aged over 20 who were employed in cotton manufacture is a suitable indicator of the importance of the industry in the districts. In the course of extracting the data it was found that, in some districts, significant numbers of women were employed in 'silk manufacture'. This information was extracted also.

The registration districts were arranged in rank order of the

---

[21] Miller, 'Hidden workforce', pp. 146–7.

[22] BPP 1852–3, LXXXVIII, *1851 Census of Great Britain, Population tables, pt. II, Ages, civil condition etc.*, II, p. 635.

Table 7.3 Relationship between the percentage of married women employed and that of women (aged over 20) employed in the cotton and silk industries: registration districts in Lancashire, 1851

Registration district	% of women employed		in both $(3)=(1)+(2)$	Rank of column (3)	% of married women employed (4)	Rank of column (4)
	in cotton (1)	in silk (2)				
Leigh	15.93	28.80	44.73	1	45.51	1
Blackburn	34.93	0.54	35.47	2	33.80	2
Oldham	25.36	9.46	34.82	3=	33.42	3
Ashton under Lyne	32.76	2.06	34.82	3=	33.42	4
Burnley	31.98	0.00	31.98	5	29.00	5
Chorley	30.51	0.15	30.66	6	27.00	6
Preston	28.49	0.01	28.50	7	26.82	7
Bury	26.55	0.48	27.03	8	23.05	9
Haslingden	23.70	0.06	23.76	9	15.64	15
Bolton	20.85	2.64	23.49	10	20.99	11
Clitheroe	21.04	0.20	21.24	11	15.13	17
Barton upon Irwell	13.20	7.11	20.31	12	19.48	13
Rochdale	19.83	0.07	19.90	13	22.68	10
Wigan	18.05	1.16	19.21	14	15.41	16
Manchester	13.92	3.56	17.48	15	25.81	8
Salford	9.47	3.27	12.74	16	19.49	12
Chorlton	9.49	0.67	10.16	17	14.04	18
Lancaster	6.26	1.02	7.28	18	8.92	20
Garstang	7.11	0.00	7.11	19	2.86	26
Warrington	4.56	1.62	6.18	20	17.07	14

Table 7.3 Continued

Registration district	% of women employed			Rank of column (3)	% of married women employed (4)	Rank of column (4)
	in cotton (1)	in silk (2)	in both (3)=(1)+(2)			
Flyde	3.85	0.00	3.85	21	8.63	22
Ormskirk	0.35	3.09	3.44	22	9.20	19
Ulverston	2.05	0.00	2.05	23	5.48	24
Prescot	0.64	0.00	0.64	24	4.13	25
Liverpool	0.31	0.02	0.33	25	8.85	21
West Derby	0.10	0.00	0.10	26	6.31	23

Sources: BPP 1852-3, LXXXVIII, *1851 Census of Great Britain, Population tables*.

percentages of women engaged in cotton or silk manufacture and also in rank order of the proportions of married women enumerated as in employment (Table 7.3). Spearman's coefficient of rank order correlation between the two resulting lists was +0.90, indicating a very strong positive correlation between women's employment in the cotton and silk industries and the proportion of married women enumerated as in employment.[23] This is emphasised by the appearance (in the same order) of the same seven districts at the top of both rankings. A similar exercise for districts ranked according to the proportion of women aged 20 and upward engaged in cotton manufacture alone (that is, comparing columns (1) and (4) in Table 7.3) produced a correlation coefficient of +0.84, indicating a similarly strong positive relationship.

This does not of course demonstrate a causal connection but it does show that in districts with a substantial textile industry, the proportion of married women enumerated as working was considerably higher than in the less industrialised areas of the county. The close correlation between the proportions of married women enumerated as working and the number of women involved in textile manufacture also suggests that enumerators and householders in the textile districts may have been more likely to record the occupations of married women than they were in other areas where work for women, particularly married women, was less regular.

Unfortunately the census reports cannot be made to identify the actual occupations followed by these married women. However, Anderson's research based on a 10 per cent sample of CEB schedules for all occupied private residences in the municipal and parliamentary borough of Preston found that, in 1851, 26 per cent of wives living with their husbands worked.[24] The census report data for the registration district of Preston (see Table 7.2) indicate a figure of 26.8 per cent. The registration district is not necessarily coterminous with the borough but it is clear that the borough must have been a substantial part of the registration district and the similarity between the two results is striking. Anderson also notes that his sample of 278 working married women included 52 per cent engaged in factory occupations.[25]

---

[23] A correlation coefficient of +1.00 would indicate a perfect match.
[24] Anderson, *Family structure*, p. 71.
[25] Anderson, *Family structure*, p. 208.

Married women workers in Lancashire in 1861

Data similar to those just described for 1851 are given in the 1861 Census Report for England and Wales: '838,856 wives are returned under other occupations' and '2,650,096 wives . . . are not otherwise described'.[26] Thus 24.0 per cent of wives were at work. The occupation tables yield a total of 318,643 farmers' wives, innkeepers' wives, etc., leaving 520,213 married women in employment, or 14.9 per cent.[27] The figures for 1851 and 1861 are set against each other in Table 7.2. It is unfortunate that in the published reports of the 1871 and subsequent censuses the all-important entry in the occupation tables of 'wives not otherwise described' is omitted, making it impossible to take the comparison beyond 1861.

The proportion of married women enumerated as in employment in England and Wales rose from 14.0 per cent in 1851 to 14.9 per cent in 1861. Over the same period, the number of married women rose by 15.7 per cent and the number of married women enumerated as in employment by 23.4 per cent. Thus the number of married women recorded as being in employment rose more than the total number of married women.

In Lancashire, the number of married women rose over the decade 1851–61 by almost 25 per cent, a substantially higher increase than for England and Wales as a whole. The number of married women enumerated as in employment rose by 39 per cent, again much more than in England and Wales. This seems to indicate clearly that the employment of married women in the county, or at least the enumeration of such employment, was still rising until 1861. The registration districts exhibit a similar pattern. In all except four the increase in numbers of married women at work was greater than the overall increase in the number of married women. This was accompanied, in all but five districts, by an increase in the *proportion* of married women enumerated as in employment. All but two of the districts identifiable with the cotton industry exhibited increases in this respect: for example, the proportion of married women at work in Preston rose from 27 to 33 per cent, in Ashton-under-Lyne from 31 to 37 per cent, and in Rochdale from 23 to 28 per cent. The relationship between the proportion of married women working and the proportion of women engaged in the manufacture of textiles was again explored.

[26] BPP 1863, LIII, pt. I, *1861 Census of England and Wales, vol. III, General report, with appendix of tables*, p. 33.

[27] BPP 1863, LIII, pt. I, *1861 Census of England and Wales, Population tables, vol. II. Ages, civil condition etc.*, Summary Table XX, pp. lvi–lxv.

Spearman's coefficients of correlation, at 0.93 for employment in the cotton and silk industries together, and 0.86 for employment in the cotton industry alone, indicate an even stronger relationship than was the case in 1851.

There are a number of possible reasons for the increase in the employment of married women over the ten years between 1851 and 1861. There may have been more jobs available in the 'mid-Victorian boom'; householders and census enumerators might have been more efficient in the identification of married women at work; there might have been a shift of married women from part-time to full-time work, which may have been more regularly recorded by enumerators. It has been suggested that the increase may have been due to male unemployment, making it necessary for wives to go out to work. Available unemployment statistics show that unemployment among trade union members was just under 4 per cent in 1851, reaching nearly 12 per cent in 1858, falling to just under 2 per cent in 1860, but rising to over 5 per cent in 1861 and 8 per cent in 1862.[28] No separate data are available for textile workers. However, it can be shown that among cotton operatives aged over 13 the proportion of males fell from 45 per cent in 1835 to 42 per cent in 1850 and 39 per cent in 1861.[29] This suggests that work for males in the cotton districts may have been becoming scarcer, producing a greater incentive for wives to contribute to the family economy.

The contribution by married women to the textile workforce cannot be measured from the census reports, but it was clearly significant. Hewitt, using a sample from the 1851 CEBs for seven registration districts regarded as typical of the Lancashire cotton area, shows that the proportion of female cotton operatives who were married women ranged from 14 per cent in Chorley to 45 per cent in Oldham.[30]

Other studies of the employment of married women in mid-nineteenth century England suggest that the availability of work for women and low pay for men are both important factors. In 1851, 56 per cent of wives in certain districts of Colyton, in Devon, were reported to be employed. The main employment was lace-making and the wives employed were in many cases the wives of labourers.[31] According to Saito, in Cardington, Bedfordshire, in 1851, a massive 63 per cent of married women were enumerated as in employment, the majority in

[28] Mitchell, *British historical statistics*, p. 122.
[29] Derived from Mitchell, *British historical statistics*, p. 377.
[30] Hewitt, *Wives and mothers*, p. 14.
[31] Wall, 'Work, welfare and the family', p. 279.

lace-making.[32] Saito compares Cardington, where the main employment for men was agriculture, with Corfe Castle in Dorset, which offered alternative employment in the clay industry to its male labour force. In Corfe Castle, less than 3 per cent of married women were employed. In Berkhamsted, Hertfordshire, straw plaiting was a major cottage industry and 34 per cent of married women were enumerated as in employment.[33] These studies all concern areas where, as in Cardington, 'the effect of cottage industry on the labour-force participation profiles of females was remarkable'.[34] Thus women's employment was important both in areas of 'cottage' industry and in areas, like Lancashire, where 'factory' industry offered employment to women. The importance of 'factory' industry is also illustrated in Dupree's work on the Staffordshire potteries. Her one in fifteen sample of all households in the parliamentary borough of Stoke-on-Trent, taken from the 1861 CEBs, shows that 18 per cent of married women were enumerated as being in employment.[35] This is considerably less than for some Lancashire districts but much higher than the national average.

Married women workers in Lancashire in 1911

Taking the discussion forward to 1911, the next census for which the reports give comparable data, in England and Wales there were 6,630,284 married women of whom 680,191 (10.3 per cent) were recorded as occupied in the tables.[36] This is less than the 14.0 per cent of 1851 but the difference may be explained, in part, by methodological changes.

It seems clear also that the decline hitherto identified as having taken place in the employment of married women between 1851 and 1911 started later than 1851. The evidence of the census reports indicates that the employment of married women was increasing until at least 1861. Changes in enumeration and collation methods in 1871 and 1881 make it impossible to be more precise. The long-term decline was also less steep than previously thought. Hunt's fall from 25 per cent in 1851 to 10 per cent in 1911 might be regarded as a steep decline. However, the conclusion offered here is that the decline was from 14.9 per cent in

---

[32] Saito, 'Who worked when?', chapter 9 below, p. 221.
[33] Goose, *Berkhamsted*, p. 38.
[34] Saito, 'Who worked when?', below, p. 226.
[35] Dupree, *Family structure*, p. 156.
[36] BPP 1913–14, LXXIX, *Census of England and Wales 1911, vol. X, pt. I, Occupations and industries*, p. 2.

Table 7.4 **Married women recorded as being in employment in 1911: Lancashire and boroughs within the county**

	Retired or unoccupied (1)	Engaged in occupation (2)	Total (3)=(1)+(2)	Percentage engaged in occupation (4)=100x(2)/(3)
Lancashire: administrative county	721,441	153,513	847,954	17.54
Blackburn	14,445	11,560	26,005	44.45
Burnley	2,461	8,820	21,281	41.44
Preston	13,913	7,600	21,513	35.32
Bury	7,903	3,558	11,461	31.04
Rochdale	13,342	4,975	18,317	27.16
Oldham	21,909	6,819	28,728	23.73
Blackpool	9,377	2,390	11,767	20.31
Bolton	28,533	5.025	33.558	14.97
Manchester	110,772	18.836	129,608	14.53
Salford	35,816	5,889	41,705	14.12
Southport	8,181	1,074	9,255	11.60
Wigan	13,731	1,437	15,168	9.47
Liverpool (city)	117,568	11,503	129,071	8.91
Warrington	11,606	1,035	12,641	8.18
Bootle	11,687	735	12,422	5.91
Barrow in Furness	11,166	506	11,672	4.33
St Helens	15,665	672	16,337	4.11
Aggregate of rural districts	37,621	4,909	43,530	11.54

Source: BPP 1913, LXXIX, 1911 *Census of England and Wales, Vol. X, occupations and industries, part II*, pp. 203–57.

1861 to 10.3 per cent in 1911, a far more gentle downward trend, and it might even be argued that these data suggest the employment of married women remained relatively stable over the second half of the nineteenth century.

It is also the case that the period from 1851 to 1911 saw large absolute increases in the number of married women and in the number of those enumerated as employed. The 6,630,284 married women recorded in England and Wales in 1911 represent an increase of 119 per cent over the number for 1851. The number of married women at work,

680,191, shows a smaller, but still substantial, increase of 61 per cent. Thus the fall in the proportion of married women in employment occurred during a period in which the numbers of married more than doubled and the numbers of married women in employment also rose, although less steeply. It seems clear, therefore, that the fall in the proportion of married women at work was due not so much to a reduction in employment opportunities as to a failure of the growth of such opportunities to keep pace with the increase in numbers.

In Lancashire in 1851, 19.9 per cent of married women in Lancashire were enumerated as in employment; in 1861 the figure was 22.2 per cent. In 1911, 17.5 per cent were employed (Table 7.4), indicating a decline in Lancashire similar to that in England and Wales as a whole. In 1911 the proportions of married women at work in the Lancashire boroughs ranged from 4 per cent in St. Helens to 44 per cent in Blackburn. It is possible that a systematic comparison between women's employment in the registration districts of 1851 and 1861 and the boroughs and county boroughs of 1911 (along the lines of the analysis described above when comparing 1851 with 1861) could be carried out, although it has not been attempted here. It can be noted, however, that some of the 1911 boroughs showed similar rates of decline to the county as a whole when compared with the associated registration districts, and some had even steeper falls. However, in the textile areas of Blackburn, Burnley, Bury, Preston and Rochdale, the proportion of married women in employment remained high and in some cases increased. In Burnley there was a rise from 28 per cent in 1861 to 41 per cent in 1911. This casts some doubt, in the case of Lancashire at any rate, on the view that the transfer of work from home to factory led to a reduction in the level of employment of married women from 1851 to 1911.

Conclusion

In Lancashire, the employment of married women in 1851 and 1861 was at a considerably higher level than in England and Wales as a whole, and in some districts more than a third of married women were enumerated as in employment. England and Wales, Lancashire and some of its registration districts showed an increase in the proportion of married women enumerated as in employment between 1851 and 1861. By 1911 the proportion of married women working had declined somewhat in the county as a whole. However, the data in the census reports which have been discussed in this paper—the only regularly recorded statistics of married women's employment—indicate that, in national terms, any decline in the proportion of married women in employment was much less than hitherto believed. The census reports indicate that for the textile districts of Lancashire the proportion of married women enumerated as in employment was much higher than the national average in 1851 and 1861 and remained high in 1911, although there was a decline between 1861 and 1911 of a similar order of magnitude to the national decline. There were, however, marked geographical variations in the level of employment of married women, across England and Wales as a whole and within the county of Lancashire,. In Lancashire, it is clear that these were related to the presence of a major industry offering employment to large numbers of women.

Finally, it is likely that the estimates of the proportion of married women employed which have been presented here do not fully reflect the actually amount of work done by women. Higgs has demonstrated that, in the case of agricultural workers, the 'low levels of women's employment recorded in nineteenth-century England and Wales may be merely a statistical illusion'.[37] The census reports for the textile districts of Lancashire in 1851, 1861 and 1911 show a high level of employment among married women. However, it remains possible— indeed probable—that female employment of a more casual nature than that in the textile mills was unnoticed by enumerators.

---

[37] Higgs, 'Occupational censuses', p. 712.

8

What can the mid-Victorian censuses tell us about variations in married women's employment?

MICHAEL ANDERSON

Introduction

It is only since 1911 that it has been possible to trace in detail the dramatic changes in patterns of employment of married women in Britain (though the 1901 census gives occupations of married and widowed women combined). Before that, only in the census reports for 1851, 1861 and (for England and Wales only) 1871, is it possible to obtain any estimates at all of the overall proportion of married women who were recorded as in employment. Otherwise, and for any detail of the occupations involved, we have to rely on the census enumerators' books (CEBs).

Following Margaret Hewitt, whose path-breaking *Wives and mothers in Victorian industry* was published in 1958, several scholars in the 1960s and 1970s used enumerators' books to analyse married women's employment in the context of the family, kinship, and the household economy.[1] While recognising that no source is perfect, most of these authors treated the reporting of women's occupations in the enumerators' books as reasonably valid and reliable indicators of the incidence of women's income-generating contribution to the family economy.

The first significant attack on the reliability and validity of the

---

[1] Hewitt, *Wives and mothers*. Hewitt took samples from the 1851 CEBs for seven Lancashire registration districts, and had similar samples prepared by the Registrar General's office from the as yet unavailable 1871 CEBs. In the book, she reports only a few findings from these data, but there is much more detail in her 1953 University of London PhD. For other early examples, Anderson, *Family structure*; Foster, *Class struggle*; Armstrong, *Stability and change*.

enumeration of married women's employment in the Victorian censuses was Higgs' work on Rochdale servants. Higgs noted that very substantial numbers of 'servants' seemed to be kin who probably assisted with domestic or business work in the households of their relatives, while most of those recorded as 'housekeepers' in the published census report were housewives responsible for managing their own households.[2] Higgs later generalised a case against the reliability and validity of the enumeration of married women's occupations, arguing that the instructions to householders and enumerators might reasonably have been interpreted in ways which would discourage the reporting of casual, seasonal and domestic industrial employment. He also produced other evidence which suggested that some male householders and some male enumerators failed to report occupations for many women, some of whom are known from other sources to have been in regular employment.[3] Extending this argument, Elizabeth Roberts subsequently argued that 'part-time work (usually undertaken by married women) was grossly under-enumerated' and that '[t]here is certainly a very big discrepancy . . . between the number of married women enumerated as working full-time in the Census . . . and the large number of women . . . who worked at some point in their lives on a casual, part-time basis—about 40% in Preston and Lancaster, and 50% in Barrow'.[4] Particularly alarming for its wider implications, Roberts presented data from John Holley's comparisons of employment revealed by the census and by wage books in the textile and papermaking industries in southern Scotland. This appears to show levels of under-enumeration of women's employment ranging from 46 per cent to 100 per cent.[5]

More recently, the work of Higgs and Roberts has been used to cast serious doubts on the reliability of census recording.[6] One particular manifestation of what is fast becoming a new orthodoxy appears in a paper published in 1995 by Sara Horrell and Jane Humphries, where they assert that,

---

[2] Higgs, 'Domestic servants'; see also his revised paper, 'Tabulation of occupations', reproduced here as chapter 11, and the further discussion of this issue in chapter 12.

[3] Higgs, 'Women, occupations and work'.

[4] Roberts, *Women's work*, p. 18; Roberts, *A woman's place*, p. 136. The 1911 Census Report gives the percentage of married women and widows in what Roberts, probably wrongly, assumes is only full-time employment as 35.0 per cent in Preston, 11.0 per cent in Lancaster, and 6.9 per cent in Barrow: see also Roberts, 'Working wives', pp. 167–8.

[5] Roberts, *Women's work*, p. 19.

[6] Not all writers have been as sceptical: see for example, Jordan, 'Female unemployment'; August, 'How separate a sphere'.

the [nineteenth-century] census enumeration of women's employment is demonstrably inaccurate . . . Checks provided by local and national evidence suggest substantial under-reporting of female work in the agricultural sector, in manufacturing, and in certain service occupations. Frequently enumerators omitted any occupational designation for married women whose work was thus particularly under-reported.

They go on to argue that '[t]he invisibility of married women's work may well have distorted views of the nineteenth-century labour force; for example, the view that factory work was confined to the young and single may be a statistical artefact'.[7]

As an alternative source, Horrell and Humphries use a large collection of family budgets as the basis of new estimates of trends in women's labour force participation, and on this basis claim, *inter alia*, that

[a]round 15% of working married women were recorded as working in factories at the turn of the [eighteenth] century and this had declined to 10% by the 1830s . . . 60% of women with husbands with factory occupations were themselves working in factories in 1831–50, a higher proportion than the 14% of married women employed in factories in Preston in 1851. In the 1840s, 38% of our women are working; this is considerably higher than the estimate of 7% in Birmingham in 1841, and again illustrates the downward bias of census estimates.[8]

Evaluation

It would be easy to read Horrell and Humphries as arguing that the reporting of married women's employment in the CEBs is so bad that the data are almost useless for serious analytical purposes.[9] But is this

---

[7] Horrell and Humphries, 'Women's labour force participation', p. 95.

[8] Horrell and Humphries, 'Women's labour force participation', p. 99, fn. 50. The references are, for Preston, to Anderson, *Family structure*, p. 72 and Barnsby, *Birmingham working people*, p. 195. Note that most of Horrell and Humphries' 'factory workers' were in fact textile workers: see Horrell and Humphries, 'Old questions, new data'.

[9] I should make clear that this is a view that, in private communication with me, both authors have said it was not their intention to convey, but it would be very easy to read such a view into their work and, given, as we shall see below (fn. 12), the ways in which scholars in this area have so frequently drawn quite incorrect implications from others' work, it seems almost inevitable that their paper will soon be added to the list of sources condemning the reporting of women's occupations in the CEBs.

really the case? A second look at much of the evidence put forward against the CEBs suggests that many concerns about reliable reporting are exaggerated. For example, women entered as domestic servants in the occupation column, but shown in the relationship column as relatives of the head of household, are easily identified in the enumerators' books.[10] If we exclude those listed as 'housekeepers' and simply as 'domestic', they make up about 13 per cent of English and Welsh 'servants' in the National Sample from the 1851 Census of Great Britain.[11] Moreover, their status is ambiguous: some, as Higgs has pointed out, were correctly returned as they were genuinely providing domestic or other services to the household in which they lived, while others, in 1851, were following a widespread custom of servants being allowed to return home for Mothering Sunday, which coincided with the census in that year. Wives, mothers and daughters who were listed as 'housekeepers' in their own households are similarly easy to spot in the enumerators' books—where, indeed, in England and Wales, this title is given in 1851 to 1.1 per cent of all married women living with husbands on census night and aged between 20 and 59. However, this use of the term 'housekeeper' to identify the person principally responsible for day-to-day household management is locally highly concentrated into the Lancashire cotton towns, with nearly half of all such occurrences in the sample occurring in Lancashire and Cheshire. Also, and offering a slightly different gloss on the position apparently identified by Higgs in Rochdale, examination of the many hundreds of enumerators' books in the National Sample shows clearly that registrars and census office checkers in many parts of the country were well aware

---

[10] As Cooper and Donald have pointed out in 'Households and "hidden" kin', there were probably significantly larger numbers of servants who had some kinship relationship to some other member of their households but were reported as servants in both the occupation and the relationship columns of the census, but the great majority of these were probably unambiguously providing domestic services, even if their recruitment, as with so many other servants at the same date, was the result of a personal connection rather than an open market operation. For a fuller discussion of this issue see chapter 12 below.

[11] The National Sample is a systematic cluster transcript of one-fiftieth of the enumerators' books from the 1851 Census (except for institutions where every fiftieth family or person is sampled and settlements with populations of less than 2,000 in England and Wales where one settlement in fifty is sampled). The whole dataset is in machine-readable form and also on computer-generated microfiche, but only subsets of the data were processed through software which generated the family and household relationships and coded the transcribed entries. Where national figures are cited in this paper, these subsets, in total some 50,000 persons, have been used.

of the possible anomaly. The result is that a minimum of 32 per cent of 'housekeepers' who were heads of households or relatives of the head are fairly unambiguously marked as having been reallocated to the residual census report category of 'persons of no stated occupations or conditions'; there are also many less clear cases, suggesting that the true extent of this reallocation was significantly higher.

Possibly more seriously, in the National Sample, about 9 per cent of married women aged between 20 and 59 and living with their husbands in England and Wales were returned only with a 'rank, profession or occupation' relating to their husband's principal economic activity (as 'labourer's wife', 'butcher's wife', 'spinner's wife', and so on). There are, however, very few enumeration districts where all married women are returned in this way and it may well often reflect not the concealment of married women's employment but the absence of anything else which could be entered against their names in the appropriate column. This is not to deny that there are some well-documented cases where there are inconsistencies in occupational recording between different enumerators in the same community, some of which do suggest under-recording of married women's employment. However, the number of well-documented examples remains small, and in the absence of much more extensive research controlling for husband's occupation and life-cycle stage, it is unclear how significant they are on a national or even a local scale.[12]

Clearly, also, the activity of those who engaged in seasonal work in sectors like agriculture and the tourist trades is not well-reported in the census, but that is arguably a correct representation of the situation at the end of March or beginning of April, where the census snapshot coincided with what in many areas was a relatively quiet time of year.

---

[12] Reviewing the footnotes supporting the case for the gross under-enumeration of married women's employment, one finds the same small number of examples used again and again. More worryingly, some writers use second-hand references, presumably without checking back to the original. The consequence is that what starts as an unsubstantiated (and probably erroneous) 'presumption' (Roberts, 'Working wives', pp. 167–8) or an undocumented 'belief' (Higgs, 'Women, occupations and work', p. 63, citing Lown, *Women and industrialization*, p. 91), or a comment on life-time employment (Roberts, *A woman's place*, p. 136) ends up as 'supporting' an assertion which implies that working-class married women's employment in London may be underestimated by two and a half times (Schmiechen, *Sweated industries*, pp. 68–9) which in turn partly underlies a further assertion that 'Women who earned wages as industrial homeworkers were especially likely to be invisible in statistical records of the nineteenth century' (Rose, *Limited livelihoods*, pp. 81–2).

This reminds us that a nineteenth-century population census was no more a budget survey than is the modern Labour Force Survey; at best it reflected—and still reflects—a situation at a particular season. As a result, when compared with a hypothetical study of year-round economic activity, it under-emphasises the significance of some forms of employment, but it also over-emphasises others. To criticise a census for failing to entirely reflect the life-time employment history of married women (as Sonya Rose, using Elizabeth Roberts' work, has implicitly done) is clearly unfair, particularly since there are very few published surveys of year-round life-time employment experience even of modern populations.[13] Moreover, as Catherine Hakim has pointed out, it is important in evaluating what to expect from a census to distinguish between work which is 'gainful', which ideally should be included, though not all women would consider home-based activities like providing domestic services for a lodger as 'an occupation'; work which is 'productive', which would normally be counted only if the product is marketed; and work which is aimed at 'expanding consumption', which, however important to the household economy, is not likely to be recorded in censuses or even in budget studies.[14]

What, though, about the criticisms of the census enumeration of factory working wives? These were clearly gainful occupations where most women were regularly employed, in 'jobs' of a 'non-domestic' kind. Clearly, no conscientious reading of the householders' or enumerators' instructions should have led to significant omission. And, indeed, on close inspection, the evidence so far available against the CEBs in this area is pretty thin. One study often footnoted in connection with doubts about the reliability of recording of women's occupations is Judy Lown's *Women and industrialization* (cited by Horrell and Humphries and, in its earlier PhD version, by Higgs). But while Lown suggests, though on the basis of no hard evidence, that many married women domestic straw plaiters, washerwomen and charwomen were under-reported in the census, her comparisons of employment

---

[13] Rose, *Limited livelihoods*, p. 230. There are, however, a few large-scale survey studies of the last 20 years in which long-term life and work histories have been collected retrospectively (for example, the *Women and employment* study and the ESRC Social Change and Economic Life Initiative). What these show, above all, is the very fragmented employment experience of many women, and, recently, also of many men. They sharpen our understanding of the often complex relationship between snapshot and life history studies, each of which has strengths for its own particular purposes.

[14] Hakim, 'Census reports', esp. p. 562; for important similar distinctions, see Pahl, *Divisions of labour*.

records at the Courtauld silk mills in Halstead with the local CEBs lead her to conclude that, among silk workers, 'there are not a great many married women . . . who evade classification'.[15] In fact, as far as I know, the only published case of significant under-enumeration of textile factory employment is John Holley's work on Walkerburn, which involved six women in the 1861 census and six in 1881.[16]

What about Horrell and Humphries' apparently devastating evidence of under-enumeration of married women's factory employment, based on comparing the 14 per cent of married women identified as employed by the present author in Preston in 1851 with the 60 per cent of the wives of factory workers reported as employed in their budget studies? Unfortunately, reference to the original source shows that Horrell and Humphries reach their conclusion only by not comparing like with like. The table they cite for Preston shows 26 per cent of all wives in the 1851 Preston enumerators' book sample as employed, and 52 per cent of these working in factory occupations, so that 14 per cent of married women in Preston were employed in factories, but this is 14 per cent of the wives of *all* men (including middle class men and men in non-factory occupations). It is quite illegitimate to compare this figure of 14 per cent with the 60 per cent of the wives of husbands in factory occupations in their budget sample, especially since only 32 per cent of married men in Preston worked in textile industries and only 22 per cent in textile factories. So what was the situation in Preston?

Married women's employment in Preston in 1851

This section of the paper uses the 10 per cent sample from the enumerators' books for Preston in 1851, originally drawn in 1965. In the light of subsequent experience, some occupations have been re-classified, and analysis is here confined to couples where both partners were resident on census night and where the husband was actively

---

[15] Lown, *Women and industrialization*, p. 91; see also fn. 12 above. Similarly, Rose, having vigorously criticised the census data, especially on homeworkers (*Limited livelihoods*, pp. 80–2, 230–2), then makes extensive use of these data, including data on Nottingham home laceworkers. For straw plaiters see chapter 5 above, pp. 97–137.

[16] Note also that both the communities which Holley studied were places where dominant firms had explicit policies to exclude married women from their works (Holley, 'Two family economies'). Evidence presented below suggests that under-enumeration at the level that Holley suggests cannot have been widespread in factory textiles in all parts of Britain.

Source: 10 per cent sample of Preston CEBs

Figure 8.1 Percentage of women in employment, by husband's occupation: Preston sample, 1851

employed.[17] This means that the results differ marginally from the figures first reported in 1971.[18]

Figure 8.1 examines married women's employment in the CEBs broken down by the occupation of their husbands. Twenty-six per cent of all wives had some recorded employment and 12 per cent worked in factories. But, of the wives of textile factory working husbands, 44 per cent were in employment, and 34 per cent worked in factories. Among all *other* married women (including wives of non-factory textile workers such as handloom weavers), only 21 per cent were in any form of employment, and a mere 5 per cent worked in factories.

Nevertheless, a figure of 34 per cent of the wives of textile workers with a factory occupation still leaves a substantial gap compared with

[17] Note, as an aside, that there is a very important distinction between the proportion of married women in employment and the proportion of wives in employment. In the 1851 census National Sample (see below), more than one-fifth of all employed married women had no spouse present.

[18] The main area of uncertainty is over the workplace of those who are recorded simply as 'weavers' (rather than 'power-loom weavers' or 'hand-loom weavers') and 'winders'. For the present purposes both these inadequately specified groups are classed as engaging in non-factory occupations, though some undoubtedly were employed in factories.

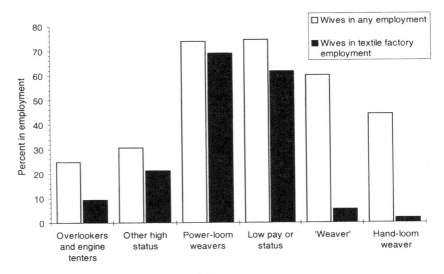

Source: 10 per cent sample of Preston CEBs

Figure 8.2 Percentage of wives of textile workers in employment, by husband's occupational group: Preston sample, 1851

Horrell and Humphries' 60 per cent. However, Figure 8.2 shows that there were very substantial variations in employment rates between the wives of men in different textile factory occupations, so comparisons must critically depend on the mix of occupations included in any non-census dataset. At one extreme (and not therefore shown on the graph), none of the wives of owners, managers and clerks employed in textile mills had a recorded occupation, and just 25 per cent of the wives of overlookers and the highly paid engine tenters; just 9 per cent of the wives of these latter groups worked in factories, and just 18 per cent of the wives of other higher paid groups like spinners and warpers. Quite different, however, was the experience of the wives of lower paid preparatory workers (for example, scutchers and carders), piecers, and factory labourers, or those whose husbands worked at the only occupation where men and women were regularly employed at the same job: power-loom weavers. Seventy-four per cent of the wives of these two groups were recorded as in employment, 62 per cent and 69 per cent respectively being in factory employment.[19]

[19] For similar findings in Clitheroe in 1881, see Rose, *Limited livelihoods*, p. 161. Note that the similarity of the employment pattern of 'weavers' and

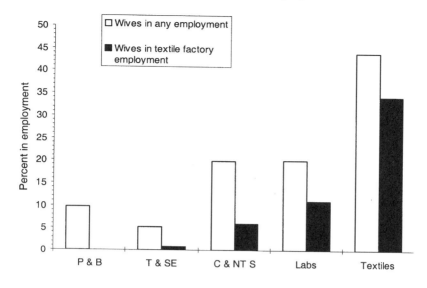

Notes: P & B   = Professional & business
        T & SE   = Trade and small employers
        C & NTS   = Craft and non-textile skilled
        Labs   = Labourers
        Textiles   = All factory textiles

Source: 10 per cent sample of Preston CEBs

Figure 8.3 Percentage of wives in employment, by husband's occupational group: Preston sample, 1851

What about the wives of non-factory workers? Figure 8.2 shows that very few wives of weavers and handloom weavers worked in textile factories. Figure 8.3 shows a marked contrast between the wives of textile factory workers and wives of the principal remaining groups of the Preston population. Very few middle-class and petit bourgeois wives had reported occupations (and almost none had factory employment). Even among men in the mass of non-textile manual occupations, only one wife in five had a reported occupation. Labourers' wives were more

'handloom weavers' in Figure 8.2 strongly suggests the likelihood that most of the former should be classified with the latter rather than with power loom weavers.

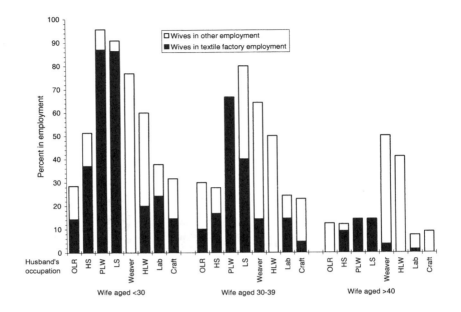

Source: 10 per cent sample of Preston CEBs
Notes: OLR   = Overlooker etc.   HS   = Other high status worker
          PLW   = Power-loom weavers LS   = Low status workers
          Weaver = Unspecified weaver HLW = Hand-loom weaver
          Craft = Craft etc.   Lab   = Labourer

**Figure 8.4 Percentage of wives in employment, by husband's occupation and
age of wife: Preston sample 1851**

likely than other non-textile groups to have factory occupations. Even
so, less than one in nine even of these wives were reported as doing
factory work. If there were large numbers of undeclared occupations, is
this especially where they will be found?

Returning to the wives of textile factory workers, there is further
reason to doubt that there was significant under-enumeration in
Preston, and this relates directly to the suggestion, made both by Higgs
and by Horrell and Humphries, that the frequently observed finding
that factory work was confined to the young and single may be a
statistical artefact of census under-reporting of married women's work.
Figure 8.4 shows the proportions of the wives of various occupational
groups with reported employment, but dividing each group of wives

into three different age groups. The results are of substantive and conceptual interest, though the small number of cases in some categories mean that the data should be treated with care. The graph shows a marked reduction in employment, and particularly in textile factory employment, as women aged. This occurs for all occupational groups (except the highly pressed families of handloom weavers where high levels of employment among married women predictably continued into late middle-age). However, the effect is much less marked among the wives of low-paid men like power–loom weavers and preparatory workers; these groups are recorded in large numbers in textile factory employment over the age of 30. Nevertheless, no group reported more than 15 per cent of their wives in textile factory employment at the age of 40 and over. It would seem difficult to identify plausible explanations of this change in terms of differential reporting by age. It thus seems reasonable to conclude that the decline in married women's textile factory employment by age is a real rather than an artefactual effect. Horrell and Humphries' conclusion is therefore almost certainly wrong.

The very high levels of reporting of occupations among younger low-paid factory textile workers also suggests that, for these occupational groups at least, reliable reporting was fairly comprehensively achieved. Ninety-six per cent of the wives of power–loom weavers aged under 30 reported some employment, as did 91 per cent of the wives of other low status factory textile workers. The very marked age effects for all occupational groups except non–factory weavers also have important implications for the use of non–census surrogates as sources for estimating overall levels of women's employment. While the census provides a representative cross-section of the population by age and family life-cycle status, representativeness is much more difficult to ensure when using other sources, such as Horrell and Humphries' budget studies. Indeed, given the interests and objectives of most of those who collected the budgets, it seems possible that they will have focused especially on families which were at the earlier and most standard-of-living critical stages of the life-cycle. They may thus have missed most of the youngest married women with no or few children who would most frequently have been in employment, but they would also have missed families at later stages of the life cycle when grown-up children were in employment and leaving home and fewer wives were working out of the home.[20] To explore these effects we move to larger data sets drawn from the National Sample from the 1851 Census of Great Britain.

[20] This is suggested by the rather large mean household sizes in Horrell and Humphries' data; see 'Old questions, new data', p. 853 and Appendix 2.

National sample data

For comparison with the Preston figures, a special dataset was prepared from the complete transcript for the 69 enumeration districts comprising the sample of Lancashire and Cheshire drawn from the 1851 census.[21] All married couples in which the husband was employed in textile manufacturing in other than a clerical or managerial capacity were selected, plus, for comparison, all couples in which the husband was a labourer of any kind (except that textile factory labourers were included under factory workers).[22] To exclude cases where occupation was not a fair reflection of the husband's income-generating capacity, couples were excluded where the husband was retired, unemployed, had a pension of some kind, or had a second occupation. The dataset contained 1,496 couples where the husband was a textile worker and 679 where he was a labourer. Occupations were grouped into the same categories as those used for the Preston analysis except that, for final presentation purposes, overseers were grouped with other high status textile factory workers.

Figure 8.5 breaks down these data by husband's occupation and age of wife, with results reassuringly similar to those for Preston. Overall, of textile factory workers whose wives were under the age of 30, 64 per cent of the wives were in employment, falling to 39 per cent for wives aged 30–39, 25 per cent for wives aged 40–49, and 8 per cent for wives of 50 and over. At least 53 per cent of textile workers' wives aged under 30 were in factory employment. At older ages, the figures fall rapidly (29 per cent at ages 30–39), with only power-loom weavers' wives continuing in factory employment in large numbers past the age of 30 (25 per cent were employed even in the age group 40–49, along with 21 per cent of the wives of lower status textile workers). While overall employment figures do not quite reach the very high levels at the younger ages recorded in the Preston data, occupational titles are given to 77 per cent of the wives of power-loom weavers under the age of 30, and 69 per cent of the wives of lower-status textile factory workers at the same age. These are clearly high levels by any criterion.

However, the highest levels of wives' employment at all age groups were found among unspecified weavers and hand-loom weavers, the figures for handloom weavers being even higher than for Preston alone.

---

[21] Strictly, there are 68 whole districts and part of one more in the sample in these counties.

[22] A small number of typically domestic textile occupations, such as wool-combing, was omitted from the analysis presented here to maintain reasonably consistent categories.

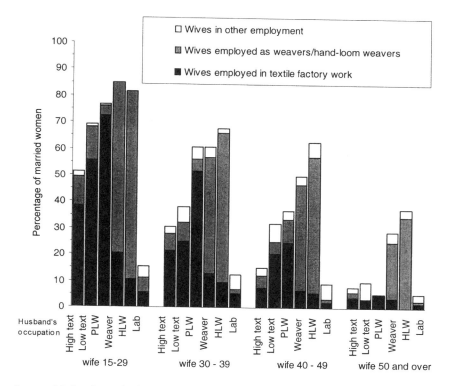

Source: National sample from the 1851 Census of Great Britain.
Notes: For key see Figure 8.4.

Figure 8.5 Percentage distribution of economic activity of married women, by own age and husband's occupation: Lancashire and Cheshire, 1851

This may reflect sampling errors from the very small numbers of these weaver groups in the youngest age category in Preston, but the Lancashire and Cheshire data also include some Cheshire silk-weaving districts, with little non-weaving employment, where entire households, even including very young children, have recorded occupations. The lower levels of employment among labourers' wives particularly reflect the large number of labourers living in the docklands areas of Birkenhead and Liverpool where there was little textile (or perhaps any other) employment for women of any kind. Indeed, one marked feature of all the data in Figure 8.5 is the very low employment rates outside textiles.

Figures 8.4 and 8.5 explored women's employment experience by reference to age. However, contemporary comment and more recent analysis strongly suggests that household economic strategies with respect to married women's employment were not so much determined by age as by: firstly, the balance struck between more income which enhanced material consumption on the one hand, and more time applied to maintaining domestic comfort on the other; and, secondly, the balance struck in allocating different kinds of family labour on the one hand to child-bearing, childcare and domestic responsibilities, and, on the other, to external resource generation. Thus, for example, referring to north Lancashire in the early twentieth century, Elizabeth Roberts has shown how 'in many families it was assumed that the mother would stop work only when the children's wages were sufficient to raise the family wage to an adequate level', or when men were promoted and incomes rose; but she also suggests that for the wife to be able to spend more time on domestic activity was a preferred option of many men *and* women, and that loss of income from termination of employment was partly compensated by reduced costs of domestic activities, notably child-minding and purchase of prepared foods.[23] Consistent with these ideas, in Preston in 1851, 44 per cent of all childless married women were in employment, 29 per cent of women with at least one child but none in employment, and just 18 per cent of those with at least one working child.

Figure 8.6 explores these life-course effects in the Lancashire and Cheshire data. Among married women under the age of 40 and with no children, employment rates are high for all groups except for the wives of labourers, who again had low levels of recorded employment at all life-cycle stages. Thus, among childless women under 40, an occupation is recorded for 85 per cent for power-loom weavers' wives, 92 per cent for hand-loom weavers' wives, and 97 per cent for the wives of unspecified weavers. Levels of under-recording of employment for these groups are clearly very low indeed. Substantively, they clearly suggest that it was normal for wives of the poorest textile workers to remain in employment until a first child was born. However, even among high status textile workers, 71 per cent of childless wives were

---

[23] Roberts, 'Working wives', pp. 144–8. A contrasting view of the pattern of employment over the life-cycle is, however, portrayed for primarily unskilled workers in three poor areas of London in August, 'How separate a sphere', esp. p. 298. In August's data, census-recorded employment is relatively flat across the life-cycle , but is at its lowest levels among those with small children, reflecting, he argues, the primacy of domestic care responsibilities at this period of life.

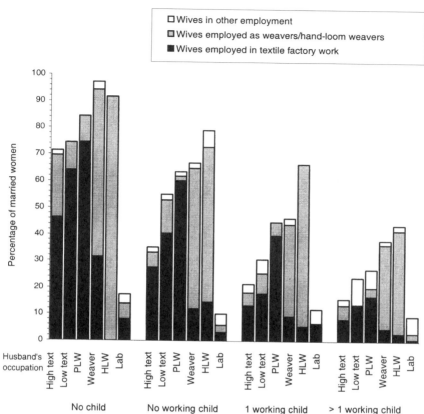

Source: National sample from the 1851 Census of Great Britain.
Notes: Data for the 'no child' categories are for wives under 40 only.
For key see Figure 8.4

Figure 8.6 Percentage distribution of stated occupations of married women, by husband's occupation and employment of children: Lancashire and Cheshire, 1851

in employment (among overlookers and engine tenters the figure was still 62 per cent), though it is interesting that, in contrast to the wives of other factory workers, significant numbers of the employed childless wives of higher status groups were engaged in domestic rather than factory textile work.

The birth of children led to a significant reduction in textile factory employment; 61 per cent of all wives of childless textile factory workers were in factory employment, compared with 40 per cent of the wives of those with at least one child but none in employment. However, inspection of the data suggest that the withdrawal from the labour force was by no means always immediate. Rather it was entry of children into the labour market that was associated with a marked reduction of wives' employment, except among power-loom and other weavers.[24] Among the wives of factory textile workers with one working child, only 19 per cent were in factory work, and among those with more than one working child the figure was a mere 12 per cent overall (17 per cent among the wives of power-loom weavers and a mere 6 per cent among the wives of overlookers and engine tenters), though the lower-paid groups compensated somewhat for the fall in textile factory earnings by increasing their levels of employment in non-textile work, including small shopkeeping and a range of outdoor domestic service activities.

To sum up so far, the patterns revealed by Figures 8.5 and 8.6, corresponding as they do with much contemporary and later commentary, confirm suggestions earlier in this paper that textile factory (and, indeed, all textile) work is well recorded by census enumerators' books in Lancashire and Cheshire.[25] Detailed examination of the 69 books from which the data are drawn supports this view. While a small number of enumerators do use the 'wife of' formula quite regularly, there is no book in which no wives are given occupations, and none in textile manufacturing areas which do not record a plausible number of wives in textile-related occupations. Indeed, with only a couple of possible exceptions, far from being suspicious about lax recording of women's occupations, what is striking is how many of the books create an impression of great care in this respect, with enumerators explicitly recording 'housework', 'housekeeper', 'domestic duties', or 'at home' against many of those wives and children of textile workers who one might have most have otherwise suspected of having been in unrecorded textile work.

So, textile employment seems to be fairly well recorded in Lancashire and Cheshire. But what about the very large numbers of women, particularly at older age groups, who are allocated no specific occupational title by the enumerators? Did they really do no gainful work and what, in particular, are we to make of the almost total lack of occupations attached to the wives of labourers in many districts? One partial answer to these questions comes from consideration of the role of women as 'lodging providers'. In this connection, various scholars

---

[24] Compare also Rose, *Limited livelihoods*, p. 165.

[25] A similar conclusion was reached by Rose in her study of women's employment in Clitheroe: Rose, *Limited livelihoods*, esp. p. 81.

have cited Leonore Davidoff's work on landladies and lodgers as evidence for under-reporting of married women's occupations, but Davidoff herself is more circumspect, pointing to the ambiguous position, at the intersection of the market and domestic economies, of most of the women in whose households the census classified some residents as 'lodgers', 'boarders' or 'visitors'.[26] Nationally, in Great Britain in 1851, lodgers or boarders were present in almost one household in eight, with substantial numbers of other households having visitors or adult relatives many, perhaps most, of whom paid for their board. In all, it seems likely that at least one-fifth of all households in Britain had one or more members who was not part of the conjugal family of the head and who was making some net financial contribution to the household economy. A majority of these 'lodgers' in the broad sense of the word were male, most were single and aged between 12 and 40, and substantial proportions in all areas were migrants, notably migrants from Ireland. More than half of lodgers specifically identified as such by the census enumerators lived in households where they were either the only lodger or one of just two.[27]

While income from lodgers made up just 3 per cent of average household income among the working classes in York at the turn of the nineteenth century, this still means that, if only one household in five had such lodgers (and it was probably significantly fewer than this), lodgers still contributed on average one-fifteenth of the income of those who took them in.[28] One 1851 Preston census enumerator reported that adult lodgers paid between 1s. and 2s. 6d. per week if, as most did, they ate meals at the same table as the rest of the household but provided their own food. Elsewhere in Lancashire, contemporary reports suggest payment averaging between 1s. and 1s. 6d. per week (sometimes including coals and candles), with a few extra pence for housewives who took responsibility for cooking the lodger's food.[29] On this basis, taking in two lodgers might contribute net to the household budget about one-third of what a woman might earn gross as a power-loom weaver

[26] Davidoff, 'Separation of home and work?'; Horrell and Humphries, 'Women's labour force participation', p. 95; Higgs, 'Women, occupations and work', p. 63, confines his specific comment to citing this paper as evidence of an area of ambiguity, but misleadingly terms the women involved as 'lodging-house keepers', missing one of Davidoff's key points and giving the activity of most of those involved a spurious degree of scale and business formality. Davidoff notes in 'Separation of home and work?', pp. 66–7, that the distinction between these categories is often arbitrary.

[27] For more detail, see Anderson, 'Households, families and individuals'.

[28] Rowntree, *Poverty*, p. 83.

[29] For more detail see Anderson, *Family structure*, p. 47.

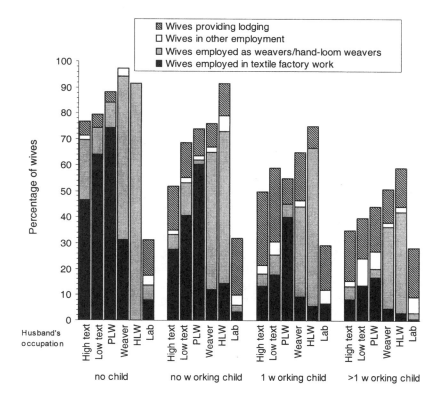

Source: National sample from the 1851 Census of Great Britain.
Notes: Data for the 'no child' categories are for wives under 40 only.
        For key see Figure 8.4

Figure 8.7 Percentage distribution of identified economic activity of married women, by husband's occupation and employment of children: Lancashire and Cheshire, 1851

(maybe half of what she might earn net) and at least one-fifth of what her husband might earn as a factory labourer. Where, as seems often to have been the case, care was provided for babies and small children of lodgers, further income will normally have accrued.

In Figure 8.7, women from the Lancashire and Cheshire data set who have been identified as 'lodging providers' have been added to the numbers in employment. Just who should qualify for inclusion in a 'lodging provider' category is a matter of judgment, since some co-resident non-conjugal family members were clearly not net providers of resource to the household (for example, some were illegitimate babies of resident unmarried daughters), and some older resident kin probably contributed by providing household services which enabled the wife of the head to remain in the labour market. For this reason, married women are only counted as lodging providers in Figure 8.7 where the household contains one or more lodger or visitor or relative (including married or widowed children if they themselves have children present) with a stated occupation and without a partner or child of their own capable of providing housework services on their behalf. This definition thus excludes married-couple lodgers where there is a non-working wife present, and it also excludes young children even where they are listed as 'nurse child' or 'orphan' with the possibility that some cash recompense might have been provided. The vast majority of these 'lodging providers' were therefore generating net income for their households and providing some domestic service on behalf of those who lived with them.

As Figure 8.7 shows, adding lodging providers to those with stated occupations markedly increases the numbers with some gainful economic activity, especially at older age groups and among better paid textile factory workers and labourers with children. For example, 8 per cent of childless overlookers' wives were lodging providers as defined here, rising to 27 per cent of such wives with children none of whom were employed, and 26 per cent of those with one employed child, then falling to 20 per cent of those with two or more working children. Comparable figures for low status textile workers are 5 per cent of the childless, 14 per cent of those with no working children and 28 per cent and 16 per cent of those with one and more than one working child respectively. In all families of factory textile workers, 5 per cent of childless wives were lodging providers, 14 per cent of those with only non-employed children, 25 per cent of those with one employed child and 18 per cent of those with more than one such child. Nineteen per cent of the wives of unclassified weavers with one employed child were lodging providers. Among labourers, such provision of lodging was undertaken by 22 per cent of the wives of labourers with children none of whom were in employment, and 18 per cent of those with one or more than one employed children. The effect of this is to treble the proportion of labourers' wives with any children who had an identifiable gainful activity from 10.2 per cent to 30.6 per cent. Among other groups, the inclusion of lodging provision only raises the proportion of childless textile factory workers with gainfully active wives from 77 per cent to 82 per cent and of all childless textile workers' wives from 82 per cent to 85 per cent. But among those in the still

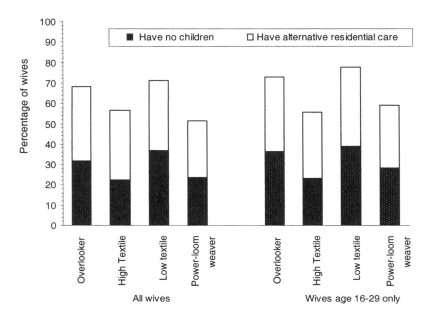

Figure 8.8 Percentage of factory working wives with no children or with alternative residential care for children: Lancashire and Cheshire, 1851

costly stage of the life-course where just one child was in employment, the figures for all factory textile workers' wives rise from 29 per cent to 54 per cent and for all textile workers' wives from 38 per cent to 60 per cent.

This lodging provision has a reverse side, also relevant for married women's employment and for their roles as wives and mothers. Most of the lodgers and financially-contributing relatives were unmarried, widowed or separated. But significant numbers were not; they were married and some had children. For these wives, living with a relative or other provider of housekeeping services allowed them to earn while delegating some housework and child care services to someone else. Some heads' wives also delegated these tasks to a co-resident relative (often a widowed mother) or specifically allocated them to a daughter, sometimes explicitly designating that person in their enumeration return as 'at home' or 'domestic duties' or 'housekeeper'. Figure 8.8 looks at the wives of factory textile workers who were themselves in textile factory employment. Overall, 27 per cent of these women had no children. Another 34 per cent had at least one child but also had a potential carer available in their house, in the form of an unoccupied female aged 8 years or over. For wives under the age of 30, who were most likely to have had dependent children, the comparable figures are 30 per cent with no children and 33 per cent with a potential carer available. Among power-loom weavers, as Figure 8.8 shows, over half of all wives and nearly three-fifths of wives aged less than 30 had either no children or a potential carer available. If we focus just on textile factory workers with a child under one year of age and no potential residential care alternative, just 8.5 per cent had wives in textile factory employment.

Conclusion

There is thus little evidence to support an argument for widespread under-recording of factory and domestic textile employment in Lancashire and Cheshire; for this group at least we can go on placing considerable trust in the census figures. Substantively, large numbers of married women continued to work in textile factories after marriage, some left when they had children and most by the time their children entered the labour force. A majority of those who continued in employment once they had children had husbands in lower paid employment and nearly half had someone else in their households who could provide household services and childcare. In a highly integrated system of interlocking family economies, most factory textile workers' wives, on leaving factory employment, almost certainly then focused most of their economic activities on what, in the absence of modern domestic technology, was potentially a full-time activity: improving the standards of life of their family by devoting more time to housekeeping, by preparing and cooking more of their own food, by spending more time in seeking bargains in the market and, no doubt, by a range of self-provisioning (productive but not gainful) activities. Many, however, supplemented the family's income to a significant degree by also providing these services to continuing full-time factory workers, including some married women who remained in textile factory employment. Among the wives of handloom weavers, most of whom worked on looms in their own home, combining household duties and productive activity was both easier and an economic necessity, given the appallingly low wages in this activity by the middle of the century. Two Lancashire enumerators specifically recognised this dual function by recording the occupations of women as 'weaver and housekeeper' or 'handloom weaver and lodging-house keeper'.[30]

---

[30] Similar inter-meshing of gainful and domestic work among poorer sections of the population is suggested by Rose, *Limited livelihoods*, pp. 86–8.

So, textile workers offer little cause for anxiety over the comprehensiveness of the recording of their paid employment. But what about the low recording of the wives of craftsmen, traders and labourers? Among the first two of these groups, we must accept that many, on a quite regular basis, assisted or participated in their husband's activities, though the extent and amount of this varied from occupation to occupation; there were probably also some life-course effects, a subject that needs further research. It is, however, important not to be over-critical of the census for not including more of these women as 'occupied'.[31] Their activities will seldom have been separately remunerated (and therefore not 'gainful' in Hakim's terms), would very often therefore not have been seen by themselves as 'an occupation' or even as 'work', and certainly will not affect our estimates of total household income.[32] Moreover, in as far as there was under-enumeration here, it continued into the present century and may not markedly affect our assessment of trends over time (and, indeed, how many shopkeepers', GPs', or MPs' wives declared their considerable contribution to their husbands' work activity to the last census?). This, however, is another area where some more sensitive, life-course based, analysis of larger samples may prove fruitful in the future.

Finally, what about the activities of labourers' wives, who could not in most cases participate directly in their husband's work? It is easy to assume that many of these women 'must' have engaged in some kind of earning activity, perhaps as homeworkers of some kind.[33] If they did

---

[31] In the published census reports for 1851 and 1861 and, for England and Wales, 1871, all the otherwise unoccupied wives of a small number of trade and craft occupations were allocated by the census authorities to the 'occupied' categories. It would clearly be open to those using enumerators' books to do the same thing for these and any other women who they believed were most probably contributors to their husbands' activity.

[32] On homeworking as not seen as 'work' see, among others, Rose, *Limited livelihoods*, pp. 82, 232.

[33] The most blatant example of the use of assumption and assertion to replace historical evidence is in Alexander, Davin and Hostettler, 'Labouring women'. Their discussion, frequently cast in terms like, 'Can we really conceive that . . . ?', and extrapolating from non-quantitatively grounded examples of casual and seasonal work without any assessment of its scale or financial significance, is based on an assertion that most labouring, and maybe most working-class, women would have wanted to work whenever they could (ignoring the significant drawbacks in terms of domestic comforts and their own energy input) and appears to assume that in most cases remunerative work acceptable to them and to their husbands was available. A similar intuitive and quantitatively unsubstantiated attack on the census, apparently ignoring the important implications for married women's employment of its (correctly)

Table 8.1 Employed labourer's wives by place and type of employment

	All	Number 'employed' by occupation of husband				All 'employed'	'Employed' %	Possible Home work %
		Possible Home work	Factory Textile	Non-factory Textile	Labourer			
Broughton	26	0	0	1	1	2	7.7	0.0
Withnel	**10**	**0**	**1**	**0**	**0**	**1**	**10.0**	**0.0**
Chester	19	1	0	0	0	1	5.3	5.3
Birkenhead	81	2	0	0	0	2	2.5	2.5
Liverpool	129	4	0	0	1	5	3.9	3.1
Toxteth	20	1	0	0	0	1	5.0	5.0
Toxteth	28	0	0	0	0	0	0.0	0.0
Everton	13	0	0	0	0	0	0.0	0.0
West Darby	16	0	0	0	0	0	0.0	0.0
Latchford	**21**	**1**	**0**	**0**	**1**	**2**	**9.5**	**4.8**
Manchester	10	2	0	0	1	3	30.0	20.0
Preston	**13**	**2**	**3**	**2**	**1**	**8**	**61.5**	**15.4**
Preston	**11**	**0**	**2**	**2**	**0**	**4**	**36.4**	**0.0**
Bury	**12**	**1**	**1**	**2**	**0**	**4**	**33.3**	**8.3**
Werneth	**12**	**1**	**3**	**0**	**0**	**4**	**33.3**	**8.3**
Wavertree	12	2	0	0	0	2	16.7	16.7
Heap	**11**	**0**	**0**	**1**	**0**	**1**	**9.1**	**0.0**
Walton-l'Dale	**13**	**0**	**4**	**0**	**0**	**4**	**30.8**	**0.0**
Macclesfield	**13**	**0**	**3**	**2**	**0**	**5**	**38.5**	**0.0**
Sanbach	10	0	1	0	0	1	10.0	0.0
Ashton-under-Lyne	**18**	**0**	**1**	**0**	**0**	**1**	**5.6**	**0.0**
Over Darwen	**20**	**0**	**0**	**4**	**0**	**4**	**20.0**	**0.0**

Note: Enumeration districts shown in bold have substantial textile employment

engage in this kind of work on a large scale, however, we must also assume that every enumerator in the Lancashire and Cheshire sample failed to include most of them, for a close inspection reveals how very few non-textile manufacturing jobs are recorded for labourers' wives in any of the enumerators' books examined. This is particularly true outside the textile manufacturing centres (see Table 8.1, which is confined to the EDs which include at least ten labourers' wives). Of course, and importantly, this does not mean that labourers' wives were not actively engaged in non-gainful but productive or consumption-enhancing activities, through foraging, self-provisioning and in many other ways.[34] Some were gainfully providing lodging services. Also, most of them, at some points in their lives, had probably sought, not always successfully, to earn money in periods of crisis or when opportunity arose, so that the census snapshot does not reflect the total numbers who may have made some economic contribution at some time in the past or who would do so at some time in the future.

Nevertheless, in terms of what a census, taken on one day, might be reasonably expected to record as a gainful (and certainly as a significantly gainful) occupation, the fact that so few labourers' wives were allocated an occupation by any enumerator must raise the possibility that levels of omission were in fact relatively low. In part, rather, low levels of gainful activity occurred because, like the wives of miners elsewhere, many wives were deeply embroiled in childcare and heavy domestic tasks, and had children who brought in significant amounts of money from diverse formal and informal resource-generating activities.[35] In addition, many, and particularly those living in docklands areas, (and again like the wives of miners) lived in places with few local opportunities for women's paid employment (at least relative to the large potential labour supply which included not only

snapshot character, is Alexander, 'Women's work in nineteenth-century London', esp. pp. 64–6.

[34] On which see, for example, Roberts, *A woman's place*, esp. pp. 148–63; Rose, *Limited livelihoods*, esp. pp. 80–1; Ross, *Love and toil*, esp. pp. 51–5, 81–4.

[35] The casual income-generating activities of children are, in fact, far more extensively referred to in the literature and in contemporary sources than are married women's gainful activities, and most budget studies suggest that their contribution in cash terms was significantly more important than those of wives; see Horrell and Humphries, 'Women's labour force participation', esp. pp. 102–3; Davin, *Growing up poor*, esp. chapter 9. Ross, *Love and toil*, p. 159, also notes that employed children expected higher standards of domestic comfort, perhaps a further incentive for mothers not to engage too heavily in gainful work themselves.

themselves but unmarried daughters and widows).[36] Moreover, a careful reading of Horrell and Humphries' paper seems actually to confirm the low contribution to the household economy of most urban married women. Overall, for the period 1846–1865, nearly half the married women in their budget data set had either a recorded occupation or non-zero earnings, though, as noted above, life-cycle variations in labour-force participation by married women probably inflates this figure compared with the population as a whole, and there must be some suspicion that families with a wide spread of income sources would have been especially likely to be selected for inclusion in budget studies in a largely pre-statistical age.[37]

Some of Horrell and Humphries' most interesting figures, however, are those which, for households where women's share is separately identifiable, show the wife's contribution to total family income.[38] Ignoring agricultural families, where some seasonal income is a well-known feature (though not one that a snapshot Spring census should have recorded in many areas), there are seven sets of observations, covering four different occupational groups and two different time periods between 1841 and 1865 (there are no cases in one of these cells, thus reducing the total from eight to seven). In only one set of observations does the mean contribution of married women to the family budget exceed 12 per cent of total family income, and this relates to a single textile family. In only one other case does the figure exceed 10 per cent. The weighted average of all seven cases is 2.5 per cent.[39]

---

[36] Jordan, 'Female unemployment'. One of the most fascinating and surely significant features of Ellen Ross's brilliant *Love and toil* is how seldom the women she studies, however hard-pressed they may be, seem to resort to the labour market, perhaps in part because they would not then have so easily been able to participate so readily in the economically vital women's networks and in the foraging and other non-gainful productive activities which she describes (see also Ross, 'Survival networks'). Even August's study, 'How separate a sphere', the abstract of which claims that 'employment was common', actually finds just 20 per cent of married women in employment and comments specifically on the relative availability of jobs in different areas: 'How separate a sphere', pp. 285, 301.

[37] Horrell and Humphries, 'Women's labour force participation', p. 98.

[38] Horrell and Humphries, 'Women's labour force participation', pp. 102–3.

[39] Even if the mean is calculated across all 19 sets of observations between 1787 and 1865, the share contributed by married women still averages out at less than 7 per cent. The share of family income contributed by wives in the ten labourers' budgets given by Rowntree in *Poverty: a study of town life* ranges from zero to 19.9 per cent with a mean of 5.8 per cent and a median of 4.9 per cent. As an example of selective illustration, note that all of Rowntree's selected married couple-headed families had children, none of whom contributed to the family budget.

Bearing in mind that some women had occupations producing considerably more than this tiny sum, the proportional contribution of the rest must have been tiny. This is not, of course, to deny its importance to the family's viability at particularly critical periods of time, but it does raise questions as to whether it would have been more rather less misleading had the 'job' it reflects featured in a census return.

So, the census undoubtedly did under-record non-agricultural married women's employment, but how significantly remains an open question. Unless we can find alternative and representative sources allowing firm estimates of the proportionate contribution to family incomes of casual and part-time work, the census enumerators' books must remain, for many parts of the country at least, the best indicator that we have of variations in married women's gainful work activity in the mid-nineteenth century.

9

Who worked when? Lifetime profiles of labour-force participation in Cardington and Corfe Castle in the late eighteenth and mid-nineteenth centuries

OSAMU SAITO

Introduction

At what age did people enter the labour force in the past? When did individuals stop working? These are straightforward questions, yet little systematic investigation has so far been made to answer them.[1] One simple method of exploring these issues is to examine the percentage of males or females in each age group who were employed. For this the CEBs are well-suited as a source. In order to gain a chronological perspective, pre-census listings of inhabitants are also analysed for Cardington, Bedfordshire, in 1782 and Corfe Castle, Dorset, in 1790, both of which are exceptionally detailed and of census-like quality.[2] A sample page from each of these two listings is reproduced on pp. 210, 212 and 213 (Figures 9.1 and 9.2). Using these sources, this chapter will analyse age and sex-specific patterns of participation in the labour force. Emphasis will also be laid on the position of the individual in the family with respect to labour supply, and the effects of cottage industry on the wife and children of the family.

The communities of Cardington and Corfe Castle

Cardington and Corfe Castle were both located in a rural setting and

---

[1] Exceptions include Conrad, 'Emergence of modern retirement'; Laslett, *Fresh map of life*, pp. 122–39; Thomas, 'Age and authority'; Plakans, 'Stepping down'.

[2] Baker, *Inhabitants of Cardington*; Hutchins, *History and antiquities of Dorset*.

1st Jany 1782. CARDINGTON. 1.

Cottage N° 1.

		Age. Y.	M.	D.
Occupier	Essex Hartop Lab^r Born at Keysur	43	–	–
Wife	Elizabeth, Maiden-name Billen, Born at Cardington And late Wid^w of William Urine. S.L.	46	–	–
Children.	By first Husband viz.			
1st	Elizabeth, Married at Warden	27	–	–
2d	Hannah, Married at Meppershall	24	–	–
Children	By her Present Husband viz.			
3d	Thomas. Works for Mr Whitbread	17	–	–
4th	Mary.	16	–	–
5th	Phebe S.L.	14	–	–
6th	Joseph Billen. at School by Mr Howard.	10	–	–

☞ Note, That S.L. means Spins Linen: S.J. Spins Jersey. S.L.&J. Spins Linen & Jersey; and M.L. makes Lace.

Figure 9.1 Sample page from the list of inhabitants of Cardington, 1782

had some similarities and some differences in economic structure. Neither Bedfordshire nor Dorset was a rich county at the turn of the century. In 1803, for example, poor-relief expenditure per head in the two counties was at about the same level, well above the average for England and Wales of about 9s., whilst the figures for the two parishes themselves, at 22s. for Cardington and 19s. for Corfe Castle, were even higher than the county averages for Bedfordshire and Dorset respectively.[3] But, as these figures suggest, Cardington may have suffered from economic difficulties at the turn of the century more than Corfe Castle. For the former parish, agriculture was the only form of employment for men, which meant it was difficult for them to be in constant employment throughout the year.[4] As a result, the majority of male children were sent out to work in service in neighbouring parishes.[5] In comparison, Corfe Castle had a small market town within the parish and its economy encompassed not only farming and trade but also other activities such as clay-cutting. This basic difference in occupational structures can be seen in Table 9.1. For the women and children of both parishes, textiles and clothing industries of the domestic type offered employment opportunities. In Cardington, lace making and spinning were carried out by women and female children, while spinning and knitting were found in Corfe Castle, although Corfe women, especially married women, were much less involved in industrial activity than were Cardington women.

Changes in local economic structure over the first half of the nineteenth century also affected the two parishes differently. It seems clear from Table 9.1 on p. 214 that there were no significant shifts in occupational structure of male household heads, which was the core of the whole economic structure. Lace making, too, which does not appear in the table, is likely to have recovered from the recession after the French Wars, despite the severe competition from its machine-based counterpart, and still occupied many Bedfordshire women in the

---

[3] BPP 1803–4, *Abstract of the Answers and Returns made pursuant to the Act 43 Geo. 3, relative to the Expense and Maintenance of the Poor.* Population figures are taken from the 1801 Census. Studies of both Bedfordshire and Dorset poor law administration and practice indicate that increases in poor expenditure in this period were not the results of maladministration but responses to growing economic distress. Therefore, we may rely upon per capita expenditure as a rough guide to the poverty problem in each parish. See Grey, 'Pauper problem in Bedfordshire', and Body, 'Administration of the poor laws'.

[4] Stone, *Agriculture of the County of Bedford, 1794,* cited by Marshall, *Reports to the Board of Agriculture,* p. 561.

[5] Schofield, 'Age-specific mobility'; Wall, 'Age at leaving home'; Schürer, 'Role of the family'.

Table: List of inhabitants of Corfe Castle, 1790

HOUSEKEEPERS — Males: Name	Condition	Age	Occupation	HOUSEKEEPERS — Females: Name	Condition	Age	Occupation	RESIDENCE	CHILDREN & GRANDCHILDREN — Males: Name	Age	Occupation	Females: Name	Age	Occupation	Name
Wm. Langtree	Married	38		Sarah Jenkins	Widow	66	Knits	Mark-pl.	Wm. Langtree	13	Breechesmaker	Mary Langtree	9		
			Butcher	Ann Rolles	Spinster	38	Baker	Ditto	Tho. Langtree	12		Eliz. Langtree	4		
Robert Whitcher	Bachelor	35	Claycutter	Martha Langtree	Married	38		Ditto	Mary Langtree	1					John Trent
William Smith	Married	32	Fisherman	Susanna Smith	Married	29		— / High-str.	William Smith	5		Susanna Smith	4		
				Miriam House	Widow	45	Schoolmistress	Ditto	John Smith	2		Elizabeth House	24	Plain work, &c	
James Chaffey	Married	36	Baker	Frances Chaffey	Married	32		Ditto	James Chaffey	7		Miriam House	22	Plain work, &c	
									William Chaffey	4		Susannah House	18	Plain work, &c	Joseph Chaffy
									John Chaffey	1½		Sarah Chaffey	9		
									Henry Chaffey	1					
Rev. John Gent	Married	49	Curate	Mary Gent	Married	29		— / Ditto	John Gent	3		Elizabeth Gent	9		
												Mary Gent	7		
												Jane Gent	1		
Robert Jenkins	Married	28	Shoemaker	Elizabeth Damon	Spinster	60	Knits	Ditto	Joseph Jenkins	1		Mary Jenkins	2		Henry Brown
William Butler	Married	60	Blacksmith	Ann Jenkins	Married	28		Ditto							
John Chipp	Married	39	Blacksmith	Elizabeth Butler	Married	54		Ditto				Mary Chipp, his base daughter	13	Knits	
				Julian Webber	Widow	67	Knits, &c.	Ditto							Thomas Ridout
				Honor Chipp	Married	31		Ditto							Tho. Ridout, jun.
				Mary Dennis	Widow	70	Midwife	Ditto							John Ridout
James Keats	Married	58	Quarrier	Alice Keats	Married	62		Ditto	John Keats	18	Quarrier	Mary Keats	15	Knits	
				Mary Hibbs	Widow	74		Quaker's M. House	Joseph Keats	11	Quarrier				Barth. Welsh
Robert Hibbs	Married	73	Shoemaker	Mary Wright	Married	50	Spins Worsted	High-str.							
Thomas Wright	Married	50	Woolcomber	Ann Conway	Married	26		Ditto				Mary Conway, dau by first wife	11		
Robert Conway	Married	43	Tallow Chand.	Mary Hounsell	Married	60		Ditto	George Hounsell	23	Claycutter	Martha Hounsell	17	Knits	Henry Day
John Hounsell	Married	49	Limeburner	Elizabeth Keats	Married	21		Ditto	William Keats			Elizabeth Hibbs	13	Knits	
Charles Keats	Married	23	Quarrier	Eleanor Hibbs	Married	40		Ditto	James Hibbs	11	Labourer	Hester Hibbs	9		
Thomas Hibbs	Married	39	Claycutter	Elizabeth Paine	Widow	57	Knits	Ditto	William Hibbs	6		Jane Hibbs			
									George Hibbs	3		Mary Paine	6	Knits, &c.	
									Robert Paine	32	Labourer	Ann Paine	11	Knits, &c.	

Figure 9.2 Sample page from the list of inhabitants of Corfe Castle, 1790

LODGERS and INMATES — Males				Females				SERVANTS and APPRENTICES — Females		TOTAL per House	PROBABLE WEEKLY EARNINGS	REMARKS
Name	Condition	age/v	Occupation	Name	age/v	Condition	Occupation	Name	age/v			
John Trent		1								1 · 1	S. Jenkins, 1s. / A. Rolles, 1s. 6d.	On Parish Pay.
				Hannah Trent	28	Married	Washes, &c.			7	R. Whitcher, 10s. / H. Trent, 2s. 6d. / W. Smith, 7s. / R. Toop, 1s. 6d.	Han. Trent's Husband run away. H. Trent on Par. Pay.
				Jane Trent	2	Spinster	Knits, &c.			4 · 6		
				Ruth Toop								
				Hetty Murphy	13		Boarder			5		
Joseph Chaffey	Bachelor	21	Claycutter					Elizabeth Sheers	19	8	Jos. Chaffey, 10s.	
								Ann Senneck	18			
										0	——	Empty House
Henry Brown	Bachelor	28	Thatcher				Knits			8	E. Damon, 1s. / H. Brown, 8s.	On Parish Pay.
Thomas Ridout	Married	40	Blacksmith	Mary Chipp, his Mother	66	Widow				1	Julian Webber, 1s.	On Parish Pay.
				Jane Ridout, dau. to Mary Dennis	40	Married	Knits			5 · 2	M. Chipp, 1s. / M. Chipp, jun. 1s. 6d.	M. Chipp, jun. on Parish Pay.
Tho. Ridout, jun.		16	Blacksmith	Mary Ridout	12					4		
John Ridout		8		Ann Ridout	6							
				Jane Ridout	3		Knits			9		
				Elizabeth Ridout	1							
Barth. Welsh	Married	74		Urs. Welsh, husb., d. of M. Hibbs	50	Married				5	James Keats, 15s. / John Keats, 10s. / Jos. Keats, 6s. / Mary Keats, 1s. 6d.	M. Hibbs, and B. Welsh, on Parish Pay. Mary Hibbs, jun. on Parish Pay. An Idiot. Robert Hibbs's Wife has eloped.
				Mary Hibbs, d. of Urs. Welsh	16	Spinster	Knits			4	U. Welsh, 1s.	
Henry Day	Widower	20	Claycutter							1	J. Hounsell, 7s.	
										2	G. Hounsell, 10s.	
										3	Mary & Martha, 2s. 6d.	
										4	C. Keats, 15s.	
										4	H. Day, 10s.	
										8	Thomas Hibbs, 10s. / James Hibbs, 1s. 6d. / Elizabeth Hibbs, 1s. / Robert Paine, 7s. / Eliz. Marr. & Ann. 1s.	

Table 9.1 Occupations of male household heads

| | Cardington | | | | Corfe Castle | | | |
| | 1782* | | 1851 | | 1790 | | 1851 | |
	n	%	n	%	n	%	n	%
Agricultural								
Farmer, Fisherman	26	17.3	29	11.8	45	21.2	29	8.4
Labourer	89	59.3	146	59.3	42	19.7	84	24.3
Non-agricultural								
Tradesman, craftsman	31	20.7	64	26.0	94	44.1	106	30.7
Clay cutter					28	13.1	93	27.0
Labourer							24	7.0
Not gainfully occupied	4	2.7	7	2.8	4	1.9	9	2.6
Total	150	100.0	246	100.0	213	100.0	345	100.0

Notes:

* Unlike other tables in this chapter, this covers all households. Unspecified labourers have been assigned to the agricultural labourer category. The figures for clay cutters in Corfe Castle include quarriers in 1790 and labourers in clay pits in 1851.

1850s.[6] However, some important changes were taking place behind the seeming stability. In Bedfordshire, agriculture, which was described by Thomas Stone in his *Report* to the Board of Agriculture in 1794 as in 'a deplorable state', had improved by the mid-nineteenth century.[7] This improvement, especially in the clay lands in the northern part of the county where Cardington is located, was attributed to successful draining, which was often combined with enclosure and engrossing. Thus, in 1857, William Bennett wrote:

> At the commencement of the present century no county in England, probably, stood in need of underdraining more than Bedfordshire, and within that period few counties have made greater progress in this department of good husbandry.[8]

In Dorset, on the other hand, while the clay industry was still prosperous in the 1850s, cottage industries, such as stocking-knitting

---

[6] For children see Horn, 'Child workers', pp. 781–2.

[7] Marshall, *Reports to the Board of Agriculture*, p. 561.

[8] Bennett, 'Farming of Bedfordshire', p. 4. Moreover, it seems that the judgement expressed in various forms that land was under-utilised had already disappeared by the 1840s: personal communication from Peter Grey, formerly of Bedford College of Education.

which was found in Corfe Castle in 1790, had disappeared as a result of competition from the east Midlands.[9] Spinning, the other industrial activity that occupied the Corfe females in 1790, and which had been introduced originally to provide jobs for the poor, could already be described by a contemporary in the mid–1790s as a failure.[10]

Thus the analysis which follows is of two communities with different economic circumstances, which can be summarised as follows. In Cardington in 1782, the problem of poverty arising from the instability of employment in farming must have been very serious, although the cottage industries offered ample employment opportunities to women and children. In 1851, however, agriculture could employ more men than in 1782, while a large number of females were still engaged in industrial activities. In Corfe Castle in 1790, males had a wider occupational choice than in Cardington and there were also employment opportunities for females. However, in 1851, while the major industry which employed males was still thriving, the industrial employment for females had all but disappeared. It is against this economic background that the patterns of labour force participation will be discussed.

The sources

Before the analysis is presented, the main sources used should be evaluated, especially in terms of the extent to which they recorded occupations accurately. First, it must be realised that the CEBs do not provide a complete picture of employment. The main concern of the General Register Office was to collect information on the numbers in gainful employment. Thus, adult males in full-time paid employment tend to be recorded quite accurately. Equally, those *usually* in full-time work but otherwise temporarily out of work should also have been recorded as such by the enumerators. Yet for others in more marginal forms of employment, those employed part-time or on a casual basis, for example, the situation is less certain.[11] The 1851 census for Corfe Castle lists a small number of individuals as 'occasionally works on farm', 'weeding' or 'stone picking', yet this is the exception rather than the rule. As a result, the enumeration of the work undertaken by women and children is especially problematic. In the case of farmers, the census

[9] Body, 'Administration of the poor laws', p. 45.
[10] Hutchins, *History and antiquities of Dorset*, p. 276.
[11] Higgs, *Clearer sense*, pp. 95–112; Mills and Schürer, 'Employment and occupations'; Morris, 'Fuller values, questions and contexts'.

of 1851 explicitly instructed that sons or daughters employed at home or on the farm should be returned as 'Farmer's son' etc., and the sample page on how to complete the census schedule gave an example of a 'Farmer's wife', on the assumption that the family of the householder would be actively involved in the work of the farm.[12] Despite the fact that the 1851 census, like those of the 1861–81, instructed that 'the occupations of women who are regularly employed from home, or at home, in any but domestic duties, [are] to be distinctly recorded', evidence points to the fact that the employment of women was prone to under-enumeration, especially when their work was on an infrequent or informal basis.[13] The same is also true of children.[14] In short, in instructing their enumerators and processing the information on employment, the officials of the General Register Office clung rather too rigidly to the simplistic and idealised notion of an adult male 'breadwinner' head of household providing for his dependent family.[15]

Since both the listings of inhabitants for Cardington and Corfe Castle were 'one off' enumerations lacking the formal procedures and administration of the CEBs, it is not so easy to comment on the completeness with which employment was recorded. Generally, like the CEBs, adult males seem to be reasonably fully recorded, yet in the case of Cardington there are two notable and unfortunate omissions. Unlike the CEBs, the families of farmers, including sons, are not designated by an occupational description. Also, although the Cardington survey provides unique information on the occupation of children of families who were resident in the village, information is lacking on servants employed in Cardington who came to the parish to work from the surrounding villages. Consequently, in the analysis that follows, the children of farmers are excluded from the Cardington figures, as are all living-in servants. Other minor adjustments are noted in the subsequent tables.

Age and sex-specific participation rates

The proportion of men and women in each age group employed in Cardington and Corfe Castle at the end of the eighteenth century and in 1851 is shown in Table 9.2, and diagrammatically in Figures 9.3 and 9.4.

---

[12] Due to the vagaries of the recording of farmers and other agricultural occupations the overall numbers working in agriculture presented in the published census reports has been questioned: Higgs, 'Occupational censuses'; Wrigley, 'Men on the land'.

[13] Higgs, 'Women, occupations and work'; Garrett, 'Women's work'.

[14] Davin, 'Working or helping?'

[15] Horrell and Humphries, 'Women's labour force participation'.

Table 9.2 Labour force participation rates by age and sex

Age group	Males								Females							
	Cardington				Corfe Castle				Cardington				Corfe Castle			
	1782		1851		1790		1851		1782		1851		1790		1851	
	%	n	%	n	%	n	%	n	%	n	%	n	%	n	%	n
5–9	0.0	39	9.8	112	10.8	83	0.0	124	23.3	43	39.0	77	13.3	83	0.7	137
10–14	2.4	42	66.3	98	55.3	76	36.4	129	66.7	39	64.9	74	69.7	76	10.7	92
15–19	80.0	5	94.7	76	96.5	57	98.2	110	80.8	26	77.9	77	79.2	53	40.5	111
20–24	80.0	10	92.6	54	92.7	41	93.9	66	79.3	29	76.3	59	67.4	43	38.7	62
25–29	95.0	20	93.0	57	100.0	36	100.0	71	89.5	19	72.1	61	42.1	57	21.4	70
30–34	94.1	17	97.7	43	100.0	38	96.4	55	87.0	23	67.3	49	34.3	35	8.7	46
35–39	100.0	12	100.0	34	100.0	46	100.0	47	73.7	19	62.5	48	24.3	37	13.2	53
40–44	100.0	15	96.8	31	100.0	23	98.3	59	61.9	21	52.9	34	34.6	26	13.0	54
45–49	100.0	16	100.0	28	100.0	24	97.9	48	72.2	18	59.4	32	22.2	27	2.9	34
50–54	100.0	15	96.6	29	100.0	22	100.0	28	35.7	14	50.0	24	39.3	28	17.6	34
55–59	90.0	11	96.2	26	100.0	18	95.2	21	50.0	10	60.0	25	26.3	19	19.2	26
60+	81.0	21	87.5	40	88.5	61	84.7	72	46.7	15	67.3	49	36.7	60	8.2	85

Notes: This table excludes all cases where age is unknown and, for Cardington in 1782, farmers, clergymen and persons of independent means and their families and servants.

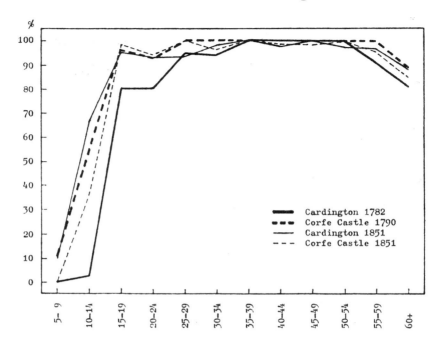

Figure 9.3 Age-specific profiles of labour force participation: males

It is clear from the two graphs that the profile for males does not vary a great deal. In all cases, except in Cardington in 1782, the rate of participation rises sharply to the age of 15, remains on a plateau during the prime working ages, and falls in the age group 60+. This pattern suggests that the age of 15 saw boys rush into the labour force in the form of either going into service away from the parental home or taking employment at home; that almost all males aged between 15 and 59 had a gainful occupation; and that some of them began to stop working after the age of 60. For Cardington in 1782, the labour-force participation rates for ages 15–19 and 20–24 are fairly low, but as the low number of observations in Table 9.2 suggest, this may be due to strikingly high rates of out-migration: 78 per cent and 85 per cent of the boys in these age groups were away from home, most of them being in service outside the village.[16] The Cardington pattern in 1782 is also distorted by the fact that the servant population in the village is not included. If it were possible to include them, the pattern would be much closer to that displayed by the three other cases.

[16] Schofield, 'Age-specific mobility', p. 265; Wall, 'Age at leaving home', Table 2.

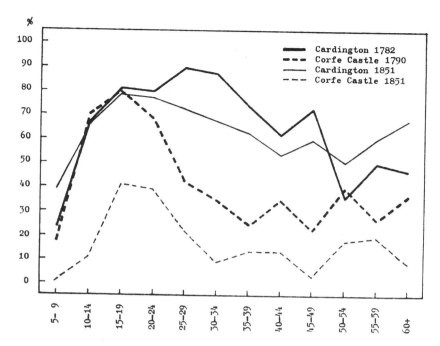

Figure 9.4 Age-specific profiles of labour force participation: females

As regards the profile for females, marked differences are found. Each pattern seems distinct, but if the levels of participation are ignored, a dividing line can be drawn between the two parishes. In Corfe Castle, both in 1790 and 1851, the rates of participation rise rapidly, reaching a peak in the age group 15–19, come down quickly to a low level, and then show a slight upward turn (although the latter is almost obscured by fluctuations in the rate between age groups). In Cardington in 1782, on the other hand, the rate continues to rise until the age group 25–29, and the lowest point does not occur in early adulthood but in the age group 50–54. In 1851, although a peak is apparent in the age group 15–19, as in Corfe Castle, the rate shows a more gradual decline after this peak than Corfe and a shallower trough in the age group 50–54 compared with the 1782 data.

It is evident that the differences between the patterns of the two parishes were mainly due to the behaviour of married women. Of those aged 25–29 about three quarters were married (79 per cent for Cardington in 1782, 76 per cent for Corfe Castle in 1851 and 70 per cent both for Cardington in 1851 and Corfe in 1970), yet the participation rate for Cardington women in 1782 was the highest for this age group. This means that most of the women in Cardington continued to work after marriage and the subsequent birth of children, whereas the majority of women in Corfe Castle dropped out of the labour force soon after marriage. A slight tendency for the rate to rise after early adulthood, observed for Corfe Castle at both dates, would also seem to indicate that married women returned to work after their children had passed infancy. It is also probable that widowhood was the occasion for a return to the labour market, the percentage widowed rising from 3 per cent for ages 20–39 to 20 per cent for 40–59 in 1790, and from 2 per cent to 15 per cent in 1851. Indeed, as is shown in Table 9.3, more widowed than married women were employed under the age of 60.[17] Evidence of such a return to the labour market is less prominent among the Cardington women. This, however, is perhaps largely due to the fact that a much greater proportion of women tended to remain in work throughout the early post-marriage and child-rearing periods.[18] Finally, although one might have expected that women, whether widowed or not, would stop working after the age of 60, this was not always true. In Corfe Castle in 1790 for example, the percentage increases after age 60. As can be seen from Table 9.3, the employment situation for elderly women is far from clear-cut.

Turning attention to the situation of children and young adults, Tables 9.4 and 9.5 confirm what has already been said concerning the economic conditions in the two communities in the late-eighteenth century. Three features of the data suggest that the Cardington boys were suffering from a lack of local employment: a very low proportion of the boys under the age of 15 were in the labour force; a very small

[17] However, this does not mean that the number of young children to be cared for had no bearing upon the decision of women to enter the labour force. A similar situation to that described by Garrett for the textile town of Keighley, Yorkshire, in which early marriage and child bearing facilitated the return to work, may have prevailed. See Garrett, 'Trials of labour'.

[18] The tendency for married women to re-enter the labour force after their children grew up was not observed in the Lancashire textile town of Preston in 1851: Anderson, *Family structure*, p. 72. However, among Irish married women in London and framework knitters' wives in Shepshed, Leicestershire, in the same year the percentage employed rose slightly from the middle to the later stages of the life-cycle: Lees, 'Mid-Victorian migration', p. 34; Levine, *Family formation*, p. 29. In Keighley Garrett found that for low-status textile workers the combination of early marriage and early fertility enabled women to rejoin the workforce, while the wives of higher status families tended not to return to the factories, but a return to work for widows was relatively commonplace: 'Trials of labour'.

Table 9.3 **Labour force participation rates for married and widowed women by age group**

| | Married | | | | Widowed | | | |
| | 1782/90 | | 1851 | | 1782/90 | | 1851 | |
	%	n	%	n	%	n	%	n
Cardington								
20–39	82.0	61	66.7	114	80.9	21	70.0	20
40–59	51.0	47	61.0	77	–	–	–	–
60+	60.0	5	55.0	20	40.0	10	72.0	25
Overall	67.5	114	63.7	211	67.7	31	71.1	45
Corfe Castle								
20–39	8.0	87	2.7	147	86.4	22	48.1	27
40–59	6.5	62	3.7	109	–	–	–	–
60+	21.8	23	0.0	40	76.5	17	11.4	35
Overall	8.7	172	2.7	296	82.1	39	27.4	62

Notes: The table excludes wives or widows of farmers. The figure for Cardington in 1782 includes wives under the age of 20.

number of those aged 15 and over were employed at home; and only a few occupations were available for them in the village. For the Corfe boys, on the contrary, almost the reverse was true, while girls in both parishes seemed to have been in a similar situation. Two-thirds of girls

Table 9.4 **Labour force participation rates for children by age and sex**

| | Males | | | | Females | | | |
| | 1782/90 | | 1851 | | 1782/90 | | 1851 | |
	%	n	%	n	%	n	%	n
Cardington								
5–14	1.2	81	37.0	189	43.9	82	60.3	121
15+	75.0	8	92.9	103	83.3	48	83.5	91
Corfe Castle								
5–14	32.1	140	18.3	241	42.5	134	1.4	208
15+	94.4	54	94.5	145	75.9	58	34.6	127

Notes: Married children resident with parent(s), servants, and the children of farmers, clergymen and persons of independent means are excluded from this table. In the case of Corfe Castle, however, children of dairywomen/men are included, for some may have been agricultural labourers and it is hard to distinguish them from graziers.

Table 9.5   Occupations of children

	Cardington				Corfe Castle			
	1782		1851		1782		1851	
	n	%	n	%	n	%	n	%
Male children								
Craft/tradesmen	5	71.4	14	8.5	28	29.2	39	21.9
Labourers								
Agricultural	–	–	144	87.8	30	31.3	74	41.6
Clay cutting	–	–	–	–	14	14.6	32	18.0
Other	–	–	–	–	4	4.2	12	6.7
Rope making	–	–	–	–	10	10.4	–	–
Other	2	28.6	6	3.7	10	10.4	21	11.8
Total	7	100.0	164	100.0	96	100.0	178	100.0
Female children								
Agriculture	–	–	–	–	–	–	9	20.0
Textiles/clothing								
Spinning	11	15.1	–	–	26	26.3	–	–
Knitting	–	–	–	–	68	68.7	–	–
Lace making	61	83.6	119	79.9	–	–	–	–
Straw plaiting	–	–	12	8.1	–	–	5	11.1
Other	–	–	11	7.3	2	2.0	19	42.2
Other	1	1.4	7	4.7	3	3.0	12	26.7
Total	73	100.0	149	100.0	99	100.0	45	100.0

Notes: Farmers' chldren are excluded from this table.

in the age group of 5–14 and more than three-quarters in the 15+ group
had an occupation, most of them being employed in cottage industries.
By 1851, as shown in Table 9.4, some changes had occurred in the
levels of participation in the labour force. Many more sons of the
Cardington cottagers stayed in the village as agricultural labourers than
had done so in 1782. For the Corfe girls, as spinning and knitting had
disappeared, the percentage employed at age 15 and above was half the
earlier level, and a number of 5–14 year-olds in the labour force had
become negligible. In contrast, the Corfe boys had not been seriously
affected, thanks to the thriving clay industry, except that they were no
longer involved in rope making, which had given employment to
younger children. While lace making in Cardington occupied roughly
the same proportion of girls in 1851 as it had in 1782, spinning had

Table 9.6   Occupations of married and widowed women

| | Cardington | | | | Corfe Castle | | | |
| | 1782 | | 1851 | | 1782 | | 1851 | |
	n	%	n	%	n	%	n	%
Agriculture	–	–	–	–	–	–	6	25.0
Textiles/clothing								
Spinning	48	49.5	–	–	8	17.0	–	–
Knitting	–	–	–	–	25	53.2	1	4.2
Lace making	37	38.1	135	81.3	–	–	–	–
Straw plaiting	–	–	13	7.8	–	–	1	4.2
Other	3	3.1	4	2.4	2	4.3	2	8.3
Other	9	9.3	14	8.4	12	25.5	14	58.3
Total	97	100.0	166	100.0	47	100.0	24	100.0

disappeared, with its place being taken by the spread of straw plaiting and other miscellaneous forms of employment.

Turning to the question of the labour force participation of women, it is clear that the disappearance of the cottage industries in Corfe Castle affected adult women more than female children. Among adult women, some contrasts are found when marital status is controlled for. About two-thirds of married women were working in Cardington, whereas less than one-tenth were recorded as employed in Corfe Castle. But the figures for widows are much less divergent and, hence, the difference between married and widowed women is wide in Corfe Castle but quite small in Cardington (see Table 9.6). In 1851 only 8 out of 296 married women were given an occupation, and the percentage for widows, who presumably had a greater need for cash income, also declined from 82 per cent to 27 per cent. On the other hand, the proportion of Cardington women in the labour force hardly changed. Looking at the figures for all age groups, slightly fewer married women and slightly more widows were employed. However, a discernible shift had occurred in the age structure of the employed female population. Fewer women at an earlier stage of married life and more at a later stage had employment in 1851 than in 1782, although the percentage for ages 20–39 was still as high as 67 per cent from 1851. This shift may be interpreted as greater care being devoted to young children than in the late-eighteenth century, and it is likely that this new situation, together with the higher proportion of male children employed at home, reflected an improvement in economic conditions which took place during the seventy years after 1782.

Economic considerations and family work

Due to the relative stability of the labour participation rates, it is possible to conclude that the duration of the working lives of adult males was quite insensitive to changes over the period in economic circumstances. The same is also true, to some extent, of male children aged 15–19, although it does seem they did have to face a choice between going into service and staying at home in under-employment when no industrial employment was available in the parish. Indeed, if employment opportunities outside Cardington had not been available for the Cardington boys in 1782, the only work available to them would have been seasonal work in the fields. On the other hand, the figures for females, both adults and children, and male children under the age of 15, showed variability according to the prevailing economic conditions of the parish. Among females, the proportion of widows and girls aged 15 and over in the labour force exceeded that of married women and of girls under 15. The difference between married and widowed women (except for those aged 60 and over) probably arises from the fact that widowhood forced them to re-enter the labour market to support their families.

In families where both parents were present, it appears that it was children who first had to take employment to supplement their father's income when the family was under pressure of poverty. Since boys over 15 were supposed to start working whatever the circumstances, it was girls, especially those over 15, who entered the labour market in response to the family's needs. Obviously, the difference between girls and boys at the point of entry into the labour force was dependent on what kind, as well as what amount, of demand for labour existed in or around the village, and hence, dependent on what amount of money could be earned, for the range of occupations for boys and their earning power was different from girls.[19] Yet it is interesting to see that the wife was probably in a more marginal position with respect to labour supply than daughters over 15, despite very little difference in the range of occupations available and wages earned among females in various age groups.[20]

[19] The 1790 Corfe Castle listing gives, though not in all cases (n=31), 'probable' weekly earnings of individuals, which show that, given the differences in occupations available, a boy under 15 could earn on average 2s. 7d., twice as much as a girl of the same age.

[20] The weekly earnings of females (all marital statuses combined) from spinning and knitting in Corfe in 1790 were given as follows: under 14, 1s. 3d.; 15–19, 1s. 4d.; 20–29, 1s. 7d.; 30–39, 1s. 4d.; 40–49, 1s. 2d.; 60+, 1s. 1d.

Table 9.7 **Working wives with at least one daughter of working age**

	Working	Daughter(s) not working	Total
Daughter's age 15+			
Cardington			
1782	6	1	7
1851	32	2★	34
Corfe Castle			
1790	4	0	4
1851	1	0	1
Daughter's age 10–14			
Cardington			
1782	5	6	11
1851	26	4	30
Corfe Castle			
1790	4	0	4
1851	1	0	1

Notes: All cases where husbands had no recorded occupation are excluded.
★ Includes one case where one of the daughters in the relevant age group was working.

This proposition can be tested by breaking down the cases of working wives with at least one daughter of working age according to whether the daughter or daughters worked or not (Table 9.7). If all, or nearly all, the daughters worked, this can be taken to mean that the wife only had to work when the family income had to be supplemented, even though the daughters had already begun to earn.[21] As far as the age group 15+ is concerned, Table 9.7 gives support to the hypothesis, for three cases in the 'not working' column turn out to be exceptions. One is the case of a daughter aged 16 with her working sister aged 14: the 16 year-old must have been unable to work for some reason. A second is a similar case where one of the two daughters, who were both over 20, did not work. A third is the case of a craftsman's wife who owned a shop, which suggests that some factors other than necessity may have played a part in determining the participation rate of the female members of that family. For the daughters aged 10–14, the results are

[21] Table 9.7 does not include wives who were not working. Rather more of these had daughters who were also non-workers. In this category there were more tradesmen and craftsmen than in the case of families with working wives. However, it is interesting that there were a significant number of families with non-working mothers but working daughters.

much less conclusive. An interpretation might be that their position in the family was as marginal as that of the wife.

Conclusion

Since information about wage rates and other factors which determine the supply of labour is scanty and indirect, it is not possible to explain these findings in precise terms. Nor is it wise to draw a general picture of the profile of labour-force participation in the past from the evidence presented in this chapter. Not only is the analysis based on only two parishes, but also the documents used provide very little information about part-time or seasonal work. Consequently, it remains unknown if productive but unpaid work was undertaken by family members. This type of work, together with seasonal work, clearly constituted an important part of the world of work in the past.

However, one thing is clear. The effect of cottage industry on the labour-force participation profiles of females was remarkable and perhaps even unique. This claim is based on the fact that none of the twentieth-century industrialised countries, where an upward trend in activity rates of married women is almost universal, shows such a high figure (82 per cent) as Cardington in 1782 produced for married women aged 20–39. The 1971 census for England and Wales, for example, records an activity rate of 58 per cent for married women aged 45–54, but this is for married women whose child-rearing period is over and the figure also includes part-time employment and those temporarily out of work.[22] If the pattern found for Cardington women in 1782 should turn out to be unique, it was probably a consequence of the combined effect of poverty and the opportunity provided by cottage industry, given the fact that the wife was in a marginal position in the family in relation to the supply of labour.[23] Some of the occupations available for women in the industrialised world can enable women to combine work and home quite easily. As the availability of part-time

---

[22] For the English experience in the twentieth century see Gales and Marks, 'Twentieth-century trends', p. 67.

[23] It is interesting that the Cardington figures for married women in employment, both in 1782 and 1851, are far greater that those for Shepshed in 1851, described as 'the most intensively industrialized village in Leicestershire—67.5 per cent and 63.7 per cent of married women in Cardington employed compared to 39.6 per cent in Shepshed, all calculations excluding farmers' wives (Levine, *Family formation*, p. 51). This might be due to the depth of poverty in Cardington, or it could be that framework knitting, in which most Shepshed wives were employed, required relatively less female labour.

jobs at office or factory has grown, child care and household work have become less of a barrier to women re-entering the labour market but, even so, this trend has not produced a pattern similar to the Cardington one. It would be too early to speculate at this stage if the victory of the factory over the domestic system has increased or decreased the aggregate demand for female labour, but the decline of cottage industry must certainly have had a great impact on the life-time profile of female labour-force participation.[24] How great this could be may be judged from the striking differences in the age pattern and participation levels between Cardington in 1782 and Corfe Castle in 1851.

---

[24] For contrasting views, see McKendrick, 'Home demand', and Richards 'Women in the British economy'.

10

Female healers in nineteenth-century England

OWEN DAVIES

Introduction

With the exception of midwifery, the history of medical provision in the nineteenth century is one primarily concerned with men. To a certain extent this is understandable, in that until the 1870s women were effectively barred from obtaining formal medical qualifications. The pioneering Elizabeth Garrett Anderson (1836–1917) was, up until then, the only woman on the Medical Register, which had been instituted in 1858 to formalise for legal and professional purposes those who were licensed 'qualified medical practitioners'. Garrett Anderson was the first woman to take and pass the Society of Apothecaries' entrance exam in 1865, but the Society swiftly changed their rules to ensure that in future women were barred.[1] As late as 1875 the Obstetrical Society rejected female members on the grounds that they were 'not by nature qualified to make good midwifery practitioners', because of their lack of physical and mental stamina.[2] In the face of this patriarchal, professional exclusion of women from licensed medical practice the London School of Medicine for Women was founded in 1874, and two years later the 1876 Medical Act ended sexual discrimination regarding the medical professions. By 1901 there were 212 women listed in the census returns for England and Wales as 'physician', 'surgeon' or 'general practitioner'.[3]

These basic facts regarding the emancipation of medical practice are fairly well known, while the main historiographical emphasis on the female medical role has focussed on midwifery and the usurpation of the

---

[1] See the entry for Elizabeth Garrett Anderson in the *New DNB*.
[2] Smith, *People's health*, p. 380.
[3] Smith, *People's health*, p. 382, Table 5.12.

position by male obstetricians from the late seventeenth century onwards, and the professionalisation of nursing in the nineteenth century.[4] Yet if we shift the focus away from midwifery, nursing and the licensed medical professions, and look hard enough, we find evidence of a little-known history of female medical practice. As Willem de Blécourt and Cornelie Usborne have observed, in the only English language study to address properly this lacuna in nineteenth-century medical history, 'the types of health care services in which women dominated were to a large extent informal and thus invisible. . . . If we as historians wish to make them visible we need a different methodology, we need to ask different questions which will lead us to new source material.'[5] Bringing together the fragmentary evidence from census returns, newspapers and ethnographic material reveals that, despite the professional and educational barriers, women were integral to most people's experience of health care in the nineteenth century. Indeed it could be argued that as petty healers, charmers, druggists, herbalists, fortune-tellers and cunning-folk, women were the mainstay of non-institutional medical provision in town and country for much of the century. Because of the paucity of work in this area, this chapter aims to provide a general overview of the activities and social characteristics of such female healers, and a consideration of the potential and limitations of the relevant source materials. What there is no room for, however, is a consideration of the role of women in self-medication *within* families, though this is obviously an important aspect of the culture of healing in nineteenth-century society.

For much of the nineteenth century the story of female healers is one of increasing official marginalisation. It would be tempting to say disempowerment as well, but as we shall see later that was not necessarily the case. In the early eighteenth century, women could, in certain circumstances, operate formally as 'surgeons', a term that equates with the role of general practitioner today. As Mary Fissell showed in her study of medicine in eighteenth-century Bristol, significant numbers

---

[4] See, for example, Forbes, 'Regulation of English midwives'; Wilson, *The making of man-midwifery*; Loudon, *Death in childbirth*; Porter and Porter, *Patient's progress*; Donnison, *Midwives and medical men*; Cody, 'Politics of reproduction', pp. 477–95; Pantin, 'Maternal mortality and midwifery'; White, *Social change and the development of the nursing profession*.

[5] de Blécourt and Usborne, 'Women's medicine, women's culture' p. 378. See also de Blécourt's book on irregular female medical providers, *Het Amazonenleger*. My thanks to Willem de Blécourt for providing me with an English summary of this work, and an unpublished paper on 'Irregular woman healers in the Dutch countryside'.

of women openly and effectively operated as 'barber-surgeons' and apothecaries. This was primarily because the city companies allowed widows to carry on their husband's business. Between 1700 and 1750 nearly half of those surgeons and apothecaries who died in mid-career were succeeded by their widows. As Fissell further points out, for women to be able to succeed in this manner suggests that they had worked alongside their husbands to some degree and possessed some medical knowledge.[6] However, during the second half of the eighteenth century fewer widows took up their husband's licensed medical businesses, in Bristol and more generally: increasingly, it would seem that the burgeoning middling-sort in society were less and less disposed towards consulting female surgeons and apothecaries. As a result the concept and title of 'surgeoness' and the 'respectable' female medical practice it denoted, became largely extinct by the early nineteenth century.[7]

The New Poor Law further pushed female healers to the edge of official recognition. Under the Old Poor Law there was plenty of scope for parish overseers to employ female healers on the basis of their reputation, cost, flexibility and propinquity. It is not unusual to come across payments made to nurses, bonesetters and doctresses in the eighteenth century poor law records. The vestry minutes for Woodstock, Oxfordshire, show, for example, that in 1758 a Mrs Southam was paid the substantial sum of two and a half guineas for curing a man's leg.[8] Under the New Poor Law, however, Unions were required to employ a licensed medical officer. Women were still employed as nurses but no longer as independent healers. The medical profession may not have liked the tendering system for posts, but the New Poor Law effectively sealed male professional domination of formal medical practice. The expansion of medical clubs encouraged by the Poor Law commissioners, and the increasingly influential role of Friendly Societies such as the Oddfellows in administering medical provision for its members by contracting licensed doctors, further reinforced the male professional grip on the medical market. Workers paying into such funds would no doubt have been reluctant to pay further sums to unlicensed medical providers if they could help it. Still, millions of working men and labourers were unable to maintain their club payments on a regular basis, while many more never joined self-help medical clubs for personal and cultural reasons. Furthermore, the

---

[6] Fissell, *Patients, power, and the poor*, p. 64.
[7] See Wyman, 'The surgeoness', pp. 38, 41.
[8] Thomas, 'The Old Poor Law and medicine', p. 2.

contracts such clubs drew up with local general practitioners generally excluded medical provision for the wives, children or female dependants of members.[9] Poor women and children were still provided for by the poor law authorities, of course, but one can understand why druggists, herbalists, and folk medical practitioners remained popular.

What's in a name?

Women healers, like many medical practitioners, have been uncomfortably forced into such categories of medicine as 'occasional', 'irregular', 'alternative', 'unorthodox', or the more pejorative 'quack', to differentiate them from the licensed professions that grew in prestige and power by servicing the rising middle classes. Yet for many people in the past the boundaries between 'orthodox' and 'unorthodox' or 'regular' and 'irregular' had no meaning. They judged medical skill and proficiency not on the basis of formal qualifications but on local reputation, hereditary knowledge, and the possession of innate powers. Within such a cultural understanding of healing, gender was not a barrier to medical practice; being a woman could actually be a positive attribute, particularly with regard to complications concerning childbirth. As de Blécourt and Usborne concluded in their article on abortion and fortune-telling in early twentieth-century Germany and the Netherlands, an examination of female cultures of healing allows us 'to cut through the alternative-official dichotomy and offer an alternative for "alternative".'[10]

We have already seen how the title of 'surgeoness' fell out of usage due to middle-class discrimination and professional protectionism. Up until the mid-nineteenth century the appropriation of the title of 'doctor', however, could not be restricted in the same way, for there was no law proscribing its use. Furthermore, in popular culture 'doctor' had quite different connotations than it does today. It denoted not only a formal knowledge of medicine but also innate, 'God-given' or magical healing abilities. As a consequence seventh sons, who had a healing touch, were often called 'doctor'.[11] It was perfectly acceptable in popular medicine, therefore, for women to also adopt or accrue the title of 'doctress' or 'doctoress'. We see it mentioned occasionally in parish records. In a churchyard near Bridgwater, Somerset, a tombstone recorded one such life: 'Sacred to the memory of Doctress Anne

---

[9] See Green, *Working-class patients and the medical establishment*, pp. 102–5.
[10] de Blécourt and Usborne, 'Women's medicine', p. 392.
[11] Davies, 'Cunning-folk in the medical market-place', p. 58.

Pounsberry, who departed this life Dec. 11, 1813, aged 73 years. Stand still and consider the wondrous works of God.'[12] Her 'wondrous' works were, in part, attributed to the fact that she was the seventh daughter of a seventh daughter. Because in popular culture there was apparently little gender discrimination in the doctoring trade, doctresses seem to have been able to compete quite well with licensed medical men, particularly in rapidly expanding urban areas of northern England. In the 1830s and 1840s the 'doctoress' Ann Cooper of Hull was prosperous enough to employ a full-time assistant.[13] One Mrs Drummond drove a thriving trade mid-century from her base in Park Square, Leeds. She and her assistant 'doctors' visited surrounding West Riding towns on market days, selling her 'Famed Herbal Tonic' and 'Aperient Canada Pills', which could cure any disease.[14]

For present purposes there is no need to consider in depth the debate about whether 'quack' is an appropriate category for use by historians. It was and continues to be used in an explicitly derogatory sense, and nineteenth-century journalists and medical professionals liberally employed it to denote anyone who was not a licensed practitioner. Ann Cooper, for example, was described as a 'quack-doctress' even though at her trial 'several surgical authorities' were quoted in support of the treatment she provided. In my opinion, though, 'quack' does serve a purpose to distinguish between those doctors and doctresses who, unlike Ann Cooper, claimed bogus qualifications and further displayed their mendacity when it came to their curative methods. Mrs Drummond, for example, claimed to be a Member of the Royal College of Surgeons. Another of the same breed was Jane Kitson, who was prosecuted under the Vagrancy Act in 1823.[15] She and her husband travelled around the country in their caravan advertising that she could cure diseases of every kind. In terms of proving her reputation, she cunningly played to every audience. She made pretence of being deaf and dumb, thereby pandering to the popular belief that those with this affliction were sometimes divinely compensated with innate healing and divinatory powers. Only a few years later, for example, another purported deaf and dumb healer, whose advertising bills ran 'Most wonderful and extraordinary cures performed by Doctress Bateman', was prosecuted at a London magistrate's court.[16] Kitson also laid claim to social respectability by professing to be the daughter of an eminent

---

[12] Snell, *Book of Exmoor*, p. 204.
[13] *The Times*, 22 July 1854.
[14] Marland, *Medicine and society*, pp. 222–3.
[15] *The Times*, 25 October 1823.
[16] *The Times*, 23 October 1827.

physician, and showed her clients bogus certificates stating as much on the authority of the King. Her medical *modus operandi* was based on a 'book of diseases' that contained entries such as 'You have a cake growing on your side, which if not removed will cause your death; I can remove it', or 'you have got the dropsy'. She would point to the relevant disease for each client and then provide him or her with bottles of medicine from the caravan. When Kitson and her husband were arrested in Soham, Cambridgeshire, constables confiscated more than £100.

As a blatant example of bogus medical practice, we can also turn to Jane Browning, who was prosecuted in 1854, for obtaining money under false pretences. Harriet Gunton, the wife of a coachman, living in Lincoln's Inn Field, had consulted her about intestinal worms. Browning said she could cure her in a day or two but it would cost £5. She accepted £2, however, as Gunton was a 'poor woman'. As to the cure, she told Gunton to undress in front of her bedroom fireplace and proceed to rub oil into her loins 'to open all the pores'. Gunton was then ordered to lie down. Browning's female accomplice held Gunton down and put her hand over her mouth to prevent her breathing while Browning probed painfully around in her anus before announcing that the worm had bitten her finger and slipped back inside. She decided another tactic would have to be adopted. Gunton was next asked to squat over a pan of hot water to force the worm out. She remained all night in this position despite the considerable pain. After a good night's sleep, Browning finally put Gunton out of her immediate misery by sticking her hand up Gunton's skirts and pulling something into the pan of water that she described as half snake half eel. It was later revealed in court that it was indeed a conger eel. Browning told Gunton that the 'worm' had been living inside her for 20 years and offered to pickle it in a jar, charging 2s. 8d.[17]

Historians are on less problematic terminological ground with 'herbalist', though herbalism encompassed a diverse group of practitioners united by core principles regarding the healing properties of herbs. They ranged from 'medical botanists', who were usually followers of the radical, anti-establishment 'system' of herbal medicine devised by the American Samuel Thomson (1769–1843) and his adherents Albert Coffin (1790/1–1866) and John Skelton, to astrological herbalists following in the footsteps of seventeenth-century astrologer-physicians like Nicholas Culpeper; and from high street

---

[17] *The Times*, 22 February 1854; 2 March 1854.

shopkeepers to village simples gatherers.[18] For some commentators, however, herbalism was merely a cover for roguery. The Reverend Sabine Baring-Gould thought, 'the professed herbalist in our country towns is very often not a herbalist at all, but a mere impostor.' Another commentator similarly declared, 'I wish it emphatically to be observed that herb-shops abound in poor neighbourhoods, and that herbs are chiefly the medicines of the poor, taken and administered empirically and ignorantly'.[19] As well as concern over the sale and administration of poisonous herbs by ill-informed herbalists, a more unspoken worry was the provision of abortions. In 1910 a government report stated, with some reason, that, 'a large number sell drugs for the purpose of procuring abortion, often at exorbitant prices.'[20] It is impossible to gauge what proportion of herbalists provided abortions but there is no doubt that most would have had knowledge of a range of long-used herbal abortifacients.[21] In 1871, for example, the husband and wife medical botanists, Charles and Sarah de Baddeley, of Lambeth, were prosecuted for supplying ergot of rye to provoke miscarriages.[22]

During the nineteenth century, druggists and chemists rose to become the most numerous dispensers of medicine and medical advice. As Hilary Marland's work has demonstrated, many did much more than just make up the prescriptions of general practitioners.[23] Some druggists also practised as dentists and medical botanists. More unusual was the Leeds druggist William Broughton who, during the mid-nineteenth-century, described himself in trade directories as a 'water caster', as did a Sheffield apothecary around the same time.[24] Up until the second half of the seventeenth century water casting or urine scrying, by which diseases could be identified from the colour and cloudiness of urine, had been an orthodox method of diagnosis. During the eighteenth century it was denounced by the medical profession as mere quackery and by the following century it was largely a practice restricted to folk medicine. Other druggists mixed the medicine trade with selling goods such as tea, perfumes and groceries. As a group, therefore, druggists

---

[18] See Brown, 'Social context and medical theory', pp. 219–23; Pickstone and Miley, 'Medical botany around 1850', pp. 140–54; Barrow, *Independent spirits*, pp. 161–73.

[19] Baring-Gould, *Devonshire characters*, p. 71; *Daily News*, 10 January 1856.

[20] Cited in Brown, 'Vicissitudes of herbalism', p. 76.

[21] See McLaren, *Reproductive rituals*, pp. 98–106.

[22] *The Times*, 23 June 1871.

[23] Marland, *Medicine and society*; Marland, 'Medical activities'.

[24] Davies, *Murder, magic, madness*, p. 39.

were highly flexible in responding to local needs both medical and non-medical, and it was the sort of business that provided women with rare entrepreneurial commercial opportunities.

Moving in to the realms of magical healing, we find the tradition of 'charming' or 'blessing' for common ailments such as toothache, bleeding, sprains and fevers. Women were just as well represented as men, largely because the transmission of certain charms was commonly, but not universally, required to be passed on to other family members or close friends contra-sexually.[25] In other words, for the charm to be effective its operator must have inherited it from the opposite sex. The charms, which were transmitted and executed in either oral or written forms depending on the ailment they cured, were thought to be God-given. A female charmer for bleeding, from Bishop's Down, Dorset, who died in 1910 at the age of 93, when asked by her son what her charm was, replied, 'Lah! Bless 'ee, I does nothin', only prays the Lord to cure 'em'.[26] Most charmers bided by a tradition of gratuity, therefore, and made their living by pursuing other mundane occupations. As a consequence, 'charmer' never appears in census records or directories.

Fortune-telling intersected with certain aspects of medical provision. As has already been mentioned, astrology was integral to the practices of some herbalists, and among simple fortune-tellers, such as card-readers and palmists, the vast majority of whom were female, we find some acting as abortionists. In 1864, for example, a fortune-teller named Julia Hayden, of St Pancras, was prosecuted for procuring an abortion by inserting a wire into the womb of her pregnant patient.[27] The amalgam of divination and medicine was most fully developed in the diverse activities of cunning-folk, roughly one third of whom were women.[28] Herbalism was integral to their multi-faceted magical practices concerning the cure of both natural and supernaturally-inspired ailments in humans and animals. Some also acted as herbal abortionists, such as the Norwich cunning-woman Sarah Whisker, who was sentenced to transportation at the Norfolk Assizes in 1846 for procuring a miscarriage

---

[25] On charmers and charming in the period see Davies, 'Charmers and charming'; Davies, 'Healing charms'; Roper, 'Typologising English charms', pp. 128–45.

[26] Rawlence, 'Sundry folk-lore reminiscences', p. 64.

[27] *Somerset County Herald*, 7 May 1864. See also Davies, 'Cunning-folk', p. 69.

[28] On the medical activities of nineteenth-century cunning-folk see Davies, *Cunning-folk*; Davies, *A people bewitched*, chapters 2 and 3; Davies, *Murder, magic, madness*, chapters 2 and 7; Davies 'Cunning-folk in the medical market-place'; Davies, 'Cunning-folk in England and Wales'.

using white hellebore.[29] It was also among cunning-folk that the practice of water casting continued the longest.[30]

Finally, there were also those who do not fall into any definable category, other than perhaps 'petty healer'. These were generally women with a good knowledge of folk remedies, who neighbours relied upon in the knowledge that they would act swiftly and provide free advice for curing common, minor ailments. Some performed this function as part of their reputation as charmers, but many did not possess any supernatural cures. An elderly Dorset woman interviewed in 1910 was one such repository of folk medical knowledge. One of her cures for boils was as follows: 'Find a place where you can cover seven or nine daisies with your foot. Then pick and eat them'. When her interviewer commented that after treading on them the daisies would be dirty, she replied 'Ther, yer must eat so much earth avore yer dies.' When questioned as to the efficacy of her cures she said, 'Bless 'e, they be a lot better than doctor's stuff.'[31] Such petty healers also existed in urban areas. In her study of religion and popular culture in Southwark during late nineteenth and early twentieth century, Sarah Williams identified several such women in the oral history archives. One account sums up such women well: 'Mrs Dixon, she wasn't a nurse or anything but she knew a bit about surgery and I'd lost a lot of blood like, you know. But she looked after me and done me well. And every time we had any other accident we were over there, she only lived across the road.'[32] Such people were the sort of women who neighbours also relied upon to lay out the dead and to help out during childbirth.

The evidence of the census

As Hilary Marland's work on medical provision in Wakefield and Huddersfield and P.S. Brown's study of Bristol have shown, trade directories and newspaper advertisements provide us with a valuable quantitative guide to the number and type of medical providers and medicine vendors on a regional and local basis. They also give us some sense of the ratio of licensed to unlicensed practitioners over time.[33] Yet,

---

[29] *The Times*, 30 March 1846.
[30] See Davies, *Cunning-folk*, pp. 105–6.
[31] Rawlence, 'Folk-lore and superstitions', p. 84.
[32] Williams, *Religious belief and popular culture*, pp. 78–9.
[33] Marland, *Medicine and society*; Marland, 'Medical activities of mid-nineteenth-century chemists and druggists'; Brown, 'Herbalists and medical botanists'; Brown, 'Providers of medical treatment'; Brown, 'Vicissitudes of herbalism', pp. 71–92. See also Inkster, 'Marginal men', pp. 128–64; King, *A Fylde country practice*; King and Weaver, 'Lives in many hands'.

as both Marland and Brown also acknowledged, neither source accurately reflects the actual number and type of healers offering services at any one time. Brown's exhaustive survey of medical provision in Bristol demonstrates how, for example, people described as herbalists in the censuses do not appear in the directories of the period and *vice versa*. The census has the potential to provide a more accurate picture of the diversity of the medical market place, and women's position in it, than do directories and newspapers. People were willing to describe their activities in terms that they would not usually advertise formally. The censuses also reveal significant numbers of working-class healers who, because of their poverty, were in neither a financial or a social position to have their occupations recorded in newspapers and directories. The problem for the historian, of course, is the logistics of combing systematically through census returns looking at occupations. The growing number of searchable electronic census databases is certainly opening up new opportunities, though unfortunately not all provide the facility to search by occupation.

As an initial survey, a search was made for the terms 'fortune-teller', 'bone setter', 'quack doctor', 'druggist', 'dentist', 'wise-woman', 'cunning-woman', 'astrologer', 'water caster', 'herbalist', 'herb doctor', 'medical botanist', 'doctoress' and 'doctress' in the 1851 censuses covering Norfolk, Devon and Warwickshire produced by the Church of Latter-Day Saints.[34] The results were poor, revealing only one female herbalist, one dentist and three 'doctoresses/doctresses'. The herbalist Martha Clarke, of Birmingham, was a 73 year-old widow, and the 'late dentist' Sophia Bott, also of Birmingham, was a widow aged 82. Two of the doctresses were also of advanced age. Sarah Salter, aged 80, of Upottery, Devon, was either widowed or separated as she was listed as married but also as the head of her household, which consisted of her unmarried daughter and a lodger. Elizabeth Hall, aged 86, a widow of King's Lynn, also took in a lodger. The other doctoress listed was a 52 year-old lodger of Padhamsleigh, Devon, who, although married, was obviously separated at the time. Two women were listed as 'fortune tellers': Sophia Allen, of Alysham, Norfolk, aged 29, the wife of a rat destroyer and labourer, and Sarah Hastings of Nuneaton, a 62 year-old pauper. The largest category, unsurprisingly, consisted of druggists. Of the 21 women listed, 14 were widows and only two were married, one of who was evidently living apart from her husband. Seven of the women also sold groceries.

[34] The Church of Jesus Christ of Latter-Day Saints, *1851 British Census (Devon, Norfolk and Warwick)*, compact disc edition (1997).

The 1851 census evidence for these three counties provides some initial indications regarding the social characteristics of female healers, suggesting that medical provision provided an important supplementary income for widows and single women, and should be seen as an aspect of the economy of makeshifts for this vulnerable group. This observation is partially born out by the far more revealing online 1881 census produced by Ancestry.co.uk, which allows searches to be made by occupation and gender across the whole country, providing the following revealing national snapshot of female healers.[35]

Water casters, quacks and fortune-tellers. There were no female water casters and only one male practitioner mentioned in the 1881 census. The last of this dying breed, according to the census, was John Wild, aged 63, born in Leeds but practising in Bingley. Two women were entered as 'quack doctors'. One was Catherine Clegg, aged 30, who was living in lodgings in Blackburn with her husband William, who was also described as a quack.[36] The other was Margaret Lamonte, a 63 year-old widow of Nantwich, Cheshire. 'Quack' was presumably not a title they bestowed upon themselves but rather the judgemental description of the enumerator. Still, considering that some of the female healers recorded in the census were Irish, though not Clegg and Lamonte, it is worth mentioning that in nineteenth- and twentieth-century Ireland the term 'quack' had no derogatory sense in popular discourse, being used to describe someone with no formal training but who possessed a healing gift.[37] The three listed fortune-tellers were a 96 year-old widow in Norwich Lunatic Asylum; Gertrude Hazelgrove a 65 year-old 'gypsy fortune teller', married to an agricultural labourer; and the pauper Rebecca Smith, aged 65, a widow residing in Birmingham Parish workhouse. The only female listed as an 'astrologer' was Susannah Smith, a widow of Lakenham, Norfolk, aged 72. The only youthful practitioner of the divinatory arts was E. Waller, an 18 year-old palmist, the daughter of a Clerkenwell bricklayer.

Doctresses. The 1881 census highlights the decline of the title of 'doctress' in popular medicine during the second half of the nineteenth century, a trend that seems to be borne out by ethnographic sources as well; only seven women were listed under this title, compared to the

---

[35] www.ancestry.co.uk.
[36] Clegg was born in Preston, and one wonders if he was related to the eighteenth-century Rochdale wise-man George Clegg; see Davies, *Cunning-folk*, pp. 43–5.
[37] See Nolan, 'Folk medicine in rural Ireland'.

three mentioned in the 1851 three-county census database. Of the seven, five were widows and one was married but separated. The other was a 'Horse & Cattle Doctoress' named Jane Stanley, the 47 year-old wife of a Yorkshire farmer. It is notable that two of the doctresses, Mary Clare of Salford and Dora Hart of Bristol, were immigrants from Ireland, where the popular conception of 'doctor'—denoting those having an innate healing ability such as being a seventh daughter—remained stronger for longer. One wonders to what extent these Irish doctresses primarily serviced Irish immigrant communities.

Bonesetters. Seven female and 19 male bonesetters were recorded. Six of the women were over the age of 55, the other being 31. Compared to the preponderance of widows in the other categories of healer discussed, and considering their age, it is significant that four of the female bonesetters were married. One husband was also a bonesetter, but two of the other husbands had no medical trade, being a strickle maker and a quarry foreman. It is likely that these female bonesetters had practised their 'art' for much of their adult lives. The widow Mary Ann Drake, a Bradford bonesetter, was listed as such in the 1861 and 1881 censuses. Bonesetting was less of a makeshift healing occupation than other categories. It was generally recognised as a skill that ran in families, and not one that could be casually adopted when needs must.[38] Hannah Bird, for instance, who was a bonesetter in Leeds during the 1850s, was the wife of a well-known bonesetter, John Bird, whose career can be traced through trade directories from the 1820s to the 1840s.[39] Similarly we find Hannah Seacroft married to a Bradford bonesetter named William Seacroft in the 1861 census, but by 1881 she was widowed and had moved back to her birthplace, Farsley in Yorkshire, where she set herself up as a bonesetter. The tradition of bonesetting as a proper occupation, rather than as an adjunct to other healing services, thrived longest in northern England, particularly in Yorkshire, perhaps due to the frequency of injuries in the mills and factories. All but one of the female bonesetters practised in Yorkshire, the other in Cumberland.

Dentists. In 1881 the census reveals 15 women making a living as dentists, as distinct from being assistants to or wives of dentists, or involved in the manufacture of dental products. There were, by

---

[38] The most famous family of bonesetters in northern England were the Taylors, who lived near Rochdale, and were popularly known as the Whitworth Doctors; see West, *The Taylors of Lancashire*; King and Weaver, 'Lives in many hands', pp. 192–3.

[39] Davies, *Murder, magic, madness*, p. 36.

contrast, well over 1,000 male dentists. Only three of the female dentists were married, three were unmarried and the rest widows, which further supports the general impression that medical practice was an important income-generator for women who had to fend for themselves. Most of them were probably basic tooth-pullers with some herbal knowledge, although Malvina Mosely was certainly an intriguing exception. This French-born, 28 year-old widow operated as a 'surgeon dentist' in Newcastle, employing two men and a boy. Her mother listed her income as 'property and investments'. It was not until 1878 that the Dentists Act instituted a register of qualified practitioners, and it only became a formal profession with the founding of the British Dental Association in 1880.[40] Before then anyone could set up a dentist's surgery and advertise their services, though it would seem that it was not a popular option for women, at least compared to the next two categories.

Druggists. Considering that there were several thousand male druggists operating in 1881, the 186 women who worked as druggists and druggists' assistants (this figures excludes such occupations as warehouse packers and labellers) constitutes only a very small percentage of the trade. Ninety-two (49 per cent) of the women were widows, 61 (32.8 per cent) were unmarried, five (2.7 per cent) married but separated, and 28 (15 per cent) married and living with their husbands. The majority of those in the unmarried category were druggists' assistants and mostly in their teens or twenties. Regarding the husbands of the married druggists, 21 (75 per cent) were also druggists, while the remaining seven (25 per cent) consisted of a tanner, hairdresser, storeroom keeper, painter, mineral water manufacturer, auctioneer, and brickyard labourer. Among the more noteworthy female practitioners was the Ramsey family of Penrith, which comprised of the 71 year-old widow Mary and her five unmarried daughters. The six women also employed a male assistant. Another prosperous example was the 65 year-old widow Hannah Jones, who ran a druggists shop in Salford with her son and employed three men and two boys.

There was a marked predominance of female druggists in Lancashire, 30 per cent of those recorded in the 1881 census working in this county. Male druggists were also particularly numerous there. The obvious reason for this is that nineteenth-century Lancashire had probably the lowest general practitioner to population ratios in the

---

[40] See Hillam, *Brass plate and brazen impudence*; Hargreaves, 'Dentistry in the British Isles'; Forbes, 'Professionalisation of dentistry'.

country, with as few as 1:5,000 outside the main urban areas.[41] Similarly in Yorkshire, which had the second largest concentration of druggists, the multiplication of druggists in the rapidly expanding towns kept pace with the population increase far better than the licensed medical profession. In Leeds, for instance, the number of druggists quadrupled between 1820 and 1854.[42]

Herbalists. Bearing in mind that a significant minority of those I have counted as druggists were assistants, and that herbalists were more likely to be involved in providing diagnoses as well as vending, it would be fair to say that the largest group of female *healers* in the 1881 census were herbalists. There were 136 female herbalists listed compared to 566 men.[43] Women, therefore, made up a significant 19.3 per cent of the trade. Breaking the figures down further, we find that 61 (44.8 per cent) of the women were widows, 23 (16.9 per cent) were unmarried, and nine (6.6 per cent) were married but were the head of the household. Of the 43 female herbalists who were married and living with their husbands 22 (51 per cent) practised as herbalists while their husbands followed a different trade, mostly as artisans or craftsmen such as shoemakers, blacksmiths, and bookbinders, although three were warehousemen and five were listed as labourers.

One draws many blanks when trying to trace the history of the female herbalists listed in 1881 through previous census returns. What the successful linkages suggest, however, is that there were two main trajectories for those widows who became herbalists. First, there were wives who took over their husbands' trade after their deaths. Some were already working as partners or assistants in the business, but others shifted occupations, such as Mary Anne Preece of Newcastle-under-Lyme. In 1861 her husband was practising as a herbalist and tailor while she worked as a milliner. He died in 1872 and by 1881 she had taken over the herb business. Other women had no apparent connection with herbalism prior to widowhood. In the 1861 census Sarah Allsebrook, of Burton upon Trent, was a 29 year-old dressmaker married to an agricultural labourer. Twenty years later we find her listed as a widowed herbalist. In 1861 Mary Ann Munn, of Maidstone, aged 44, was the wife of a painter. After his death in 1865 she pursued the occupation of herbalist. Likewise Jane Stripe of Portsea, Hampshire, aged 59, was listed

---

[41] King, *A Fylde country practice*, p. 34.
[42] Davies, *Murder, magic, madness*, p. 37.
[43] This figure excludes those described as wives of herbalists, but does include assistants.

in the 1871 census as the wife of William Stripe, a carpenter and joiner. He died in 1874 and she subsequently earned a living selling herbal remedies. It is possible that these women were engaged in herbalism during their married life, or course, but the evidence suggests that at least some learned—or formalised—the trade when faced with the restricted choices open to widows seeking an independent income.

As well as the 136 'herbalists', a further seven women were described as 'medical botanists', four of whom were widows. It is likely they were followers of Thomson or Coffin, but then again, like some male practitioners, they may have merely adopted the title to give themselves a more distinguished and learned air. There were just over 100 male medical botanists listed, meaning that women made up a much smaller percentage compared with herbalists generally. This is somewhat surprising considering that women had a significant representation in certain aspects of medical botany. Thomson claimed much of his herbal knowledge derived from a New England wise-woman, and he gave recognition to the role of female healing more generally, while Coffinites also condemned the use of male midwives. A woman ran at least one of the Botanic Colleges set up in the Midlands and northern England during the 1850s and 1860s.[44] Yet as Logie Barrow observed, most practitioners were men, a fact confirmed by the 1881 census.[45] Despite the movement's sympathetic attitude towards the medical role of women, perhaps its attempt at professionalisation through the creation of societies and colleges tacitly reinforced male control and hindered female participation.

As with the druggist trade, it is clear from the figures that female herbalists, like their male counterparts, predominated in urban industrial areas, and for the same reason. Thirty-nine women worked in Lancashire alone and 29 in London. This geographical bias was recognised at the time. In 1856 it was observed that it was 'the densely populated manufacturing districts, where medical quackery and medical superstition take disastrous effect upon the working classes, chiefly through the medium of herbs and herbalists.'[46] A 1910 report also observed that herbalists were particularly profuse in Lancashire, the West Riding of Yorkshire, Nottinghamshire and Derbyshire. Turning to historical analyses, P.S. Brown found a dramatic rise in herbalists in industrialising South Wales between 1871 and 1921.[47] In contrast, no

---

[44] Smith, *People's health*, p. 340.
[45] Barrow, *Independent spirits*, p. 164
[46] *Daily News*, 10 January 1856.
[47] Brown, 'Vicissitudes of herbalism', p. 72.

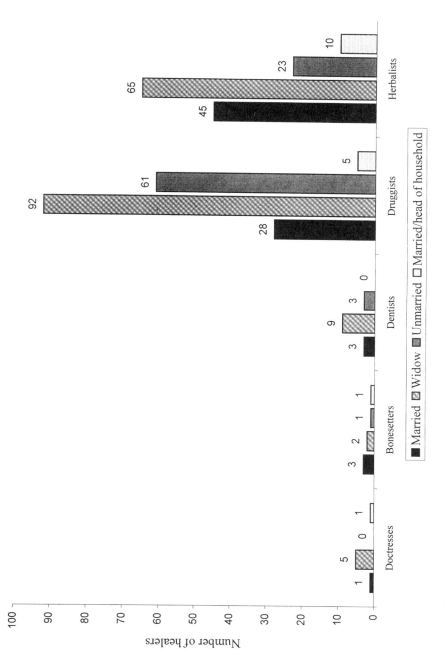

Figure 10.1 Marital status of female healers in the 1881 census

female herbalists were recorded in rural counties like Oxfordshire, Sussex, Wiltshire and Buckinghamshire, just as none were found in the 1851 census for Devon and Norfolk, and the only one in Warwickshire worked in Birmingham. This does not mean, of course, that there were no female herbalists operating in these rural counties. Rather it suggests that in rural areas women were more likely to practise herbalism on a casual basis, in conjunction with other activities such as midwifery, or as part of the package of services provided by cunning-folk.

A rural county case study

Considering the understandable preoccupation of historians with unofficial medical provision in industrial urban communities, I want to redress the balance a little, and thereby support the above observation regarding rural herbalism, by focusing briefly on the evidence for female healers in Somerset. The 1881 census mentions three female herbalists operating in the county. One was a labourer's wife named Anna Hern from the parish of Milborne Port, regarding whom more will be said later. The second was Merion Mathews, a 56 year-old widow serving a sentence in Shepton Mallet prison, for whom no further details could be traced. The third was Sarah May of Bridgwater, the 55 year-old wife of a gravedigger. In 1861 May's occupation was listed as 'wife', and in 1871 as the 'sextoness of St Mary's Church', Bridgwater, while her husband, John, was employed as an agricultural labourer. In 1891 we find her widowed and acting as a nurse. None of these women were mentioned in contemporary trade directories.

Just as the limitations of directories and advertisements have been pointed out, similarly the censuses provide only a partial representation of female medical practice. Even directories, advertisements and census returns combined provide only a glimpse of the everyday role of women in petty healing within households and between neighbours, and they reveal practically nothing about charmers and cunning-women. It is only by turning to prosecution records, newspaper trial reports, and ethnographic sources that the extent and nature of female medical activities becomes more apparent.

Two women whose medical activities we would have known little or nothing about unless they had been prosecuted were Ruth Marshman and Esther Peadon. Marshman was recorded in the 1851 census as a 40 year-old silk worker, married to a labourer, and in 1861 as having no occupation. At her trial before the Shepton Mallet petty sessions in 1856, however, it was revealed that she had the reputation of being a 'wise woman' and a 'fortune-teller'. The prosecution was brought by one of her patients, Elizabeth Bathe, who had been seriously ill for several months. Marshman told her she was under the spell of the Devil and to counter his evil influences she went through a ritual involving the placement of a card and a piece of paper in the bottom of a box. The magistrates sentenced her to six weeks imprisonment. This evidently did not deter her from continuing her occult trade, as in 1862 she was prosecuted again for fortune telling.[48]

Esther Peadon was tried for manslaughter in 1858 after the death of one of her patients, a farmer's wife named Sarah Palmer. Prior to her marriage in 1852, to Elias Peadon, coachman to the rector of Dowlish Wake near Chard, Esther Perry had evidently prospered as a herbalist. In the 1851 census we find her described as a 'herbal doctress', aged 33, living in Dowlish Wake with a son and a servant woman. It is likely that she was related to the famed cunning-man John Perry, who lived in nearby Chard and died in 1850.[49] In the winter of 1857 Sarah Palmer, who had recently given birth, was suffering from 'lowness of spirits'. She consulted her local surgeon but his medicine did nothing for her depression and so she paid a visit to Peadon, who provided her with two boxes of pills and two bottles of medicine. As well as taking the medication, Palmer was instructed to cut her toe and fingernails and a lock of hair, which she was to tie around one of the bottles until it perished away, in an act of sympathetic magic. After taking some of the medicine provided by Peadon, Palmer died in considerable pain on New Year's Day. When the renowned chemist William Herapath analysed Palmer's stomach and the contents of the bottles, he found a toxic, hallucinogenic mix of belladonna, bryony, tobacco, hemlock and dropwort. Because there was no conclusive proof that Palmer's death was a direct consequence of taking Peadon's medicine, the herbalist was acquitted with a severe reprimand from the judge and a caution 'as to her future conduct.'[50] Whether she decided to heed this warning, or due to the consequent loss of her local reputation, three years later we find Peadon and her husband living in the town of Axmouth, some 13 or so miles south of Dowlish, where she was ostensibly employed as a housekeeper while her husband worked as a groom. Ten years later she was listed in the census as a butler's wife. Had she really been put off her magico-medical practice, or is her true occupations hidden in the census?

Turning to the ethnographic record, a good example of the sort of

[48] *Western Flying Post*, 4 November 1856; Davies, *A people bewitched*, pp. 44–7.
[49] Davies, *A people bewitched*, p. 31.
[50] *Somerset County Herald*, 27 March 1858.

female healer whose occupation evaded all formal mention was an elderly woman named Nanny Holland, who the working-class memoirist Roger Langdon recalled from his Somerset youth in the 1820s. He described her as 'a sort of oracle in the village, besides being a kind of quack doctor'. She had long had a reputation in his village as a skilled midwife and as a bonesetter. Although she had a fearsome reputation, she 'was always ready to assist her neighbours in cases of sickness. She would go when called upon, whether by night or by day; and if any one hesitated to call her, she would not be any better pleased'. This was in contrast to the local doctor who was often 'too drunk to attend.'[51] At the other end of the century, Frances Harriott Wood recounted her experience of a similar character who lived in Wood's brother-in-law's parish of Walton, near Street. The woman was a seventh child of a seventh child, and like Nanny Holland seems to have mixed divination with healing. She was a very religious person who always used prayer in her cures and never demanded money for her services. 'She looked on herself as set apart,' said Wood, 'and never married'. It was not only the labouring classes in the parish who consulted her. When Wood's sister, who lived in Durham, suffered from 'gatherings' (suppurating swellings) after childbirth, she came to visit her family in Somerset. As Wood acerbically put it, her doctor in Durham 'let her come south, "lest she should die in his hands."' She was gravely ill and as a last resort the healer was called in and provided an effective salve. When Wood's brother-in-law was afflicted with carbuncles the healer recommended he take brewer's yeast, which cured the infection.[52] In both these cases, as in numerous others recorded in such sources, the male, licensed medical profession was painted in a bad light while the untrained but experienced village healer received glowing reports. The difference was primarily portrayed as one between educated laziness and arrogance and humble folk wisdom, but one also detects a gendered undertone contrasting natural female empathy with male insensitivity.

What can appropriately be called the occult or hidden careers of female healers and the nature of their practices is highlighted by one Somerset healer about whom we do know a fair bit—the aforementioned Anna Hern of Milborne Port parish, who was listed as a 'herbalist' in the 1881 census.[53] She was aged 38, married to an agricultural labourer named George Hern, and had a 19 year-old son,

---

[51] Langdon, *The life of Roger Langdon*, pp. 15, 20.
[52] Wood, *Somerset memories and traditions*, pp. 50–1.
[53] In other sources she is referred to as Mother Herne.

Tom, also a labourer. George died in 1893 and two years later Anna married another labourer named George Wills. In the 1901 census she was listed as having no occupation. From the census entries it might be presumed that she collected and sold herbs merely to supplement the meagre salary of her husbands and son. But ethnographic sources from the early twentieth century reveal that she was a popular and widely consulted cunning-woman whose services ranged far beyond the selling of herbs. She died in the 1920s and her cottage was subsequently pulled down, but a couple of first-hand accounts of her in old age are revealing about her character, reputation and way of life.[54]

One visitor described Hern as a 'little woman, looking shabby and dirty' whose cottage 'was full of smoke, old bottles, and litter of various kinds.' Another visitor noted how 'the low ceiling was hung with bunches of herbs' and that a cauldron hung over an open hearth. She shared her dwelling with a black cat, a dog, some chickens and a guinea pig. By the sound of it she looked and knowingly acted the part of the stereotypical witch. Yet, while few in the surrounding area dared slight her, she had a very good reputation as a healer, fortune-teller and witch doctor and would make use of the train to visit clients too sick to travel long distances. As to the nature of her medical practices, she cured a wide range of simple ailments such as boils, toothache and skin complaints with herbs gathered at sunrise and at full moon to boost their potency. It was also understood that she had magical healing powers that she could transmit to patients without the need for herbal ointments. She also offered basic advice, such as when she told a boy with a dislocated and swollen knee, 'Go home, my boy, bathe it in water as hot as you can bear, and bind it with bandages soaked in vinegar. It will soon be well'.[55] More serious cases were likely to be blamed on witchcraft. Around 1900 a farmer consulted her after having badly twisted his ankle falling from a ladder. He was laid up in bed for a month and had to walk on crutches after that, to the obvious detriment of the running of the farm. He consulted all the doctors in the neighbourhood, but when their treatment proving ineffective he resorted to the wise-woman. A female neighbour went on his behalf, and was informed by Hern that the farmer's fall had been caused by an evil eye cast upon him by a farm worker. She advised that the man should be sacked, and also prescribed some bay leaves, which were to be boiled and wrapped tightly around the farmer's foot. It was known

---

[54] *Somerset County Herald*, 3 July 1926; Knott and Legg, *Witches of Dorset*, pp. 33–9; Rawlence, 'Folk-lore and superstitions', pp. 85–7.
[55] *Somerset County Herald*, 3 July 1926.

that women in the area requested Hern to perform abortions, but it was said that she refused to help, though she did take in and look after one unfortunate girl until the illegitimate child was born.

There is a strong emphasis on the healing powers of elderly women in the ethnographic sources, which is also reflected, in part, in the number of widows listed as healers in the census data. This presumably relates to the perception that the accumulation of wisdom and knowledge through experience, particularly of childbirth and death, conferred greater medical skills on the aged. The flip side of this portrait was that age and widowhood were, partly for the same reasons, also attributes of the stereotypical witch in nineteenth-century popular culture. An analysis of 25 prosecutions brought by women in nineteenth-century Somerset in response to having been abused or assaulted as witches, reveals that three quarters were aged over 50, and a third were widows, while two others were spinsters.[56] As one Somerset commentator observed, 'Besides witches proper there is a class of old ladies who can hardly be distinguished from them . . . Partly it is their age, partly their look, partly their temper, but above all the possession of certain uncanny accomplishments'.[57] The folklorist F.B. Kettlewell, recalling life and beliefs in a Somerset village during the 1880s, remembered the life one such elderly woman: 'She was a great friend of mine and often talked to me about her "gifts," for she believed that she had the power of healing and could cure the King's evil.' Amongst her arsenal of charms were a baby's caul and an old black letter Bible. She also had a reputation for divining future events. She was respected by her neighbours, possessed some education, wore horn-rimmed spectacles, and had once taught the local girls. Few had the temerity to pass her door at night, however, and after her death her lasting reputation was as a witch and not as a healer.[58]

Conclusion

With the recent availability of online searchable census databases and trade directories there is huge potential for researching women's role in both unofficial and official medical provision. The evidence presented in this chapter is sufficient to demonstrate that to understand properly the popular experience of medicine in the nineteenth century, historians need to pay more attention to female healers, and that future work

---

[56] Davies, *A people bewitched*, p. 116.
[57] Snell, *Book of Exmoor*, p. 219.
[58] Kettlewell, *Trinkum-Trinkums*, pp. 39–43.

needs to be sensitive to regional and local differences in medical practice. At the broadest level it is apparent that the experience of female medical provision was different in urban and rural communities, but further localised research might reveal distinct variations in the types of medical service provided by women in provincial towns and villages. The obvious factors determining regional patterns of female medical practice have been highlighted, such as population size, the number of available general practitioners and industrial working conditions, but more attention needs to be paid to the influence of smaller-scale regional and local economies. I would suggest, for instance, that in dairying areas, such as southern Somerset, there was more scope for female medical practice than in predominantly arable farming communities, due to the demand for veterinary services as well as human medical attention. There are many questions to be answered, of course, and until more extensive surveying of local newspapers becomes feasible, some will remain difficult to address. One of the most important gaps in our knowledge is an understanding of patients' perceptions of female healers. Were women more likely to consult a female herbalist or druggist than a male one, and vice versa? It is possible that, here again, regional and local cultures perceived women's social role and therefore medical proficiency differently. To identify such subtle differences in behaviour, mentality and practice, historians of medical occupation patterns will need to move beyond the obvious quantitative data sources and tease out the ethnographic insights buried in parochial news reports and the folklore archive.

11

The tabulation of occupations in the nineteenth-century census, with special reference to domestic servants

EDWARD HIGGS

The published returns

The statistical abstracts contained in the parliamentary census report are our principal source for reconstructing the occupational structure of Victorian society. As such they have been widely used by historians, sociologists and economists, and are a vital component of all statistical models of the economy of that period. However, despite the obvious importance of the source, very little work has been done to gauge its accuracy. With notable exceptions, most students of the period have been content to accept the figures contained in the census reports at face value.[1] The present chapter is not an attempt to measure the overall discrepancies in the occupational totals quoted in the census reports. It can merely suggest some way in which such discrepancies may have occurred and encourage others to undertake the local census studies which may allow such an evaluation to be made. An example of the problems involved in the interpretation of such published occupational tables will be given with reference to the employment of domestic servants in one northern district in the period 1851–71.

When examining these statistics it is important to recognise that they are several stages removed from the reality of nineteenth-century society. They represent a series of interpretations of fact made in turn by the householders who filled in the original schedules, by the enumerators who collected these and copied them into their enumeration books, and by the clerks in the central Census Office who tabulated the results. Each would have interpreted the subtle distinctions

[1] Tillot, 'Sources of inaccuracy', pp. 82–133.

between household relationships according to their own experience and values. When evaluating the reliability of these data it will therefore be necessary to look at the process of taking the census from the differing points of view of the individuals involved. It is also necessary to examine the assumptions underlying the interpretation of these statistics by modern historians.

These strictures certainly apply when dealing with terms such as 'servant' and 'domestic employment'. 'Service' in the nineteenth century was a legal term rather than the description of an occupation. It related to a certain relationship between employer and employee, and could be applied equally to living-in farm labourers and to housemaids in aristocratic households. Thus in the nineteenth-century census schedules the term 'servant' could appear in the column reserved for information on an individual's relationship to the household head, as well as in the column giving occupations. On the other hand, 'domestic' occupations such as that of housekeeper might not imply any contractual or legal relationship within the household, but rather a function carried out by a member of the family within the home. A 'housekeeper' could merely be the keeper of the house, in other words, a housewife. But such a function could also be performed by a distant relative who in every social sense was regarded as outside the family unit, and who might even be paid on a contractual basis. Such subtle, but nevertheless important, distinctions would be difficult to communicate through a census form, and were easily lost in the process of transcription and interpretation which the compilation of the nineteenth-century census involved. In dealing with such matters it is necessary to distinguish between 'domestic service' as a description of a legal and social system, and the term 'housemaid' as a description of a person performing a set of duties in the home of their employer. In nineteenth-century usage, however, such distinctions were often blurred.

The administration of the census

The taking of a Victorian census for the whole of England and Wales, and the derivation of statistics from the results, was a considerable administrative task. After the passing of the necessary Census Act, the department in charge of taking the census (from 1841 the General Registry Office, hereafter GRO)) established a temporary Census Office in London. This, staffed by temporary clerks, undertook the tabulation of the information compiled locally. Until 1841 the census was supervised in the field by the overseers of the parishes, but with the establishment of civil registration in 1837 and the transfer of responsibility for the census to the GRO following Rickman's sudden death in 1840, the districts employed by the local Registrar of Births and Deaths became the local units of administration. This official had to divide his district into enumeration districts, and to appoint an enumerator for each. The latter, also employed on a temporary basis, distributed household schedules to each householder, who filled them out on the night of the census. The enumerator had to copy these into books which were then sent to London for tabulation under various headings.[2]

Such an administrative system could only produce consistent statistical results if there was a clear policy on tabulation at the centre, and if the staff involved were properly trained and supervised. Since the Census Office was only a temporary institution, none of these conditions could be adequately fulfilled in the nineteenth century. The Registrar General and his predecessors appear to have been too preoccupied with the establishment of the Census Office, and its staffing, to give much time to the serious consideration of such policy. The temporary clerks employed were not of a high quality, and appear to have received little training in methods of tabulation.[3] It was admitted in 1890 that these clerks could not be adequately supervised, and this must have applied to an even greater extent to the local enumerators and to the householders who filled in the original schedules.[4]

Given this administrative system modern researchers must be alive to the numerous difficulties in interpreting the statistics presented in the official census reports. We have no means of gauging how far Victorian householders could understand the census schedules, or how far the enumerators standardised the entries they copied into their books for despatch to London. Nor do we know how the clerks working in the Census Office interpreted these schedules, or how they may have revised them. Such revisions certainly took place, as when multiple occupations were reduced to a single component for ease of tabulation. Thus in extant schedules the term 'farmer and butcher' is often reduced to 'farmer' or 'butcher' by the deletion of the other, complementary, occupation.

---

[2] See Higgs, *Clearer sense*, pp. 15–16, for fuller details.
[3] BPP 1890, LVIII, *Report of the Committee appointed by the Treasury to inquire into certain Questions connected with the taking of the Census . . .*, p. viii.
[4] BPP 1890, LVIII, p. viii.

The example of servants

More work needs to be done on the relationship between the enumerators' books and the tabulations in the published census reports, for which they formed the raw material. The example which follows examines domestic servants and their employers in the Registrar General's District of Rochdale in the period 1851–71. This work was based on one-in-four random samples of households containing domestic servants in the CEBs for this district in the censuses of 1851–71.[5] As has been suggested already, a 'domestic servant' could be defined in two ways, either by occupation or by relationship to the head of the household. In the analysis which follows a 'servant-employing household' is defined by occupation: that is, it includes an individual designated as one of a variety of the terms 'servant' and 'maid', or as a 'butler', 'footman', 'groom', 'coachman', 'gardener', 'governess' or 'nurse'.

As can be seen from Table 11.1, the sample of such households from the 1851 CEBs produced totals of persons aged 20 and over in the various servant occupations which were, in general terms, comparable to those found in the published census report.[6] The match was very close in the case of housekeepers. This led to the conclusion that the clerks in the Census Office merely summed the occupational entries in the schedules to arrive at the total number of domestic servants in the district. However, a large number of these individuals in the sample were not enumerated as servants in terms of the relationship to the head of household in which they lived. Out of the total sample of 367 persons in servant occupations aged 20 years or over, 160, or 43.6 per cent, were not enumerated as such, the vast majority of these being related by kinship to the household head.[7] In Table 11.1 the number of persons in particular servant occupations in the sample who were also designated as servants in relationship to the household head is given in the second column under the heading 'true servants', the remainder being either lodgers or relatives.

These figures can be interpreted in several different ways. Such servants resident with kin may have been normally employed as living-

[5] TNA, HO 107/3032–3051; RG 10/4112–4132. The wider work of which this analysis forms part is presented in Higgs, *Domestic servants and households*. See also Higgs, 'Domestic service and household production'.

[6] BPP 1852–3, LXXXVIII, *1851 Census of Great Britain:Population tables, pt. II, vol. II*, pp. 636–47.

[7] The term 'kinship' is being used here in its widest sense to indicate any relationship by marriage or birth.

Table 11.1   Servants aged 20 years or over, Rochdale district sample, 1851

Servant types	Sample total	'True servants'	Census total (divided by 4)
General (F)	217	158	244.75
Butler	1	1	0.00
General (M)	21	9	17.25
Coachman	3	1	0.25
Groom	4	0	0.25
Gardener	16	2	0.00
Housekeeper	66	10	65.70
Cook	5	5	8.75
Housemaid	18	9	13.25
Nurse	9	6	5.75
Governess	3	2	0.00
Ladies Maid	2	2	0.00
Laundry Maid	1	1	0.00
Kitchen Maid	1	1	0.00
Footman	0	0	0.00
Companion	0	0	0.00
Total	367	207	356.25

Source: BPP 1852–3, LXXXVIII, *1851 Census of Great Britain, Population tables, pt. II. vol. II*, pp. 636–47.

Notes: The published census totals are divided by four to make them compatible with one-in-four census samples. For the definition of 'true servants' see text.

in domestics but may have been temporarily out of work. This would, however, have represented a very high level of unemployment. Conversely, this might indicate a large population of day-servants, who worked in the homes of their employers by day and who returned to lodge with their relatives at night. A third possibility is that these 'domestics' not only lodged with their kin but also worked in their homes.

The Victorian Registrar Generals and modern historians have often tended to assume a dichotomy between life in the home and work in the outside world. Our conception of an occupation has tended to be conditioned to our expectation that 'work' is an activity carried on outside the home which can be measured by the money equivalents of wages or profits. Thus it has often been assumed that the number of persons in servant occupations in the nineteenth-century census tabulations represented the number of men and women working for board, lodging and wages in the homes of middle-class employers with whom they had some contractual arrangement.[8] There is some evidence, however, that many of the Rochdale householders who filled in their schedules on the night of the census saw 'service' as a set of functions which could be carried on within the family. Thus, among the 66 'housekeepers' of all ages found in the 1851 sample, only 10 were also servants in relationship to the head of the household in which they resided. Of the remaining 56 women, no fewer than 23 were the heads of the households in which they lived, and another 15 were the wives of the head of the household.

Similarly out of the 38 'nurses' living with kin enumerated in the Rochdale district sample of 1851, 18 were aged under 10 and only 3 were not members of the nuclear family. Such children were probably part of that vast army of child-minders so familiar in nineteenth-century textile towns, where so many married women worked. Amongst the 36 households containing such 'nurses', 27.8 per cent contained 3 or more children aged under 10, compared with 16.0 per cent amongst a control sample of 201 randomly selected Rochdale households. Since these figures are aggregate percentages drawn from samples one cannot be certain that they are a true reflection of the actual figures which would have been obtained from a study embracing all households or all servant employing households. However, statistical theory allows us to estimate, at various levels of confidence, the degree to which sample proportions will deviate from the true figures in the underlying population. In this case we can be at least 80 per cent certain that this difference in the two proportions quoted was not caused by sampling error.[9]

---

[8] See, for example, Perkin, *Origins of modern English society*, p. 143; McLeod, *Class and religion*, p. 26.

[9] This is achieved by calculating the difference between the two percentages involved and then comparing this with the likely magnitude of the statistical error given by the formula:

$$\text{Sampling error (t statistic)} = \sqrt{\frac{PS_1\,(1 - Ps_1)}{n_1 - 1} + \frac{Ps_2\,(1 - Ps_2)}{n_2 - 1}}$$

Where:
Ps_1 = first sample percentage treated as a proportion of one
Ps_2 = second sample percentage treated as a proportion of one
n_1 = number of cases in population from which first proportion derived
n_2 = number of cases in population from which second proportion derived
The t statistic is a computed value which can be reduced in size to correspond to certain confidence levels. Thus if we wish to be 95 per cent certain that the

Among the remaining 88 female 'kin servants', who were neither housekeepers, nurses, nor specifically 'working at home', some, if not all, may have been 'day-servants' or temporarily unemployed. However, certain aggregate characteristics of the households in which they lived suggest that many may have been working at home. Thus, in 1851, out of 69 households containing such servants, 31, or 44.9 per cent, contained a head who was widowed, compared with 17.9 per cent amongst the control sample.[10] Similarly, amongst the former group of households, 57.1 per cent contained five or more persons, compared with 46.3 per cent amongst the control sample.[11] Many of the households containing such 'kin servants' were headed by persons of relatively high social status. Thus 34.3 per cent of these households were either retailers or farmers, compared with only 16.5 per cent amongst the control sample.[12] These aggregate characteristics suggest that many of these women were probably working at home, often standing-in for absent wives, in fairly prosperous homes. In addition, of these 88 women, 43.1 per cent were not members of the nuclear family, compared with a mere 7.0 per cent amongst the 478 females in the control sample.[13] This indicates that such 'servants' were a feature of relatively unusual extended families.

None of these individuals can automatically be said to be mis-enumerated. However, the position of many of them within the households of their kin, and the aggregate characteristics of such households, suggest that a significant number will have worked at home as 'home-helps'. As Anderson has pointed out, in nineteenth-century Lancashire there was a heightened propensity for relatives to provide each other with support within the home, especially at times of family

difference between two proportions is statistically significant we multiply the results of the equation to the right of the t statistic in the formula by the value of t at 95 per cent, that is 1.96. If the resulting sampling error is smaller than the difference actually observed between the sample proportions then we can be 95 per cent certain that this discrepancy was not solely due to sampling error but represents a true difference between the underlying populations. In the case quoted above the difference is not significant at 95 per cent, but by reducing the t statistic to the 80 per cent confidence level we get a positive result. In other samples from the 1861 and 1871 censuses the differences between the analogous percentages were significant at the 80 and 95 per cent levels respectively.

[10] Difference statistically significant at the 95 per cent level of confidence.
[11] Difference statistically significant at the 80 per cent level of confidence
[12] Difference statistically significant at the 95 per cent level of confidence.
[13] Difference statistically significant at the 95 per cent level of confidence.

crisis.[14] The extent to which widows remained at home as 'housekeepers' while their children were at work, or children acted as 'nurses' for the babies of the female factory wives during the widowhood of the household head, all reflect the importance of this tradition of 'huddling'. The fact that such relationships could be regarded as occupations reflects the recognition of their importance by such families.

This propensity of householders to interpret occupations in ways alien to our own preconceived notions can also be found amongst census enumerators. Thus, in 1861, out of 234 households in one enumeration district in the Castleton area of Rochdale, the enumerator described 49 housewives as 'housekeepers' in his copy of the original schedules. Similarly, in the same census, out of the 249 households in an enumeration district in Wardleworth, the enumerator described 141 housewives in the same manner. For these officials the term 'housewife' and 'housekeeper' appear to have been synonymous.[15]

How did the clerks in the central Census Office interpret the results of the census? The short answer is that we do not know. However, examination of the census schedules for the Rochdale district and the census reports for the period 1851–71 suggest that some attempt was made to compensate for the type of mis-enumeration mentioned above. Although the match between the 1851 census sample and the tables in the 1851 census report shown in Table 11.1 is close, this is not the case for 1861. In that year the census sample gave a total of 628 persons aged over 19 in servant occupations, while the census report gave a total of 1,533 for the same age group, or 383.25 when divided by four to bring the figure in line with the one-in-four census sample.[16] The same report recorded 253 housekeepers of that age, although the census sample would have led us to expect none fewer than 968 ($\pm$14). The inference to be drawn is that the clerks did not merely add together all the occupations to get the occupational totals. On the other hand they did not do so by adding up all those persons recorded as 'servant' in the column headed 'Relationship to the Head of the Household'. An examination of all households in the 1861 Rochdale census reveals that this figure would have been only 1,321 for all servants of all ages.

An examination of the census reports for other areas over the same period suggests that similar attempt were made to rectify the 'mis-

---

[14] Anderson, *Family structure*.

[15] TNA, RG 9/3032–3051.

[16] BPP 1863, LIII, *1861 Census of England and Wales, Population tables, pt. II*, pp. 634–47.

specification' of servant occupations. Thus in 1851, the Borough of Blackburn was recorded in the census report as having 733 persons employed as 'housekeepers', nearly 38 per cent of the entire servant population.[17] By 1861, the number of 'housekeepers' recorded had fallen to 51, or under 3 per cent of the servant total.[18] Over the same period the number of 'housekeepers' in the Borough of Oldham rose from 48 to 146.[19] It is evident that some alterations were being made to the raw statistics contained in the census schedules, but to what system and with what consistency cannot be determined.

Even assuming that the census reports accurately reflected the number of traditionally defined living-in domestic servants, it would still be unwise to use them uncritically to reconstruct changes in local occupational structures over time. Just as the term 'domestic servant' might represent the work of a woman in the home of her relatives, it might also cover other types of work which are today regarded as separate occupations. Thus, during the period 1851–71, between a third and a quarter of all living-in servants in Rochdale worked for retailers. Most of these servants would have worked in the shop, a supposition confirmed by other local sources. The distinction between the servant and the shop assistant is therefore an artificial one. Those who attempt to explain the decline of domestic service in the late nineteenth century by the rise of alternative employment, especially in shops, may be mistaking the cause for the effect: the decline of the domestic may not be linked to the 'rise' of the shop assistant, rather to the change of nomenclature as the home-based, family shop was replaced by the lock-up shop and the chain store. As retailing ceased to be a domestic business, so workers in this section of the economy ceased to be called domestic servants.[20]

Conclusion

If such mis-specifications were a general feature of the nineteenth-century census, it might lead us to revise our views on the economic

---

[17] BPP 1852–3, LXXXVIII, *1851 Census of Great Britain, Population tables, pt. II, vol. II*, p. 652.

[18] BPP 1863, LIII, *1861 Census of England and Wales, Population tables, pt. II*, p. 652.

[19] BPP 1852–3, LXXXVIII, *1851 Census of Great Britain, Population tables, pt. II, vol. II*, p. 652; BPP 1863, LIII, *1861 Census of England and Wales, Population tables, pt. II*, p. 652.

[20] For a broader discussion of the GRO's handling of the census data see Higgs, *Clearer sense*, pp. 154–68.

and social role of women in Victorian England and Wales.[21] If we assume that all the 'servants' who lived with relatives in Rochdale worked at home, then out of 2,065 persons, described as working in servant occupations in 1851, only 1,113 or 53.9 per cent, were properly enumerated. If such a discrepancy was found over the whole country then approximately a half million women may have been wrongly enumerated in the nineteenth-century census reports. This may be a gross overestimation, but the precise level of this discrepancy can only be gauged by detailed studies of the role of 'kin-servants' in industrial and agricultural communities. It is to be hoped that the present chapter has raised enough questions about the mechanics of the Victorian census to encourage others to undertake such studies.

At the heart of the matter lies the definition of an occupation and work, and the relationship between economic work and the home. Confusion between 'domestic' and 'business' activities may have existed in the homes of retailers, farmers, and in all small businesses where the help of the servant, wife, or children was indispensable.[22] Victorian ideology attempted to keep the two spheres of home and work separate, but we must not fall into the trap of believing that all Victorians shared these beliefs, or that such a division always existed in practice.

[21] See Higgs, 'Women, occupations and work', for an extension of this point.
[22] For the problems of interpretation with the agricultural workforce, see Higgs, 'Occupational censuses'.

12

Mis-specification of servant occupations in the 1851 census: a problem revisited

MICHAEL ANDERSON

Introduction

In a paper originally published in *Local Population Studies* in 1982, reprinted as chapter 11 in the present volume, Edward Higgs drew attention to the problem faced, both by the census authorities at the General Register Office and by researchers using the CEBs today, when men and women were listed with domestic service occupational titles in the column headed 'Rank, Profession or Occupation' but as something other than 'servant' in the column 'Relation to Head of Family'.[1] In Higgs's one in four sample from the CEBs for Rochdale in 1851, he found that 40 per cent of the females ages 20 and over with 'servant' occupational titles did not have 'service' relationships to the head of their household. The inconsistency was especially frequent among what he called 'General servants' (27 per cent of whom were not recorded with a 'servant' relationship), 'Housemaids' (half were inconsistent) and, above all, among 'Housekeepers', where 85 per cent had a non-servant relationship, more than a third being reported as heads of households and more than another fifth being the wives of household heads. In some ways even more disturbing was Higgs's suggestion that the published census figures for Rochdale for 1851 appeared to have included all these 'familial housekeepers' as domestic servants, thus markedly over-reporting the numbers in service in the town. The same problem of housekeeper recording recurred in the CEBs for 1861 and 1871, but at these censuses the procedures in the Census Office seemed to have changed, implying that in some way the checkers were rectifying what Higgs neatly calls this 'mis-specification of servant occupations'.

---

[1] Higgs, 'Tabulation of occupations'.

An England and Wales perspective

How typical was Rochdale? And are there any further clues in the census returns that may point to how this problem may have been handled in 1861 and thereafter? This chapter seeks to throw some light on this issue, using data for England and Wales from the National Sample from the 1851 Census of Great Britain.[2] The National Sample comprises the total population of 2 per cent of all 'settlements' with populations of less than 2,000 (the 'rural' sample), and every 50th enumeration book from the remainder of the country (the 'non-rural sample). The complete data set contains more than 400,000 people, but the subset used here consists of three separate 2.5 per cent systematic sub-samples from the rural sample and six separate 2.5 per cent sub-samples from the non-rural sample; where national estimates of percentages are provided, the rural sample has been double-weighted, but the numbers of cases shown in the tables are the unweighted figures. The analysis is confined to female servants in 'domestic service' occupations, thus excluding such groups as dairymaids, farm servants, laundresses and nurses. Removing those servants who were in institutions, or whose occupational title included supplementary information such as 'Pauper, 'Formerly', or 'Out of Place', left the 2,114 girls and women whose occupational titles are summarised in the first column of Table 12.1.

The main body of Table 12.1 shows how these 2,114 'servants' were described in the relationship column of the CEBs. In all, the population equivalent of 72.5 per cent were designated as 'servants' of some kind, and another 6.1 per cent had either no entry or were recorded, potentially quite 'correctly', as lodgers or visitors. As in Higgs's work, there were considerable differences in relationships between the different categories of 'servant', but there were two groups that were especially likely not to have a 'servant' designation. One was the substantial number of persons who were given simply the designation 'Domestic' or 'Dom'. Only a maximum of 12.5 per cent of this group appear to have had anything approaching a 'purely open market' relationship to their head of household, and it seems very likely that this designation was in general use simply to describe a person primarily responsible for housework activity—and that the census checkers tabulated it as such. The other group where non-servant relationships

---

[2] The complete National Sample machine-readable dataset and associated documentation is held by the ESRC Data Archive as the University of Essex. A microfiche transcript was published by Chadwyck-Healey in 1987. For a brief account see Anderson, 'Households, families and individuals'.

Table 12.1 Relationship to head of household of female servants

Occupational title	No entry	Head or wife	Daughter	Other kin	Lodger or visitor	Servant	All	Unadjusted No.
Servant or general servant	4.4	0.8	17.6	5.5	5.0	66.7	100.0	519
Domestic servant	5.4	0.0	10.7	0.0	3.6	80.4	100.0	54
House servant	1.6	0.6	5.3	2.9	1.2	88.4	100.0	819
Maid (excluding lady's or nurse)	6.9	1.9	5.6	2.3	2.8	80.6	100.0	185
Lady's maid or companion	0.0	4.8	2.4	4.8	11.9	76.2	100.0	38
Nursemaid	3.7	0.0	9.3	3.7	5.6	77.8	100.0	43
Cook	2.8	4.2	0.0	1.4	1.4	90.3	100.0	128
Housekeeper or assistant housekeeper	5.0	34.2	10.2	21.7	2.2	26.7	100.0	272
'Domestic'	0.0	50.0	23.2	8.9	5.4	12.5	100.0	56
All except housekeeper and 'Dom'	*3.1*	*1.1*	*8.6*	*3.4*	*2.8*	*81.0*	*100.0*	*1,786*
All	3.3	6.4	9.1	5.9	2.8	72.5	100.0	2,114

Source: see text.

were in a majority is 'Housekeepers', though the figure is somewhat below that recorded by Higgs in Rochdale. When these two groups are set aside, 81 per cent of the population with service occupational titles had relationships to the household head as 'servants', the major remaining exceptions being the considerable numbers of daughters who are recorded as 'Servant', 'General servant' or 'Domestic servant'.

A regional and local view

The problem identified by Higgs for Rochdale thus also appears in 1851 at the national level, but it occurs at a markedly lower frequency. Moreover, when its occurrence is examined at a regional level, a clear pattern seems to emerge. In the National Sample, Census Division VIII (Lancashire and Cheshire) had 14 per cent of the population in 1851, but it had 28 per cent of the female 'servants' who were identified in the relationship column as heads of households or as kin of the head, and 48 per cent of all 'Housekeepers' in such a situation, these being concentrated particularly in the Lancashire textile manufacturing towns. Division IX (Yorkshire) had 10 per cent of the 1851 population, but 13 per cent of servants listed as heads or with a kin relationship to the head. It had only 5 per cent of 'Housekeepers' in this position, but it contained 55 per cent of all heads or kin of heads who were described simply as 'Domestic'. However, unlike in Lancashire where 'Housekeepers' were widely distributed through the sample enumeration districts, a substantial majority of the Yorkshire occurrences of 'Domestic' were clustered in just two enumeration books, and this may therefore reflect the practice of particular enumerators or a very localised use of the term.

It would thus seem that, while it was quite a common practice nationally for women to be listed with a servant title in the occupation column but as kin in the relationship column, the misleading appearance of the description 'Housekeeper' may have been disproportionately common in the Lancashire textile towns. There are clearly, as Higgs points out, several plausible reasons why some of those engaged in service occupations should be listed as relatives of the head: many were in households where the head was a farmer, an innkeeper or engaged in some other kind of business where servants would need to be employed. In these cases, relatives might quite reasonably be doing jobs in the family business and were thus quite correctly returned as engaged in service occupations. A particular extension of this kind of case may be the significant number of girls in all-female households where the head was described as 'laundress' or 'charwoman'; presumably in these cases the girls helped the head with her work. In other cases, some of the grand-daughters, cousins and nieces, for example, were probably taken on preferentially as servants in direct substitution for a non-relative (perhaps because they were orphans or their families had fallen on hard times, or just as a favour), and these women would have worked and perhaps been treated in ways little different from a non-relative in a similar role.[3] Some others would have been living-out servants, going daily to their employer, or perhaps employed only during the week. And some would have been 'ordinary' domestic servants, normally resident with their employers, but visiting their parents' home on census night or for a few days.[4] In this connection, it is significant that the 1851 census was held on Mothering Sunday when, in certain parts of the country, it was conventional to give servants leave to pay a visit to their parents.

However, in the textile districts of Lancashire and Cheshire, and perhaps also in the West Riding of Yorkshire, in a situation where large numbers of married women were in factory or domestic manufacturing employment, there may well have been a very different origin to the listing of so many widowed heads of household, wives, daughters and sisters as employed in 'service' occupations. Examination of all the 69 Lancashire and Cheshire enumeration books in the National Sample gives a clear impression that many enumerators quite explicitly recorded 'housework', 'housekeeper', 'domestic duties', or 'at home' against wives, children and other relatives of textile workers who might otherwise have been employed in textile work. In doing so, enumerators (and perhaps—but by no means certainly—heads of household who completed schedules) may well have quite explicitly been identifying those particular women and girls who were playing a key role in the household economy by undertaking the task of the domestic minder of the house where all other members were in remunerated employment.

---

[3] Indeed, as Cooper and Donald have pointed out ('Households and "hidden" kin'), there were probably significant numbers of servants who had some kinship relationship to some other member of their households but were reported as servants in both the occupation and the relationship columns of the CEBs. The great majority of these were probably unambiguously providing domestic services, even if their recruitment, as with so many other servants at the same date, was the result of a personal connection rather than open market activity.

[4] See also Higgs, 'Women, occupations and work'; Higgs, 'Domestic service'.

Census Office tabulation

This in turn links to the other important question raised by Higgs: how did the census office officials deal with such cases? In Rochdale, where these domestic minders were listed by the enumerator as 'housekeeper', Higgs suggests that almost all were included under that domestic service heading in the tabulations that became in due course the publish census statistics. But this was clearly not always the case. Examination of photocopied pages from any CEB clearly shows marks made by the census office checkers, and sometimes also shows corrections made by the registrars before the books were forwarded to London. Most of the checkers' marks are simply ticks made against entries to assist tabulation (for example, there are usually ticks against all female ages and against all birthplaces which are outside the county of residence). But some marks are rather different, showing how checkers interpreted particular entries—for example, where they underlined the occupation that they had selected for tabulation when a multiple occupation (such as 'farmer and weaver') was returned. Sometimes, additionally, checkers crossed through whole entries or wrote annotations against them—and it is this practice that provides some clue as to how they handled servants who were also kin. Unfortunately, when working from photocopies it is not always easy to be sure when a checker has made a mark, or just what he has written. Nevertheless, in many cases the marks are unambiguous.

In order to explore the consequence of the checkers' work, each of the 467 'servants who were also kin' in the dataset used for Table 12.1 were looked for in the photocopies from which the National Sample was produced, and 465 of them were located. Of these, 132 occupational entries had unambiguously either been crossed through or had been annotated by a registrar or checker in a way that clearly showed that the person had not been allocated to a domestic service occupation. In at least another 15 cases (and probably a number more) there was a reasonable presumption that this had happened, but these cases were not included in the analysis that follows.

Table 12.2 shows the effect of removing from the analysis the cases where either a registrar or a checker had unambiguously excluded the entry from the 'servant' occupational category. Now 78 per cent of those listed as 'servants' in the occupation column are classified as servants in the relationship column. This figure rises to 84 per cent if housekeepers and entries saying simply 'domestic' are ignored. By far the largest exclusions are from the category of 'Housekeeper', where at least 22 per cent were removed before tabulation, though even so this

Table 12.2 Relationship to head of household of female servants, after omission of cases excluded by Census Office checkers

Occupational title	No entry	Head or wife	Daughter	Other kin	Lodger or visitor	Servant	All	Unadjusted no.	Percentage cut before tabulation
Servant or general servant	4.7	0.9	12.2	4.5	5.4	72.2	100.0	485	7.7
Domestic servant	5.4	0.0	10.7	0.0	3.6	80.4	100.0	54	0.0
House servant	1.7	0.3	3.3	2.7	1.2	90.9	100.0	798	2.7
Maid (excluding lady's or nurse)	7.1	1.9	3.3	2.4	2.8	82.5	100.0	181	2.3
Lady's maid or companion	0.0	4.8	2.4	4.8	11.9	76.2	100.0	38	0.0
Nursemaid	3.9	0.0	5.9	2.0	5.9	82.4	100.0	40	5.6
Cook	2.8	3.5	0.0	1.4	1.4	90.9	100.0	127	0.7
Housekeeper or assistant housekeeper	6.0	32.0	5.6	20.4	1.6	34.4	100.0	210	22.4
'Domestic'	0.0	55.1	18.4	6.1	6.1	14.3	100.0	49	12.5
All except housekeeper and 'Dom'	*3.2*	*0.9*	*5.7*	*3.0*	*2.9*	*84.2*	*100.0*	*1,723*	*3.9*
All	3.5	5.3	5.9	4.9	2.8	77.5	100.0	1,982	6.0

Source: see text.

still leaves only 34 per cent of all 'housekeepers' with a servant relationship to the head.

However, examination of the regional distribution of the deletions hints at a surprising finding, but one which may provide a clue to the question raised by Higgs when he points out that while the term 'housekeeper' continued to be used in the 1861 and 1871 CEBs for Rochdale to describe the person responsible for housework, in the published tabulations for these censuses most of these individuals have been excluded. In the 1851 CEBs in the National Sample, deletions of this group of women seem to vary considerably between different parts of England, presumably mainly reflecting some mixture of random sampling error, varying checker practice, and genuine differences in the situations within which 'housekeepers' found themselves. But in the sub-sample used here, in the six Welsh books in which such 'housekeepers' appear, all 16 cases are deleted. And it is not just 'housekeepers' that were treated in this way. Of the 34 cases (spread across more than a dozen sample CEBs) where the holder of any 'servant' occupation is recorded as head of household or as having a kinship relationship to the head, 25 were unambiguously deleted and three more probably were. This is a far higher rate than the England and Wales figures shown in Table 12.2, or than is found in any Division in the sample data. The deleted cases include a number that arguably would have been appropriately classified as servants: for example two daughters of a victualler where the daughters almost certainly did serve customers.

One distinct possibility that this raises is that occupational analysis of the Welsh books was undertaken rather late (or even last) in the sequence of tabulation and that at about this time the problem of servants who were also relatives was confronted in the Census Office and new instructions issued. This then led to many more such cases being excluded from the occupational tabulation.[5] This lesson was then kept in mind in the planning of the census for 1861 and thereafter. Indeed, what is more generally striking about the Welsh CEBs in the National Sample is a markedly higher level of all kinds of explicit annotation which is not in the enumerators' hand, so the treatment of

---

[5] Examination of the published tables shows that 'housekeepers' form a very low proportion of all servants in Wales, at 7.4 per cent compared with an average for England and Wales of 10.9 per cent, and a Lancashire and Cheshire figure of 15.6 per cent. But the lowest figure is for London (5.2 per cent), and the highest (21.2 per cent) is for East Anglia, for reasons which remain unclear and may merit further investigation. The east Midlands have the second highest recorded rate.

servants may not be the only area affected by a new and more rigorous approach.

Conclusion

This chapter raises several issues which might be developed in future work. First, it reminds us on the one hand of the dangers of national averages and on the other the need to be aware of local and regional diversity in generalising from data from the CEBs for one place. Second, it invites further investigation of the circumstances under which relatives of the head may sometimes be returned in the occupation column of the CEBs, and, in particular, it suggests that, in areas where married women were commonly in paid employment, household heads and/or enumerators may have been especially likely to identify one or more women in a household as the person engaged in domestic duties in ways which can confuse the unwary but may in fact provide interesting insight into a largely unknown aspect of the workings of the household economy.[6] Third, the findings suggest that there may be some interesting further work to be done in studying on a comparative basis an almost unexplained topic: the work of the Census Office checkers at the nineteenth-century censuses.

---

[6] I understand from a discussion with Bob Morris that a similar phenomenon can be observed in at least one textile village in Fife.

13

Gender and the rhetoric of business success: the impact on women entrepreneurs and the 'new woman' in later nineteenth-century Edinburgh[1]

STANA NENADIC

Introduction

The essay arises out of a conundrum. Towards the end of the nineteenth century there was a major movement by women in Britain, as elsewhere in the western world, to gain a greater role in the public sphere of politics and paid employment and to secure greater independence of action outside family and marriage. This was reflected in the agitation for voting rights, pressures for access to higher education and to previously male-only professional employments, demands for property rights within marriage and for equality under the law in such areas as divorce. The ideal 'new woman'—a largely middle class phenomenon, it must be admitted—emerged in the later nineteenth century as educated, independent and capable of leading a life of considerable autonomy and freedom of action.[2] She was a very different creature to the early Victorian ideal of the 'angel in the home'—nurturing and family-centered, devoted to husband and children and eschewing the need for engagement in the public sphere.[3]

Yet despite the very real aspirations for a new style of life and new opportunities among young women of the post–1870 generation, there

[1] This essay arises from an Economic and Social Research Council funded project entitled 'Women in the garment trades: Edinburgh 1775 to 1891', ESRC No: R000234068.
[2] Gorsley, 'Old maids and new women'; Vicinus, *Independent women*; Ardiss, *New woman*.
[3] See, for example, Branca, *Silent sisterhood*.

was no discernible pressure for access to business ownership as a desirable career choice.[4] White collar employment in big business was clearly attractive and access to the professions was keenly sought, but independent entrepreneurship was not.[5] At a point when women were increasingly active outside the home and pushing for entry to previously male-dominated domains, a paradox emerges in the character of female career choices and labour markets, with their rates of entry into business continuing the long downward slide that had begun in the later eighteenth century. With the effective demise of the traditional female business sectors in the inter-war years, notably bespoke garment-making for women customers, twentieth-century business ownership became an almost exclusively male phenomenon, only to change again in the past few decades.[6] This chapter, which is illustrated with a case-study of the business community in the city of Edinburgh, suggests that there were two dimensions to the apparent indifference of the 'new woman' to a career in business ownership.[7] The few areas of business in which women conventionally had had a significant presence were, by the later nineteenth century, of a character that still exploited traditional images of womanhood and a petite bourgeois reliance on family associations to achieve business success and were likely, therefore, to repel or actively exclude ambitious, educated and independent-minded women of the middle classes. Moreover, the majority of business areas where men had a dominating presence were defined by an increasingly masculine rhetoric of entrepreneurship that equally excluded those women who might have looked towards such sectors for a potential career. These two phenomena were linked to growing competition within the domestic and international economies and to the cultural crises that emerged with Modernism from the 1870s. The friable and contested nature of gender identities, it is argued, underpinned all notions of legitimate business behaviour and shaped a rhetoric of business success.

---

[4] In 1910, the following careers were suggested by the woman's magazine *The Lady's Realm* as suitable for their readership (middle class and with a 'new-woman bias'): stage actress, nurse and manicurist.

[5] On office work, see, Wilson, *Disillusionment*.

[6] Carter and Cannon, *Female entrepreneurs*.

[7] The project noted in footnote 1, was based on extensive record linkage of firms in existence in Edinburgh between 1861 and 1891. The method and sources are described in Nenadic, 'Record linkage'. The core case studies of 53 long-surviving firms were enhanced through the construction of the family histories of the women entrepreneurs, using standard family reconstitution techniques.

Gender and business ownership

In Scotland in 1891, 11 per cent of all commercial employers were women. This rose to 13 per cent in towns and cities over 10,000 people and in Glasgow, the largest and most industrial city in the country, it was 20 per cent.[8] Most of these commercial employers were concentrated in a few sectors. Dressmaking and millinery was by far the most important, with 38 per cent of Scottish and 42 per cent English female commercial employers concentrated here. In Edinburgh, a city with a large market for goods of personal consumption, dressmakers and milliners comprised 45 per cent of all female commercial employers. Food retail occupied about a quarter of all women and hotel and lodging-keeping was also significant. Women commercial employers clearly formed a large component of the late nineteenth-century business community but, when compared with male entrepreneurs, they had a disproportionate presence in business areas that stressed traditional women's skills of garment making for women and children, food retail and the provision of accommodation. Though male commercial employers were also dominated by such sectors as food retail and clothing production, sectoral concentration was not so extreme as among women and the implications for business participation were not loaded with 'gendered' considerations.[9] Women were able to engage successfully in business areas such stationer and bookseller—indeed, 6 per cent of both male and female commercial employers were in this sector in Edinburgh in 1891—but major areas of the local economy, notably the building trades, metal processing and manufacture and engineering had no women entrepreneurs.

Over the course of the nineteenth century changes had clearly taken place. Although it is difficult to define the comparative scale of business ownership with any precision, it is broadly assumed that there were proportionately greater numbers of women in business in the eighteenth and early nineteenth centuries than was usual by the end of the nineteenth century and that they engaged in a wider spectrum of businesses.[10] Localised case studies, mainly based on city directories, tend to suggest a figure that ranged between 20 to 30 per cent of business owners, and that this was fairly consistent throughout early nineteenth-

[8] *1891 Census of Scotland*, Vol 2, Part 2.

[9] For male entrepreneurs in Edinburgh see, Nenadic, 'Small family firm'. The largest group of male commercial employers in Edinburgh in 1891 was the 25 per cent in food retail.

[10] For eighteenth-century Edinburgh see Sanderson, *Women and work*; Davidoff and Hall, 'Hidden investment'.

century Britain, Europe and North America.[11] Although women's garment making was clearly important—as it had been in the eighteenth century—there were many women to be found in areas of business that by the end of the nineteenth century were exclusively male domains.[12] Some of these women had served conventional apprenticeships and they apparently engaged in business on an equal footing with their male competitors.[13] The 'ghettoisation' of women's entrepreneurship in the first half of the nineteenth century is conventionally attributed to the intensification among the middle classes of 'separate spheres' notions of appropriate behaviour for men and women, with the necessary corollary that the status of men came to be built around the ideal of a 'leisured' wife and daughters, consuming rather than producing and engaged in the conspicuous construction of an idealised home and family life.[14] The fact that ideal and reality often diverged—for many women could not expect a life of leisure and were obliged to support themselves through their own efforts—inevitably meant that the forms of economic activity that were most likely to be culturally acceptable to women were those with a feminine character, circumscribed by domesticity or servicing the needs of other women or children. The dramatic expansion of the garment-making sector in the decade from 1881 to 1891 allowed women to retain a foothold in business while other opportunities were being eroded.[15]

But entering business was a dangerous career decision for women with ambitions to make their own way in the world, as it was, of course, for men, because the average experience of business ownership was one of instability and volatility. Of the 1,384 women-owned businesses that were making women's garments in Edinburgh between 1861 and 1891, 59 per cent had a life span of three years or less. For male-owned firms in all sectors the equivalent figure was 55 per cent.[16] Only 16 per cent of women's firms in the 1861–91 cohort survived for over ten years. Economic modernisation at the end of the nineteenth century,

---

[11] See, Crossick and Haupt, *Petite bourgeoisie*, p. 93. It is worth noting that in the late twentieth century there was a similar percentage of women in the managerial labour force of businesses in finance, accounting and marketing: see Cooper and Davidson, *Women in management*, p. v.

[12] A detailed study is given in Crowston, *Fabricating women*.

[13] See details included in Sanderson, *Women and work*.

[14] Described in Davidoff and Hall, *Family fortunes*.

[15] Milliners and dressmakers in England and Wales increased by 16.5 per cent over the decade: *Census of England and Wales, 1891*, p. 53. On the same in the U.S., see Gamber, *Female economy*. The male clothing trades also grew rapidly at this time, as explored in Honeyman, *Well suited*.

[16] Nenadic, 'Small family firm'.

including the rise of big business, clearly increased opportunities for small enterprises to exist, while simultaneously rendering them more fragile and vulnerable to pressures from outside.[17] In Edinburgh in 1851 there was one woman-owned firm in the garment trades for every 883 people in the population (183 firms in all) and by 1891 there was one firm for every 473 of the population (562 firms in all). Most of the growth was at the small-scale and low-skill end of the business spectrum. Cut-throat competition, an uneasy dependence on overpriced wholesale supplies from merchants who often encouraged business start-up in the absence of any capital from the entrepreneur, and the want of adequate legal structures for business regulation inevitably gave rise to high rates of firm formation and terrifyingly high rates of failure. It is not surprising that the sons of small business owners in the nineteenth century so often elected to pursue an education in order to enter white-collar employment or, if lucky, to make a career in the professions.[18] Women from similar backgrounds made similar decisions. By the latter part of the nineteenth century there were new employment opportunities for able young women as clerks or teachers or shop assistants in departmental stores and contemporaries lamented the poor quality of recruits to the bespoke dressmaking industry.[19]

Women in business

Success in business was hard to achieve, but even those that were successful were unlikely to represent attractive role models for potential women entrepreneurs. Based on detailed case studies of 53 long-surviving women-owned firms in Edinburgh between 1861 and 1891, it is clear that business behaviour and the relationship between the business and the personal circumstances of the owner were so defined by narrowly feminine and traditional preoccupations as to repel the modern 'new woman' with ambition. Such businesses were capable of generating a comfortable income and allowed their owners to leave a comfortable fortune when they died. Of the 17 women whose wealth at death could be traced, the average fortune was £416, which put them on a par with other areas of small business ownership and certainly above the average wealth-at-death of most male white collar workers.[20] But there was a high personal price to pay for such success.

---

[17] Observed by the economist Marshall, among others. See Westall, 'Competitive environment'.
[18] Crossick and Haupt, *Petite bourgeoisie*, pp. 84–5.
[19] Irwin, *Women's work*, p. 35.
[20] Nenadic, 'Structure, values', chapter 2.

One of the distinctive characteristic of those women entrepreneurs who enjoyed long-run success was that they were relatively old when their businesses were founded, having spent long periods of training, usually in the form of an informal apprenticeship, with many additional years in the employment of others as 'improvers' while they learned the business before entry into ownership on their own account.[21] The average age of business start-up for such women was 34 years, seven years older than the average age of business entry among men.[22] In their mid-thirties, one assumes that the women in question had managed to accumulate capital and business contacts and, being mature in age and judgement, that they were more likely to achieve success than younger women. Yet the route to independence was a hard one. Apprenticeships in dressmaking were devoid of any formal regulation, the wages were notoriously low and the work was arduous and exploitative. Many contemporary complaints were directed towards workshop mistresses who kept their apprentices and 'improvers' in a state of ignorance of the details of how the trade was conducted, in order to minimise future competition.[23] Though apprentices commonly aspired to enter a partnership with their mistress, this rarely happened.[24] The best that could be hoped for was that a trained employee could rise through the business in order to buy it when the owner retired or, more probably, when she died. A rare example of a forewoman who purchased a successful business from her deceased employer is provided by the firm of Catherine Cranston, dressmaker in Edinburgh between 1868 and 1894. The business was founded when Cranston was 32 years old and was operated with great success for 26 years, employing up to eight workers. Cranston died a spinster at the age of 58 leaving a personal fortune of £775 and the firm continued after her death in the hands of the forewoman, Miss Margaret Taylor on the understanding—defined in Cranston's will, who had negotiated the terms with Taylor at some point prior to her death—that she pay £50 per annum for ten years to the trustees of the estate, for the benefit of the first owners family.[25]

Those women that did manage to move from an apprenticeship to

---

[21] The usual system of training is described in *The unprotected*; also in Irwin, *Women's work* .

[22] Age is based on the 53 case studies of long surviving firms; equivalent figures for male entrepreneurs are given in Nenadic, 'Small family firm'.

[23] Examples were provided by Mayhew mid century; see Thompson and Yeo (eds), *Unknown Mayhew*, pp. 428–39; see also *The unprotected*.

[24] For a famous literary evocation of this aspiration, see the experience of Kate Nickleby in Charles Dickens, *Nicholas Nickleby*, first published in 1848.

[25] National Archives of Scotland [hereafter N.A.S.], SC70/4/275 pp. 291–300.

business ownership or entered the ranks of the self employed were largely drawn from prosperous artisan or lower middle class family backgrounds and commonly had family connections in related areas of business. As remarked by one contemporary, 'unless girls have bien [comfortable] homes they can't take up the Dressmaking. It's reckoned a very genteel trade, and there's many a one sends their girls to it that wouldn't let them to a factory or even to serve in a shop. But it's not a good trade unless a girl has friends and capital at her back'.[26] Of the 53 Edinburgh business histories that form the heart of the present study, only two were of working-class family origins. The majority came from small trade and shopkeeping families, with a scattering of white collar workers among the fathers of the women in question. Twenty-nine of the businesses were directly connected with male-owned family firms in related sectors. Usually these were owned by fathers or brothers engaged in business as tailors, upholsterers, drapers, or boot and shoe makers, or as travellers and agents for textile merchants. Such dovetailing between related trades and occupations was a common strategy in small business families, allowing privileged sources of supply and customer contacts. It was a way of side stepping many competitive pressures, it allowed the reduction of transaction costs and facilitated a between-firms strategy of internalisation that generally worked to the advantage of the family in question. Inevitably, however, it was not a strategy aimed at profit maximisation, expansion or product innovation, though it may have generated many comfortable small businesses that were capable of supporting the entrepreneur and his or her family and be regarded as successful in those terms.[27] A good example is provided by the Misses Hollis, four sisters with an age range between 20 and 30 years when they set up in business in 1841 as dressmakers and milliners. Initially based in the premises of their father, who was a master tailor employing three men in 1851, the sisters remained in business for 34 years. All but one was a life-long spinster. Other male members of the Hollis family included a clothier in London and a bookseller in Peebles.[28]

Most of the women who were in business on their own account were born into a culture of small enterprise, with family situations that increased their chances of success in a competitive sector and a petite bourgeois preoccupation with maintaining independence on the basis of

---

[26] Irwin, *Women's work*, p. 33.

[27] There is a growing literature on the economic advantages that were gained by family firms in the nineteenth century. See Jones and Rose, *Family capitalism*; Rose, 'Family firm'; Owens, 'Inheritance'.

[28] Details derived from Census household schedules supplemented with family reconstitutions based on registers of births, marriages and deaths.

small capital. Theirs was a social world composed of shopkeepers and travelling salesmen, skilled artisans such as tailors, as well as clerks and teachers. Their female relatives were shopkeepers, lodging house-keepers and also, increasingly, teachers—the latter a useful source of customer contacts. They belonged to a social stratum that was commonly viewed with contempt by those above them in class—a social stratum that was characterised as narrow-minded, xenophobic and preoccupied with meanly-defined notions of respectability.[29] Like the Hollis sisters, such women were also predominantly life-long spinsters, living in households that were largely composed of women. Their marital situations and their domestic arrangements coloured contemporary perceptions of their worth and inevitably contributed to a marginalised social existence. Thirty-seven of the 53 Edinburgh businesses were composed of female family partnerships, two-thirds being sister partnerships, the rest comprising widowed mother and spinster daughters.

Female family partnerships allowed women entrepreneurs to exploit dove tailed skills in different areas of garment production and by living in the same household, to minimise their living costs.[30] A large house could double as a workshop and allowed the cheap accommodation and easy supervision of apprentices and other employees. Commonly, the most successful firms were those that could draw on several female relatives. A partnership of two was particularly vulnerable if one of the sisters became ill or died, or, more rarely, if one of them married. But these extended family partnerships, particularly those of spinster sisters, were also the most restrictive on the lives of the women involved since they tended to give rise to large all-women households and a commensurate narrowing of social opportunities. The relatively late age of business formation among women entrepreneurs suggests that the women in question had probably relinquished all expectation of marriage as a route in life. Once they were contained within such households, particularly those comprising spinster sisters, they were engaged in a form of business that was demanding of time and involved predominantly female customer contacts, and hence few women ever found the opportunity to marry. This was the experience of the Misses Lamb, milliners and dressmakers in Edinburgh between 1860 and 1888. The business was formed by four spinster sisters, aged between 32 and 39 years, living in a high-rental house with 18 rooms in the elite commercial district of Edinburgh which additionally provided

---

[29] See Crossick and Haupt, *Petite bourgeoisie*.
[30] Such survival strategies have a long history: see Hufton, *Prospect before her*.

accommodation for an elderly widowed mother and an elderly spinster aunt. Ten non-related 'assistants' also lived in the house, with ages ranging from 15 to 23 and there were two domestic servants. There were 18 women in the household in total, which doubled as workshop and place of business. None of the sisters ever married. One of them died in the 1870s and the firm ended when the sisters left Edinburgh— possibly for East Lothian, where they had family connections—when they were all in their sixties. Given the scale of the enterprise, they had almost certainly generated enough wealth from the business to enjoy a reasonably comfortable old age in retirement. But this was contingent on a dovetailed partnership strategy that had tied the women together for life.

Partnerships comprising widowed mother and daughters were less restrictive, as seen in the case of a firm that was founded in Edinburgh in 1864 by a family of women comprising a mother aged 44 and her four unmarried daughters, following the suicide of the head of the household, who was a printer with a substantial firm facing financial ruin. It is unlikely that the elder daughters had any training in dressmaking prior to the founding of the business, though the younger girls were probably formally 'apprenticed' to their mother once the business was established. The mother was the daughter of a London silk mercer and had probably served an apprenticeship in dressmaking prior to her marriage. The suicide of the father, the family's loss of fortune and the business activities of the daughters, did not appear to have a long-term impact on their social status or life chances since one of the sisters married an accountant and another married a solicitor.[31] A fifth sister did not enter the trade, but was employed as a music teacher, which provided complementary contacts for the family business. The brother of the family became a sugar merchant and the firm of Misses Hofford, dressmakers and milliners, with a substantial shop in central Edinburgh, flourished for over 40 years with a workforce of ten in 1891.

Male entrepreneurs rarely formed partnerships among siblings, preferring to keep their independence even where brothers were engaged in similar types of enterprise and thus retain the possibility of forming their own household and establishing a family.[32] Some women entrepreneurs similarly engaged in loose arrangements of individual firms informally connected within a family network, particularly where the women in question were married. Three of the firms that feature in

[31] Family reconstitution details.
[32] For discussion of this see Nenadic, 'Small family firm'.

the 53 Edinburgh case studies were of this type, all connected with a single family. The women behind the firms were Marie Pauline Souyris, née Roques, a French woman, the daughter of a linen weaver, sister of a merchant in London and married to a mercantile shipping clerk in Edinburgh, who was in business as a dressmaker between 1867 and 1898. The second was Isabella Roques, née Wight, married to Casimir Roques who was a perfumer in Edinburgh and brother to Marie Pauline Souyris. Isabella Roques was in business as a milliner and dressmaker between 1862 and 1907, sometimes in partnership with a cousin called Christina Wight, who was married to Henry Bourdeaux, another Frenchman and a master hairdresser by trade. The firm of Roques and Wight existed between 1863 and 1892. This complex of businesses and trades, embracing women's garment making, perfumery and hairdressing—all conducted from elite business premises in central Edinburgh, contained within a tight family network and with high status 'French' associations—was clearly successful in supporting the families in question.[33] When she died in 1898, Marie Souyris, a widow of 58, left a fortune of almost £700.[34]

It is not surprising that the 'new woman' should have manifested little desire to enter such a business sector when age of start-up was so late, relevant family connections were critical, the prevailing tone was so distinctly 'petite bourgeois' and the most successful entrepreneurs were characterised by life-long spinsterhood and household situations that were intensely feminised and inevitably, therefore, socially marginalised. The concentration on a female market place resulted in a further characteristic of this most significant area of women-owned business that was likely to act as a disincentive to women who were seeking a career in the public world. This was manifested in the simple fact that most businesses in the women's garment sector invested great efforts into the minimisation of their business presence in the public eye, and conspicuously cultivated non-businesslike behaviour as the best route to profitability. In order to sell an image of desirable products to elite women it was necessary to engage in a highly personalised bespoke service and conduct the business from a domestic environment of conspicuous gentility and femininity. In essence, such businesses traded successfully by exploiting and actively reifying 'separate spheres' ideologies in their contacts with the market. Such characteristics

---

[33] For similar connections in 20th century USA see Scranton, *Beauty and business*.

[34] Details taken from City Directories, Census and family reconstitutions. Also from the inventory of wealth at death of Marie Souyris. N.A.S. SC70/1/372, pp. 617–25.

allowed women to secure stable and loyal customers among the elite and to attract socially aspirant women seeking to engage in the consumption of a luxury product with intense cultural associations. But it militated against the pursuit of business expansion and certainly limited opportunities for forward integration into mass production or the large-scale retail of ready-made clothing. Relationships with suppliers and wholesalers were wholly businesslike, governed by the market and based on the pursuit of efficiency and good prices, but relationships with customers were culturally defined.[35]

Women and advertising

The absence of a desire to cultivate a significant public profile among such businesses, particularly when compared with those of men engaged in the same sector, is well illustrated through advertising. The use of advertising in the industries of personal consumption reached the level of a fine art in the second half of the nineteenth century.[36] Newspapers, magazines and other regular publications such as city directories were full of advertisements, often detailed and elaborately illustrated, designed to make new markets and gain advantages over rivals. Sophisticated advertising was more closely associated with big companies with a national market and particularly with branded products than with smaller firms, but localised producers and businesses with an emphasis on bespoke production also employed many of the classic advertising techniques. Women in business in the garment trades, even those with large firms, were, however, poorly represented in the advertising pages of local publications. There were 1,834 such businesses in existence in Edinburgh between 1861 and 1891 that were recorded in the annual trade lists of the *City Directory*, yet during these years only 31 women employed separate advertising in the substantial advertiser's index of the same publication. Of the 53 case studies of long-surviving and successful firms for whom detailed case histories have been constructed, none engaged in any form of business-generating advertising in local publications, including newspapers. Of course, it was possible to advertise the existence of a business through means other than printed publications. There was a wide use of shop-front signs to signal the presence of business at a particular location—as can be identified through business inventories when trade was suspended following sequestration—but these were discrete because the most important

---

[35] For a detailed account see Nenadic, 'Social shaping'.
[36] Richards, *Commodity culture*.

route for gaining new markets was through personal recommendation through informal networks of customer contacts and friends.[37]

Two-thirds of the women entrepreneurs that used advertisements did so for the most basic of reasons, merely to announce the existence of a newly formed firm and inform potential customers of their place of business. Five out of the 31 cases were simple change-of-address notices given by existing firms of standing and stability. One of the advertisers was the widow of John Conway, a substantial clothes dealer engaged in both ready-made retail and bespoke production for men and women, who sought to inform her customers that she remained in business to carry on the trade following his death.[38] Only four firms associated with the women's garment trades and in the ownership of women made sophisticated use of advertising to project their business and engage directly with the competition. All were active in the 1870s, which seems to have been a critical decade in women's attempts to establish a stronger profile in the business world. Three of these very unique businesses traded conspicuously on an association with a prior and long-established firm with a high market profile. Miss Taylor, proprietor of the 'Millinery and Dressmaking Establishment' in 4 Hope Street,

---

[37] These were available in a standard format by the later nineteenth century, supplied by mail order by the big dressmakers warehouses and advertised in publications like *Weldon's Ladies Journal*, which catered for the trade and for home dressmaking.

[38] This was announced in the following way, *Edinburgh Directory, 1845–6*, p. 505:
'CLOTHING DEPOSITORY, No. 4, ST MARY'S WYND – Mrs Conway begs to return thanks to the numerous supporters of her late Husband for the last twenty-three years, and to intimate that she continues to carry on the business, in all its branches, exclusively, at No. 4, ST MARY'S WYND, where a complete assortment of every article connected with the trade may be obtained at very moderate prices. Observe – J. CONWAY, No. 4, ST MARY'S WYND, Second Shop from Cannongate'. The next year she placed a second advertisement in the same publication, with a somewhat different text, suggesting that as a woman alone she was encountering difficulties in at least one area of her established business:
'CLOTHING DEPOSITORY, No. 4, ST MARY'S WYND – Mrs Conway, in returning grateful thanks for the continued support she has received, begs to intimate, that the business is still carried on (in all its branches) in the same Equitable Manner which has secured such Decided Preference for the last Twenty-Four years. Mrs C. can with confidence assure her friends, that her foreman is highly qualified, by long experience, to make up, in the first style of fashion, Gentlemen's and Boy's Apparel, which will be sold at very Moderate Prices....'. By the early 1850s the firm, still trading from the same premises, was in the hands of Patrick Conway, probably a son. Mrs Conway, although still alive, had retired from business.

Charlotte Square made the following declaration in her advertisement of 1868, which was repeated in successive years:

> Mary Taylor, from the late Madame Chaffard's, 2 Castle Street, begs to inform the Ladies of Edinburgh and Vicinity that she is now in full possession of the above premises, where she will be happy to receive their orders. Miss T. trusts that, from her experience in Madame Chaffard's business, and the satisfaction expressed by those Ladies who patronised that Establishment, that she will receive and continue to merit their approbation.

Madame Chaffard, of the Magasin Francais in Castle Street, had also employed elaborate advertising in the form of an engraved trade card for a few years in the 1850, when she herself first entered business. Mary Taylor moved to a less salubrious business location in 1871 and remained in business for the next 20 years without again resorting to advertising.[39]

Another entrepreneur was Miss Ogg, a corset maker by trade, who engaged in a variety of partnerships with female relatives in the garment sector between the 1860s and 1890s, some running simultaneously, suggesting a complex business network and aggressive entrepreneurship. She advertised the London Straw Hat and Millinery Warehouse in the mid-1870s, the business of Laing and Ogg, late of 'Mitchell and Heriot', the latter firm having been in trade since the 1830s.[40] Madame Wortham, a lace cleaner and mender, married to Henry Wortham, a silk and woollen dyer of Queen Street and London Street in Edinburgh, operated a parallel business with her husband from the same premises and advertised in 1858 that she was the 'daughter of Mrs Curling, Woodstock Street, London, Lace mender and cleaner to HER MAJESTY and the Court'. By 1862, she was describing herself—with what veracity is not certain—as lace mender to Her Majesty.[41]

In each of these relatively rare cases of elaborate marketing through directory advertising the strategy was the same: to project the credentials and status of the individual entrepreneur by virtue of association with a notable well-established name, rather than to promote the product that they produced. The link with fashionable French names and titles was a further aspect of this strategy of selling an individual and their genteel or fashionable associations, rather than selling a standardised product. The absence of a culture of product innovation or business expansion is

---

[39] *Edinburgh Directory, 1869–70*, p. 64.
[40] *Edinburgh Directory, 1877–78*, p. 105, plus case-study details.
[41] *Edinburgh Directory, 1864–65*, p. 111.

striking. There was, indeed, only one woman-owned firm in Edinburgh broadly associated with garment production to employ full-page advertising of the 'puff' variety, with an emphasis on the product, as seen so commonly in the marketing strategies of male entrepreneurs. Miss J.S. Miller of the 'General Sewing Machine Depot', in addition to illustrating her advertisement of 1870 with an engraving of a sewing machine and providing detailed costings of the different machines available, declared that 'All kinds of first-class hand and treadle machines [were] sold, taught, cleaned and repaired on the shortest notice'. The career of J.S. Miller illustrates some of the problems of women who endeavoured to move beyond the narrow range of feminised business activities in garment making. For five years prior to becoming a sewing machine agent, one of only two women in Edinburgh to enter this predominantly male pursuit in the 1870s, she was a dressmaker in partnership with a sister and running a business from home. On becoming a sewing machine retailer and agent—possibly following the marriage or death of her sister-partner—she moved into separate commercial premises and advertised vigorously for two years. But the business was not a success. In 1872 the commercial premises and retail aspect to the firm were relinquished and she returned to home-based self-employment as a 'teacher of Singer sewing machines'. She continued in this line of work for five years and vanished from the Edinburgh records in 1878.[42]

The advertising of male-owned small businesses in the garment trades, though clearly dominated by simple information on the location of firms, reflects a more complex product-dominated engagement with the market, rather than an image-conscious and personal-service-focused strategy. Male businesses were more likely to be advertised through detailed descriptions including costings of the products on offer, suggesting aggressive price competition and product innovation, with an emphasis on the product itself rather than the producer as a particular type of personality. Such advertising was more likely to employ printed illustrations of the product and also, commonly, illustrations of business premises, which were often distorted in such a way to suggest that the firm was more substantial and illustrious that in reality.[43] There are no examples of women-owned firms employing advertising that included illustrations of the shop or workshop. Indeed, we know from evidence elsewhere that

---

[42] *Edinburgh Directory, 1870–71*, p. 61, plus case-study details.
[43] See Nenadic, 'Business advertising'.

women went to considerable efforts to disguise the business-character of their business premises.[44]

Dramatic claims such as 'cheapest in Edinburgh' or other attempts to achieve an image of distinctiveness were employed by male entrepreneurs in conjunction with complex advertising narratives that included detailed descriptions of the antecedents of the firm, the entrepreneur's connections with other firms and strong statements of the number of years in business. It was also common among large, well-established firms to engage in an advertising strategy that linked the history of the firm to the history and political affairs of the city in which they were located. This was done by the firm of J.R. Allan, silk mercers and clothiers that had risen to become one of the premier departmental stores in Edinburgh by the later nineteenth century and published a book in 1900—an elaborate advertising 'puff' ostensibly intended to celebrate the millennium—charting the advance of Edinburgh along with an account of changing fashions and linked to a laudatory history of the firm.[45] By stressing the political and public service dimensions of male-owned business, entrepreneurs—who were frequently represented on town councils and played a prominent role in local charitable and cultural institutions—enhanced the status of their businesses in the public eye.[46] Women entrepreneurs, inevitably divorced from the formal political process, never engaged in such marketing devices. The exploitation of male family connections in the business's name was also a common marketing strategy, sometimes undertaken without any foundation in fact. 'John Smith and Son' was not necessarily a father and son firm, it was merely the adoption of a name that gave an impression of long standing.[47] Though most successful women-owned businesses were family partnerships, this was never made explicit in the name of the firm because longevity and details of family relationships were potentially counter-productive in the sale of a fashionable image.

Spatial distribution of the garment trades

To be successful, women entrepreneurs in the garment trades did not have to make use of business advertising: indeed, to do so could undermine those images of exclusivity and intimacy on which

---

[44] In 1861 49 per cent of businesses of this type in Edinburgh were conducted from domestic premises; by 1891 this had risen to 79 per cent: *Edinburgh city rate books*.

[45] Gilbert (ed.), *Edinburgh in the nineteenth century*.

[46] The best account of this is provided by Hennock, *Fit and proper persons*.

[47] Examples are given in Nenadic, 'Small family firm'.

businesses tended to trade. Customers were cultivated through personal contact, they were also made aware of the existence of firms by a pattern of intense geographical concentration that characterised the sector.[48] From the 1820s, most firms of any substance were located in the New Town area of Edinburgh, in a part of the city that was rapidly developing as a central business district, characterised by luxury retail and prestige offices. An analysis of one of these New Town streets— Frederick Street between 1851 and 1871—reveals the degree to which substantial firms were located in domestic tenements alongside massive lodging-houses for apprentices, other garment workers and young men employed in retail and commerce. The most substantial of these lodgings in 1861 was owned by William Maxwell, a draper with a 37 room lodging house at 45 Frederick Street, which accommodated, in addition to his own family and four servants, nine young women boarders described as milliners and 46 young men variously employed as clerks and draper's assistants. The 'National Registry for Servants' was in Frederick Street, alongside other businesses directed towards wealthy female customers such as upholsterers, carvers and gilders, painters and decorators, china merchants, portrait artists, and teachers of music, drawing and languages. In 1851, the tenemented blocks in this relatively short street contained 16 women-owned businesses in the garment trades. Twenty years later there were 23 and numbers were rising. Several were among the successful and long-surviving firms that appear in the 53 case studies. Certain tenements were dominated by the trade, suggesting that major market benefits were gained by concentration. Number 13 Frederick Street accommodated two dressmakers, a milliner, a lace cleaner, a clothier and a tailor in 1861.[49]

From the 1850s to 1870s, in addition to this central concentration of elite firms, new areas of suburban concentration were emerging, particularly on the eastern side of the city running along Leith Walk to the north and to the south along Nicholson Street, leading to the developing middle-class suburbs of Newington and Grange. Intense suburban concentration continued at several points of new lower middle class and artisan housing in the years from 1870 to 1890, notably in the Bruntsfield, Tollcross, Morningside and Haymarket areas.[50] The suburban firms of the late nineteenth century were more likely to be classified as self-employed or private dressmakers catering for less

---

[48] This appears to have been greater than in other areas of small business, though the evidence for this is sparse: see Scola, *Feeding the Victorian city*.

[49] Details taken from census schedules linked to rate book information.

[50] Suburban building development for the lower middle classes is described in Rodger, *Transformation of Edinburgh*.

wealthy clients than the central firms of the New Town, but they were similarly concentrated. Spatially, the distribution of businesses was an accurate mirror of customer type and product, conforming to a geography that was gender-defined by virtue of both the producers and the customers.

Conclusion: masculine business rhetoric and the 'new woman'

When seeking opportunities to make their way in the world, young middle-class women did not see business ownership in the garment trades as an attractive option. The gendered geography of the sector merely underlined their negative perceptions. Moreover, by the later nineteenth century, reflecting the middle-class antipathy, new entrants to the sector were increasingly likely to be drawn from a working-class background, from among women who saw business ownership as a route to upward social mobility and were able to circumvent the need for a lengthy apprenticeship or family connections through exploiting newly available commercially-produced scientific systems of cutting and commercial paper patterns.[51] Why, therefore, did middle class women and in particular the ambitious 'new woman' looking for a career not seek access to other areas of business? The answer here is that, just as the traditional women's sectors of business were defined and circumscribed by notions of femininity, those of men were shaped by ideas of masculinity, and this masculinity was of a variety that by the later part of the nineteenth century was intensely inimical to female entry and participation in most areas of business.

Two masculine ethics emerged in the early years of the nineteenth century which together defined the middle-class sense of maleness.[52]

---

[51] One contemporary commentator cites the following example of such a woman in Glasgow: 'She had started life as a factory worker, but had felt she might do well in dressmaking if she could only get the training. She managed to save money to send to America for charts and instructions pertaining to a scientific method of dressmaking, "which was a new thing in these days". She then set to work with a girl friend to master the system in their evenings after their hard days work was over. By and by, after a little practice on their own frocks, they ventured to rent a back kitchen in the neighbourhood and took in dresses from friends. These they made in the evenings and on Saturdays. In time the orders became so numerous that the mill work was given up, and my informant had fairly launched herself in to the world as a professional dressmaker. When I visited her she was established in an excellent business and presiding over fifteen girls': Irwin, *Women's work*, p. 36.

[52] See Rosen, *Changing fiction*; Hall, *Muscular Christianity*; Roper and Tosh (eds), *Manful assertions*.

The professional ethic was the first to evolve, building on earlier traditions of service to church and court. The professional ethic stressed intellectual accomplishment and the exercise of the rational mind. There was emphasis upon service to the public good, which validated professional involvement in the political sphere and justified the relatively controlled competitive environment in which professionals, protected by their associations and by government legislation, increasingly operated. Overt moral probity was regarded as the basis of professional rights to exercise authority.[53] The business ethic, though less formally codified than the professional ethic, was founded on Darwinian principles of competitive struggle and the 'survival of the fittest'. Rationality was there, but of equal importance was enterprise and daring. Physical energy was a necessary condition for engagement in business in ways that were not apparent in the professions. The provision of employment and the creation of wealth for the nation as well as for the individual entrepreneur were seen as moral virtues, and validated rights to engage in national and local politics.[54]

Each of these two ethics was quintessentially masculine. Rationality, physicality, individualism, competitive struggle and political involvement were not compatible with idealised notions of womanhood. Yet masculinity was a contested arena in the nineteenth century, particular because of the cultivation in the middle decades of the century of the domesticated and sensitive family man as a central pillar of middle-class morality. This can be seen in a number of guises, notably in early-Victorian 'condition of England' fiction, such as Charles Dickens' *Dombey and Son* (first published in 1848) where the ruthless businessman Dombey is tamed into domestic submission by the vagaries of business failure and fraud. [55] Or in the biographies of the period, most powerfully in the exemplary details of entrepreneurs, their wives and their families, that were provided by Samuel Smiles in his endeavours to promote 'self help' and 'thrift' among the working classes.[56] There is some evidence in the 1860s and early 1870s— illustrated, for example, in the experience of Miss Miller, the sewing machine agent described above—that women entrepreneurs were beginning to make their way into business areas beyond the traditional spheres of the garment trades, just as they were starting to gain entry into the formerly male-only professions and were calling for equal access

---

[53] Perkin, *Professional society*, chapter 1.
[54] Some of these issues are raised in Nenadic, 'Businessmen'.
[55] See Russell, *Novelist and Mammon*.
[56] Smiles, *Self help*; Smiles, *Thrift*.

to legal and political rights. Arguably, they were exploiting the 'softening' tendencies in ideas about mid-Victorian manhood. But this had ended by the 1880s in the sphere of business, probably due to a redefining of the business ethic contained within a new-masculinity backlash.

Shifting notions of masculinity coexisted with shifting notions of desirable femininity. The 'newly-masculine man' of the late nineteenth century was matched by the 'new woman'. But though 'new women' emerged to challenge men in the public spheres of politics and the professions, they singularly avoided, as they did through much of the twentieth century, attempts to seek entry into the world of business entrepreneurship. The post-1880 backlash in business had given rise to a male-only, anti-female culture of extreme physicality, tempered by Christian morality or by imperial-militaristic adventuring.[57] Falling rates of marriage among middle class men; the rise of male-only business clubs with a strong air of anti-domesticity; the popularity of the Volunteer and Masonic movements, both important for business networking; jingoism; and growing fears of international competition in business, were inevitably communicated through the rhetoric of business success.[58] The image of big business became increasingly alien to middle-class women, despite their successful endeavours to enter the masculinised domains of work and politics and active permeation of the public service professions, with the successful adoption of the scientific-rational and competitive ethos that was necessary for the latter. The image of big business was also increasingly alien to other sectors of society and criticised for its growing amorality and ruthlessness.[59]

The intensely aggressive, new-masculine tone of late nineteenth-century and Edwardian business, kept the 'new woman' out of most areas of entrepreneurial opportunity just as effectively as the intensely feminine tone of the conventional areas of female entrepreneurship acted to repel those women who were not from a specific cultural and family background. This remained the case well into the twentieth century. As small businesses in all sectors went into rapid decline in the interwar years and as the bespoke dressmaking trades were finally replaced by the ready-made industry, the number of women engaged in business entered an all-time low. Although young women sought an

---

[57] See Dawson, *Soldier heroes.*
[58] Nenadic, 'Victorian middle classes'.
[59] Perhaps most famously in the Edwardian period, in E. M. Forster's *Howard's End* (first published in 1910) which was deeply hostile to the characterisation of British national identity and business life (in the form of the Wilcox family, wealthy colonial rubber importers) as imperialist, masculine and brutal.

ever-widening range of careers in the 1920s and 1930s, business ownership was rarely, if ever, considered.[60] The legacy of this nineteenth-century 'gendered' characterisation of entrepreneurship and a particular rhetoric of business success continues to be felt in Britain today.[61]

---

[60] See Orr, 'Continuity and change'.

[61] Scase and Goffee, *Women in charge*. The situation in the United States, where women historically had a more prominent role in business, is different: see Bird, *Enterprising women*.

14

From Hartland to Hartley: marital status and occupation in the late nineteenth century

CHRISTINE JONES

Introduction

Several contributors to this volume have focused on the work done by married women. This chapter focuses on the work done by never-married women, contrasting it with that recorded for their ever-married sisters and neighbours. It also covers geographical, temporal and occupational areas not explicitly addressed elsewhere in this volume, by selecting women born before 1837 and still alive at the time of the 1881 census in five groups of parishes. The term never-married is used in preference to 'single' since in some other works 'single' includes widows as well as spinsters. An age was required after which few women tended to marry for the first time to distinguish the permanently never-married from the not-yet-married. Forty-five years is the age used by most previous researchers in work involving marital status, although Froide argues for a younger age.[1]

Five contrasting areas are examined. The first area is formed by a group of non-contiguous agricultural parishes in west and south Devon—Hartland, Thurlestone, Ipplepen and Bridford.[2] The second area consists of two parishes in Essex—Terling and Great Oakley—again non-contiguous and forming a contrasting agricultural region.[3]

---

[1] Wall, 'Woman alone'; Anderson, 'Social position of spinsters'; Litchfield, 'Single people in the nineteenth-century'; Wrigley and Schofield, *Population history of England*; Bennett and Froide (eds), *Singlewomen*; Froide, 'Old Maids'; Froide, 'Hidden women'.

[2] For more information on these parishes see Bouquet, *Family, servants and visitors*; Snowdon, *Born to farm in Devon*.

[3] For more information on agriculture in Terling see Gavin, *Ninety years of family farming*.

Another group are the market towns of Banbury (Oxfordshire) and Gainsborough (Lincolnshire).[4] The domestic rather than factory-based textile industry is represented by Gedling and Carlton (Nottinghamshire) where framework knitting predominated, and by Alcester (Warwickshire) which was the site of another localised domestic industry, needle making.[5] The final locality is made up of the mining communities in the parish of Earsdon (Northumberland) including Hartley.[6]

Evaluation of sources

Data for this chapter are taken from the machine-readable version of the 1881 census of England and Wales, available from the UK Data Archive, University of Essex.[7] Previous work on the census enumerators' books (hereafter CEBs) has been based on place of enumeration. It is only with the development of the national index to the 1881 census that it has become possible to undertake a study by birthplace, regardless of current place of residence.[8] The index to the 1881 census enables a search to be made across all enumeration districts by place of birth. This overcomes the problem experienced by many researchers of identifying the 'movers'.[9] In evaluating the CEBs as a source, several contributors to this volume and elsewhere comment on possible inaccuracies in the recording of occupations and ages.[10]

---

[4] For more information on these market towns see Trinder, *Victorian Banbury*; Beckwith, *Book of Gainsborough*. For a contemporary description of life in Banbury see Herbert, *Shoemaker's window*; and for a feminine point of view see Beesley, *My life*.

[5] For more information on these areas of domestic industry see Jacks, *Confession of an octogenarian*, pp. 40–9; Gloger and Chester, *More to a needle than meets the eye*.

[6] For more information on this mining district see Jones, 'Personal tragedy or demographic disaster'.

[7] Genealogical Society of Utah, Federation of Family Historians, *1881 Census for England and Wales, the Channel Islands and Isle of Man* [computer file] (Colchester, Essex, The Data Archive [distributor], 1997). SN 3643. For an account of how this was created see Woollard, 'Creating a machine-readable version of the 1881 census', pp. 98–101.

[8] Williams, 'Migration and the 1881 census index'.

[9] Levine, 'Reliability of parochial registration'; Ruggles, 'Migration, marriage, and mortality'; Sharpe, 'Locating the "Missing Marryers"'; Robin, *From childhood to middle age*; Levine, 'Sampling history'; Razzell, 'Conundrum'; Ruggles, 'Limitations'.

[10] In addition to those in this volume see Higgs, *Clearer sense*, pp. 78–82; Mills and Schürer (eds), *Local communities*, pp. 74–7.

However, the reliability of the reporting of marital status does not appear to have been studied. Higgs suggests that there may be some cases of doubtful enumeration. He cites as possibilities engaged women describing themselves as married, female married heads of household who may be separated, widows who still regarded themselves as married and separated individuals describing themselves as widowed. He concludes that 'these and similar questions must remain in the realms of speculation, and each case must be considered on its merits'.[11]

Considering those aged 45 years and over, reliability is likely to be greatest among those still living in the parish where they were born, especially if that was a rural community. Reporting errors, whether intentional or accidental, are more likely to occur in communities where the person's past is unknown, and particularly in urban areas. Reporting errors are most likely to occur in institutions, especially where, because of mental or physical handicap, assumptions are made about the individual by staff completing the schedule. In nineteenth-century workhouses and asylums, particularly where the inmate was elderly and described as deaf, dumb, imbecile, idiot, or lunatic, little reliance can be placed upon the marital status recorded.[12] Staff may have assumed people to be married when they were single or assumed them to be widowed when they still had a spouse living.

Marital status by region and locality

Table 14.1 shows the distribution of women aged 45 and over in 1881 across the five localities by marital status. For England and Wales as a whole in 1881 the proportion of women aged 45 and over who were never-married was 11.2 per cent, but this figure disguises considerable regional and local variation.[13] The proportions of women born in these localities who were never-married stood below the national average in all areas except the area of domestic industry.

Occupations by marital status and region or locality

Other contributors to this volume have discussed the possible under-recording of women's occupations in the CEBs.[14] Table 14.2 compares the proportions of women for whom the occupation field was left blank

[11] Higgs, *Clearer sense*, pp. 77–8.
[12] Higgs, *Clearer sense*, pp. 87–90.
[13] BPP 1883, LXXX, *1881 Census of England and Wales. Population, ages, condition as to marriage*, p. 89. For the geographical variation see Jones, 'Those whom God hath not joined', pp. 44–80.
[14] See chapter 2, pp 32–42; chapter 5, pp. 101–3; chapter 8.

Table 14.1 Women aged 45 and over in 1881 by area of birth and marital status

Areas	Never-married No.	%	Ever-married No.	%	Total No.
Devon rural	77	9.7	718	90.3	795
Essex rural	32	7.6	391	92.4	423
Market towns	200	10.4	1,714	89.6	1,914
Domestic industry	105	11.2	836	88.8	941
Mining communities	66	8.7	693	91.3	759
Total	480	9.9	4,352	90.1	4,832
England and Wales	292,151	11.2	2,312,644	88.8	2,604,795

Sources: 1881 CEBs and BPP 1883, LXXX, p.89.

by area of birth and by marital status. This field was far more likely to be completed for never-married women than for ever-married women. Those most likely to have an entry in the occupation field were the never-married women born in the market towns. The ever-married women born in the Devon rural parishes were more likely to have an entry in the occupation field than ever-married women born in other areas.

The likelihood of the occupation field being completed would seem to be strongly related to other forms of support. Many ever-married women were described by their husband's occupation even when it was not an occupation in which she could have assisted or continued the

Table 14.2 Women for whom occupation field was left blank, by area of birth and marital status

Areas	Never-married No.	%	Ever-married No.	%
Devon rural	15	19.5	319	44.4
Essex rural	8	25.0	240	61.4
Market towns	26	13.0	995	58.1
Domestic industry	21	20.0	448	53.6
Mining communities	14	21.2	490	70.7
Total	84	17.5	2,492	57.3

Source: 1881 CEBs.

Table 14.3 Ever-married women described by the occupation of a male family member

Areas	No.	%
Devon rural	164	22.8
Essex rural	53	13.6
Market towns	179	10.4
Domestic industry	50	6.0
Mining communities	63	9.1
Total	509	11.7

Source: 1881 CEBs.

business after his death—for example rector's wife, pilot's mother, solicitor's widow. Table 14.3 shows the numbers and percentages of ever-married women described by the occupation of a husband or son. Women born in the rural Devon parishes were over three times as likely to be described by the occupation of a male family member as women born in the areas of domestic industry. However, only four of the 440 never-married women were described by the occupation of a male relative—for example vicar's aunt, coal miner's sister, farmer's daughter. This demonstrates how few was the number of male relatives that elderly never-married women could rely upon for financial support. Contemporaries believed that never-married women were frequently themselves contributing to the support of parents, siblings and nieces.[15] Demographic simulation for women born before 1855 suggests that 53 per cent of those aged 45 would not have had a parent still alive and a further 39 per cent would only have had one parent alive. Similarly while 92 per cent of women aged 45 would have siblings, by the age of 60 this had fallen to 86 per cent.[16]

A few women had an entry in the column headed 'Rank, Profession or Occupation' that was not a job in the twenty-first century meaning of the word occupation, although it may have kept them fully occupied. Examples of these are wife, housewife, domestic duties, at home, lady, gentlewoman, retired, boarder, visitor, and old age.[17] Table 14.4 shows

[15] Jameson, *Memoirs and essays*, pp. 296–7. See also Boyd-Kinnear, 'Social position of women', p. 332.
[16] Zhao, 'Demographic transition', Tables 7, 9 and 11.
[17] My favourite is from another rural Devon parish, Kenton, in which Mary Bond, an 86 year-old widow, who was nonetheless enumerated as the head of the household, stated her occupation as 'principally in bed'.

Table 14.4   Non-employment entries, by marital status and area

Areas	Never-married		Ever-married	
	No.	%	No.	%
Devon rural	2	2.6	42	5.8
Essex rural	1	3.1	5	1.3
Market towns	9	4.5	61	3.6
Domestic industry	6	6.3	20	2.4
Mining communities	2	1.7	11	1.6
Total	20	4.1	139	3.2

Source: 1881 CEBs.

how these types of non-employment entry were distributed across the areas by marital status. The numbers and percentages are very small and are only significant when combined with the other categories of unemployed women.

A great many women from the age of 45 onwards, whether they had ever been married or not, were living on income from some form of investment, annuity, interest or dividend, or property in the form of land or houses.[18] Table 14.5 shows the distribution of women living on investments by marital status and by area. The proportion of never-married women living on investments was highest in the market towns,

Table 14.5   Women living on investments, by marital status and area

Areas	Never-married		Ever-married	
	No.	%	No.	%
Devon rural	13	16.9	39	5.4
Essex rural	5	15.6	11	2.8
Market towns	47	23.5	93	5.4
Domestic industry	16	15.2	27	3.2
Mining communities	6	9.1	33	4.8
Total	87	18.1	203	4.7

Source: 1881 CEBs.

[18] For a study of alternative strategies for securing an income other than employment see Green and Owens, 'Gentlewomanly capitalism?'.

Table 14.6   Women who were paupers, by marital status and area

Areas	Never-married		Ever-married	
	No.	%	No.	%
Devon rural	0	0.0	12	1.7
Essex rural	0	0.0	5	1.3
Market towns	5	2.5	23	1.3
Domestic industry	0	0.0	5	0.6
Mining communities	1	1.5	2	0.3
Total	6	1.3	47	1.1

Source: 1881 CEBs.

where nearly a quarter of all never-married women were living on annuities, interest or property, compared with less than 10 per cent in the mining communities. Among ever-married women the proportions were lower in each locality since it was mainly the widows rather than the wives who drew their support from investments. Again the proportion was relatively high in the market towns.[19]

At the other end of the social scale were women described as paupers or on parish relief.[20] Table 14.6 shows the distribution of paupers. None of the never-married women born in the rural areas or the area of domestic industry were recorded in the census as receiving relief. However, the proportion of never-married women born in the market towns and in the mining communities reported as receiving relief was greater than the proportion of ever-married women.

When the numbers in Tables 14.2 to 14.6 are combined and subtracted from those in Table 14.1 the remaining numbers are those women who had a declared occupation that, following the nomenclature of Higgs, might be termed 'true' work.[21] Table 14.7 presents this calculation for never-married women and Table 14.8 the equivalent calculation for ever-married women. Between 56 and 62 per

[19] The proportion of widows living on investments in the mining areas may be inflated by those supported by the Hartley Relief Fund, see Jones, 'Personal tragedy'.

[20] However, the margin between independence and poverty was a very fine line and some annuitants may have been living on little more than some paupers. For a description of genteel poverty see Gaskell, *Cranford*, especially chapters 1 and 14.

[21] Higgs, 'Tabulation of occupations', chapter 11 above.

Table 14.7 Never-married women with and without 'true' work by area

	Devon rural	Essex rural	Market towns	Domestic industry	Mining communities	Total
All aged 45 and over	77	32	200	105	66	480
Occupation field blank	15	8	26	21	14	84
Described by occupation of male relative	0	0	1	1	2	4
Non-employment entries	2	1	9	6	2	20
Investments	13	5	47	16	6	87
Paupers	0	0	5	0	1	6
Residual = numbers with 'true' work	47	18	112	61	41	279
Percentage with 'true' work	61.0	56.3	56.0	58.1	62.1	58.1

Source: 1881 CEBs.

Table 14.8 Ever-married women with and without 'true' work by area

	Devon rural	Essex rural	Market towns	Domestic industry	Mining communities	Total
All aged 45 and over	718	391	1,714	836	693	4,352
Occupation field blank	319	240	995	448	490	2,492
Described by occupation of male relative	164	53	179	50	63	509
Non-employment entries	42	5	61	20	11	139
Investments	39	11	93	27	33	203
Paupers	12	5	23	5	2	47
Residual = numbers with 'true' work	142	77	363	286	94	962
Percentage with 'true' work	19.8	19.7	21.2	34.2	13.6	22.1

Source: 1881 CEBs.

cent of never-married women were engaged in work compared with between 14 and 34 per cent of ever-married women.[22] The highest proportions were among never-married women born in the mining communities and the Devon rural areas, whereas these were the areas from which ever-married women were least likely to be engaged in work. Conversely among those born in the market towns, never-married women were less likely to be engaged in work, while ever-married women were more likely to be working, though those born in areas of domestic industry were most likely to be working. This begins to point to differences in the nature of the work being done by never-married and ever-married women.

Work undertaken by women by marital status

To examine female employment by occupational group the figures for the residual values from Tables 14.7 and 14.8 will be used for calculating percentages rather than the population figures from Table 14.1. Since the numbers involved in each occupational group at the level of the region are small the areas will be combined to examine the differences between never-married women and ever-married women.

Thirty years earlier a great many of the 4,832 women born in these five areas would have been in some form of domestic service, but service has usually been regarded as a life-cycle stage.[23] Here the women aged 45 and over enumerated in domestic service are observed, and the variations in their proportions by marital status.[24] Table 14.9 includes all those women classified by the Registrar General as working in 'Domestic Service or Offices', both domestic servants and those in the other service occupations, such as charwoman. It presents them by marital status and by type of occupation. The general servants also include a chambermaid and a housemaid. They and the housekeepers may include women who were serving their relatives.[25] Cooks, laundresses (which includes those described as washerwomen) and charwomen were less likely to be mis-specified.[26]

---

[22] These rates are low compared with those found by Goose in the St Albans region of Hertfordshire in 1851: *St Albans*, Table 7, p. 90.

[23] Horn, *Rise and fall of the Victorian servant*, p. 25.

[24] It is not possible to tell from census data alone whether they had remained in domestic service since their late teens or had returned to domestic service later in life.

[25] See chapters 11 and 12 by Higgs and Anderson, above.

[26] Charwomen includes those where the enumerator actually wrote 'chairwoman'.

Table 14.9   Women in domestic service or offices

Type of servant	Never-married		Ever-married	
	No.	%	No.	%
General	43	15.4	41	4.3
Housekeepers	46	16.5	83	8.6
Cooks	25	9.0	18	1.9
Laundresses	8	2.9	140	14.6
Charwomen	8	2.9	81	8.4
Total in domestic service or offices	130	46.6	363	37.7
Women with 'true' work	279	100.0	962	100.0

Source: 1881 CEBs.

Table 14.9 shows that, while a higher proportion of never-married working women than ever-married working women were engaged in domestic service and service occupations, the distribution within the occupations varied by marital status. Never-married women were more likely to be working as general or minor servants, as housekeepers or as cooks, occupations that were often residential, so providing accommodation as well as income, while ever-married women were more likely to be working as laundresses and charwomen, work done on a daily or weekly basis from their own homes.[27] That the proportion of ever-married housekeepers was also high may add weight to the suggestion that some of them were housewives.[28] No other occupational group involved even half as many women as those in domestic service or offices. The next most numerous group of women workers were those involved in the clothing trade as dressmakers, tailoresses and milliners, also including a shirt maker, corset and stay makers, and in most parishes anyone described as seamstress or needlewoman, but omitting those specifically making gloves or stockings.[29]

Another substantial group were the retailers. This was to be expected in the market towns, but was also found to be a significant way of earning a living for women from the mining areas and for never-married

[27] In one case the enumerator specifically wrote 'go out to day work (charwoman)' [sic].

[28] To check for this it would be necessary to examine the household composition for each of the women.

[29] The exceptions are seamstresses in Gedling who were working in the hosiery industry and needlewomen in Alcester who were working in the needle making industry. These two groups will be described later.

women from the areas of domestic industry. Among retailers are included all the varieties of shopkeeper together with dealers and hawkers. Davies discusses the role of alternative female healers.[30] In the areas studied here women were well represented as nurses and midwives and as companions, who may have been carrying out personal care functions, one being described specifically as an 'invalid lady's companion'. Women have also traditionally been providers of accommodation as boarding- or lodging-house keepers, innkeepers and licensed victuallers.[31] Education is another traditional sphere of female involvement common to all five geographic areas.

As Sharpe shows, the number of women recorded in the 1851 census in Essex as working in agriculture was small.[32] Snell, using settlement examinations, argued for a decreasing participation by women in agricultural work in arable areas.[33] However, Miller, comparing farm account books with CEBs, found a far wider range of agricultural work undertaken by women in the former than the latter.[34] Higgs is convinced that both the female and the male agricultural workforce were under-enumerated, the former more than the latter.[35] In this study agriculture includes both farmers and farm labourers, together with those in the dairy industry and market gardening. Accepting that agriculture was an occupational category in which women were particularly likely to be under-enumerated, it is nonetheless true that a higher proportion of women were involved in agriculture in the mining areas than in either of the rural areas.

Turning to the domestic industries, needle manufacture was specific to women born in and still living around Alcester. Women born in Alcester and enumerated as 'needlewoman', as well as those described as fish hook bender or maker, or as needle-driller, needle-eyer, needle-filer, needle forewoman, needle-hander, needle-header, needle-maker, needle-paperer, needle-picker, needle-spitter or needle-straightener were all assumed to be part of this domestic industrial process. Hosiery manufacture, although centred on Gedling, also involved women born in Banbury and Earsdon. Women born in Gedling who were enumerated as 'seamstress' were assumed not to be the equivalent of dressmaker in other areas, but to be the equivalent of hose seamer, hose

---

[30] See chapter 10, above.
[31] For a discussion of the position of women as landladies see Davidoff, 'Separation of home and work?'.
[32] Chapter 3 , above, p. 56.
[33] Snell, *Annals*, pp. 15–66.
[34] Miller, 'Hidden workforce'.
[35] Higgs, 'Occupational censuses'.

Table 14.10   Women in other occupational groups by marital status

Type of occupation	Never-married		Ever-married	
	No.	%	No.	%
Clothing trades	50	17.9	164	17.0
Retailers	30	10.8	111	11.5
Medical attendants	14	5.0	59	6.1
Food and lodging	7	2.5	52	5.4
Agriculture	7	2.5	33	3.4
Education	19	6.8	14	1.5
Needle manufacture	5	1.8	26	2.7
Hosiery	6	2.2	55	5.7
Other textiles	11	3.9	33	3.4
Miscellaneous	0	0.0	52	5.5
Women with 'true' work	279	100.0	962	100.0

Source: 1881 CEBs.

stitcher, hosiery hand, hosiery maker up, seamer or stocking seamer. The other textile involvement was in both silk and lace making in Nottinghamshire and, outside of the main area of the industry discussed by Goose, in straw hat manufacture in Oxfordshire and Lincolnshire.[36] There were a few other isolated domestic workers still undertaking spinning and weaving, while some women had moved from their birthplaces to work in the mills as spinners.

This leaves a few miscellaneous occupations which do not fall neatly into any category such as book and boot binders, carpenters, gate and lodge keepers, labourers, millers, postmistresses, a barber, a basket maker, a Bible woman, a blacksmith, a brush maker, a cab proprietor, a district visitor, a house painter, a plumber, a potter, a salt maker, an upholsteress, workers at a paper mill in Banbury, and women who were assistants on a barge and at a concert hall.

Table 14.10 presents these categories of workers by marital status. In many of the categories the proportions of never-married women and ever-married women are similar, but never-married women are over-represented in education while being under-represented in food and lodging and in hosiery. Never-married women were prominent among both governesses and schoolteachers.[37] While a few never-married

---

[36] See chapter 5, above.

[37] For a description of the life of one woman who worked in both capacities see Smith, *Autobiography*.

women kept boarding and lodging houses, there was only one never-married innkeeper. In hosiery, although there were seven female framework knitters (all ever-married) most of the knitting was done by men. It was their wives who sewed up the stockings. Their never-married daughters lived on investments (13 per cent) or followed other employment, as domestic servants (26 per cent), as dressmakers (15 per cent), as retailers, in education, in agriculture or mending lace or silk (5 per cent each).

Women as employers

A few women were employers and, although the numbers are small, as a proportion of women with 'true' work twice as many never-married women were employers as ever-married women. The women included two partners in an unspecified business from Hartland, a superintendent from Banbury, the matron of a girls' institution, the mistress of a private school and two grocers. Most of the female employers were farmers, cultivating a total of 786 acres, providing employment for eighteen men, nine boys and two girls. Other business women were a bookseller and printer employing three men and three boys, a confectioner employing two men and two boys, a glass and earthenware dealer employing one man and one boy, a brush maker employing three men and one woman, a coal merchant employing one man, a house painter employing three men and one boy, and a carver and gilder employing one man and one boy. Together these women provided employment for over 54 people.

Migration, marital status and work opportunities

Recent research using lifetime residential histories has added considerably to our understanding of the structure and processes, and to the social and cultural meaning, of migration.[38] Although the dataset created by Pooley and Turnbull included a lower percentage of never-married people than in the 1851 and 1891 censuses, they found that never-married people moved greater distances than ever-married people and were less constrained in their migration choices.[39] It would appear that around 56 per cent of the moves of never-married people were due to work, compared with 40 to 44 per cent of the moves of ever-married

---

[38] Pooley and Turnbull, *Migration and mobility*, Table 6.7, p. 215, summarises the characteristics of moves by never-married people.

[39] Pooley and Turnbull, *Migration and mobility*, pp. 43–4, 49, 68–9.

people.[40] Large cities attracted a disproportionate number of never-married migrants.[41] By contrast, never-married people were less likely than ever-married people to move between small places.[42] The occasions upon which never-married people moved were on entry to the labour market, following the death of a parent or after a family dispute.[43] Domestic servants, agricultural labourers and professionals were the employment categories most likely to move.[44]

Defining migration by regions rather than by parishes is not easy. At the beginning of this chapter five areas were described. Migration is taken to be movement out of one of these areas.[45] Movement from one parish to another of a similar type within the five study areas will not be considered as migration. Thus movement between agricultural parishes in west and south Devon will not be classed as migration, but movement to a city, such as Plymouth or Exeter, or to a different agricultural region would be considered to be migration. Movement between agricultural parishes in Essex will not be classed as migration, but movement to a different agricultural region, to towns, such as Colchester or Chelmsford, or into London would be considered to be migration. Similarly movement from Banbury or Gainsborough to a similar market town will not be classed as migration, but movement to a rural area or to a city would be considered as migration. Movement around Nottinghamshire, Leicestershire and Derbyshire, to other parishes where domestic textile production predominated will not be classed as migration, but movement to the factory-based textile industries of Yorkshire or Lancashire would be considered as migration. Movement from Alcester to Redditch (Worcestershire) will not be classed as migration since large numbers of the needle makers are known to have relocated to be closer to improved canal and rail transport facilities.[46] Movement into Birmingham is more difficult to classify since some women might have gone there to continue needle making while others would have gone into domestic service or taken advantage of the wider opportunities in trade, commerce or industry. Inspection of the

---

[40] Pooley and Turnbull, *Migration and mobility*, pp. 73–4.
[41] Pooley and Turnbull, *Migration and mobility*, pp. 119–21.
[42] Pooley and Turnbull, *Migration and mobility*, p. 133.
[43] Pooley and Turnbull, *Migration and mobility*, pp. 162, 260.
[44] Pooley and Turnbull, *Migration and mobility*, p. 157.
[45] This is at variance with the standard definition of migration: Pooley and Turnbull, *Migration and mobility*, pp. 7–19.
[46] BPP 1862, L, *Population tables. Vol. I. Numbers and distribution of the people, with index to names of places,* p. 481; see also Gloger and Chester, *More to a needle than meets the eye.*

Table 14.11   **Proportions of women who had migrated by area and marital status**

Areas	Never-married			Ever-married		
	migrants	all women	% migrant	migrants	all women	% migrant
Devon rural	30	77	39.0	243	718	33.8
Essex rural	15	32	46.9	150	391	38.4
Market towns	22	200	11.0	197	1,714	11.5
Domestic industry	26	105	24.8	199	836	23.8
Mining communities	13	66	19.7	102	693	14.7
Total	106	480	22.1	891	4,352	20.5

Source: 1881 CEBs.

enumerations shows that none of those born in Alcester who were living in Birmingham were working in any branch of needle making. Movement into Birmingham will therefore be considered as migration. Finally, movement between the mining communities of the Northumberland and Durham coalfield will not be classed as migration since it was an almost annual occurrence.[47] However, movement to coalfields in Lancashire, Staffordshire or South Wales, or to non-mining communities will be considered as migration.

Applying these definitions, the proportions of women who migrated by area and by marital status is shown in Table 14.11. Because the definition of migration from each area is different it is not possible to compare proportions of migrants within marital status across areas. However, each definition was consistently applied to women of each marital status and so it is possible to compare never-married with ever-married women within each area. It can be seen that a higher proportion of the never-married women than the ever-married women had migrated from each area except the market towns. It is more illuminating to compare migration and marital status for those with and without 'true work'. The results of this comparison are seen in Table 14.12. While for all women aged 45 and over the proportion of never-married women who had migrated was higher than the proportion of ever-married women who had migrated, this did not hold for those

[47] For migration between mining communities see Fynes, *Miners of Northumberland and Durham*, pp. 134, 260; see also Burt, *Autobiography*, p. 24; Tonks, 'A kind of life insurance', pp. 49–50.

Table 14.12 Women with and without 'true work' by marital and migration status

Work status	Never-married all women				Ever-married all women			
	migrants	all women	% migrant		migrants	all women	% migrant	
All aged 45 and over	106	480	22.1		891	4,352	20.5	
Occupation field blank	24	84	28.6		497	2,492	19.9	
Described by occupation of male relative	1	4	25.0		83	509	16.3	
Non-employment entries	4	20	20.0		33	139	23.7	
Investments	18	87	20.7		61	203	30.0	
Paupers	0	6	0.0		9	47	19.1	
Residual = numbers with 'true' work	59	279	21.1		208	962	21.6	

Source: 1881 CEBs.

with non-employment entries, those living on investments, or for paupers. None of the never-married paupers had migrated from the type of area in which they were born, although if they were enumerated in an institution such as a workhouse that might be located in a different parish within the Union. Thus they might have migrated according to the narrower definition of having left their parish of birth. Many of the never-married women living on investments were receiving an income from property inherited from their fathers and so were unlikely to move away from the area. The reasons for never-married women with non-employment entries to remain in the same area are less clear.

Among those women with 'true work' the proportions migrating are similar for never-married and ever-married women. It is these women that will now be examined in more detail. Table 14.13 presents women in the various types of domestic service and service occupations by marital and migration status. Across all types of service occupation never-married women were more likely to have migrated than ever-married women. Cooks and general servants who had remained single were particularly likely to have migrated compared with ever-married women working in these capacities. The opposite is true of housekeepers, an abnormally high proportion of ever-married housekeepers having migrated. Table 14.14 presents women in other occupational groups by marital and migration status. For those in the clothing trades, medical attendants, those supplying food and lodging, and those in agriculture the proportions migrating were similar for the never-married and the ever-married; nor were they very far removed from the overall average for women with 'true work'.

One group where there was a marked difference was the retailers. Ever-married shopkeepers and hawkers were slightly less likely than other workers to have migrated, but never-married shopkeepers and hawkers were even less likely to have migrated. Indeed never-married women working as retailers were very likely to be serving their local communities, either in the parish in which they were born or in a similar neighbouring parish. Education was another area in which the experiences of ever-married and never-married women differed. While the migration level of ever-married women was similar to that in other forms of employment, never-married women were predominantly educating children from backgrounds similar to their own, teaching in local schools or giving home tuition to the children of their own locality. This finding is somewhat unexpected as it might be thought that teaching skills would have been transportable, allowing single women a greater degree of geographical mobility. It is not surprising that migration rates should be low among the ever-married women

Table 14.13 Women in domestic service or offices by marital and migration status

Type of servant	Never-married			Ever-married		
	migrants	all women	% migrant	migrants	all women	% migrant
General	12	43	27.9	8	41	19.5
Housekeepers	12	46	26.1	26	83	31.3
Cooks	12	25	48.0	4	18	22.2
Laundresses	0	8	0.0	31	140	22.1
Charwomen	0	8	0.0	21	81	25.9
Total in domestic occupations	36	130	27.7	90	363	24.8

Source: 1881 CEBs.

Table 14.14 Women in other occupational groups by marital and migration status

Occupational group	Never-married			Ever-married		
	migrants	all women	% migrant	migrants	all women	% migrant
Clothing trades	12	50	24.0	35	164	21.3
Retailers	2	30	6.7	18	111	16.2
Medical attendants	4	14	28.6	16	59	27.1
Food and lodging	2	7	28.6	16	52	30.8
Agriculture	1	7	14.3	6	33	18.2
Education	1	19	5.3	3	14	21.4
Needle manufacture	1	5	20.0	1	26	3.8
Hosiery	0	6	0.0	3	55	5.5
Other textiles	0	11	0.0	0	33	0.0
Miscellaneous	0	0	0.0	20	52	38.5
Totals	23	149	15.4	118	599	19.7

Source: 1881 CEBs.

engaged in the domestic industries since the boundaries of what was to be regarded as the local area, within which movement was not to be considered as migration, were deliberately drawn to include the adjacent parishes, even across the county boundaries, where the same trades were practised. The higher rate among never-married women in needle manufacture is probably distorted by the very small numbers involved. Similarly, the apparently high rate of migration among the ever-married women in miscellaneous occupations is distorted by the disparate nature of these occupations; for example a woman from the Essex agricultural area working at an iron works in Poplar, another working as a potter in Stoke on Trent, the woman from Banbury working her barge round the canal system probably fetching coal from the Midlands, the woman from Gedling running a painting and decorating business in York, and the women from Alcester making salt in Droitwich or running businesses in Birmingham.

Overall the higher rates of migration were among those in domestic service, particularly cooks and housekeepers, among those providing food and lodging and among medical attendants (nurses and midwives). The greatest differences in migration rates between never-married and ever-married women (ignoring those where the rates are distorted by very small numbers) were in education and in retailing, where never-married women were less likely to migrate than ever-married women, and among cooks, where never-married women were more likely to migrate than ever-married women. As was noted earlier never-married women living on investments were less migratory than ever-married women.

A wider perspective

How far did the patterns of marital status, occupation and migration in the localities described here reflect the specialised nature of these communities and how far were they typical of the country as a whole? The 5 per cent sample of the 1881 census created by the Historical Censuses and Surveys Group of the University of Essex from the enumerations of 823 parishes enables the behaviours observed in these local areas to be put into a national context.[48]

---

[48] This is a random sample of the parishes of Great Britain, created by listing all the parishes, allocating to each parish a number between zero and one produced by a random number generator, and selecting all those less than or equal to 0.05. The records of all persons enumerated in these 823 parishes were extracted and combined in a database, available from the UK Data Archive. Schürer and Woollard, *National sample of the 1881 census.*

Table 14.15   Comparison of never-married women in study areas with those in census sample (percentages)

	Study areas	Census sample
45 and over never-married	9.9	10.0
With 'true work'	58.1	58.7
Domestic service or offices	27.1	29.0
Clothing trades	10.4	10.2
Medical and education (professionals)	6.9	5.0
Hosiery and other textiles (textile fabrics)	3.6	5.4
Food and lodging	1.5	3.6
Agriculture	1.5	1.8
Needle manufacture (mineral substances)	1.0	0.2
Retailers	6.3	unknown

Source: 1881 CEBs.

Note: retailers are spread across several categories in the census sample.

As observed earlier, the proportion of never-married women aged 45 and over born in the five study areas was below the national average. Other features of the population may also be atypical. The proportion of women aged 45 and over in the 5 per cent sample was also below the national average, in fact very close to the level in the five study areas. Analysis of the 1881 census 5 per cent sample showed that 41 per cent of never-married women, 89 per cent of wives and 54 per cent of widows in this age range were without specified employment.[49] In the five study areas the proportions were 42 per cent of never-married women and 78 per cent of ever-married women (wives and widows combined). In the census 5 per cent sample 29 per cent of never-married women were engaged in domestic service and service occupations, 10.2 per cent in dress, 5.4 per cent in textile fabrics, 5 per cent were professionals (mainly education and medical care), 3.6 per cent in food and lodgings, 1.8 per cent in agriculture, and 0.2 per cent in minerals substances. Table 14.15 compares the never-married women in the five study areas with the never-married women from the 5 per cent sample. The figures for the five study areas have been recalculated to represent proportions of all never-married women in this age group, not merely those with 'true work', and categories have been combined

[49] For this analysis see Jones, 'Those whom God hath not joined', pp. 145–54.

to correspond with the occupational orders used in the 5 per cent sample. There is no direct equivalent in the census sample to the group described as retailers in the five study areas. It will be seen that the employment patterns of the never-married women in the five study areas are similar to those in the census 5 per cent sample with certain exceptions. The proportion in domestic services and service occupations in the five study areas is slightly lower than the proportion in the 5 per cent sample. The proportion of professionals is higher despite being limited to medical and educational professions only. The proportion in textiles is lower, the domestic textile industry in this area providing, as noted earlier, work mainly for ever-married women in contrast to the factory-based textile industry of Lancashire and Yorkshire which employed a higher proportion of never-married women. The proportion in food and lodging in the five study areas was lower than that in the 5 per cent sample, but the sample would include food retailers. Needle manufacture was a special case peculiar to the study area, which accounts for its over-representation.

Conclusion

This study has shown that marital status did have an effect on the occupations of women in the late-nineteenth century. The enumerator was far more likely to have completed the occupation column for never-married women than for ever-married women. Those most likely to have an entry in the occupation column were the never-married women born in the market towns. While ever-married women were often described by reference to their husband's occupation, very few never-married women were described by the occupation of a male relative, demonstrating how few male relatives never-married women could rely on for financial support once their fathers had died. The proportion of never-married women living on investments was higher than that of ever-married women in each locality and was highest in the market towns, where nearly a quarter of all never-married women were living on annuities, interest or property. On average, 58 per cent of never-married women had a declared occupation compared with only 22 per cent of ever-married women. That there was variation across the five areas suggested differences in the nature of the work being done by never-married and ever-married women. This was clearly demonstrated within the Registrar General's broad classification of 'domestic service or offices'. Never-married women were more likely to be working as general or minor servants, as housekeepers or as cooks, occupations that were often residential, thus providing accommodation as well as an income. Ever-married women were more likely to be working as laundresses or charwomen, work done on a daily or weekly basis from their own homes. The numbers of women in other occupational classifications were small and in many categories the proportions of never-married and ever-married women were similar. However, never-married women were over-represented among governesses and schoolteachers but under-represented in food and lodging and in hosiery. Twice as many never-married as ever-married women were employers of labour.

With the exception of the market towns, a higher proportion of the never-married women than the ever-married women had migrated from the area of their birth. However, migration was also shown to vary by occupational status. Among those where the occupation field was left blank and those described by the occupation of a male relative a higher proportion of never-married than ever-married women had migrated; but among those with non-employment entries, those living on investments and paupers a lower proportion of never-married women than ever-married women had migrated. Across all types of service occupation never-married women were more likely to have migrated than ever-married women. Cooks and general servants who had remained single were particularly likely to have migrated compared with ever-married women working in these capacities. The opposite is true of housekeepers, an abnormally high proportion of ever-married housekeepers having migrated. The greatest differences in migration rates between never-married and ever-married women were in education and in retailing, where never-married women were less likely to migrate than ever-married women. Never-married women working as retailers were very likely to be serving their local communities, either in the parish in which they were born or in a similar neighbouring parish. Similarly, never-married women were predominantly educating children from backgrounds similar to their own, teaching in local schools or giving home tuition to the children of their own locality. This finding was unexpected, as it might have been thought that teaching skills would have been transportable, allowing single women a greater degree of geographical mobility.

By comparing the results from the five study areas with the national 5 per cent sample from the 1881 census it was shown that many of these effects were similar to those experienced by never-married women at a national level. It is therefore important when considering women's work in industrial England to consider not merely the geographical perspective but also the marital perspective, the working experiences of older never-married women being different from those of wives and widows. This study elaborates the finding of Anderson when analysing the 1861 census returns that 'migrant women could hope for either marriage or for a job, but would have been rather lucky to get both'.[50]

---

[50] Anderson, 'Marriage patterns', p. 71.

15

The dawning of a new era? Women's work in England and Wales at the turn of the twentieth century[1]

EILIDH GARRETT

Introduction

The appearance of women in white collar jobs at the end of the nineteenth and the beginning of the twentieth centuries seemed to contemporaries to herald a new increase in the number of working women. The proponents of women's rights suggested that the entry of women into formerly male fields meant the dawn of a new era. . . . Some of the women who entered white-collar jobs came from the middle classes. For them work for wages was a new development, a departure from the enforced leisure of middle-class daughters and wives. Commentators tended to equate the experience of these middle class women with the experience of all women. Hence they concluded that jobs for women increased absolutely in this period and even suggested that the existence of these jobs reflected new attitudes about women's position and abilities.[2]

Such beliefs, based as they were on early twentieth century, middle class perceptions, belied the experience of the majority of women in earlier

[1] This paper was first published in *Histoire Sociale/Social History*, XXVIII, no. 56 (1995). We are grateful to the editors for their kind permission to reproduce it in this volume. Thanks are due to Alice Reid, Tamzin Close, Kevin Schürer, Richard Wall, Simon Szreter, Charles Pattie and several anonymous referees for their help and advice. A particularly big 'thank you' is owed to Kris Inwood. Data presented in this paper are reproduced with permission of Controller of H.M.S.O. The support of the Economic and Social Research Council is gratefully acknowledged. The work formed part of the programme of the ESRC Research Centre for History of Population and Social Structure.
[2] Tilly and Scott, *Women, work and family*, p. 150.

centuries and proved over optimistic in their prognosis for the coming decades, as Louise Tilly and Joan Scott demonstrate. Their statement above, however, highlights the significance attached to women moving into 'the world of men' and how closely that world was associated with working 'for wages'. The ability of contemporary commentators to mislead future generations, unless their views can be tempered by a liberal dose of statistics showing the 'true' state of affairs, is also evident. In Great Britain, Canada and the United States the decennial censuses from the turn of the century provide us with 'official statistics' depicting the course of male and female employment. In the case of women, however, such statistics may be at least as misleading as the more qualitative pictures painted by contemporary reporters.

The history of 'women's work' is be-devilled by problems of definition and conceptualisation. These occur at several levels. Firstly there is the question of exactly what qualifies as 'work' and how this differs by gender. Secondly there are the difficulties surrounding the collection and publication of 'official statistics' on the subject, and thirdly there are the problems faced by those who wish to analyse and interpret these statistics to compare and contrast women's experience of work over time and across space.

In the dictionary the noun 'work' is defined as 'employment', while the verb 'work' means 'to be occupied in business or labour'.[3] The same source defines 'employment' as 'occupation', 'to employ' as 'give work to' and 'occupation' as 'the state of being employed or occupied'. 'Work' therefore has connotations of things 'done, achieved or made', of time spent productively. Increasingly over the nineteenth century, however, industrialisation and capitalism engendered the closer association of 'work' with a 'living earned' and a 'productive role in the economy'; when one spent one's time working to make money one was 'gainfully occupied'.[4] A person could have his or her time fully committed to 'useful employment', but if monetary remuneration was not forthcoming then he or she did not have a 'paid job', was not 'gainfully occupied', and therefore could not be seen as 'a worker'. The unpaid roles of wife and mother, while essential to maintain the reproductive functions of any economy, were, and still are, not viewed as 'gainful' under such a framework and therefore, despite taking up a great deal of time and energy, have been treated in many respects as 'non-occupations' since the final decades of the nineteenth century. As the spheres of 'paid work' and 'home' became inexorably separated as

---

[3] *Chambers English Dictionary.*
[4] See Hill, 'Women, work and the census', pp. 78–94.

industrialisation progressed, so the status of women's reproductive tasks steadily diminished as social, and indeed analytical, emphasis was increasingly placed on 'ability to contribute productively to the economy'.[5]

While conceptions of work altered, the language used to signify its different aspects did not evolve in step. Thus even today a woman cooking and cleaning for her family, unpaid, still does 'house*work*'; someone 'out *working* in the garden' is understood not to be receiving any wages (unless doing so as a professional gardener), but to be occupied in tasks contributing to the reproductive function of the household; whereas someone reported to be '*out at work*' is recognised as being away from home pursuing the employment by which he or she earns a living. All three individuals are 'fully occupied' at the time at which they are observed, we have no indication from the language used, however, whether these are 'full-time occupations' or not. As the disassociation of the 'workplace' and 'home' progressed, paid employment became more and more something one 'went out' to. As women 'stayed in' to do housework this disqualified their activities from being real 'employment'. Such reasoning suggests why there was so much concern over 'home-working': not only was it symptomatic of the notorious practice of sweating but it also contravened the 'home/work' dichotomy.[6]

Collectors of statistics on 'occupation' or 'work' therefore have a three-fold task. They have first to decide which particular aspect of work they wish to survey. Are they interested in how people 'spend their time', or in the occupations which people pursue in order to 'earn a living'? Do they wish to monitor their subject's occupational status in the long run (what job a respondent generally does, or which job that person is trained for) or at a specific time (what occupation is a person pursuing at the time of the survey)? Or do they wish to view occupation in terms of contribution to the economy: whether people are 'gainfully occupied', 'retired' or 'unemployed' and, if the latter, then how this should be defined—whether, for instance, 'seeking work' should be treated in the same way as 'housework'?

The second task in the statistics collection process is wording the survey questions to ensure that the responses given are compatible with the conceptual framework from which the questions originate: the subjects of the survey have to be clear about what they are being asked

---

[5] Hill argues that this conception of work arose from the thinking of classical economists such as Smith, Malthus, Ricardo, Mill and Bentham: 'Women, work and the census', p. 81

[6] On sweating see Morris, 'Characteristics of sweating'.

and how they should answer. Those collecting the information also have to be given precise instructions. For instance, in the era when the census-taking process involved enumerators copying out each household's completed schedule into an 'enumerator's book', which was then dispatched to the Census Office, instructions had to be drawn up for the enumerators in an effort to reduce untoward bias or misrepresentation of the original responses.[7]

Having collected the responses to the questionnaires the collectors of statistics must, thirdly, create a digest of their findings for publication. At this stage both the conceptual framework of the survey, plus contemporary beliefs and prejudices, may influence the process of classifying numerous individual responses into classes or orders of occupation for easier tabulation. Eddy Higgs has shown, for instance, that the original occupational classification system of the mid-nineteenth-century census reports of Great Britain, based on the material individuals worked with, was used because information was being sought on the health implications of particular occupations.[8] As we will see below, any changes in the classification procedure in the course of a series of surveys could compromise comparability across time. Both Margo Conk and Bridget Hill have demonstrated how different classification systems have made the comparison of published census statistics between nations extremely difficult, even when the questions asked have been very similar.[9]

The final level, involving problems of definition and conceptualisation concerning occupation, particularly women's occupations, is the use of the published statistics derived from a census or survey. An increasing literature in this field divides into three schools, all of which agree that women's work was consistently under-recorded. The first school may be typified by the work of Margo Conk and Catherine Hakim and unpacks the census machinery for collecting statistics on occupation, showing how and why anomalies in the final reports occur.[10] The second body of literature comes largely from

---

[7] Enumerators' books were used in all of the British censuses where individual level data was collected from 1841 to 1901. Not only did the enumerator have to copy out the responses into his or her book but very often could fill out the forms for the less literate householders. The enumerator would thus impose his interpretation of the situation he was recording on the collected data: see Higgs, *Making sense of the census*. From 1911 onward the original schedules were sent directly to the Census Office for analysis.

[8] Higgs, 'Disease, febrile poisons and statistics'.

[9] Conk, 'Labor statistics'; Hill, 'Women, work and the census'.

[10] Conk, 'Labor statistics'; Hakim, 'Census reports'.

economic history where the changing nature and extent of women's contribution to the economy is the object of study. This literature takes the stance that it should be possible, making certain assumptions, to estimate the extent of any under-enumeration and therefore to 'correct' the statistics. Examples of this approach are found in the work of Higgs and of Marjorie Abel and Nancy Folbre.[11] The latter authors estimate that, on the basis of 'probable participation' and several complementary assumptions in two Massachusetts settlements in 1880, married women's observed market participation rates of 10 per cent should be inflated to 47 and 68 per cent. The authors call for further efforts to revise and refine measures of women's participation in the market economy. The third school, represented by Hill among others, argues that while such revision may be desirable it is not advisable because we would 'be perpetuating the same error as those who have manipulated [the data] in the past. Their prejudices which many of us are only just beginning fully to appreciate will be replaced by our own.'[12] Hill and others of her ilk warn against uncritical acceptance of statistical material concerning women's labour force participation, but are of the opinion that researchers should live with the limitations of the figures, while attempting to avoid such shortcomings in any data we might create and leave behind for future generations.

The approach taken here probably fits somewhere between the first and the third schools involved in the debate. Having examined the picture of 'women's work' painted in the published reports of the turn of the century censuses, we set out to discover what changes were observable in women's work from a series of individual level census returns taken from a selection of 13 registration districts (or locales) scattered across England and Wales from the 1891, 1901, 1911 and 1921 censuses. By employing the same coding frame for each of the four censuses we hope to obviate the problems of comparability that arise in the use of material from the published reports. However, this exercise highlights the importance of continuity in the wording of questions from one census to another if comparability is to be achieved, and therefore the census questions concerning occupation are scrutinised in detail.

The period from 1891 to 1921, while perhaps too short and too late to be ideal for a study of the evolution of the concept of work for the two genders, is nevertheless of interest because individual level data for

---

[11] Higgs, 'Women, occupations and work'; Abel and Folbre, 'Female market participation'.
[12] Hill, 'Women, work and the census', p. 92.

1901 to 1921 would not normally be available to present day scholars, English and Welsh census data being subject to a 100 year confidentiality rule.[13] Furthermore, this period saw substantial revision of both the census questions employed to elicit information concerning occupation and of the methods of tabulation used in the census reports, bringing the problems engendered by these two features of the data collection process into sharp focus. In the absence of access to the individual level data, interpretation of the published reports for this period has proven particularly troublesome. B.R. Mitchell and Phyllis Deane found, when trying to compile standardised occupational statistics for males and females from the published census material, that complete comparability was elusive.[14] We examine the national census results of Great Britain for the years 1881 to 1921 presented by Mitchell and Deane in order to set out the problems they faced and also to place the findings of our study in a wider context.

Problems in interpreting census results

Jane Lewis, in *Women in England 1870–1950*, describes the late nineteenth to early twentieth-century pattern of women's work derived from the census reports of the period as showing that the 'overall female participation rate (excluding those in unpaid domestic work) actually declined from 1871 to 1901, increased 1911, declined 1921 and then rose to 1951'.[15] Across the Atlantic in the United States, according to Abel and Folbre, the picture was one of steadily increasing participation rates between 1870 and 1900, followed by a peak in 1910 which would not be surpassed until the 1940 census.[16]

The difficulties of analysing trends in women's occupations on both sides of the Atlantic via the published census reports have long been

---

[13] Since this paper was first published in 1995 the 1901 census enumerators' books have been released to the public.

[14] Mitchell and Deane, *Abstract of British historical statistics*, p. 56.

[15] Lewis, *Women in England*, Table 5, p. 147. The figures Lewis gives are for England and Wales and suggest that participation rates for women aged 15 and over stood at approximately 42 per cent in 1871 (although this is a poor base as the number included the retired), 34.5 per cent in 1901, 35.6 per cent in 1911 and 33.7 per cent in 1921.

[16] Abel and Folbre, 'Female market participation', Figure 1, p. 168. The level of their figures is rather lower than that of Lewis' as they calculate participation rates for those aged 10 and over. The 1910 peak is, however, more marked than that of 1911 in England and Wales.

acknowledged.[17] The number of persons recorded as pursuing a particular occupation could alter for any one of several different reasons. Of course, the actual number of workers in a particular niche in the labour market could certainly vary. The data had to pass through several stages before appearing in a published table, however, and at any of these points changes from one census to the next might alter the number of persons recorded under a given heading, even though in actuality the number of workers remained the same.

At the conceptualisation stage the census authorities might decide to revise the question or questions they were going to ask, either in form or in substance. They might alter the instructions, causing those who were collecting the data to enter or omit information. It might also be decided to tabulate the data in a different way, redefining the classification system. Respondents might have reasons for altering the way in which they answered the question. It must also not be forgotten that what has been referred to as 'individual level' responses were in fact household level responses with one member of the household (sometimes assisted by the enumerator) filling out the form for all the other residents. Answers may well have differed depending on who was appointed to fill out the schedule.

Table 15.1 illustrates some of the problems of comparability which result from a combination of such effects. This table is derived from Mitchell and Deane who have standardised as best they can on the occupational classification scheme used in the 1911 census report.[18] While ideally, in terms of the present discussion, the table should show only England and Wales, Mitchell and Deane do not disaggregate their statistics below the level of Great Britain. The figures in panel A depict the proportion of those men reporting an occupation in each of the five censuses who were in particular sectors of the labour force; the equivalent figures for women are shown in panel B.

Let us first take the figures at their face value. Among the male workers perhaps the most noticeable change over the 40-year period is the declining proportion in agriculture, which falls from being by far the largest employer to only the fourth behind metal manufacturing, transport and the 'all others occupied' category. Closer inspection of Panel A in Table 15.1 also reveals considerable decline in the proportion

[17] See for example: Abel and Folbre, 'Female market participation'; Hudson and Lee *Women's work*, esp. chapter 1; Jordan, 'Female unemployment in England and Wales', pp. 186–7; Hakim, 'Census reports as documentary evidence'; Davies, 'Making sense of the census'; Rose, *Limited livelihoods*, pp. 79–82.

[18] Mitchell & Deane, *Abstract of British historical statistics*, p. 59; OPCS, *Guide to census reports*.

Table 15.1 Percentages of A) male and B) female workers in particular categories of occupation: Great Britain, 1881–1921

	A Males					B Females				
	1881	1891	1901	1911[a]	1921[a]	1881	1891	1901	1911[a]	1921[a]
Public Administration	1.23	1.46	1.65	2.10	2.82	0.23	0.38	0.61	0.92	1.42
Armed Forces	1.29	1.34	1.52	1.71	1.74	0.00	0.00	0.00	0.00	0.00
Professional Occupations	2.87	2.87	3.01	3.19	3.05	5.22	5.88	6.85	7.08	7.74
Domestic/Personal Services	2.69	2.93	2.95	3.53	2.73	45.19	45.34	42.12	39.31	32.37
Commercial Occupations	3.97	4.49	5.17	5.71	6.65	0.28	0.58	1.60	2.90	10.30
Transport & Communications	9.82	11.03	12.20	12.15	11.25	0.39	0.45	0.57	0.70	1.26
Agriculture etc.	17.13	14.21	11.60	11.11	9.88	2.99	1.78	1.81	2.16	1.84
Fishing	0.65	0.53	0.44	0.41	0.38	0.08	0.02	0.00	0.00	0.00
Mining & Quarrying	6.82	7.50	8.06	9.30	9.12	0.21	0.16	0.17	0.11	0.16
Metal Manuf., Machines etc.	11.03	11.50	12.86	13.88	15.63	1.26	1.31	1.77	2.37	3.07
Building and Construction	9.88	8.98	10.53	8.82	6.57	0.05	0.07	0.06	0.09	0.09
Wood, Furniture etc.	2.09	2.06	2.31	2.22	3.76	0.54	0.56	0.63	0.65	0.54
Bricks, Cement, Pottery, Glass	1.25	1.19	1.32	1.12	0.74	0.69	0.71	0.78	0.78	0.79
Chemicals etc.	0.81	0.89	1.00	1.20	0.68	0.23	0.38	0.65	0.85	0.61
Skins, Leather, Hair, Feathers	0.82	0.80	0.75	0.70	0.53	0.41	0.45	0.57	0.59	0.58
Paper, Printing etc.	1.51	1.78	1.84	1.96	1.42	1.36	1.74	2.33	2.66	2.12
Textiles	6.26	5.93	4.82	4.94	3.01	19.17	17.70	16.72	16.08	12.30
Clothing	4.28	4.09	3.66	3.34	2.32	17.16	16.90	16.65	15.25	10.56
Food, Drink, Tobacco	5.58	5.97	6.07	6.23	1.68	2.52	3.63	4.54	5.69	2.16
Gas, Water, Electricity	0.27	0.38	0.54	0.67	–	0.00	0.00	0.00	0.00	0.00
All others occupied	9.73	10.08	7.68	5.73	16.07	2.01	1.98	1.58	1.81	12.07

Table 15.1 continued

	A Males					B Females				
	1881	1891	1901	1911[a]	1921[a]	1881	1891	1901	1911[a]	1921[a]
Total number occupied	8,852	10,010	11,548	12,927	13,656	3,887	4,489	4,751	5,413	5,699
Total number of working age[b]	10,628	12,038	13,790	15,093	15,659	11,504	13,026	14,980	16,788	17,667
% of total who are 'unoccupied'	16.7	16.8	16.2	14.3	13.3	66.2	65.5	68.3	67.7	67.7

Source: Mitchell and Deane, *Abstract of British historical statistics*. For original figures and comprehensive notes see pp. 59–61.

Notes: a) Mitchell and Deane stress that figures from 1911 and 1921 are only in a few instances directly comparable.
b) 1921 figures are the proportion of persons aged 12 and over, in the other years the proportion is of those aged 10 and over.

of males working in the textiles, clothing and food categories. Other sectors underwent noteworthy increases; roughly speaking both public administration and the commercial occupations doubled their contribution to the male workforce. The growth of the heavy industries during this period is reflected in the rising proportion of miners and metal workers, the latter category also including those working in vehicle-making and ship-building, as well as instrument and toy makers.

Among women the relative decline in the number reported to be in domestic service, textiles and clothing is clear, as is the increasing role of commerce and the professions. It should be remembered that, as the final line of the table shows, those women who had an occupation returned in the census were in the minority at this period. Approximately 34 in every 100 women of working age were reported as having an occupation in the published census results of 1881 and 1891. In 1901 and 1911 this fell to about 32 per cent and remained around this figure in 1921, although by then the census authorities saw 'those of working age' to be 12 years or over, rather than the 10 years or over of previous decades.[19] A further feature worthy of note in Panel B of Table 15.1 is the continuing concentration of women in only a small number of occupational classes. In 1881 87 per cent of those reporting an occupation were working in just four sectors of the economy: service, textiles, clothing and professions. Forty years later 63 per cent of women reporting an occupation were still in these four sectors, although by then there were also proportionately more women working in commercial occupations than in the professions. These five sectors now encompassed 73 per cent of the reported female workforce, so some diversification appears to have been occurring.

Certain aspects of Table 15.1 suggest that the trends depicted should be interpreted with caution, however. Mitchell and Deane admit that, despite their attempts at standardisation, 'changes in each census render exact comparisons usually impossible'.[20] There is in fact an irremediable disjuncture in the figures presented. In the census reports prior to 1921 individuals were classified according to the materials they worked with, rather than by the jobs they did within a particular sector of industry. Hence, for instance, pre-1921 dealers and labourers would be found scattered across most of the occupational categories listed. In 1921 a new categorisation procedure collected 'those doing similar jobs' together,

[19] Mitchell and Deane, *Abstract of British historical statistics*, pp. 59–61. The authors, like the census authorities, take the working ages to be 10 and over 1881–1911 and twelve and over in 1921 so the 1921 figures suggest there had been a decline in female participation rates. Statistics refer to Great Britain.

[20] Mitchell and Deane, *Abstract of British historical statistics*, p. 59.

explaining the decline in certain categories such as food among both men and women while contributing to the apparent growth in others such as commerce between 1911 and 1921 as 'dealers' were redistributed. Mitchell and Deane suggest that very few of the categories shown in Table 15.1 are truly comparable for the 1911–1921 decade. Nineteenth-century trends in occupation cannot, therefore, be followed beyond 1911 using the published British census reports, even when standardised.

Even the pre-1921 trends depicted in Table 15.1 could be compromised without changes in the occupational classification system. The Registrar General noted that the number of workers whose occupation was difficult to classify was much reduced between 1901 and 1911 because in the latter year the census schedules included a question on the nature of the business undertaken by the respondent's employer.[21] Thus someone giving his occupation simply as labourer in 1901 would have had to be classified in the 'all others occupied' category as it was unclear with which materials he worked. In 1911, although he again returned himself as a 'labourer', he might have noted that his employer was a tanner, for instance, and therefore been classified in the 'shoes, leather, hair' category. Our ability to usefully compare the overall proportion in the 'all others occupied' category between 1901 and 1911 is thus affected, and has repercussions for the proportions in other categories.

The uncertainties affecting the numbers in each employment category from one census to the next have implications for analysis at even slightly more complex levels. Table 15.2 shows the proportion of each occupational category made up of women and girls. If an alteration differentially prevented males from being reported in a particular occupational category, then that category will appear to have experienced greater feminisation than was truly the case.[22] For instance,

---

[21] The Registrar General remarks that 'indefinite classes' of occupation were much reduced by the inclusion of the question concerning the respondent's employer's business; *Census of England and Wales 1911*, p. 98. Thus the number of 'warehousemen' declined 34 per cent, that of 'factory hands' by 67 per cent and that of 'machine workers' by 75 per cent: *Census of England and Wales 1911*, p. 100.

[22] In his report on the 1911 Census the Registrar General noted that an abnormally large number of men were absent from home in 1901 on account of the Boer War: *Census of England and Wales 1911*, p. 58. This may have had some impact on the male/female balance in certain occupations, further distorting our view of the 'feminisation' process. However, women formed a slightly smaller proportion of the total reported workforce in 1901 than in any of the other census years shown in Table 15.2, rather than increasing as might be expected, given the Registrar General's comment.

Table 15.2   Percentage of workers in each occupational category who are female: Great Britain, 1881–1921

	Census Date				
	1881	1891	1901	1911	1921
Public Administration	8	10	13	16	17
Armed Forces	0	0	0	0	0
Professional Occupations	44	48	48	48	52
Domestic/Personal Services	88	87	85	82	83
Commercial Occupations	3	5	11	18	39
Transport & Communications	2	2	2	2	4
Agriculture etc.	7	5	6	8	7
Fishing	5	2	0	0	0
Mining & Quarrying	1	1	1	0	1
Metal Manuf., Machines etc.	5	5	5	7	8
Building and Construction	0	0	0	0	1
Wood, Furniture etc.	10	11	10	11	6
Bricks, Cement, Pottery, Glass	20	21	20	22	31
Chemicals etc.	11	16	21	23	27
Skins, Leather, Hair, Feathers	18	20	24	26	31
Paper, Printing etc.	28	30	34	36	39
Textiles	57	57	59	58	63
Clothing	64	65	65	66	66
Food, Drink, Tobacco	17	21	24	28	35
Gas, Water, Electricity	0	0	0	0	–
All others occupied	8	8	8	12	24
All occupied	30	31	29	30	30

Source: Mitchell and Deane, *Abstract of British historical statistics*.

we must ask whether the increasing proportion of women in the 'all others occupied' category between 1901 and 1911 is exclusively due to a move of women into new spheres of work, or if it may be partially explained by the number of labourers, mostly male, being classified elsewhere. Many categories, such as public administration, skins, food and paper, show apparently steady feminisation from 1891 to 1921, while others see more dramatic increases, particularly in the final decade. Given the caveats discussed above, any attempt to explain the markedly increased proportion of female workers 1911–1921 among those in commerce, the professions, bricks and 'all others occupied' must unravel whether it entailed an important and long-lasting shift in occupational structure, a more short term aftermath of World War I or, more prosaically, changes in collection or classification procedures by the Census Office. We must also contemplate the possibility that the answer may be different for each of the four occupational categories.

This brief look at (standardised) figures derived from the published reports of the British censuses of 1881–1911 has shown how for men they depict a decline in the agricultural sector but a rise in heavy industry and the tertiary sector, while for women the most dramatic change is the decline of domestic service. The tables have come with several 'health warnings', however, and therefore we cannot, for instance, use the figures to illustrate dramatic changes in the structure of the workforce over the decade of World War I. The momentous rise in the proportion of women reported to have worked in commercial occupations and the accelerated decline in those reported as servants and as textile or clothing workers could simply be the result of changing classification practices.

To ascertain whether these changes are 'real', access to a series of individual census schedules is required so that the occupations can be classified to a standardised scheme, held constant from one census to the next. Our dataset, drawn from 13 registration districts scattered across England and Wales and spanning the 1891, 1901, 1911 and 1921 censuses, enables us to avoid the problems arising from changing classification schemes, but is still affected by the ways in which the census questions concerning occupation altered over time.

Problems relating to census questions

The censuses between 1841 and 1881 were relatively uniform in the information which they recorded on occupation. In 1841 the 'occupation of every person, regardless of age or sex, was required to be stated other than wives or sons or daughters, living with their husbands or parents and not receiving wages'.[23] The four succeeding censuses had a column headed 'rank, profession or occupation' on their schedules; as Higgs points out the responses did not necessarily equate with 'paid economic activity'.[24] However, in all four decades, the instructions accompanying each schedule contained a section addressing 'Women and children', where it was stated: 'The occupation of those regularly employed away from home, or who follow any business at home, is to

---

[23] OPCS, *Guide to census reports*, p. 19. Although censuses had been taken in Britain on a decennial basis from 1801, the 1841 census was the first to record individual occupations. The form of the question emphasises that *paid* occupation was to be recorded.

[24] Higgs, *Making sense of the census*, p. 78.

be distinctly recorded.'[25] Thus the individual level manuscript returns should indicate whether a woman saw herself or wished to be seen, or was seen by the person filling out the form, as having regular employment, although payment for that employment was only implicit. Up until 1871 the published census tables classified women who were engaged in the domestic chores of their household as having an occupation.[26] From that date on, however, the emphasis appears to have changed from gathering information on 'tasks in which one's time was spent' to 'tasks for which one received financial remuneration'. This re-conceptualisation was emphasised by the inclusion from 1891 onwards of new questions concerning 'employment'.[27] By 1921 respondents were even being asked to supply the names of their employers.[28] From 1881 women 'wholly engaged in domestic labour at home' were classified in the published reports as being 'unoccupied'.

The 1881 census therefore marks something of a watershed regarding the collection and analysis of occupational data, particularly in regard to women. From 1891 to 1921 the census schedules were further revised and expanded. The alterations were not without problems. Ambiguity in the instructions printed on the schedules led to unexpected discrepancies in responses to questions from one census to the next. Attempts to tighten up laxity in earlier instructions resulted in comparability being compromised even further. As women's work is the focus here we will discuss those instructions from each census principally affecting the female portion of the workforce.[29]

In the general instructions on the 1891 census schedules the respondent was directed to state 'the occupations of women and children . . . as well as those of men', although the examples given tended to be couched in terms of males: for example 'Sons or other relatives of farmers employed on the farm should be returned as

---

[25] The wording shown here is from the instructions of 1881: *Census of England and Wales: 1881*, p. 116. The wording differs slightly in other years from 1851 to 1881, but the sense remains the same.

[26] Lewis, *Women in England*, p. 146; Hakim, 'Census reports'.

[27] To follow the evolution of the employment questions see the 1891, 1901, 1911 and 1921 census instruction sheets provided as Appendices A to D in the census reports. The originals of the first three can be found in *Census of England and Wales, 1891*; *Census of England and Wales, 1901*; *Census of England and Wales, 1911* Appendix A. The 1921 Report was published by HMSO in 1927. See also Rose, *Limited livelihoods*, pp. 80–1.

[28] 1921 Census schedule, instruction 11.

[29] These questions have been abstracted for convenience in the Appendix to this chapter.

"farmer's son", "farmer's brother" etc.'[30] Also men employed on farms
and living in the farmer's house could return themselves as 'farm
servants' but this term was not to be used for domestic servants in a
farmhouse. Domestic servants, it was noted in special instruction 13,
should indicate 'the nature of their service'.[31] In an attempt to separate
workpeople from their masters, and to suit the needs of the Board of
Trade, the 1891 schedule included three new columns headed
'employer', 'employee', and 'neither employer or employee'.[32] A cross
was to be inserted in the appropriate column by those working in trade
or industry, but *not* by domestic servants. It was further noted, in general
instruction 5, that 'Married women assisting their husbands in their
trade or industry are to be returned as "Employed"'.[33] Such women
were not, however, instructed to return an occupation in the 'profession
or occupation' column. The report on the 1891 Census cast
considerable doubt on the validity of the 'employer/employee' data, as
a large number of people had not crossed any box, or had returned
themselves as belonging to more than one category.[34] We can only
speculate that the uncrossed boxes might indicate that a person was
unemployed as this contingency does not appear to have been allowed
for in the instructions. Multiple crosses would seem to be a perfectly
logical response for someone under contract who in turn hired the rest
of the labour he or she needed.

In 1901 the census instructions stated that vague terms such as
'manager', 'dealer', and 'factory hand' must not be used alone: 'Full and
distinctive description of the occupation' had to be given.[35] The
instruction to farmers' relatives remained, but agricultural workers were
now told to enter themselves according to the particular type of work
in which they were usually engaged. The terms 'cattleman', 'horse
keeper' and 'carter on farm' were to replace 'agricultural labourer'.[36]

---

[30] 1891 Census schedule, special instruction 10.
[31] 1891 Census schedule, special instruction 13.
[32] Higgs, 'Disease'; OPCS, *Guide to census reports*.
[33] 1891 Census schedule, general instruction 5.
[34] Schürer, 'The 1891 Census', pp. 24–6. Schürer argues that the Registrar
General's failure to analyse the 'employer/employee' data might have arisen
from a fit of pique as, against his judgement, the questions had been included
at the behest of the Treasury Committee. Schürer further suggests that this data
does in fact hold considerable research potential.
[35] 1901 Census schedule, instruction 3. As discussed previously, however, many
persons still answered this question in very general terms and only with the
addition of a question in 1911 on the nature of the respondent's employer's
business was much of the troublesome 'vagueness' removed.
[36] 1901 Census schedule, instruction 10.

Shopkeepers and shop assistants received instructions to return themselves as such, but also to state their 'branch of business', while those who worked in a shop but were principally engaged in manufacture and repair were instructed *not* to return themselves as 'shopkeepers'.[37] (In 1891 there had been no distinction made between the two sorts of 'shopwork'). Nurses were asked to specify the type of nursing they undertook.[38] Servants once again had to enter the nature of their service. They were to make sure to enter the word 'domestic' in their replies if this was appropriate.[39] In combination these instructions may well have contributed to the decline between 1891 and 1901 in the proportion of men and women having to be classified in the catch-all 'all others occupied' category in Table 15.1.

The distinction between 'shopkeepers' and 'makers of goods in shops' had obviously not been totally resolved by the 1901 instructions, as instruction 2 on the 1911 schedule reiterated that, 'Dealers, Shopkeepers . . . as distinct from Makers, Producers or Repairers . . . should leave no doubt as to whether they are Dealers or Makers'.[40] Someone who was both a dealer and a maker had to distinguish whether they were 'chiefly' one or the other. There followed an explicit instruction that persons 'out of work' (that is, 'unemployed' in the modern sense) were to state their 'usual occupation'. There was nowhere allocated for them to indicate that they were unemployed at the time of the census.

Another instruction pertained explicitly to women: 'The occupations of women engaged in any business or profession, including women *regularly engaged in assisting relatives in trade or business*, must be fully stated'.[41] As a logical corollary of this, under the instruction concerning farmers' relatives, the term 'Farmer's daughter' was included amongst the examples for the first time. Women involved solely in domestic duties were, under the 1911 instructions, to have the occupation box left blank.

In 1921, for the first time, those occupied 'mainly' in unpaid domestic duties were to have the term 'Home Duties' entered as their occupation. The use of the word 'mainly' implies that some other form of occupation was also possible. The first instruction on the schedule

---

[37] 1901 Census schedule, instruction 11.
[38] Davies suggests that this was to enable hospital (or sick) nurses to be distinguished from those nursing (children) as a form of domestic service: 'Making sense of the census', p. 598.
[39] 1901 Census schedule, instruction 14.
[40] 1911 Census schedule, instruction 2.
[41] 1911 Census schedule, instruction 4.

concerning those 'working for payment or profit' had directed people with more than one occupation to 'state that by which (their) living was mainly earned', a form of words also used in 1911.[42] Prior to this a person was supposed to list their occupations in order of importance.[43] Employees, apart from domestic servants, also had to enter the name of their employer on the schedule, along with the nature of the employer's business. The unemployed were to enter their last employer's name, adding 'out of work'.[44]

While in 1911 respondents had been instructed that women *regularly* engaged in assisting relatives were to be recorded as occupied, the equivalent 1921 instruction read: 'For a member of the household who is *chiefly* occupied in giving unpaid help in a business by the head of household . . . state the occupation as though it were a paid occupation'.[45] Thus in 1921 the household member concerned could be either male or female, and the help had to be that person's main occupation, whereas in 1911 the women involved simply had to be helping on a regular basis in order to have an occupation recorded.

To illustrate the impact of such revisions to the census questions, we examine the implications of the changing instructions concerning women helping their relatives in trade or business. The fact that the word 'regularly' was not defined in the 1911 instructions is of considerable significance for our understanding of women's work patterns and how the census does or does not capture these.

The published census reports, and indeed many of the individual returns, give the impression that all the occupations recorded were pursued on a full-time basis. It can be demonstrated, however, that reality fell short of this. Men were not asked to specify if, and by what means, they supplemented their 'main' income, nor were they asked to state that they 'helped out' friends and relations if they reported having an occupation of their own.[46] Thus while 'apparent full-time occupation' probably overstates men's contribution to the formal economy (part–time work, under-employment and, in some years,

---

[42] 1921 Census schedule, instruction 9; 1911 Census schedule, instruction 1.

[43] See for example 1901 Census schedule, instruction 2. Classification schemes would, however, use the first occupation listed thus reducing any list to one occupation.

[44] 1921 Census schedule, instruction given at the top of the 'Employment' column.

[45] 1911 Census schedule, instruction 4; 1921 Census schedule, instruction 7.

[46] Pre 1921 censuses did give the option for respondents to enter more than one job, in order of importance, but some means of supplementary income may well not have been seen as 'jobs'.

unemployment going unacknowledged), their contribution to the informal and reproductive economies was very much under-recorded. Hakim suggests that over the nineteenth century there emerged the notion of a 'personal occupation'—a 'one career imperative'—and this does seem to be the model to which the census authorities were working in designing their schedules by the turn of the century: an 'occupation' was not only gainful, it was also pursued full-time.[47] While such a model was probably accurate for middle class males pursuing a career it undoubtedly fell short of the experience of the many semi- and unskilled working-class men who endured casual, under and unemployment, and bore little relation to the lives of the majority of women with their 'duality of roles'.[48] In both the latter cases the recording mechanism of the censuses would have failed to capture the full complexity of the occupational strategies involved in balancing the household economy.

In comparing the work of men and women one fundamental difference has to be borne in mind. If a man left his 'occupation' box blank it would be impossible to assign him to any group within a classification scheme except 'not known'; a wife or daughter returning no occupation could be assumed to be undertaking 'domestic duties', or doing 'housework'. The man had no identity but his economic, gainfully occupied one; the woman operated in two spheres, and the assumption could be made that if she was not found in one she must be in the other. The dimensions of possible overlap were never clearly defined, and thus, while the census probably misrepresents the occupational experience of men to some extent, it does so at a much smaller level of magnitude than appears in its failure to represent accurately the contribution of women to the productive economy. It can also be argued that those women who did return an occupation would, in the terms of the logic of the census, have been seen as full-time paid workers, and therefore their reproductive role goes unacknowledged.

If males and females are to be treated within the same logical framework, then 'main occupations' have to be viewed as the 'main way one spends one's time' to allow housewifery to be an occupation, albeit not a 'gainful' one. 'Apparent full-time' housewifery may not have qualified as *employment*, but it was certainly viewed as a legitimate, indeed an ideal, *occupation* for women. It was undeniably often very hard *work*:

---

[47] Hakim, 'Census reports', p. 561.
[48] McBride, 'Women's work', p. 65.

the life of the married women of the working class is often extremely hard, taking into account the large amount of work done by them at home, cooking, cleaning, washing, mending and making of clothes, . . . also baking of bread, tendance of children and of the sick, over and above and all but simultaneously with the bringing of babies into the world.[49]

The late nineteenth-century belief in the desirability of the 'family wage', the increasingly money-oriented economy, and the spatial separation of 'home' and 'work', not only served to relegate the role of housewife to an inferior status, but also confused the terminology of 'work', 'occupation' and 'employment'.

Whatever the philosophy of the census takers, peoples' answers to the questions posed would be influenced by the way the questions were phrased, as this would affect their understanding of the nature of the information they were asked to supply. It is arguable that many people, poring over the 1911 census schedule in England and Wales, supplied the information requested concerning women's occupations exactly as instructed. With no guidance as to what constituted 'regular' assistance women who helped out a relative once or twice a week, or maybe just every Saturday afternoon for a few hours, were entered as having an occupation, one which would then be analysed as though it were pursued full time. The emphasis in the instruction that no occupation should be returned for women *wholly* engaged in domestic duties, probably served to bolster the conviction that any regular assistance at all qualified as an occupation. If this was the case, the logic that the census elicited a woman's *main* occupation was subverted in 1911. The authorities responsible for census taking appear to have believed that this is what happened, because in 1921 the equivalent instruction was changed so that only those (and now both sexes were included) who were *chiefly* occupied in giving help in a business carried on by the head of the household were to be returned as though in a (full-time) 'paid occupation'.

In both England and Wales in 1911 and in the United States in 1910, when very similar wording was used, the proportion of women reporting an occupation in the census rose sharply, and authors such as Abel and Folbre argue that this should have prompted 'reconsideration of estimates [of women's gainful economic activity] from previous years'.[50] Certainly, if the census had been attempting to monitor all forms of activity contributing to the market economy then the 1911

---

[49] Hutchins, *Women in modern industry*.
[50] Abel and Folbre, 'Female market participation', p. 169.

wording probably did a better job at catching certain aspects of women's participation in the labour force than did other censuses. However, given the 'main occupation' framework under which the census operated, then the 1911 figures were anomalous. If one set about adjusting data on female occupation from other years to bring them into line with those of 1911, then for the sake of equality one would have to adjust the data on males as well to bring their part-time, possibly unpaid, secondary occupations into the picture. At this stage it becomes obvious that the census is being asked to supply data which it was not designed to collect. For the purposes of comparative history it is preferable to assume that the 1911 census over-represents the number of women in the paid, full-time workforce and to adjust our interpretation of the trends we observe accordingly.

Perhaps the most confusing step taken by the census authorities in the light of the conceptual framework under which they were operating, and certainly their greatest disservice to women, was their decision in 1881 to classify 'housewifery' and 'domestic duties' in the category 'unoccupied' in their tables for publication. As a result, the main occupation of the majority of married women acquired resonances of being 'without work' and 'unproductive', while the truth is that industrial economies would have foundered without the full-time reproductive labour of wives and mothers. To clarify the rather confused picture of women's work which we have so far uncovered, we move on to examine individual responses drawn from manuscript returns from the censuses for England and Wales of 1891, 1901, 1911 and 1921.

The manuscript census returns for England and Wales

Under the rules laid down by the Office of Population Censuses and Surveys (OPCS), manuscript census returns for England and Wales are only released once 100 years have elapsed after their original collection. The latest micro-level census data available to the public in microfilm form are thus the returns for 1901, although researchers have access to confidential individual level data from the 1971, 1981, 1991 and 2001 census data via the Longitudinal Study conducted by OPCS and to anonymised individual data through the Sample of Anonymised Records (SARs) released from the 1991 and 2001 censuses.[51] Unlike the

---

[51] On the 1991 census material see Dale, 'OPCS longitudinal survey' and Marsh, 'Sample of anonymised records'. For the 2001 census see: the Office of National Statistics Website at http://www.statistics.gov.uk/census2001/ sar_update.asp.

United States, England has no public use sample of material from the early part of the twentieth century. The Cambridge Group for the History of Population and Social Structure was, however, privileged to acquire from the OPCS the anonymised, machine readable census records of between 80,000 and 103,000 individuals from each of the censuses of England and Wales for 1891, 1901, 1911 and 1921.[52]

The individual records, copied from the census enumerators' books of 1891 and 1901, and directly from the enumeration schedules of 1911 and 1921, were taken from clusters of enumeration districts within 13 'locales'. The 1891 Registration Districts in which these locales fell are shown in Figure 15.1, as are the three letter codes used for each of the 13 study areas. Thus within the Registration Districts of Hendon and West Ham, for example, lie respectively our 'locales' of Pinner (PIN) and Walthamstow (WAL).

The 13 locales are by no means a random sample; they were chosen to provide as wide a spectrum of life as possible at the turn of the century. Morland (MOR) and Saffron Walden (SAF) were chosen to represent rural areas, with Banbury (BAN), a thriving market town in the heart of an agricultural area, and Axminster (AXM), including both a lace-making centre and developing holiday resort set in a rural hinterland, also contributing to the rural picture.[53] Bolton (BOL), a cotton centre, Earsdon (EAR), a mining community and Stoke (STO) or more accurately Hanley, one of Bennett's 'Five Towns' forming the Potteries, were chosen to represent industrial centres.[54] Both Bolton and Stoke had substantial roles for women in their labour markets. York (YOR) and Swansea (SWA) were both sizable urban centres with considerable retailing sectors, but they too contribute to our industrial profile. The Welsh town of Abergavenny (ABY) served a market function, and it had, like York, some railway works. Its neighbour, Blaenavon, while having a considerable portion of its workforce in the metal industry, also contributes a further dimension to our view of the mining industry. In addition we have enumeration districts taken from the rural areas nearby. The importance of London to the national

---

[52] To ensure confidentiality all names and addresses were removed by OPCS before the Cambridge Group received the data

[53] The area dubbed 'Axminster' does not, in fact, include any part of that town. More accurately this locale contains the town of Colyton and its near neighbour, Colyford, plus their agricultural surroundings, plus the nearby centres of Seaton and Beer.

[54] In reality there were six pottery towns: Stoke, Burslem, Tunstall, Longton, Hanley and Fenton. Arnold Bennett omitted the last from his count in *Anna of the five towns*.

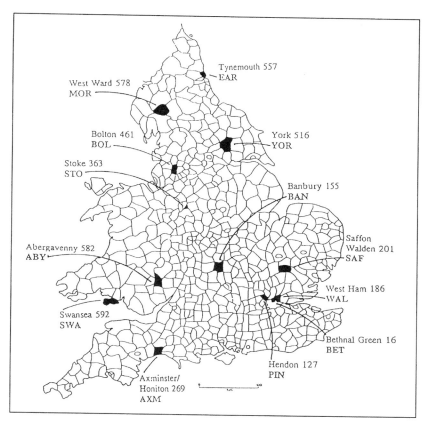

Note:
York - name of registration district in which locale lies,
516 - number of registration district in 1891,
YOR – three letters used to identify a particular locale.

Source: Grateful thanks are extended to Prof. R.I. Woods, Department of Geography, University of Liverpool, for permission to use his outline map of registration districts in this diagram.

Figure 15.1 The location of the registration districts in England and Wales which contain the OPCS locales

picture was acknowledged by our choice of three locales to represent its diversity. Walthamstow (WAL) was a growing working class suburb to the north-east, Pinner (PIN) a burgeoning middle class suburb to the north-west, and Bethnal Green (BET) was an acknowledged area of poverty encompassing a large immigrant population in the 'East End'. In combination we refer to the inhabitants of the 13 locales as the 'OPCS population'.

These 'locales' should not be seen as representative of the nation as a whole. Rather they should be seen as separate case studies, each with their own idiosyncrasies providing a spatial dimension for comparison of women's experiences across different regions and economies, an opportunity not often granted in studies dealing with census data at the level of the individual. Our ability to recode individual replies to the occupational questions ensures greater comparability from one census to the next and avoids the major disjunctures evident when the tables in the published reports are compared in series. The individual returns also allow examination of personal characteristics such as age and marital status as well as observation of the household and family structures in which the women lived. It is possible to conduct cross-locale studies or to examine the experience of the OPCS population *en masse*. Both approaches are employed in the following discussion.

As we have seen, the published census reports for 1891, 1901 and 1911 treated persons of 10 years of age and over as being of working age. By 1921 the minimum working age was considered to be 12. Here, however, we will look at those individuals who were 15 years old or over. This allows comparability across censuses, and also enables the population to be divided more easily into equal five-year age groups.

The 1891 OPCS population includes approximately 27,000 women aged 15 and over in observation. By 1921 this had risen to just under 39,000. Over the first three censuses the proportion of married women in the OPCS population remained at a constant 51 per cent.[55] The proportion of single women rose from 37 to 39 per cent, while declining mortality contributed to reducing the proportion widowed from 11.7 to 10.2 per cent. In contrast, the 1921 figures partially reflect the impact of the First World War. The proportion of single women fell slightly to 36 per cent, while the proportion married rose by two percentage points. Levels of widowhood rose again, but at 11.1 per cent

---

[55] The proportion married includes all women stating that they were so, whether or not their husbands were present on census night. We have only two divorced women recorded; both in 1921. The latter women are not included in the tables which follow.

Table 15.3   **Percentage of ever-married women who are widowed by age group: women aged 15 or over, OPCS population 1891–1921**

Age group	1891	1901	1911	1921
15–	2.1	1.5	6.8	3.2
20–	1.0	1.1	0.4	1.0
25–	2.3	1.9	1.3	3.7
30–	4.5	3.6	2.4	5.9
35–	6.6	6.0	5.0	6.4
40–	11.6	9.7	8.1	8.3
45–	15.4	14.6	13.1	11.3
50–	24.8	23.6	19.1	17.2
55–	29.1	30.9	26.3	23.7
60+	56.2	54.8	55.8	52.4

Source: Office of Population Censuses and Surveys (OPCS) census records.

did not reach 1891 proportions. As can be seen from Table 15.3 the rise in widowhood in 1921 was age selective: only the 20–34 age group experienced 1921 levels of widowhood greater than those of 1891; the levels for older women continued to decline, hence the relatively small overall rise in the proportion widowed between 1911 and 1921.[56]

Table 15.4 unravels women's changing experience further. Between 1891 and 1911, the proportion of single women rose in every age group. Comparing the 1911 figures with those of 1921, however, we see that this trend was abruptly reversed amongst the 20–34 year-olds, although it continued amongst those aged over 40. As single women were more likely to be reported as having an occupation, the OPCS population appears to have had an increasing pool of potential workers on which to draw, particularly between 1891 and 1911.

Over the decade from 1911 to 1921 marriage chances for younger women actually appear to have improved, despite the loss of young men during the First World War. Had the chance of marriage remained at 1911 levels there would have been 7 per cent more single women in their twenties in 1921 than the actual numbers indicate. These figures have to be treated with caution, however. The census snapshot of our 13 areas may not be revealing changes in marriage patterns so much as changes in occupation. As will be demonstrated below, the proportion

---

[56] There is some evidence that remarriage after the death of a spouse was an increasing possibility for both men and women. This would to some small degree reduce the number of widows recorded.

Table 15.4 **Percentage of each age group who remain single: women aged 15 or over, OPCS population 1891–1921**

Age group	1891	1901	1911	1921
15–	97.8	98.6	98.8	98.1
20–	68.8	71.2	74.9	70.9
25–	36.9	39.0	43.1	39.0
30–	23.2	20.8	25.2	24.0
35–	14.8	16.8	18.8	18.7
40–	12.0	14.8	15.2	16.0
45–	10.7	11.2	14.1	15.5
50–	10.2	10.0	12.1	14.0
55–	9.7	8.8	10.3	12.7
60+	9.9	8.4	9.8	10.8

Source: as Table 15.3.

of women recorded as domestic servants fell dramatically between 1911 and 1921. Servants were predominantly unmarried, and if they were no longer being employed in such numbers and were seeking alternative employment elsewhere then areas in which they had previously been concentrated would see a decline in the proportion of single women in the female population.[57] At the national scale the potential servants would have been enumerated as single women elsewhere, but they may well have migrated 'out of observation', thus distorting the marital status distribution in the OPCS population.

Figure 15.2 demonstrates, for 1891, how diverse the proportions in the various marital states could be from place to place. Single girls formed less than 30 per cent of the female population aged 15 and over in Bethnal Green, Earsdon and Saffron Walden, whereas in middle-class Pinner they outnumbered married women, forming almost half of the adult female population. In Bethnal Green and Earsdon marriage came early, and here and in Saffron Walden those not marrying left to find jobs elsewhere. Pinner's middle-class population married late and there were large numbers of places for domestic servants, creating a concentration of unmarried females.[58]

---

[57] National figures suggest that the proportion of women ever married rose between 1911 and 1921; if the migration of servants did contribute to the reduced proportions single in the OPCS population, this only enhanced the more general picture of increased marriage chances. See Lewis, *Women in England*, p. 3.

[58] By 1921 the proportion of the adult female population single had not altered dramatically, although certain locales, such as Pinner and Swansea with a

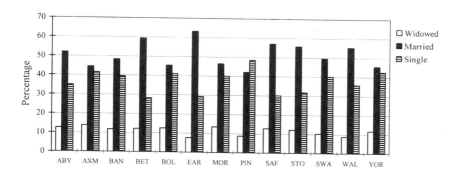

Source: as Table 15.3.

Figure 15.2 All women aged 15 and over: percentage by marital status, by OPCS locale, 1891

Marital and occupational status were closely related. In most of our 13 locales the majority of single women were returned as working in the labour market. The column second from the right in Table 15.5 shows for the OPCS population the percentage of women of each marital status who were returned as having an occupation in each of the four censuses. Approximately 70 per cent of single women are so recorded, with a peak in 1911 of 73.5 per cent. Among married women whose husbands were living with them on census night, at most 1 in 10 returned an occupation, again with the peak rate occurring in 1911, whereas among widows apparent employment rates lay at over 40 per cent until the dawn of the new century, but then dropped steeply. The apparent participation rates by age (not shown) indicate that the drop in employment rates among widows between 1901 and 1911 is mainly restricted to those aged 65 and over, suggesting the introduction of the old age pension in 1908 may have been playing a part.[59] The proportionately greater drop between 1911 and 1921 is evident in all age groups, however. Given the absence of widow's pensions until

relatively large middle-class component showed larger than average declines in the proportion of single women, adding weight to the 'decline of service' argument. Nevertheless 41 per cent of Pinner's adult female population remained single while the proportion in Earsdon was only 28 per cent.

[59] Initial legislation in Britain set the qualifying age for receipt of a state pension at 70 and was by no means universal: Macnicol and Blaikie, 'Politics of retirement', pp. 25–6.

Table 15.5 Percentage of women aged 15 and over returning a labour market occupation[a] in each census, by marital status and age, OPCS population 1891–1921

| | | | | | Age Groups | | | | | |
	15–	20–	25–	35–	45–	55–	65+	All	N
Marital Status									
Single									
1891	69.6	75.7	73.4	67.5	61.9	50.4	26.2	70.7	10,035
1901	69.4	75.5	71.4	64.3	65.0	47.8	29.6	69.8	12,101
1911	74.6	79.7	75.7	66.6	60.6	55.1	29.5	73.5	14,184
1921	68.5	77.5	71.3	64.1	57.2	47.1	26.4	68.2	13,845
Married – Spouse Absent									
1891	(66.7)[b]	(30.6)	45.5	48.1	42.9	42.1	(34.2)	43.7	704
1901	(25.0)	31.2	31.9	44.0	39.0	43.5	26.1	37.2	893
1911	(0.0)	35.7	37.9	41.1	47.4	45.4	31.4	40.9	1,030
1921	(43.7)	25.6	27.4	30.5	29.9	31.0	8.1	27.9	1,180
Married – Spouse Present									
1891	13.2	15.0	9.6	9.6	9.2	7.8	6.8	9.5	13,171
1901	9.5	10.1	6.8	8.0	7.1	7.5	5.7	7.5	15,390
1911	(12.5)	11.8	12.2	10.5	10.3	9.7	6.9	10.8	17,730
1921	14.9	12.1	8.2	8.0	7.0	6.2	3.3	7.6	19,320

Table 15.5 Continued

		Age Groups							
	15–	20–	25–	35–	45–	55–	65+	All	N
Widowed									
1891	(50.0)	(66.7)	69.9	70.3	54.9	43.0	23.6	42.5	3,202
1901	–	(60.0)	73.1	63.9	55.0	39.1	22.9	40.4	3,461
1911	(75.0)	(60.0)	74.3	66.8	51.3	36.2	17.1	34.9	3,740
1921	(66.7)	(28.6)	44.8	42.1	42.1	27.2	10.8	25.5	4,306

Notes:

a) Women not returning a labour market occupation include those returned as 'scholars' or 'students', those returned as 'housewives' or considered to be undertaking 'home duties', those stating that they were not working for some reason and those whose 'occupation' box was left blank.

b) The numbers in parenthesis indicate percentages derived from fewer than 50 women.

Source: as Table 15.3.

1925, this drop is much more difficult to account for, particularly as until 1911 widows under the age of 45 had participation rates on a par with single women, but in 1921 were only two thirds as likely to return an occupation.[60] A fourth group of women, those reportedly married but whose husbands were not present on census night, show apparent participation rates more akin to those of widows than of wives—an unsurprising discovery given that some of these women would have been abandoned by, or separated from, their husbands on a long-term basis. Others may well have been single mothers attempting to disguise their unmarried state and in need of employment to support themselves and their children. It is also possible that the absence of her husband may have left a woman freer to return an occupation than might have been the case had he been at home. However, in common with widows, the 'married spouse absent' women display a marked decline in their reported participation rates between 1911 and 1921. This perhaps suggests a problem in the consistency of reporting occupations among these groups, rather than a welfare or cultural development, a point which remains to be investigated.

The proportion of women reporting an occupation diminished with age in every marital status category, although rates remain relatively buoyant for those in their late forties and early fifties. Beyond this, and particularly for those over the age of 65, rates drop rapidly. Possibly by this stage women could call on relatives for support, maybe by exchanging 'home duties' for financial and material assistance. It is also possible that the activities of older women in the labour market might have been of a kind overlooked by the census.

Figure 15.3 illustrates how diverse regional experience of 'women's work' could be. In 1911 in Stoke, Bolton and Bethnal Green over 80 per cent of single women reported having a paid occupation, while the norm for other areas lay between 60 and 80 per cent. In the mining community of Earsdon only 40 per cent of single women returned an occupation, reflecting the fact that there were few job opportunities for women outside the home and a large demand for help with domestic tasks within. Where the demand for women's industrial labour was high, as in the potteries of Stoke, the textile mills of Bolton, and the workshops of Bethnal Green, the level of married women's reported participation in the workforce was also high at around 20 per cent. Elsewhere closer to 10 per cent of wives reported having a labour market occupation, Earsdon again having the lowest rate with only one

---

[60] Macnicol and Blaikie, 'Politics of retirement', p. 28; Lewis, *Women in England*, p. 64.

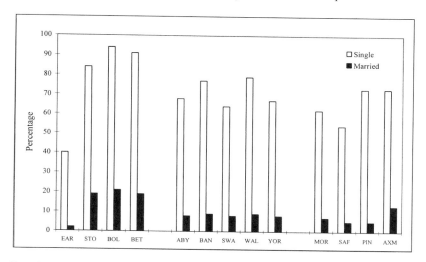

Note: a) 'Married' does not include those women whose spouse was absent on census night.
Source: as Table 15.3.

Figure 15.3 The percentage of women aged 15 and over returning an occupation, by marital status[a] and OPCS locale, 1911.

in every 50 married (spouse present) women reporting an occupation. Middle-class Pinner, while having relatively high rates of single women's work, had the second lowest apparent participation rate amongst married women. The role of the young, single, mobile servant in such areas is thus highlighted once again. Taking the two extremes of Bolton and Earsdon in Table 15.6 we can see that work in the labour market was virtually universal for single women under the age of 45 in the former, but reported by fewer than half of the women in this age group in the latter. The growing proportion of single women reporting an occupation with age in Earsdon suggests that having a job enabled one to keep one's independence longer. Among married women in Bolton apparent labour force participation diminished with age: as women's families grew they found it increasingly difficult to remain out at work and as their children grew older they could replace their mother's earning capabilities, freeing her to devote herself entirely to domestic chores.[61] The women of Bolton certainly do not appear to have found it necessary to give up work on marriage, whereas in Earsdon full-time, paid work and marriage appear to have been almost

[61] See Garrett, 'The trials of labour', Figure 5, p. 131; Roberts 'Women's strategies'.

Table 15.6   Percentage of women returning a labour market occupation[a] by marital status and age, Bolton and Earsdon, 1911

	Age Groups								
	15–	20–	25–	35–	45–	55–	65+	All	N
Single									
Bolton	95.8	97.1	93.4	90.3	(84.4)[b]	(95.4)	(46.7)	94.0	1,007
Earsdon	33.7	40.8	47.7	(50.0)	(70.0)	(80.0)	(66.7)	40.1	1,461
Married – Spouse Present									
Bolton	–	30.6	27.0	21.0	13.1	14.8	(8.1)	20.7	1,060
Earsdon	–	2.6	1.4	1.5	3.5	2.6	(0.0)	2.0	1,013
Widowed									
Bolton	–	–	(100.0)	(77.4)	59.7	38.6	18.5	43.8	290
Earsdon	–	–	(60.0)	(52.9)	(14.3)	14.7	2.0	16.7	126

Notes: as Table 15.5.
Source: as Table 15.3.

totally incompatible. Similarly Bolton's apparent participation rate for widows was by far the highest of the 13 locales in 1911: the availability of job opportunities in addition to the past labour market experience of women must have played a large part in enabling widows to return to employment. Elsewhere, if widows were eking out a living, they were doing so in ways that did not enrol them in the census returns as apparent full-time, paid employees.

In an attempt to demonstrate how 'earning money' does not necessarily equate with an apparent full-time occupation, Figure 15.4 depicts the percentage of all (spouse present) married women in each locale for whom an occupation was reported in conjunction with the proportion who had at least one boarder in their household on census night in 1911. Keeping a boarder tended to be seen as a woman's activity; although men shared the house with the boarders they are seldom described as keeping them, a reflection of the fact that most of the services boarders required were domestic functions.[62] Obviously circumstances would determine both the demand for places as boarders and the ability for such demands to be fulfilled. In areas of large families but small houses, such as Bethnal Green, space for boarders was limited, and in those agricultural areas such as Saffron Walden which were

[62] Davidoff, 'The separation of home and work?', pp. 74–6, 82–3.

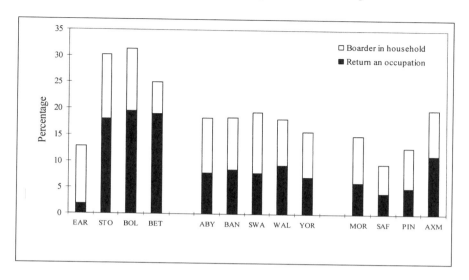

Note: a) Wives returning an occupation *and* keeping a boarder are included amongst the 'return an occupation' category.
Source: as Table 15.3.

Figure 15.4 The percentage of all 'wives of head of household' returning an occupation, and the percentage housing at least one boarder[a], OPCS locales, 1911.

experiencing out-migration, few people sought to board. If we were to treat keeping a boarder as an apparent full-time occupation then an extra 5 to 10 per cent of wives in each area could be viewed as having paid employment, a feature the published census returns render invisible.[63]

In sum, the data presented here do not indicate a dramatic, nor even a moderate, rise in the proportion of women having their main occupation reported as lying outside the home. The surge upward in

---

[63] Boarders who slept and ate as members of the household are much more easily identified in the censuses of this period than are lodgers, despite their many similarities. Census instructions directed that lodgers, who did not eat with their host family, should be recorded as living in separate households. The proportions of women having an extra income from renting out space in their homes is thus underestimated in Figure 15.4. It is possible that there was considerable, but unquantifiable, regional variation in the extent of this undercount. The low level of boarders in Bethnal Green, for instance, may reflect a preference for lodging in that area. Figure 15.4 does, nevertheless, indicate that earning strategies were available to women who appear to be without full-time paid occupation in the census returns.

reported participation in 1911, probably created by the different phraseology of the occupation question, gives an illusion of a rising trend. Indeed, among husband–absent married and widowed women the underlying trend was a markedly downward one. The number of women working certainly rose, but this appears to be due more to a growth in the population, rather than to women increasingly infiltrating the 'apparent full-time labour market'.

The changing nature of women's employment

If the proportion of those occupied was not altering dramatically, the jobs which women were doing were changing demonstrably. At the national level (Table 15.1) the four main sectors where women were to be found in 1891 were domestic service, commerce, clothing and textiles. Those working in the latter category were concentrated in the cotton and woollen areas of Lancashire and the West Riding of Yorkshire. The other three categories were dispersed more evenly across the country. Knowing that our locales were not a representative sample of the national experience, we appreciated that our view of textile workers would be highly coloured by the experience of Bolton. We applied the same logic to the pottery workers of Stoke, and therefore did not include these two groups in the following analysis.[64] Instead we look at workers in dress, those who worked as dealers or dealers assistants, those who were domestic servants, and all other women who returned a non–textile, non–pottery occupation, whom we have designated as being in 'non-major occupations'.[65]

---

[64] The levels of married women's occupation outside the home can act as a barometer, not only of the state of the industry in which the women are working, but also of the industries in which their husbands work. If male unemployment or under-employment is high in an area then the number of married women reported to be out at work increases. See Garrett, 'Trials of labour'. Bolton and Stoke saw considerable change in their fortunes over the 30 year period in question. To include the changing proportion of textile workers and potters in the following calculations would have had repercussions for the measurement of the proportion of women employed in other sectors; they were therefore omitted.

[65] 'Non-major' is here used in the sense of 'not making up a major component' of the workforce. In combination these occupations do make up a considerable proportion of the workforce, but the constituent occupational groups each contribute only a relatively small proportion of the total. The 'Non-major' category thus includes all women reporting labour market participation except those in dress, dealing, domestic service, textiles and pottery. Tables 15.1 and 15.2 give a full list of the categories included.

Table 15.7   **Percentage of women aged 15 and over reportedly employed in industries other than textiles or pottery who are in dress, dealing, domestic service or 'non-major' occupations, by marital status, OPCS population 1891–1921**

	1891	1901	1911	1921
Single women				
Dress[a]	15.7	17.9	16.2	11.2
Dealers[b]	7.9	7.6	8.9	12.2
Dealers' assistants	0.3	1.3	1.8	2.9
Domestic servants[c]	54.9	48.4	42.7	31.9
Non-major occupations[d]	21.3	24.9	30.3	43.2
Number reporting employment in the occupations listed	6,107	7,253	9,039	8,383
Married women[e]				
Dress	23.6	21.3	12.0	9.9
Dealers	16.9	17.0	14.9	21.6
Dealers' assistants	0.2	0.2	12.1	2.9
Domestic servants	30.5	29.1	24.7	17.4
Non-major occupations	28.9	32.5	36.5	48.2
Number reporting employment in the occupations listed	1,209	1,166	2,161	1,557
Widows				
Dress	13.7	13.6	9.9	6.9
Dealers	18.9	20.5	17.9	17.7
Dealers' assistants	0.0	0.1	0.5	0.2
Domestic servants	43.8	39.6	44.0	44.0
Non-major occupations	23.6	26.2	27.7	31.2
Number reporting employment in the occupations listed	1,282	1,315	1,297	1,025

Notes:

a) 'Dress' includes all 'dressmakers', 'tailoresses', 'milliners', 'corsetmakers' and others in the making and repairing of clothes.

b) 'Dealers' are all those reported to be 'shopkeepers', 'dealers', 'shop assistants', etc., no matter in what commodity they are dealing.

c) 'Domestic servants' are all those returned under an occupation with the words 'domestic' or 'domestic servant' appended to it, as well as those described by these terms alone and thus would include kitchen maids, maids, domestic nurses, domestic governesses, domestic kitchen and laundry hands, mothers' helps, day servants and charwomen if they describe themselves as 'in service'.

d) The 'non-major' category includes all women reporting labour market participation, excluding those in dress, dealing, domestic service, textiles and pottery (see Tables 15.1 and 15.2 for full list of possible categories).

e) 'Married women' include both spouse–present and spouse–absent wives.

Source: as Table 15.3.

In Table 15.7 women in the OPCS population have again been divided by marital status. Among single women the greatest occupational change was the decline of domestic service and of dress, replaced by jobs in other sectors of the economy. In 1891 every second never-married adult woman recording an occupation outside of textiles and pottery in the OPCS population was a domestic servant. By 1921 this had fallen to fewer than one in three. Among married working women too the proportion returned as domestic servants fell from one in three to fewer than one in five. In this group the decline in dress-making was even more dramatic. Elizabeth Roberts suggests that, with the increase of factory-made clothing and the rise of foreign competition, the demand for dress-makers and tailoresses diminished, married women being first, as usual, to withdraw their labour.[66] It may also be that opportunities for home-working in the industry diminished and thus married women were no longer able to participate to the same extent as when they had been able to combine work and child-care.[67] Participation in dress declined among widows too, but service, atypically, retained a fairly constant proportion of those widows returning an occupation. The proportion returning non-major occupations rose as well, but not as rapidly as among the other two marital status groups. It might be suggested that the changes experienced at the opening of the new century worked through the population via generations of young workers who explored avenues of employment which had not been open to their elders. It was not that women moved wholesale out of the more traditional employments: young women apparently preferred not to enter them. Legally enforceable compulsory education had only been in place for approximately ten years by 1891. By 1921 the daughters of parents with only basic literary skills were entering the labour market equipped with more sophisticated reading, writing and arithmetic abilities, and were looking for jobs in which to use these.[68] The jobs no longer being filled by the youngsters

---

[66] Roberts, *Women's work*, p. 30.

[67] The decline in women's reported participation in the dressmaking industry may in part be attributed to the fact that the 1921 Census was taken in June, rather than the more usual time of late March or early April, because of threatened industrial action at the latter time. See OPCS, *Guide to census reports*. Morris, however, reports that the busiest times of the year for dressmakers were March to August and October to December. These dates were for the London bespoke trade, and other regions of the country may have experienced different 'off-seasons': Morris, 'Characteristics of sweating'.

[68] The 1902 Education Act formed the foundation stone for a national secondary system. Initially fees were charged but in 1907 grants to the schools were made, provisional on 25 per cent of places being provided free for pupils from

increasingly became the provenance of those in the later stages of their life cycle.

The figures in Table 15.7 also bring into sharp focus the impact of the change in wording in the 1911 census concerning women helping or assisting relatives on a regular basis. Previously, apparent participation rates have been shown to rise amongst single and married women in 1911 only to decline again in 1921. Table 15.7 is more specific, showing the proportion of married women returned as 'dealer's assistant' soaring from 0.2 per cent in 1901 to 12.1 per cent in 1911 but falling to only 2.9 per cent in 1921. Among single women, dealers' assistants saw steady percentage growth with no 'bounce' in 1911. This suggests that the wives of dealers were more likely than their daughters to be helping out on a 'part-time but regular' basis in the family business. Knowing from the census manuscripts how individual household members are related to one another we can test this supposition. Predictably, the story is not clear-cut.

All women returned as being either a 'dealer' or a 'dealer's assistant' were identified from the returns and all those reported to be the wife or daughter of the household head were selected. They were then divided by whether or not the household head was a dealer and further divided into age groups. The results of this exercise are depicted in Figures 15.5a (for wives) and 15.5b (for daughters).

Relatively few wives of dealers were under the age of 30, dealing being an occupation requiring some accumulation of capital, perhaps involving the inheritance of premises or stock and thus favouring rather older persons who would in turn have rather older spouses. In 1891 and 1901 the OPCS population included approximately 1,200 men reported to be dealers. In 1911 there were 1,382 and in 1921 1,094. Around 3 per cent of these men had wives who were reported to be dealers or dealers' assistants in the first two censuses, but 20 per cent did so in 1911 and 13 per cent in 1921. The great surge in the number of dealers' wives reportedly working in dealing in 1911 followed by a decline in 1921 suggests that many dealers' wives helped out in the shop on a regular basis but far fewer did so on a relatively full-time basis, a situation captured by the wording of the 1911 and 1921 censuses in combination. The wives of non-dealers reported to be involved in dealing also rose in

publicly run elementary schools. Halsey, *Trends in British society*, Table 6.2, shows that by 1911, 18,900 12–14 year olds and 33,000 15–18 year olds were receiving 'grant aided' secondary education. By 1921 the figures had grown to 186,000 and 82,000 respectively. See also Bourke, *Working class cultures*, pp. 116–18.

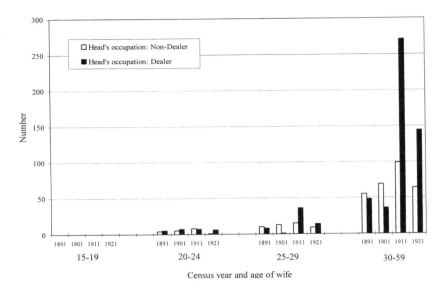

Source: as Table 15.3.

Figure 15.5a The number of 'dealers' and 'dealer's assistants' who were also returned as 'wife of head of household' by head's occupation and by age of wife, OPCS population, 1891–1921

1911. Under the 1911 instructions women could have been assisting relatives who resided in another household. It is possible that married women were helping out nearby kin in their enterprises on a part-time basis, but this is very difficult to prove.

The fortunes of dealers' daughters take quite a different path to that of non-dealers' daughters (Figure 15.5b). Among the former the number employed as dealers or dealers' assistants remained fairly constant over the first two censuses in each age group, but took the now familiar 1911 upswing followed by a downturn in 1921. The 1911 wording captured the help given by daughters in the family shop, but the experience of these women is eclipsed by the growing number of shop workers who came from families who did not own or run a shop. The new consumer era heralded a rise in demand for 'shop assistants' to control stock and serve customers. The growing influence of large stores at the expense of small, family shops greatly expanded this job market, a demand met by a better educated, working-class female pool of labour with a desire to be respectable and work in a shop, much as Eliza

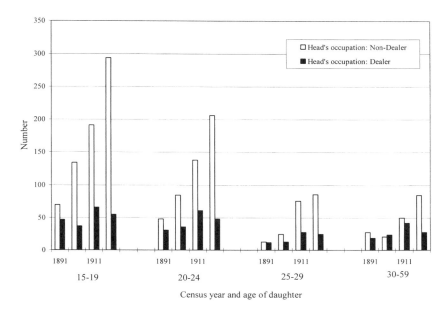

Census year and age of daughter

Source: as Table 15.3.

Figure 15.5b The number of 'dealers' and 'dealers' assistants' who were also returned as 'daughter of head of household' by head's occupation and by age of daughter, OPCS population, 1891–1921

Doolittle dreamed of in *Pygmalion*.[69] The dimensions of dealing and shop work thus altered over our study period, not only in the number of women reported as participating, but also in the nature and the conditions of the work undertaken.

The changing nature of work as experienced by women is also evident if we examine women who were married, but whose husbands were not present with them on census night. It has been shown that such women comprise between 5 and 6 per cent of all married women

[69] McBride highlights the fact that the advent of large stores reduced the opportunities for married women to work in family-run shops: 'Women's work', p. 76. It may also have contributed to the declining number of men reported to be 'dealers' evident in the OPCS population, but this point requires further investigation. Roberts (*Women's work*) makes the point that 'for many working class females working in [a] shop carried more social status than working in either a factory or in domestic service'. The importance of 'respectability' is rehearsed in Rose, *Limited livelihoods*.

Table 15.8   Percentage of married women aged 15 and over in various occupations living apart from their husbands on census night, OPCS population 1891–1921

	1891	1901	1911	1921
Pottery	12.9	14.2	13.7	8.8
Textiles	12.8	18.6	19.9	12.6
Dress[a]	15.8	15.7	19.0	25.7
Dealers[b]	23.1	20.7	12.2	13.8
Dealers assistants	–	–	2.1	2.6
Domestic servants[c]	28.0	37.2	36.3	24.2
Non-major occupations[d]	19.8	21.4	12.5	16.4
Those not returning an occupation	3.1	3.7	3.7	4.5
All	5.0	5.5	5.5	5.7

Notes: as Table 15.7.
Source: as Table 15.3.

in the OPCS population. However, much higher proportions of absent husbands are evident among married women reporting an occupation. Table 15.8 shows the percentages of married women in various occupations who were living apart from their husbands on census night. In certain occupations, such as domestic service, separation from one's spouse might be an expediency of the job, but overall the impression given by the table is that many married women worked because they had to support themselves and their families in the absence of their husbands.[70] It is possible that, if the family lived in straightened economic circumstances, husband and wife might choose to separate so that each could find employment in a different locality, but this cannot be ascertained from the census returns, nor can we gauge how long such

---

[70] Comparing the living arrangements of those returned as servants across the censuses of 1891 to 1921, one finds some evidence that there was a decline in the proportion of servants who 'lived in', particularly in 1921 after the First World War. Unlike other employees domestic servants were not required to supply the name of their employer in the 1921 census, thus we cannot determine whether a shift in the nature of service had taken place, with more servants living locally and going daily to their employers, or whether the rescheduling of the 1921 census to the summer months meant that more servants were observed having travelled home to spend Sunday with their families. As previously suggested, where a woman's husband was absent she might be more likely to report having an occupation than when he was present.

Table 15.9   Percentage of single women in various age groups employed in the domestic service and non-major occupation categories and not returning a labour market occupation: OPCS population, 1891–1921

Age	1891	1901	1911	1921
Domestic service[a]				
15–	32.4	26.1	24.6	16.6
20–	35.6	31.9	29.0	20.2
25–	37.0	35.2	31.6	22.0
30–	30.6	28.6	28.2	22.3
60+	16.8	13.8	16.0	13.4
Non-major occupation[a]				
15–	11.8	16.0	19.0	25.7
20–	13.9	15.7	21.6	32.6
25–	15.9	13.6	21.2	28.7
30–	12.2	13.5	17.1	22.2
60+	8.3	8.2	10.0	12.1
Not returning a labour market occupation[b]				
15–	30.3	30.6	25.3	31.5
20–	24.1	24.5	20.2	22.5
25–-	25.5	26.5	21.8	25.4
30–	32.9	34.9	32.7	36.0
60+	62.4	60.7	59.5	62.7

Notes:
a) Definition as in Table 15.7
b) Definition as in note a, Table 15.5.

Source: as Table 15.3.

a separation might last. It is noticeable that as the dress category became a less favoured occupation for married women (Table 15.7) so the proportion of spouse-absent women working in it rose (Table 15.8), possibly signifying a decline in social status for this group of occupations. The marked drop in the proportion of spouse-absent wives in the dealers and non-major occupational categories in 1911 may reflect a greater number of wives being reported as assisting their husbands, resulting in higher numbers of women having been counted in these categories, thus reducing the proportion formed by the spouse-absent wives. Levels amongst the latter do not return to their 1901 base in

1921, however, suggesting that other factors may be at play. The June date for the 1921 census, rather than the usual March/April date, may have affected the likelihood of spouses being separated on census night, for instance.[71]

The complexity of factors underlying the proportion of women in particular situations reported as having an occupation is thus further highlighted, and the need to standardise for age or marital status is underlined. In focussing further on the changing nature of women's work at the beginning of the twentieth century, we will concentrate on single women who indisputably formed the bulk of the female paid labour force. In Table 15.7 the major feature among this group was the decline in domestic service and the rise in non-major occupations. The proportion of women reportedly occupied in the latter category doubled over the 30 year study period. Table 15.9 indicates how different age groups of single women were affected. For comparison, the proportion of women in each age group not returning an occupation is included. Allowing for the problems with data from 1911, we can suggest that the proportion of single women in all age groups returning an occupation saw only marginal changes between 1891 and 1921.

The sort of jobs young women were doing changed markedly in the 30 years between 1891 and 1921, however. Among teenagers the proportion in service fell by 50 per cent, and single women in their early twenties reported a 43 per cent decline. Again, bearing in mind the problems of the 1911 figures, all ages experienced a significant upturn in employment in the non-major occupational category by 1921, but those between 20 and 24 saw the greatest relative rise in this form of employment. The oldest age group was, perhaps not surprisingly, least affected by the encroaching changes.

What were the 'non-major' occupations into which single women were moving? Table 15.10 breaks down this category into its component sectors, and shows how the contribution of each to the whole category was changing. While it is impossible to discuss here in detail each individual sub-category, it is worth noting that the most dramatic rise was obviously among the white collar occupations, within which the major contribution to growth was made by women employed in clerical jobs. Even though the number of women reporting professional occupations such as teaching rose from fewer than 300 in 1891 to over 500 in 1921, this group experienced a substantial

---

[71] Higgs, 'Women, work and occupations', suggests that the March/April dates had been chosen for the census to avoid distortions created by summer migration patterns.

Table 15.10   The percentage of single women aged 15 and over and reported to be employed in 'non-major occupations'[a] in each of the occupational sub-categories, OPCS population, 1891–1921

	1891	1901	1911	1921
White-collar				
Government service	1.6	2.6	3.3	3.5
Professional	22.7	20.6	19.6	14.8
Clerical	2.0	4.7	8.4	21.8
Total white-collar	26.3	27.9	31.3	40.1
Non-white-collar				
Transport and communications	1.6	1.1	1.1	2.6
Agriculture	10.4	4.9	6.1	2.3
Printing, bookbinding, paper	6.2	15.8	11.9	6.8
Food	22.9	26.8	26.0	18.9
General work	11.7	5.6	8.6	16.0
Other occupations in the 'non-major' category	21.0	17.9	14.9	13.2
Total non-white-collar	73.7	72.1	68.7	59.9

Note: a) for definition see Table 15.7.

Source: as Table 15.3.

proportional decline. It is also noticeable that within the non-major occupations the diversity of employment experience contracted dramatically in 1921. In the previous three censuses approximately 70 per cent of women reporting occupations in the 'non-major category' were returning non-white collar jobs. By 1921 this had dropped to 60 per cent. In the 13 OPCS locales the pace of women's movement into the white-collar sector and the level of their participation in 1921 varied widely. Table 15.11 shows that while the proportion of women reporting 'commercial' (predominantly clerical and secretarial) white collar jobs grew markedly between 1911 and 1921 in all 13 locales, almost one in every five single women aged 15 and over was reported as employed in this category in 1921 in predominantly working-class Walthamstow.[72] In middle-class Pinner the equivalent ratio was almost

[72] Under the classification scheme used here 'commercial' workers include: commercial clerks, those in bank service, salesmen and buyers, insurance clerks, those in advertising, and secretaries, as well as merchants, brokers and factors. The great majority of women so classified were secretaries or clerks.

Table 15.11   **The number of single women in 'commercial' white-collar occupations, per 1,000 single women age 15–64, by locale, OPCS population, 1891–1921**

	1891	1901	1911	1921
ABY[a]	1	2	5	20
AXM	4	1	8	17
BAN	4	7	13	40
BET	4	6	18	67
BOL	–	2	2	23
EAR	3	2	6	26
MOR	–	2	–	8
PIN	9	9	22	98
SAF	–	2	7	25
STO	3	3	12	31
SWA	2	7	11	52
WAL	14	37	77	198
YOR	–	9	17	88

Note: a) for definition of abbreviations, see text.

Source: as Table 15.3.

one in ten; if servants are excluded from the calculation, which is necessary as there are five servants reported in Pinner for every one in Walthamstow, then Pinner's 'commercial' ratio becomes one in six. The 'metropolitan influence' on the creation of such non-professional white collar opportunities for women is demonstrated by the fact that the 'commercial' ratio for 'East End' Bethnal Green was surpassed only by York, a major regional centre, of the other OPCS locales. The other regional centre, Swansea, showed reported levels of women's 'commercial' work on a par with those in Bethnal Green. With servants removed from the calculation York, Bethnal Green and Swansea had respectively 108, 70 and 69 per 1,000 single women aged 15 and over reporting 'commercial' occupations in 1921. Women were moving out of domestic service and into the 'service sector'.

Conclusion

To conclude this examination of 'women's work' as reported by the censuses as the twentieth century dawned let us return to the contemporary reports of an increase in the number of working women.

The published census reports, the instructions on the census schedules and individual replies given on the completed schedules for 1891 to 1921 reveal that it is likely that women did not experience a rise in full-time, paid employment, which they could report as their 'main occupation'. The national picture of women slowly infiltrating the workforce between 1891 and 1911, then withdrawing into the home again in the wake of the Great War, appears to be an artefact of the census-taking process. The anomalous wording of the 1911 census reveals, however, that many women, particularly married women, who spent most of their time on domestic tasks could have been helping in family enterprises on a part-time basis. When such women went out to work in the labour market and were paid, this might be termed 'direct earning', for they brought back money which could then be spent on goods required by the household. However, when the women helped out in the family shop or business without pay they were 'earning indirectly' in that the family saved money because they did not have to pay someone else to do the work; the family may actually have made more money because a sister, mother, or daughter was able to do work over and above that normally possible. It is difficult to judge from a present day standpoint whether the women involved saw themselves as 'working' or as undertaking their 'duty' to family and household, just another facet of 'housework'.

Women were no more likely to be reported in employment after the First World War than they were 30 years earlier; indeed married women and widows were rather less likely to be so. With the increasing idea that 'work' was something one went out to, was paid for, and undertaken on a full-time basis, so the number of wives and widows who thought of themselves as being in the 'workforce' diminished. With rising living standards many working-class wives may have been very relieved to discard the 'double burden' of paid labour in conjunction with labour in the home.[73] The decline in reported occupations among widows remains a puzzle worthy of further research. Certainly the numbers in the female workforce were growing, but this appears to have been a result of population growth, plus a greater proportion of women remaining single at each age, at least between 1891 and 1911. The proportion of unmarried women over the age of 40 continued to grow over the war decade. More single women meant

[73] Bourke, *Working class cultures*, p. 127 quotes Roberts, *A woman's place* in this regard: 'Women who worked full-time were certainly not regarded as emancipated by their contemporaries, rather as drudges. Women whose husbands earned sufficient money to clothe, feed and house the family preferred to have a reduced workload rather than extra income.'

greater numbers of potential workers to be reported, even if their recorded participation rates remained static.

The proportion of single women in apparently full-time paid work may not have changed but the nature of the work they were doing was altering, in such a way as to make women and their work more visible to men. From the contemporary reports cited by Tilly and Scott it seemed as though greater numbers of women were working because they appeared 'in formerly male fields'. It may be more accurate that women workers increasingly appeared in the public field and therefore middle-class male observers became more aware of them. A man who had previously encountered servants in his home may not have thought of them as 'women workers': they were after all in women's proper place—the domestic sphere, 'at home'. The great majority of the middle classes had little call to venture into the textile factories, the pottery works, the sweatshops, or the fields where those not in service found paid employment. With the growth of the tertiary sector, however, middle-class men would increasingly encounter women 'going out to work'; sharing their trains and trams as they travelled to their workplaces, taking their notes, doing their typing, filing their correspondence, serving them in the burgeoning department stores. While some of these women would have been middle-class, many came from working-class districts. The new white-collar jobs may have meant subordination in the work place for the women involved, but it was certainly a step up from the servitude they would have experienced had they taken the more traditional path into domestic service. With the movement of women into the public arena the definition of work as something that one 'went out to do' became stronger and the status of 'housework' as an occupation dwindled. As we have observed, the census does not capture all the nuances of women's paid work, and it may also fall short in this respect in the case of men. Because the census was apparently designed to capture 'how one spent the majority of one's time' many women are recorded as (or simply imputed to be) housewives. Yet we know very little about the labour that went on under this umbrella title. From the lady running her household of servants to the poverty-stricken single mother juggling part-time and casual jobs, child care, and survival, there is a spectrum of 'home duties' about which the census remains stubbornly silent.

If we really wish to uncover the changes in women's work at the dawn of the twentieth century we need a picture of women in the private, as well as the public sphere. The census, however, was conducted on the basis of logic conceived in the male, public sphere. While individuals within a household were listed, it was deemed sufficient to list 'occupation', the criterion by which a man is placed on the social scale, to judge the individual's contribution to society. The census authorities failed to acknowledge the importance of the reproductive role played by the female of the household. Thus we have in some respects even less knowledge of 'women's labour' in the home and how much paid work it might actually have encompassed, than we do of 'women's work' in the apparently full-time, paid labour market. Our understanding of the broad, national picture of the latter between 1891 and 1921 comes to us from the published results of the decennial censuses, refracted through the questions posed, the answers given, and the classification schemes used to tabulate the published statistics. While the ability to examine the manuscript census returns does not enable us to clarify the picture totally, it does allow us to compensate for the refraction. This permits greater understanding of the view of society held by contemporary census-takers, and also forces a reappraisal of certain present-day conceptions of exactly what comprises 'work for women'.

Appendix 15.1 Instructions given on census schedules 1891–1921, with reference to female occupations

1891[a]	1901[b]	1911[c]	1921[d]
G.1.1. The precise nature of the occupation must be inserted.	1. The precise nature of the occupation must be inserted.	1. Describe the occupation fully. If more than one occupation is followed state that by which living is mainly earned.	9. If more than one occupation is followed, state only that by which the living is mainly earned. The occupation should be stated . . . whether the worker is at work or not at the time of the census. (Instruction 1 at head of 'Employment' columns: If at present out of work [state name of] last employer adding 'out of work').
G.1.2. A person following several distinct occupations must state each of them in order of their importance.	2. A person following more than one occupation should state each of them in order of their importance.	3. OUT OF WORK – if out of work . . . at the time of the census, the *usual occupation* must be stated.	
		5. CHILDREN AT SCHOOL AND STUDENTS – for all persons over 10 years of age attending school write 'school' . . . if also engaged in any employment state the employment as 'School, Newsboy'.	2. EDUCATION – for persons attending a school or other institution for the purpose of receiving education write 'whole time' if attending daily . . . For children under 12 [columns referring to occupation should be left blank].'
G.1.4. The occupations of women and children, if any, are to be stated as well as those of men.	4. Children attending school and also engaged in a trade or industry should be described as following the particular trade or industry.		5. For a member of a private household . . . who is mainly occupied in domestic duties at home write 'Home Duties'. . .
G.1.5. Married women assisting their husbands . . . are to be returned as 'Employed'		4. THE OCCUPATIONS OF WOMEN engaged in any business or profession, including women *regularly engaged in assisting relatives in*	7. For a member of a household who is chiefly occupied in giving unpaid help in a business carried on by the head of the household . . . state the occupation . . . as though it were a *paid occupation*

S.I.9. SONS or other RELATIVES of FARMERS employed on the farm should be returned as 'Farmer's Son' . . . etc.

S.I.10. Men employed on farms and living in the Farmer's house may return themselves as FARM SERVANTS, but this term should not be used for domestic servants in a farm house

S.I.11. SHOPMEN and WOMEN should state in what branch of business they are employed – as 'Draper's Assistant'.

S.I.13. DOMESTIC SERVANTS should state the nature of their service, adding in all cases 'Domestic Servant'.

9. SONS or other RELATIVES of FARMERS employed on the farm should be returned as 'Farmer's Son' . . . etc.

11. SHOPKEEPERS and SHOP ASSISTANTS should return themselves as such and should also state their branch of business . . . persons wholly or principally engaged in manufacture or repair . . . should return themselves as such and not 'Shopkeepers' . . .

14. DOMESTIC SERVANTS should be entered according to the nature of their service adding in all cases 'Domestic'.

trade or business, must be fully stated. No entry should be made in the case of wives, daughters or female relatives wholly engaged in domestic duties at home.[e]

8h. FARMER. State whether 'Farmer', 'Grazier' or 'Farm Bailiff'. Farmer's sons and other relatives assisting in the work of the farm should be returned as 'Farmer's Son working on Farm' . . . 'Farmer's Daughter, Dairy Work' . . . etc.

8l. FARM SERVANT state nature of work, and indicate if mainly in charge of horses, cattle, etc.

2. DEALERS, SHOPKEEPERS or SHOP ASSISTANTS as distinct from MAKERS, PRODUCERS or REPAIRERS . . . should be so described as to leave no doubt whether they are DEALERS or MAKERS.

8n. DOMESTIC SERVICE state nature of service.

10b. Shopkeepers, Retail Dealers or . . . if selling only . . . or if chiefly selling should use the word 'shopkeeper' [if] chiefly engaged in making or producing, though also selling, should add 'maker'.

In the case of Domestic Servants . . . the word 'Private' should be entered in [the 'Employment' column] . . . the name and business of the employer must NOT be stated.

18. LABOURERS . . . should specify the nature of their employment – as 'Navvy' 'Bricklayer's Labourer', 'General Labourer'.

19. PERSONS FOLLOWING NO PROFESSION, TRADE . . . deriving their income from land, houses, dividends or other private sources should return themselves as 'Living on their own means'.

19. LABOURERS . . . should specify the nature of their employment – as 'Navvy' 'Bricklayer's Labourer', 'General Labourer'.

13. NURSES, the term 'Nurse' by itself too indefinite. The kind of nurse should be stated as 'Hospital Nurse' . . .

21. LIVING ON OWN MEANS – Persons . . . deriving their income from private sources, should return themselves as 'Living on own means'.

8o. SERVANTS, WAITERS IN HOTELS, CLUBS, RESTAUR-ANTS AND BOARDING HOUSES state nature of employment and service to which engaged as 'Hotel Cook'.

LABOURER . . . state nature of employment as 'Bricklayer's Labourer' etc.

8p. NURSE state whether 'Nurse (Domestic)', 'Sick Nurse' etc.

7. PRIVATE MEANS – for persons neither following, nor having followed a profession or occupation, but deriving their income from private sources write . . . 'Private Means'.

10g. *Labourers* should always state fully the type of work done . . . but those accustomed to employment of different kinds of work should describe themselves as 'General Labourer'. The term 'labourer' must not be used alone.

10e. *Nurses* state whether 'nurse (domestic)' . . . etc.

8. For persons . . . who are mainly dependent on others' earnings or upon private means write 'None' or 'Not occupied for a living'.

1. *Relationships* any relative present in the dwelling . . . who usually lives elsewhere should . . . be described as 'Visitor' and not as 'Son', 'Aunt' etc.

Sources:
a) Census Report, General Report 1893, cd. 7222; b) 1901 Census Report, General Report 1904, cd. 2174; c) 1911 Census Report, General Report 1917–18, Appendix A:; d) 1921 General Report, cd. 84–91; e) Stated in 1911 Report to particularly affect farmers' wives, lodging-house keepers' wives and dealers'/traders' wives.

Consolidated bibliography

Abel, M. and Folbre, N., 'A methodology for revising estimates: female market participation in the US before 1940', *Historical Methods*, 23 (1990).

Alexander, S., 'Women's work in nineteenth-century London: a study of the years 1820–50', in Mitchell and Oakley (eds), *Rights and wrongs of women*.

Alexander, S., Davin, A. and Hostettler, E., 'Labouring women: a reply to Eric Hobsbawm', *History Workshop Journal*, 8 (1979).

Alexander, S., *Becoming a woman and other essays in 19th and 20th century feminist history* (London, 1994).

Allen, R.C., 'The growth of labour productivity in early modern English agriculture', *Explorations in Economic History*, 25 (1988).

Allen, R.C., *Enclosure and the yeoman. The agricultural development of the south Midlands, 1450–1850* (Oxford, 1992).

Anderson, M., *Family structure in nineteenth century Lancashire* (Cambridge, 1971).

Anderson, M, 'The study of family structure', in Wrigley (ed.), *Nineteenth-century society*.

Anderson, M., 'Marriage patterns in Victorian Britain: an analysis based on Registration District data for England and Wales 1861', *Journal of Family History*, 1 (1976).

Anderson, M., *Approaches to the history of the western family 1500–1914* (London, 1980).

Anderson, M., 'The social position of spinsters in mid-Victorian Britain', *Journal of Family History*, 9 (1984).

Anderson, M., 'Households, families and individuals: some preliminary results from the National Sample from the 1851 Census of Great Britain', *Continuity and Change*, 3 (1988).

Anderson, M., 'Mis-specification of servant occupations in the 1851 census: a problem revisited', *Local Population Studies*, 60 (1998).

Anderson, M., 'What can the mid-Victorian censuses tell us about variations in married women's employment?', *Local Population Studies*, 62 (1999).

Ankarloo, B., 'Agriculture and women's work. Directions of change in the west, 1700–1900', *Journal of Family History*, 4 (1979).

Anon., *An account of the Essex society for the encouragement of agriculture and industry* (Bocking, 1793).

Anon., *The unprotected or facts in a dressmaking life, by a dressmaker* (London, 1857).

Apfel, W. and Dunkley, P., 'English rural society and the New Poor Law, 1834–47', *Social History*, 10 (1985).

Ardiss, A.L., *New woman, new novels: feminism and early Modernism* (New Brunswick, 1990).

Armstrong, W.A., *Stability and change in an English country town: a social study of York, 1801–51* (Cambridge, 1974).

Armstrong, A., *Farmworkers in England and Wales. A social and economic history, 1770–1980* (London, 1988).

August, A., 'How separate a sphere?: poor women and paid work in late-Victorian London', *Journal of Family History*, 19 (1994).

Ault, W.O., 'By-laws of gleaning and the problems of harvest', *Economic History Review*, 14 (1961).

Baker, D. (ed.), *The inhabitants of Cardington in 1782*, Bedfordshire Historical Record Society, 52 (1973).

Ball, M. and Sunderland, D., *An economic history of London 1800–1914* (London, 2001).

Banks, J.A., *Prosperity and parenthood. A study of family planning among the Victorian middle classes* (London, 1954).

Baring-Gould, S., *Devonshire characters and strange events* (London, 1908).

Barker, H., *The business of women: female enterprise and urban development in northern England 1760–1830* (Oxford, 2006).

Barker, T. and Drake, M. (eds), *Population and society in Britain, 1850–1980* (London, 1982).

Barnsby, G.J., *Birmingham working people* (Wolverhampton, 1979).

Barrow, L., *Independent spirits: spiritualism and English plebeians 1850–1910* (London, 1986).

Baudino, I., Carré, J. and Révauger, C. (eds), *The invisible woman. Aspects of women's work in eighteenth-century Britain* (Aldershot, 2005).

Baudino, I., 'Eighteenth-century images of working women', in Baudino, Carré and Révauger (eds), *The invisible woman*.

Beachy, R., Craig, B. and Owens, A. (eds), *Women, business and finance in nineteenth-century Europe* (Oxford, 2006).

Beckwith, I., *Book of Gainsborough* (Buckingham, 1988).

Beesley, S., *My life* (privately printed, 1892).

Beneria, L. and Sen, G., 'Accumulation, reproduction and women's role in economic development: Boserup revisited', *Signs*, 7 (1981).

Bennett, A., *Anna of the five towns* (1902, Harmondsworth, 1967).

Bennett, J.M., *Women in the medieval English countryside* (Oxford, 1987).

Bennett, J.M. and Froide, A.M. (eds), *Singlewomen in the European past* (Philadelphia, 1999).

Bennett, W., 'The farming of Bedfordshire', *Journal of the Royal Agricultural Society of England*, 18 (1857).

Berg, M., *The age of manufactures: industry, innovation and work in Britain 1700–1820* (London, 1985).

Berg, M., 'Women's work, mechanisation and the early phases of industrialisation in England', in Joyce (ed.), *Historical meanings*.

Berg, M., 'What difference did women's work make to the industrial revolution?', in Sharpe (ed.), *Women's work*.

Berg, M. and Hudson, P., 'Rehabilitating the industrial revolution', *Economic History Review*, 45 (1992).

Berlanstein, L.R. (ed.), *The Industrial Revolution and work in nineteenth century Europe* (London, 1992).

Bird, C., *Enterprising women* (New York, 1976).

Black, C., *Married women's work: being the report of an enquiry undertaken by the Women's Industrial Council* (Virago edn, London, 1983; 1st published 1915).

Blackburn, S.C., '"No necessary connection with homework": gender and sweated labour, 1840–1909', *Social History*, 22 (1997).

Blécourt, W. de and Usborne, C., 'Women's medicine, women's culture: abortion and fortune-telling in early twentieth-century Germany and the Netherlands', *Medical History*, 43 (1999).

Blécourt, W. de, *Het Amazonenleger: irreguliere genezeressen in Nederland, ca. 1850–1930* (Amsterdam, 1999).

Body, G.A., 'The administration of the poor laws in Dorset 1760–1834, with special reference to agrarian distress' (unpublished Ph.D. thesis, University of Southampton, 1965).

Bonfield, L., Smith, R. and Wrightson, K. (eds), *The world we have gained: histories of population and social structure* (Oxford, 1986).

Boserup, E., *Women's role in economic development* (London, 1970).

Botelho, L. and Thane, P. (eds), *Women and ageing in British society since 1500* (Harlow, 2001).

Bouquet, M., *Family, servants and visitors: the farm household in nineteenth and twentieth-century Devon* (Norwich, 1985).

Bourke, J., 'Housewifery in working-class England 1860–1914', *Past and Present*, 143 (1994).

Bourke, J., *Working class cultures in Britain 1891–1960* (London, 1994).

Boyd-Kinnear, J., 'The social position of women in the present age', in Butler (ed.), *Woman's work*.

Boyer, G., *An economic history of the English Poor Law, 1750–1850* (Oxford, 1989).

Bradley, H., *Men's work, women's work. A sociological history of the sexual division of labour in employment* (Cambridge, 1989).

Branca, P., 'A new perspective on women's work: a comparative typology', *Journal of Social History*, 9 (1975).

Branca, P., *Silent sisterhood: middle class women in the Victorian home* (London, 1975).

Branca, P., *Women in Europe since 1750* (London, 1978).

Brewer, J. and Porter, R. (eds), *Consumption and the world of goods* (London, 1993).

Brown, P.S., 'The providers of medical treatment in mid-nineteenth-century Bristol', *Medical History*, 24 (1980).

Brown, P.S., 'Herbalists and medical botanists in mid-nineteenth-century Britain', *Medical History*, 26 (1982).

Brown, P.S., 'The vicissitudes of herbalism in late nineteenth- and early twentieth-century Britain', *Medical* History, 29 (1985).

Brown, P.S, 'Social context and medical theory in the demarcation of nineteenth-century boundaries', in Bynum and Porter (eds), *Medical fringe & medical orthodoxy.*

Brown, R., *Society and economy in modern Britain, 1700–1750* (London, 1991).

Burman, S. (ed.), *Fit work for women* (London, 1979).

Burnett, J. (ed.), *Useful toil* (London, 1974).

Burnette, J., 'Testing for occupational crowding in eighteenth-century British agriculture', *Explorations in Economic History*, 33 (1996).

Burnette, J., 'An investigation into the female-male wage gap during the Industrial Revolution in Britain', *Economic History Review*, 50 (1997).

Burnette, J., 'Labourers at the Oakes. Changes in the demand for female day-labourers at a farm near Sheffield during the agricultural revolution', *Journal of Economic History*, 59 (1999).

Burnette, J., 'The wages and employment of female day-labourers in English agriculture, 1740–1850', *Economic History Review*, 57, (2004).

Burt, T., *An Autobiography* (London, 1924).

Butler, J. (ed.), *Woman's work and woman's culture* (London, 1869).

Bynum, W.F. and Porter, R. (eds), *Medical fringe & medical orthodoxy 1750–1850* (London, 1987).

Bythell, D., *The handloom weavers: a study in the English cotton industry during the Industrial Revolution* (Cambridge, 1969).

Bythell, D., *The sweated trades: outwork in nineteenth century Britain* (London, 1978).

Bythell, D., 'Women in the workforce', in O'Brien and Quinault (eds), *The Industrial Revolution.*

Caird, J., *English agriculture in 1850–51* (reprinted London, 1967, 1st published London, 1852)

Cannadine, D.N., 'The present and the past in the English Industrial Revolution 1880–1980', *Past and Present*, 103 (1984).

Carter, S. and Cannon, T., *Female entrepreneurs: a study of female business owners: their motivations, experiences and strategies for success* (London, Department of Employment Research Paper, 65, 1988).

Caunce, S., *Amongst farm horses: the horselads of East Yorkshire* (Stroud, 1991).

Chambers English Dictionary (Edinburgh, 1990).

Chinn, C., *They worked all their lives: women of the urban poor in England, 1880–1939* (Manchester, 1988).

Clapham, J.H., *An economic history of modern Britain*, 3 vols (Cambridge, 1926–38).

Clark, A., *Working life of women in the seventeenth century* (reprinted London 1992, 1ˢᵗ published 1919).

Cobbett, W., *Cottage economy* (reprinted Oxford, 1979, 1ˢᵗ published 1822).

Cody, L. F., 'The politics of reproduction: from midwives' alternative public sphere to the public spectacle of man midwifery', *Eighteenth-Century Studies*, 32 (1999).

Coker Egerton, J., *Sussex folk and Sussex ways* (1924).

Coleman, D.C., 'Labour in the English economy of the seventeenth century', *Economic History Review*, 3 (1956).

Collins, E.J.T., 'Harvest technology and the labour supply in Britain, 1790–1870', *Economic History Review*, 22 (1969).

Conk, M., 'Labor statistics in the American and English census: making some invidious comparisons', *Journal of Social History*, 16 (1983).

Conrad, C. 'The emergence of modern retirement: Germany in international comparison (1850–1960)', *Population* (English selection), 3 (1991).

Cooper, D. and Donald, M., 'Households and "hidden" kin in early nineteenth-century England: four case studies in suburban Exeter, 1821–1861', *Continuity and Change*, 10 (1995).

Cooper, G.L. and Davidson, M.J., *Women in management* (London, 1984).

Cooter, R. (ed.), *Studies in the history of alternative medicine* (Basingstoke, 1988).

Crafts, N.F.R., 'A cross-sectional study of legitimate fertility in England and Wales, 1911', *Research in Economic History*, 9 (1984).

Crafts, N.F.R., *British economic growth during the Industrial Revolution* (Oxford, 1985).

Crafts, N.F.R., 'Duration of marriage, fertility and women's employment opportunities in England and Wales in 1911', *Population Studies*, 43 (1989).

Crompton, C.A., 'Changes in rural service occupations during the nineteenth century: an evaluation of two sources for Hertfordshire, England', *Rural History*, 6 (1995).

Crossick, G. and Haupt, H.G., *The petite bourgeoisie in Europe, 1780–1914* (London, 1995).

Crowston, C.H., *Fabricating women: the seamstresses of Old Regime France, 1675–1791* (Durham, N.C., 2001).

Cunningham, H., 'The employment and unemployment of children in England, *c.* 1680–1851', *Past and Present*, 126 (1990).

Dale, A, and Marsh, C., *The 1991 census user's guide*, (London: HMSO, 1993).

Dale, A., 'The OPCS Longitudinal Survey', in Dale and Marsh, *The 1991 census user's guide*.

Davidoff, L. and Hall, C., *Family fortunes: men and women of the English middle class 1780–1850* (London, 1987).

Davidoff, L. and Hall, C., '"The hidden investment": women and the enterprise', in Sharpe (ed.), *Women's work*.

Davidoff, L., 'The family in Britain', in Thompson (ed.), *Cambridge social history*, vol. 2.

Davidoff, L., 'The separation of home and work? Landladies and lodgers in nineteenth- and twentieth-century England', in Burman (ed.), *Fit work*.

Davies, C., 'Making sense of the census in Britain and the USA', *Sociological Review*, 28 (1980).

Davies, D., *The case of the labourers in husbandry* (reprinted New Jersey, 1977, 1st published 1795).

Davies, O., 'Charmers and charming in England and Wales from the eighteenth to the twentieth century', *Folklore*, 109 (1998).

Davies, O., 'Cunning-folk in England and Wales during the eighteenth and nineteenth centuries', *Rural History*, 8 (1997).

Davies, O., 'Cunning-folk in the medical market-place during the nineteenth century', *Medical History*, 43 (1999).

Davies, O., 'Healing charms in England and Wales 1700–1960', *Folklore*, 107 (1996).

Davies, O., *A people bewitched: witchcraft and magic in nineteenth-century Somerset* (Bruton, 1999).

Davies, O., *Witchcraft, magic and culture 1736–1951* (Manchester, 1999).

Davies, O., *Cunning-folk: popular magic in English history* (London, 2003).

Davies, O., *Murder, magic, madness: the Victorian trials of Dove and the Wizard* (London, 2005).

Davin, A. 'Working or helping? London working-class children in the domestic economy', in Smith, Wallerstein and Evers (eds), *Households and the world economy*.

Davin, A., *Growing up poor: home, school and street in London, 1870–1914* (London, 1996).

Dawson, G., *Soldier heroes: British adventure, empire and the imagining of masculinities* (London, 1994).

Day, A., *Glimpses of rural life in Sussex during the last hundred years* (Oxford, 1927).

De Vries, J., 'Between purchasing power and the world of goods. Understanding the household economy in early modern Europe', in Brewer and Porter (eds), *Consumption and the world of goods.*

Degler, C., 'Women and the family', in Kammen (ed.), *The past before us.*

Devine, T.M. (ed.), *Farm servants and labour in Lowland Scotland* (Edinburgh, 1984).

Devine, T.M., 'Women workers, 1850–1914', in Devine (ed.), *Farm servants.*

Donnison, J., *Midwives and medical men: a history of the struggle for the control of childbirth* (London, 1977).

Dony, J.G., *A history of the straw hat industry* (Luton, 1942).

Dunn, R.S. and Dunn, M.M. (eds), *The world of William Penn* (Philadelphia, 1986).

Dupree, M.W., 'Family structure in the Staffordshire Potteries 1840–1880' (unpublished D.Phil. thesis, University of Oxford, 1981).

Dupree, M.W., *Family structure in the Staffordshire potteries 1840–1880* (Oxford, 1995).

Earle, P., 'The female labour market in London in the late seventeenth and early eighteenth centuries', *Economic History Review*, 42 (1989).

Eden, F.M., *The state of the poor: or an history of the labouring classes in England*, 3 vols (reprinted Bristol, 2001, 1st published London 1797).

Edinburgh and Leith Post Office Directory, (Edinburgh, 1845–91).

Emsley, C., *British society and the French wars* (London, 1979).

Engels, F., *The condition of the working class in England*, translated by W.O. Chaloner (Oxford, 1958).

Engels, F., *The origins of the family, private property and the state* (1972 edn, 1st published 1884).

Farncombe, J., 'On the farming of Sussex', *Journal of the Royal Agricultural Society of England*, 11 (1850).

Feinstein, C., 'Pessimism perpetuated: the standard of living during and after the Industrial Revolution', Tawney lecture at the Economic History Society Annual Conference, University of Oxford, March 1999.

Festing, S., *The story of lavender*, 2nd edn (Sutton edn, 1989, 1st published, 1982).

Fissell, M. E., *Patients, power, and the poor in eighteenth-century Bristol* (Cambridge, 1991).

Floud, R. and Johnson, P. (eds), *The Cambridge economic history of modern Britain. Vol. 1: Industrialisation, 1700–1860* (Cambridge, 2004).

Forbes, E.G., 'The professionalisation of dentistry in the United Kingdom', *Medical History*, 29 (1985).

Forbes, T.R., 'The regulation of English midwives in the eighteenth and nineteenth centuries', *Medical History*, 15 (1971).

Foster, J., *Class struggle and the Industrial Revolution. Early industrial capitalism in three English towns* (London, 1974).

Fraser, W.H. and Maver, I. (eds), *Glasgow, 1830–1912* (Manchester, 1996).

Freeman, C., *Luton and the hat industry* (Luton, 1953).

Froide, A., 'Old maids: the lifecycle of single women in early modern England' in Botelho and Thane (eds), *Women and ageing*.

Froide, A.M., 'Hidden women: rediscovering the singlewomen of early modern England', *Local Population Studies*, 68 (2002).

Fynes, R., *The miners of Northumberland and Durham: a history of their social and political progress* (Sunderland, 1873).

Gales, K.E. and Marks, P.H., 'Twentieth-century trends in the work of women in England and Wales', *Journal of the Royal Statistical Society*, series A, 137 (1974).

Gamber, G., *The female economy: the millinery and dressmaking trades, 1860–1930* (Chicago, 1997).

Garrett, E.M., 'The trials of labour: motherhood versus employment in a nineteenth-century textile centre', *Continuity and Change*, 5 (1990).

Garrett, E.M., 'The dawning of a new era? Women's work in England and Wales at the turn of the twentieth century' *Social History/Histoire Sociale*, 28 (1995).

Gaskell, E., *Mary Barton: a tale of Manchester life* (Penguin edn, Harmondsworth, 1970, 1st published 1848)

Gaskell, E., *Cranford* (London, 1853).

Gavin, W., *Ninety years of family farming: the story of Lord Rayleigh's and the Strutt and Parker Farms* (London, 1967).

Genealogical Society of Utah, Federation of Family Historians, *1881 Census for England and Wales, the Channel Islands and Isle of Man* [computer file] (Colchester, Essex, The Data Archive [distributor], 1997). SN 3643.

Geographical Editorial Committee University of Sussex, *Sussex: environment, landscape and society* (Gloucester, 1983).

Gilbert, W.M. (ed.), *Edinburgh in the nineteenth century with an account of the building of South Bridge and a sketch of the fashions, chiefly in ladies' attire during the last 100 Years*, edited by W.M. Gilbert for J. & R. Allan, Ltd, 80–86 South Bridge Street (Edinburgh,1901).

Gielgud, J., 'Nineteenth-century farm women in Northumberland and Cumbria: the neglected workforce' (unpublished D.Phil. thesis, University of Sussex, 1992).

Gilboy, E.W., 'Labour at Thornborough: an eighteenth century estate', *Economic History Review*, 1ˢᵗ series, 3 (1932).

Gittins, D., 'Marital status, work and kinship, 1850–1930', in Lewis (ed.), *Labour and love*.

Gleadle, K., *British women in the nineteenth century* (Basingstoke, 2001).

Gloger, J.A. and Chester, P., *More to a needle than meets the eye: a brief history of needle making past and present* (Redditch, 1999).

Goose, N., 'Farm service in southern England in the mid-nineteenth century', *Local Population Studies*, 72 (2004).

Goose, N., *Population, economy and family structure in Hertfordshire in 1851. Vol. 1 The Berkhamsted region* (Hatfield, 1996).

Goose, N., *Population, economy and family structure in Hertfordshire in 1851. Vol. 2 St Albans and its region* (Hatfield, 2000).

Goose, N. (ed.), *The Hertfordshire census 1851: family history edition*, CDRom (Hatfield, 2005).

Goose, N., 'Poverty, old age and gender in nineteenth-century England: the case of Hertfordshire', *Continuity and Change*, 20 (2005).

Goose, N., 'Farm service, seasonal unemployment and casual labour in mid nineteenth-century England', *Agricultural History Review*, 54 (2006).

Goose, N., 'How saucy did it make the poor? The straw plait and hat trades, illegitimate fertility and the family in nineteenth-century Hertfordshire', *History*, 91 (2006).

Goose, N., 'Cottage industry, migration and marriage in nineteenth-century England', *Economic History Review*, on-line early (2007).

Gorsley, S., 'Old maids and new women: alternatives to marriage in English women's novels, 1847–1915', *Journal of Popular Culture*, 8 (1973).

Green, D.G., *Working-class patients and the medical establishment* (Aldershot, 1985).

Green, D.R. and Owens, A., 'Gentlewomanly capitalism? Spinsters, widows, and wealth holding in England and Wales, *c.* 1800–1860', *Economic History Review*, 56 (2003).

Green, J.A.S., 'A survey of domestic service', *Lincolnshire History and Archaeology*, 17 (1982).

Grey, E., *Cottage life in a Hertfordshire village* (St Albans, 1935).

Grey, P., 'The pauper problem in Bedfordshire from 1795 to 1834' (unpublished M.Phil. thesis, University of Leicester, 1975).

Gritt, A.J., 'The census and the servant: a reassessment of the decline of farm service in early nineteenth-century England', *Economic History Review*, 53 (2000).

Grof, L.L., *Children of straw. The story of a vanished craft industry in Bucks, Herts, Beds and Essex* (Buckingham, 1988).

Guerriero Wilson, R., *Disillusionment or new opportunities? The changing nature of work in offices, Glasgow 1880–1914* (Aldershot, 1998).

Gutchen, R.M. (ed.), *On the sanitary condition of the Hitchin Union Workhouse 1842* (Hoddesdon, 1972).

Haines, M., *Fertility and occupation: population patterns in industrialisation* (London, 1979).

Hakim, C., 'Census Reports as documentary evidence: the census commentaries', *Sociological Review*, 28 (1980).

Hall, D.E., *Muscular Christianity: embodying the Victorian age* (Oxford, 1994).

Hall, R., *Women in the labour force: a case-study of the Potteries in the nineteenth century*, Dept. of Geography and Earth Science, Queen Mary College, London, Occasional Paper no. 27 (London, 1986).

Halsey, A.H., *Trends in British society since 1900* (Basingstoke, 1972)

Hardy, T., *Tess of the D'Urbervilles* (1985 edn, 1st published 1891).

Hareven, T.K., 'The history of the family and the complexity of social change', *American Historical Review*, 96 (1991).

Hargreaves, A., 'Dentistry in the British Isles', *Clio Medica*, 72 (2003).

Harrsion, B., *Not only the 'dangerous trades': women's work and health in Britain, 1880–1914* (London, 1996).

Hartwell, R.M., *The industrial revolution and economic growth* (London, 1971).

Harvey, C. and Press, J. (eds), *Databases in historical research* (London, 1996).

Hassell Smith, A., 'Labourers in late sixteenth-century England. A case study from north Norfolk [Part I]', *Continuity and Change*, 4 (1989).

Hassell Smith, A., 'Labourers in late sixteenth-century England. A case study from north Norfolk [Part II]', *Continuity and Change*, 4 (1989).

Henderson, J. and Wall, R. (eds), *Poor women and children in the European past* (London, 1994).

Hennock, P., *Fit and proper persons: ideal and reality in nineteenth-century local government* (London, 1973)

Herbert, G., *Shoemaker's window: recollections of Banbury before the railway age* (Oxford, 1848).

Hewitt, M., *Wives and mothers in Victorian industry* (London, 1958).

Higgs, E., 'The tabulation of occupations in the nineteenth century census with special reference to domestic servants', *Local Population Studies*, 28 (1982).

Higgs, E., 'Domestic servants and households in Victorian England', *Social History*, 7 (1983).

Higgs, E., *Domestic servants and households in Rochdale, 1851–1871* (New York, 1986).

Higgs, E., 'Domestic service and household production', in John (ed.), *Unequal opportunities.*

Higgs, E., 'Women, occupations and work in the nineteenth century censuses', *History Workshop Journal*, 23 (1987).

Higgs, E., 'Disease, febrile poisons and statistics: the census as medical survey, 1841–1911', *Social History of Medicine*, 4 (1991).

Higgs, E., 'Occupational censuses and the agricultural workforce in Victorian England and Wales', *Economic History Review*, 48 (1995).

Higgs, E., *A clearer sense of the census* (London, 1996).

Higgs, E., *Making sense of the census revisited* (London, 2005).

Hiley, M., *Victorian working women: portraits from life* (Boston, 1979).

Hill, B., *Women, work and sexual politics in eighteenth-century England* (London, 1989).

Hill, B., 'Women, work and the census: a problem for historians of women', *History Workshop Journal*, 35 (1993).

Hillam, C., *Brass plate and brazen impudence: dental practice in the provinces, 1755–1855* (Liverpool, 1991).

Holley, J., 'The re-division of labour: two firms in 19th century south-east Scotland' (unpublished Ph.D. thesis, University of Edinburgh, 1978).

Holley, J., 'The two family economies of industrialism: factory workers in industrial Scotland', *Journal of Family History*, 6 (1981).

Honeyman, K., 'Gender divisions and industrial divide: the case of the Leeds clothing trade, 1850–1970', *Textile History*, 28 (1997).

Honeyman, K., *Well suited: a history of the Leeds clothing industry, 1850–1990* (Oxford, 2000).

Honeyman, K., *Women, gender and industrialisation in England, 1700–1870* (Basingstoke, 2000).

Hoppit, J., 'Counting the Industrial Revolution', *Economic History Review*, 43 (1990).

Horn, P., 'Child workers in the pillow lace and straw plait trades of Victorian Buckinghamshire and Bedfordshire', *Historical Journal*, 17 (1974).

Horn, P., *The rise and fall of the Victorian servant* (Dublin, 1975).

Horn, P., 'Victorian villages from census returns', *The Local Historian*, 15 (1982).

Horn, P., *Labouring life in the Victorian countryside* (Stroud, 1987, 1st publ. Dublin, 1976).

Horn, P., *Life and labour in rural England, 1760–1850* (London, 1987).

Horn, P., *Victorian countrywomen* (Oxford, 1991).

Horn, P.L.R., 'The Buckinghamshire straw plait trade in Victorian England', *Records of Buckinghamshire*, 19 (1971).

Horrell, S. and Humphries, J., 'Old questions, new data, and alternative perspectives: families' living standards in the Industrial Revolution', *Journal of Economic History*, 52 (1992).

Horrell, S. and Humphries, J., 'Women's labour force participation and the transition to the male breadwinner family, 1790–1865', *Economic History Review*, 48 (1995).

Horrell, S., 'Women and the industrious revolution', First Modern Labour Market Seminar paper, 22 September 2006: http://www.labourmarkets.bham.ac.uk.

Hostettler, E., 'Women farm workers in eighteenth and nineteenth-century Northumberland', *North East Labour History*, 16 (1982).

Howkins, A., 'Peasants, servants and labourers: the marginal workforce in British agriculture, 1870–1914', *Agricultural History Review*, 42 (1994).

Howkins, A., 'The English farm labourer in the nineteenth century. Farm, family and community', in Short, (ed.), *English rural community*.

Hudson, P. (ed.), *Regions and industries: a perspective on the Industrial Revolution in Britain* (Cambridge, 1989).

Hudson, P. and Lee, W.R. (eds), *Women's work and the family economy in historical perspective* (Manchester, 1990).

Hudson, P. and Lee, W.R., 'Women's work and the family economy in historical perspective', in Hudson and Lee (eds) *Women's work*.

Hudson, P., *The industrial revolution* (London, 1992).

Hudson, P., *History by numbers: an introduction to quantitative approaches* (London, 2000).

Hudson, P., 'Industrial organization and structure', in Floud and Johnson (eds), *Cambridge economic history*, vol. 1.

Hudson, R. and Williams, A., *The United Kingdom* (London, 1986).

Hufton, O., *The prospect before her: a history of women in Western Europe* (London, 1995).

Humphries, J., 'Protective legislation, the capitalist state and working class men: the case of the 1842 Mines Regulation Act', *Feminist Review*, 7 (1981).

Humphries, J., '"…The most free from objection…". The sexual division of labor and women's work in nineteenth-century England', *Journal of Economic History*, 47 (1987).

Humphries, J., 'Female-headed households in early industrial Britain: the vanguard of the proletariat?', *Labour History Review*, 63 (1998).

Humphries, J., 'Enclosures, common rights and women. The proletarianisation of families in the late eighteenth and early nineteenth centuries', *Journal of Economic History*, 50 (1990).

Humphries, J. and Rubery, J., 'The reconstitution of the supply side of the labour market: the relative autonomy of social reproduction', *Cambridge Journal of Economics*, 8 (1984).

Hunt., E., *British labour history* (London, 1981).

Hussey, S., 'Out in the fields in all weathers. Women's agricultural work in north Essex, 1919–1939', *Essex Journal*, 28 (1993).

Hutchins, B.L., *Women in modern industry* (London, 1915, reprinted New York, 1980).

Hutchins, J., *The history and antiquities of the County of Dorset*, 2nd edn (1976).

Inkster, I., 'Marginal men: aspects of the social role of the medical community in Sheffield 1790–1850', in Woodward and Richards, *Health care and popular medicine*.

Inkster, I. et al. (eds), *The Golden Age. Essays in British social and economic history, 1850–1870* (Aldershot, 2000).

Irwin, M.H., *Women's work in tailoring and dressmaking: report of an inquiry conducted for the Scottish Council for Women's Trades* (Glasgow, 1908).

Jacks, L., *Confession of an octogenarian* (London, 1942).

Jameson, A., *Memoirs and essays* (London, 1846).

Jeffreys, M. (ed.) *Growing old in the twentieth century* (London, 1991).

John, A.V., 'Introduction', in John (ed.), *Unequal opportunities*.

John, A.V. (ed.), *Unequal opportunities: women's employment in England 1800–1918* (Oxford, 1986).

Jones, C., 'Personal tragedy or demographic disaster?', *Local Population Studies*, 66 (2001).

Jones, C., 'Those whom God hath not joined: a study of never-married people in England and Wales in the nineteenth century' (unpublished Ph.D. thesis, University of Essex, 2004).

Jones, G. and Rose, M.B. (eds), *Family capitalism* (London, 1993).

Jordan, E., 'Female unemployment in England and Wales, 1851–1911', *Social History*, 13 (1988).

Joyce, P., *Work, society and politics: the culture of the factory in later Victorian England* (Brighton, 1980).

Joyce, P. (ed.), *The historical meanings of work* (Cambridge, 1987).

Joyce, P., 'Work', in Thompson (ed.), *Cambridge social history*, vol. 2.

Kammen, M. (ed.), *The past before us: contemporary historical writing in the United States* (Ithaca and London, 1980).

Kent, D.A. 'Ubiquitous but invisible: female domestic servants in mid-eighteenth century London', *History Workshop Journal*, 28 (1989).

Kertzer, D.I. and Schaie, D.W. (eds), *Age structuring in comparative perspective* (New Jersey, 1989).

Kettlewell, F.B., *Trinkum-Trinkums* (Taunton, 1927).

King, P., 'Gleaners, farmers and the failure of legal sanctions in England, 1750–1850', *Past and Present*, 125 (1989).

King, P., 'Customary rights and women's earnings. The importance of gleaning to the rural labouring poor, 1750–1850', *Economic History Review*, 44 (1991).

King, P., 'Legal change, customary right and social conflict in late eighteenth-century England. The origins of the Great Gleaning Case of 1788', *Law and History Review*, 10 (1992).

King, S. and Tomkins, A. (eds), *The poor in England 1700–1850: an economy of makeshifts* (Manchester, 2003).

King, S. and Weaver, A., 'Lives in many hands: the medical landscape in Lancashire, 1700–1820', *Medical History*, 45 (2000).

King, S., *A Fylde country practice: medicine and society in Lancashire, circa 1760–1840* (Lancaster, 2001).

Kingman, M.J., '"Doing the beads": by-employment for women and children in rural Warwickshire, 1865–6', *Warwickshire History*, 10 (1966–7).

Kirby, M.W. and Rose, M.B. (eds), *Business enterprise in modern Britain from the eighteenth to the twentieth century* (London, 1994).

Kirby, P., *Child labour in Britain, 1750–1870* (Basingstoke, 2003).

Kirby, P., 'A brief statistical sketch of the London child labour market in mid-nineteenth century London', *Continuity and Change*, 20 (2005).

Kirby, P., 'How many children were "unemployed" in eighteenth and nineteenth century England?', *Past and Present*, 186 (2005).

Kitteringham, J., 'Country work girls in nineteenth-century England', in Samuel (ed.), *Village life*.

Knott, O. and Legg, R., *Witches of Dorset* (Tiverton, [1961] 1996).

Kussmaul, A., *Servants in husbandry in early modern England* (Cambridge, 1981).

Land, H., 'The family wage', *Feminist Review*, 6 (1980).

Landau, N., 'The law of settlement and the surveillance of immigration in eighteenth-century Kent', *Continuity and Change*, 3 (1988).

Landau, N., 'The eighteenth-century context of the laws of settlement', *Continuity and Change*, 6 (1991).

Lane, P., 'Work on the margins: poor women and the informal economy of eighteenth and early nineteenth-century Leicestershire', *Midland History*, 22 (1997).

Lane, P., Raven, N. and Snell, K.D.M. (eds), *Gender, work and wages in England, 1600–1850* (Woodbridge, 2004).

Langdon, R., *The life of Roger Langdon* (London, 1909).

Laslett, P. and Wall, R. (eds), *Household and family in past time* (Cambridge, 1972).

Laslett, P., 'Mean household size in England since the sixteenth century', in Laslett and Wall (eds), *Household and family in past time.*

Laslett, P., *A fresh map of life. The emergence of the third age* (London, 1989).

Lee, C.H., *British regional employment statistics: 1841–1971* (Cambridge, 1979).

Lee, C.H., 'Regional growth and structural change in Victorian Britain', *Economic History Review*, 34 (1981).

Lee, C.H., 'The service sector, regional specialization, and economic growth in the Victorian economy', *Journal of Historical Geography*, 10, (1984).

Lee, C.H., *The British economy since 1700: A macro-economic perspective* (Cambridge, 1986).

Lee, W.R., 'Women's work and the family. Some demographic implications of gender-specific rural work patterns in nineteenth-century Germany', in Hudson and Lee (eds), *Women's work.*

Lees, L., 'Mid-Victorian migration and the Irish family economy', *Victorian Studies*, 20 (1976).

Lehman, G., 'The birth of a new profession: the housekeeper and her status in the seventeenth and eighteenth centuries', in Baudino, Carré and Révauger (eds), *The invisible woman.*

Leslie, K. and Short, B., *An historical atlas of Sussex* (Chichester, 1999).

Levine, D., 'The reliability of parochial registration and the representativeness of family reconstitution,' *Population Studies*, 30 1976).

Levine, D., *Family formation in an age of nascent capitalism* (London, 1977).

Levine, D., 'Industrialization and the proletarian family in England', *Past and Present*, 107 (1985).

Levine, P., *Reproducing families: the political economy of English population history* (Cambridge, 1987).

Levine, D., 'Sampling history: the English population', *Journal of Interdisciplinary History*, 28 (1998).

Lewis, J., *Women in England 1870–1950* (Hemel Hempstead, 1984).

Lewis, J. (ed.), *Labour and love: women's experience of home and family 1850–1940* (Oxford, 1986).

Lewis, J., 'Introduction: reconstructing women's experience of home and family', in Lewis (ed.), *Labour and love.*

Litchfield, R.B., 'Single people in the nineteenth-century city: a comparative perspective on occupations and living situations', *Continuity and Change*, 3 (1988).

Long, J., *Conversations in cold rooms. Women, work and poverty in nineteenth-century Northumberland* (Woodbridge, 1999).

Loudon, I., *Death in childbirth: an international study of maternal care and maternal mortality 1800–1950* (Oxford, 1992).

Lown, J., *Women and industrialization: gender and work in nineteenth-century England* (Oxford, 1990).

MacEwan-Scott, A., 'Women and industrialisation. Examining the "female marginalisation thesis"', *Journal of Development Studies*, 22 (1986).

Macfarlane, A., *The origins of English individualism* (Oxford, 1978).

Macnicol, J. and Blaikie, A., 'The politics of retirement' in Jeffreys (ed.), *Growing old.*

Malcolmson, P., *English laundresses: a social history, 1850–1930* (Urbana and Chicago, 1986).

Marland, H., 'The medical activities of mid-nineteenth-century chemists and druggists, with special reference to Wakefield and Huddersfield', *Medical History*, 31 (1987.)

Marland, H., *Medicine and society in Wakefield and Huddersfield 1780–1870* (Cambridge, 1987).

Marsh, C., 'The sample of anonymised records', in Dale and Marsh, *The 1991 census user's guide.*

Marshall, W., *The review and abstract of the county reports to the Board of Agriculture,* 5 vols (York, 1808–1817).

Mathias, P. and Davis, J.A. (eds), *Enterprise and labour from the eighteenth century to the present* (Oxford, 1996).

Mathias, P., 'Labour and the process of industrialisation in the first phases of British industrialisation', in Mathias and Davis (eds), *Enterprise and* labour.

McBride, T., 'Women's work and industrialisation', in Berlanstein (ed.), *The Industrial Revolution.*

McIntosh, M.K., *Working women in English society 1300–1620* (Cambridge, 2005).

McKay, J., 'Married women and work in nineteenth-century Lancashire: the evidence of the 1851 and 1861 census reports', *Local Population Studies*, 61 (1998).

McKendrick, N. (ed.), *Historical perspectives. Studies in English thought and society* (London, 1974).

McKendrick, N., 'Home demand and economic growth: a new view of the role of women and children in the industrial revolution', in McKendrick (ed.), *Historical perspectives.*

McLaren, A., *Reproductive rituals: the perception of fertility in England from the sixteenth to the nineteenth century* (London, 1984).

McLeod, M., *Class and religion in the late Victorian city* (London, 1974).

Middleton, C., 'The familiar fate of the *famulae*. Gender divisions in the history of wage labour', in Pahl (ed.), *On work*.

McMurry, S., 'Women's work in agriculture: divergent trends in England and America, 1800 to 1930', *Comparative Studies in Society and History*, 34 (1992).

Miller, C., 'The hidden workforce: female fieldworkers in Gloucestershire, 1870–1901', *Southern History*, 6 (1984).

Mills, D.R., *Lord and peasant in nineteenth-century Britain* (London, 1980).

Mills, D. and Schürer, K, (eds), *Local communities in the Victorian census enumerators' books* (Oxford, 1996).

Mills, D. and Schürer, K., 'Employment and occupations', in Mills and Schürer (eds), *Local communities*.

Mingay, G.E. (ed.), *The agrarian history of England and Wales, VI, 1750–1850* (Cambridge, 1989).

Mitchell, B. and Deane, P., *Abstract of British historical statistics* (Cambridge, 1962).

Mitchell, B.R., *British historical statistics* (Cambridge, 1988).

Mitchell, J. and Oakley, A. (eds), *The rights and wrongs of women* (Harmondsworth, 1976).

Morris, C. (ed.), *The journeys of Celia Fiennes* (London, 1947).

Morris, J., 'The characteristics of sweating: the late nineteenth century London and Leeds tailoring trades', in John (ed.) *Unequal opportunities*.

Morris, R.J., 'Fuller values, questions and contexts: occupational coding and the historian', in Schürer and Diederiks (eds), *Use of occupations*.

Nardinelli, C., 'Child labour and the factory acts', *Journal of Economic History*, 40 (1980).

Nardinelli, C., *Child labor and the industrial revolution* (Bloomington, Indiana, 1990).

Neeson, J., *Commoners. Common right, enclosure and social change in England, 1770–1820* (Cambridge, 1993).

Nenadic, S., 'The Structure, values and influence of the Scottish urban middle class: Glasgow 1800–1870' (unpublished PhD thesis, University of Glasgow, 1986).

Nenadic, S., 'Businessmen, the urban middle classes and the "dominance" of manufacturers in nineteenth-century Britain', *Economic History Review*, 44 (1991).

Nenadic, S., 'Business advertising and the nineteenth-century city', *History Teaching Review Yearbook*, 6 (1992).

Nenadic, S., 'Record linkage and the small family firm: Edinburgh 1861 to 1891' *Bulletin of the John Ryland Institute of Manchester*, 74 (1992).

Nenadic, S., 'The small family firm in Victorian Britain', *Business History*, 35 (1993).

Nenadic, S., 'The Victorian middle classes' in Fraser and Maver (eds), *Glasgow*.

Nenadic, S., 'The social shaping of business behaviour in the nineteenth-century women's garment trades', *Journal of Social History*, 31 (1998).

Nolan, P.W., 'Folk medicine in Rural Ireland', *Folk Life*, 27 (1988–9).

O'Brien, P.K. and Quinault, R. (eds), *The Industrial Revolution and British society* (Cambridge, 1993).

Office of Population Censuses and Surveys (OPCS) *Guide to Census Reports, Great Britain 1801–1966* (London: HMSO, 1977).

Orr, K., 'Continuity and change in female identity: the experience of women in Edinburgh, 1919 to 39' (unpublished PhD thesis, European University Institute, Florence, 1996).

Orwin, C.S. and Felton, B.I., 'A century of wages and earnings in agriculture', *Journal of the Royal Statistical Society*, 92 (1931).

Osterud, N.G., 'Gender divisions and the organisation of work in the Leicester hosiery industry', in John (ed.), *Unequal opportunities*.

Overton, M., *Agricultural Revolution in England. The transformation of the agrarian economy, 1500–1850* (Cambridge, 1996).

Owens, A., 'Inheritance and the life-cycle of family firms in the early Industrial Revolution', *Business History*, 44 (2002).

Page, W. (ed.), *The Victoria History of the County of Hertfordshire*, 4 vols. (London, 1904–14).

Pahl, R.E. (ed.), *On work. Historical comparative and theoretical approaches* (Oxford, 1988).

Pahl, R.E., *Divisions of labour* (Oxford, 1984).

Pantin, C.G., 'A study of maternal mortality and midwifery in the Isle of Man, 1882–1961', *Medical History*, 40 (1996).

Penn, S.A.C., 'Female wage earners in late fourteenth-century England', *Agricultural History Review*, 35 (1987).

Pennington, S. and Westover, B., *A hidden workforce: homeworkers in England, 1850–1985* (Basingstoke, 1989).

Perkin, H., *The origins of modern English society, 1780–1880* (London, 1969).

Perkin, H., *The rise of professional society* (London, 1989).

Perkyns, A., 'Birthplace accuracy in the censuses of six Kentish parishes, 1851–1881', *Local Population Studies*, 47 (1991).

Perkyns, A., 'Age checkability and accuracy in the censuses of six Kentish parishes, 1851–1881', *Local Population Studies*, 50 (1993).

Phillips, N., *Women in business, 1700–1850* (Woodbridge, 2006).

Pickstone, J.V. and Miley, U., 'Medical botany around 1850: American medicine in industrial Britain', in Cooter (ed.), *Studies in the history of alternative medicine*.

Pinchbeck, I., *Women workers and the Industrial Revolution, 1750–1850* (reprinted London, 1981, 1st published London, 1930).

Plakans, A., 'Stepping down in former times. A comparative assessment of retirement in traditional Europe', in Kertzer and Schaie (eds), *Age structuring*.

Pleck, E., 'Two worlds in one: work and family', *Journal of Social History*, 10 (1976).

Pooley, C. and Turnbull, J., *Migration and mobility in Britain since the eighteenth century* (London, 1998).

Pooley, C. and Whyte, I.D. (eds), *Migrants, emigrants and immigrants. A social history of migration* (London, 1991).

Porter, D. and Porter, R., *Patient's progress: doctors and doctoring in eighteenth-century England* (Stanford, 1989).

Pounds, N.J.G., 'Barton farming in eighteenth-century Cornwall', *Journal of the Royal Institution of Cornwall*, 7 (1973).

Prochaska, 'Female philanthropy and domestic service in Victorian England', *Bulletin of the Institute of Historical Research*, 55 (1981).

Purdy, F., 'On the earnings of agricultural labourers in England and Wales, 1860', *Journal of the Royal Statistical Society*, 24 (1861).

Rawlence, E.A., 'Folk-fore and superstitions still obtaining in Dorset', *Proceedings of the Dorset Natural History and Antiquarian Field Club*, 35 (1914).

Rawlence, E.A., 'Sundry folk-lore reminiscences relating to man and beast in Dorset and the neighbouring counties', *Proceedings of the Dorset Natural History and Antiquarian Field Club*, 37 (1916).

Razzell, P., 'The evaluation of baptism as a form of birth registration through cross-matching census and parish register data', *Population Studies*, 26 (1972).

Razzell, P., 'The conundrum of eighteenth century English population growth', *Social History of Medicine*, 11 (1998).

Reay, B., *Microhistories: demography, society and culture in rural England, 1800–1930* (Cambridge, 1996).

Reed, M., 'Indoor farm service in nineteenth-century Sussex: some criticisms of a critique', *Sussex Archaeological Collections*, 123 (1985).

Richards, E., 'Women in the British economy since about 1700: an interpretation', *History*, 59 (1974).

Richards, T., *The commodity culture of Victorian England: advertising and spectacle, 1851–1914* (London, 1990).

Roberts, E.M., 'Working wives and their families', in Barker and Drake (eds), *Population and society*.

Roberts, E.M., *A woman's place: an oral history of working-class women, 1890–1940* (Oxford, 1984).

Roberts, E.A.M., 'Women's strategies 1890–1940, in Lewis (ed.) *Labour and love.*

Roberts, E., *Women's work, 1840–1940* (Cambridge, 1988).

Roberts, M., 'Sickles and scythes. Women's work and men's work at harvest time', *History Workshop Journal*, 7 (1979).

Robin, J., 'Family care of the elderly in a nineteenth-century Devonshire parish', *Ageing and Society*, 4 (1984).

Robin, J., *From childhood to middle age: cohort analysis in Colyton, 1851–1891*, (Cambridge, 1996).

Rodger, R., *The transformation of Edinburgh: land, property and trust in the nineteenth century* (Cambridge, 2001).

Rogers, H., '"The good are not always powerful, nor the powerful always good": the politics of women's needlework in mid-Victorian London', *Victorian Studies*, 40 (1997).

Roper, J. (ed.), *Charms and charming in Europe* (Basingstoke, 2004).

Roper, J., 'Typologising English charms', in Roper (ed.), *Charms and charming in Europe.*

Roper, M. and Tosh, J. (eds), *Manful assertions: masculinities in Britain since 1800* (London, 1991).

Rose, S.O., 'Gender at work: sex, class and industrial capitalism', *History Workshop*, 21 (1986).

Rose, S.O., *Limited livelihoods: gender and class in nineteenth-century England* (Berkeley, California, 1991).

Rose, S.O., 'Widowhood and poverty in nineteenth-century Nottinghamshire', in Henderson and Wall (eds), *Poor women and children.*

Rosen, D., *The changing fictions of masculinity* (London, 1994).

Ross, E., 'Survival networks: women's neighbourhood sharing in London before World War I', *History Workshop Journal*, 15 (1983).

Ross, E., *Love and toil: motherhood in outcast London, 1870–1918* (Oxford, 1993).

Rouyer-Daney, M-C., 'The representation of housework in the eighteenth-century women's press', in Baudino, Carré and Révauger (eds), *The invisible woman.*

Rowntree, B.S., *Poverty: a study of town life* (London, 1901).

Ruggles, S., 'Migration, marriage, and mortality: correcting sources of bias in English family reconstitutions,' *Population Studies*, 46 (1992).

Ruggles, S., 'The limitations of English family reconstitution', *Continuity and Change*, 14 (1999).

Rule, J., *Albion's people* (London, 1992).

Russell, N., *The novelist and Mammon: literary responses to the world of commerce in the nineteenth century* (Oxford, 1986).

Saito, O., 'Who worked when? Lifetime profiles of labour-force participation in Cardington and Corfe Castle in the late-eighteenth and mid-nineteenth centuries', *Local Population Studies*, 22 (1979), reprinted in Mills and Schürer, *Local communities.*

Samuel, R. (ed.), *Village life and labour* (London, 1975).

Samuel, R., 'Workshop of the World: steam power and hand technology in Mid-Victorian Britain', *History Workshop*, 3 (1977).

Sanderson, E.C., *Women and work in eighteenth-century Edinburgh* (Edinburgh, 1996).

Sayer, K., *Women of the fields. Representations of rural women in the nineteenth century* (Manchester, 1995).

Scase, R. and Goffee, R., *Women in charge: the experience of female entrepreneurs* (London, 1985).

Schmiechen, J.A., *Sweated industries and sweated labour: the London clothing trades, 1860–1914* (London, 1984).

Schofield, R.S., 'Age-specific mobility in an eighteenth century English parish', *Annales de Démographie Historique* (1970).

Schürer, K., 'The 1891 Census and local population studies', *Local Population Studies*, 47 (1991).

Schürer, K., 'The role of the family in the process of migration', in Pooley and Whyte (eds), *Migrants.*

Schürer, K. and Diederiks (eds), *The use of occupations in historical analysis* (St Katharinen, 1993).

Schürer, K. and Woollard, M., *National sample of the 1881 census of Great Britain* [computer file], University of Essex, Genealogical Society of Utah [original data producers], Colchester, Essex: UK Data Archive [distributor], 2003. SN: 4375.

Schürer, K. and Woollard, M., *The national sample of the 1881 census of Great Britain. A user guide and workbook* (Colchester, 2001).

Schwarz, L.D., *London in the age of industrialisation: entrepreneurs, labour force and living conditions, 1700–1860* (Cambridge, 1992).

Schwarzkopf, J., *Unpicking gender: the social construction of gender in the Lancashire cotton weaving industry, 1880–1914* (Aldershot, 2004).

Scola, R., *Feeding the Victorian city: the food supply of Manchester, 1770–1870* (Manchester,1992).

Scott, J.W., 'Women in history: the modern period', *Past and Present*, 101 (1983).

Scranton, P. (ed.), *Beauty and business: commerce, gender and culture in modern America* (New York, 2000).

Seccombe, W., 'Patriarchy stabilized: the construction of the male breadwinner wage norm in nineteenth-century Britain', *Social History*, 11 (1986).

Seccombe, W., 'Starting to stop: working-class fertility decline in Britain', *Past and Present*, 126 (1990).

Seccombe, W., *Weathering the storm: working-class families from the Industrial Revolution to the fertility decline* (London and New York, 1993).

Shammas, C., 'The world women knew. Women workers in the north of England during the seventeenth century', in Dunn and Dunn (eds), *The world of William Penn*.

Sharpe, P., 'Literally spinsters. A new interpretation of local economy and demography in Colyton in the seventeenth and eighteenth centuries', *Economic History Review*, 44 (1991).

Sharpe, P., 'Locating the "missing marryers" in Colyton, 1660–1750', *Local Population Studies*, 48 (1992).

Sharpe, P., 'The women's harvest: straw-plaiting and the representation of labouring women's employment, c. 1793–1885', *Rural History*, 5 (1994).

Sharpe, P., 'Continuity and change: women's history and economic history in Britain', *Economic History Review*, 48 (1995), reprinted in Sharpe (ed.), *Women's work*.

Sharpe, P., 'Time and wages of West Country workfolks in the seventeenth and eighteenth centuries', *Local Population Studies*, 55 (1995).

Sharpe, P., *Adapting to capitalism: working women and the English economy, 1700–1850* (Basingstoke, 1996).

Sharpe, P. (ed.), *Women's work: the English experience, 1650–1914* (London, 1998).

Sharpe, P., 'The female labour market in English agriculture during the Industrial Revolution: expansion or decline?', *Agricultural History Review*, 47 (1999).

Short, B. (ed.), *The English rural community. Image and analysis* (Cambridge, 1992).

Short, B., 'The changing rural economy and society of Sussex, 1750–1945', in Geographical Editorial Committee, *Sussex*.

Short, B., 'The decline of living-in servants in the transition to capitalist farming: a critique of the Sussex evidence', *Sussex Archaeological Collections*, 122 (1984).

Shrimpton, C., 'The landed society and the farming community of Essex in the eighteenth and early nineteenth centuries' (unpublished PhD thesis, University of Cambridge, 1965) (published New York, 1977).

Simonton, D., *A history of European women's work, 1700 to the present* (London, 1998).

Simonton, D, 'Claiming their place in the corporate community: women's identity in eighteenth-century towns', in Baudino, Carré and Révauger (eds), *The invisible woman.*

Smelser, N.J., *Social change in the Industrial Revolution: an application of theory to the Lancashire cotton industry 1770–1840* (London, 1959).

Smiles, S., *Self help* (London, 1859).

Smiles, S., *Thrift* (London, 1875).

Smith, C.F., 'In harvest time', *Essex Review*, 48 (1903).

Smith, F.B. *The people's health 1830–1910* (London, [1979] 1990).

Smith, J., Wallerstein, I. and Evers, H. (eds), *Households and the world economy* (London, 1984).

Smith, M., *The autobiography of Mary Smith, school mistress and non-conformist: a fragment of a life* (London, 1892).

Smith, R., 'Fertility, economy and household formation in England over three centuries', *Population and Development Review*, 7 (1981).

Snell, F.J., *A book of Exmoor* (London, [1903] 1923).

Snell, K.D.M., *Annals of the labouring poor: social change and agrarian England 1660–1900* (Cambridge, 1985).

Snell, K., 'Pauper settlement and the right to poor relief in England and Wales', *Continuity and Change*, 6 (1991).

Snowdon, H., *Born to farm in Devon: by horse and handtool at Thurlestone 1918–39* (Newton Abbot, 1998).

Speechley, H., 'Female and child agricultural day labourers in Somerset, *c.*1685–1870' (unpublished PhD thesis, University of Exeter, 1999).

Spencely, G.F.R., 'The English pillow lace industry 1845–80: a rural industry in competition with machinery', *Business History*, 70 (1970).

Stedman Jones, G., *Outcast London* (Oxford, 1971).

Stone, L., *The family, sex and marriage in England, 1500–1800* (London, 1977).

Stone, L., 'Family history in the 1980s: past achievements and future trends', *Journal of Interdisciplinary History*, 12 (1981).

Sundin, J. and Soderlund, E. (eds), *Time, space and man: essays in microdemography* (Stockholm, 1979).

Szreter, S., 'The decline of marital fertility in England and Wales *c.* 1870–1914' (unpublished PhD thesis, University of Cambridge, 1984).

Szreter, S., *Fertility, class and gender in Britain 1860–1940* (Cambridge, 1996).

Thomas, E.G., 'The Old Poor Law and medicine', *Medical History* 24 (1980).

Thomas, K., 'Age and authority in early modern England', *Proceedings of the British Academy*, 62 (1976).

Thomson, D., 'Age reporting by the elderly and the nineteenth-century census', *Local Population Studies*, 25 (1980).

Thompson, E.P. and Yeo, E. (eds), *The unknown Mayhew: selections from the Morning Chronicle, 1849–50* (London, 1971).

Thompson, F.M.L. (ed.), *The Cambridge social history of Britain 1750–1950*, vol. 2 (Cambridge, 1990).

Tillott, P.M., 'Sources of inaccuracy in the 1851 and 1861 censuses', in Wrigley (ed.), *Nineteenth-century society*.

Tilly, L. and Cohen, M., 'Does the family have a history? A review of theory and practice in family history', *Social Science History*, 6 (1982).

Tilly, L., 'Demographic change in two French industrial cities: Anzin and Roubaix 1872–1906,' in Sundin and Soderlund (eds), *Time, space and man*.

Tilly, L.A. and Scott, J.W., *Women, work and family* (London, 1987).

Tonks, D., 'A kind of life insurance: the coal-miners of north-east England 1860–1920', *Family and Community History*, 2 (1999).

Tranter, N.L., 'The social structure of a Bedfordshire parish in the mid-nineteenth century. The Cardington census enumerators' books, 1851', *International Review of Social History*, 18 (1973).

Trinder, B., *Victorian Banbury* (Chichester, 1982).

Ure, A., *The philosophy of manufactures* (reprinted London, 1967, 1ˢᵗ published 1835).

Valenze, D., 'The art of women and the business of men. Women's work and the dairy industry, *c.* 1740–1840', *Past and Present*, 130 (1991).

Valenze, D., *The first industrial woman* (Oxford, 1995).

Verdon, N., 'Changing patterns of female employment in rural England, c.1790–1890' (unpublished Ph.D. thesis, University of Leicester, 1999).

Verdon, N., '"Physically a splendid race" or "hardened and brutalised by unsuitable toil"? Unravelling the position of women workers in rural England during the Golden Age of agriculture', in Inkster et al. (eds), *The Golden Age*.

Verdon, N., 'The rural labour market in the early nineteenth century: women's and children's employment, family income, and the 1834 Poor Law Report', *Economic History Review*, 55 (2002).

Verdon, N., *Rural women workers in nineteenth-century England: gender, work and wages* (Woodbridge, 2002).

Verdon, N., 'A diminishing force? Reassessing the employment of female day labourers in English agriculture, *c.*1790–1850', in Lane, Raven and Snell (eds), *Gender, work and wages*.

Vicinus, M., *Independent women: work and community for single women, 1850–1920* (Chicago, 1985).

Wach, H.M., 'A "still small voice" from the pulpit: religion and the creation of social morality in Manchester, 1820–1850', *Journal of Modern History*, 63 (1991).

Wall, R., 'The age at leaving home', *Journal of Family History*, 3 (1978).

Wall, R., 'Woman alone in English society', *Annales de Démographie Historique*, (1981).

Wall, R., 'Work, welfare and the family: an illustration of the adaptive family economy', in Bonfield, Smith and Wrightson (eds), *The world we have gained*.

Wells, R., 'The development of the English rural proletariat and social protest, 1700–1850', *Journal of Peasant Studies*, 6 (1978–9).

West, J.L., *The Taylors of Lancashire: bonesetters and doctors 1750–1890* (Worsley, 1977).

Westall, O.M., 'The competitive environment of British business, 1850–1914' in Kirby and Rose (eds), *Business enterprise*.

Whipp, R., 'Women and the social organization of work in the Staffordshire pottery industry 1900–1930', *Midland History*, 12 (1987).

Whipp, R., *Patterns of labour: work and social change in the pottery industry* (London, 1990).

Whipp, R., 'Kinship, labour and enterprise: the Staffordshire pottery industry, 1890–1920', in Hudson and Lee (eds), *Women's work*.

White, R., *Social change and the development of the nursing profession: a study of the poor law nursing services 1848–1948* (London, 1978).

Whitehead, C., 'On recent improvements in the cultivation and management of hops', *Journal of the Royal Agricultural Society of England*, 2nd series, 6 (1870).

Wilkes, A.R., 'Adjustments in arable farming after the Napoleonic Wars', *Agricultural History Review*, 28 (1980).

Williams, I., 'Migration and the 1881 census index: a Wiltshire example', *Local Population Studies*, 69 (2002).

Williams, S., 'Earnings, poor relief and the economy of makeshifts: Bedfordshire in the early years of the New Poor Law', *Rural History*, 16 (2005).

Williams, S.C., *Religious belief and popular culture in Southwark c. 1880–1939* (Oxford, 1999).

Williams-Davies, J., 'Merched y Gerddi: a seasonal migration of female labour from rural Wales', *Folk Life*, 15 (1977).

Wilson Fox, A., 'Agricultural wages in England and Wales during the last fifty years', *Journal of the Royal Statistical Society*, 66 (1903).

Wilson, A., 'The making of man-midwifery' (unpublished M.A. thesis, University of Cambridge, 1995).

Winstanley, M., 'Industrialisation and the small farm. Family and household economy in nineteenth-century Lancashire', *Past and Present*, 152 (1996).

Wood, F. H., *Somerset memories and traditions* (London, 1924).

Woods, R., 'Approaches to the fertility transition in Victorian England', *Population Studies*, 41 (1987).

Woods, R. and Shelton, N., *An atlas of Victorian mortality* (Liverpool, 1997).

Woodward, D. (ed.), *The farming and memorandum books of Henry Best, 1642*, British Academy Records of Social and Economic History, new series, 8 (1984).

Woodward, D., *Men at work. Labourers and building craftsmen in the towns of northern England, 1450–1750* (Cambridge, 1995).

Woodward, J. and Richards, D., *Health care and popular medicine in nineteenth century England* (London, 1977).

Woodward, M., *The mistress of Stantons' farm* (Lowestoft, 1938).

Woollard, M., 'Creating a machine-readable version of the 1881 census of England and Wales', in Harvey and Press (eds), *Databases*.

Wrigley, E.A. (ed.), *Nineteenth-century society: essays in the use of quantitative methods for the study of social history* (Cambridge, 1972).

Wrigley, E.A., 'Baptism coverage in early nineteenth-century England: the Colyton area', *Population Studies*, 29 (1975).

Wrigley, E.A., 'Reflections on the history of the family', *Daedalus*, 106 (1977).

Wrigley, E.A., 'Population history in the 1980s', *Journal of Interdisciplinary History*, 12 (1981).

Wrigley, E.A., 'Men on the land and men in the countryside: employment in agriculture in early-nineteenth-century England', in Bonfield, Smith and Wrightson (eds), *The world we have gained*.

Wrigley, E.A., *Continuity, chance and change: the character of the Industrial Revolution in England* (Cambridge, 1988).

Wrigley, E.A. and Schofield, R.S., *The population history of England, 1541–1871: a reconstruction* (London, 1981).

Wrigley, E.A., *Poverty, progress and population* (Cambridge, 2004).

Wyman, A.L., 'The surgeoness: the female practitioner of surgery 1400–1800', *Medical History*, 28 (1984).

Young, A., 'A tour in Sussex', *Annals of Agriculture*, 11 (1789).

Young, A., *General view of the agriculture of the county of Hertfordshire* (reprinted Newton Abbot, 1971, 1st published 1804).

Young, M. and Willmott, P., *The symmetrical family* (Harmondsworth, 1977).

Zhao, Z., 'The demographic transition in Victorian England', *Continuity and Change,* 11 (1996).

Zimmeck, M., 'Jobs for the girls: the expansion of clerical work for women, 1850–1914', in John (ed.), *Unequal opportunities.*

Index